MUSIC IN DISNEY'S ANIMATED FEATURES

MUSIC IN
DISNEY'S
ANIMATED FEATURES

Snow White and the Seven Dwarfs to *The Jungle Book*

JAMES BOHN
FOREWORD BY JEFF KURTTI

University Press of Mississippi • Jackson

www.upress.state.ms.us

Publication of this book was supported by the Bridgewater
State University College of Humanities and Social Sciences and
the office of the provost of Stonehill College.

Designed by Peter D. Halverson

The University Press of Mississippi is a member of the Association of
American University Presses.

First printing 2017
∞

Library of Congress Cataloging-in-Publication Data

Names: Bohn, James Matthew, 1970– author.
Title: Music in Disney's animated features : Snow White and the Seven
Dwarfs to The jungle book / James Bohn ; foreword by Jeff Kurtti.
Description: Jackson : University Press of Mississippi, [2017] | Includes
bibliographical references and index.
Identifiers: LCCN 2016058506 (print) | LCCN 2016059255 (ebook) | ISBN
9781496812148 (cloth : alk. paper) | ISBN 9781496812155 (epub single) |
ISBN 9781496812162 (epub institutional) | ISBN 9781496812179 (pdf single) |
ISBN 9781496812186 (pdf institutional)
Subjects: LCSH: Motion picture music—United States—History and
criticism. | Animated films—United States—History and criticism. | Disney,
Walt, 1901–1966—Criticism and interpretation. | Walt Disney Productions.
Classification: LCC ML2075 .B64 2017 (print) | LCC ML2075 (ebook) | DDC
781.5/42—dc23
LC record available at https://lccn.loc.gov/2016058506

British Library Cataloging-in-Publication Data available

LOVINGLY DEDICATED TO MY PARENTS,
LAWRENCE AND MARY BOHN,
FOR FORTY-SOME YEARS OF LOVE AND SUPPORT

CONTENTS

FOREWORD

Walt Disney once wrote, "I cannot think of the pictorial story without thinking about the complementary music which will fulfill it." Like so much of the creative work that was inspired by his artistic vision, Walt Disney's music catalogue is frequently regarded (and sometimes dismissed) at face value, with little further attention. Like "Disney movies," the term "Disney music" is a blanket expression applied to a vast number and remarkable variety of works created during Walt Disney's lifetime.

"Some people will tell you that music was a key ingredient of Walt Disney's success," film historian Leonard Maltin wrote. "Don't you believe it. Music was the *foundation* of Walt Disney's success. That statement may seem extreme, but remember that the cornerstone of Walt's career was *Steamboat Willie* in 1928. What made *Steamboat Willie* a hit was the novelty of animated characters moving in rhythm to a musical soundtrack, enhanced by colorful sound effects. Everything depended on that jaunty musical score."[1]

"He did know an astonishing amount about music," longtime collaborator and Disney Imagineer John Hench said, "which always amazed everybody, because he kept arguing with the musicians, and did frequently, when he put the films together."[2]

Music continued to play an essential role in his film and television projects, for the rest of his career, and when he expanded to the creation of live spectacles and his innovative amusement park, music was always a part of his storytelling instincts.

"He couldn't read music," Oscar-winning composer Richard Sherman says. "He couldn't play an instrument. But Walt was innately musical. He understood how it worked, and he had an instinct about how to make it work for his projects."[3]

Walt's leadership style has, in fact, frequently been compared to that of an orchestra conductor—certainly not able to play a symphony alone, but erudite and able to cast the parts, and get the right talent to fit his desired creative goals.

The music of Walt Disney's films created a seemingly simple but actually sophisticated songbook for millions of children (of all ages, as the saying goes) around the world. This work has been almost ritually passed along to succeeding generations, along with rich cultural memories and memorable entertainment experiences, to gain an even deeper meaning in the ensuing decades.

Within *Music in Disney's Animated Features:* Snow White and the Seven Dwarfs *to* The Jungle Book, James Bohn has assembled an abundant and informative history of the music and musical techniques in Walt Disney's animated films, the circumstances of their creation, and a detailed biographical and professional understanding of the many creative people who coalesced, collaborated, and created a rich and diverse musical score that has collectively come to be regarded, with great esteem and affection, as "Disney music."

Introducing us to the many and varied people and events behind "Disney music," Bohn not only gives a fascinating and enlightening insight to a particular creative process, he also—rather than diminishing Walt Disney's genius by explicitly giving proper credit to his employees—*adds* an extra appreciation for a unique kind of creative vision, and a style of leadership that demands—and achieves—a collaborative creative goal.

Music in Disney's Animated Features: Snow White and the Seven Dwarfs *to* The Jungle Book is an edifying and entertaining volume about perhaps the most important cultural contributions of the twentieth century's most enduring and influential creative personality, Walt Disney.

JEFF KURTTI

ACKNOWLEDGMENTS

My gratitude goes out to Stonehill College and Dean Maria Curtin for providing support for two research trips to the Walt Disney Archives, as well as providing funds to cover most of the image licensing costs for this volume. Further thanks are due to Bridgewater State University and Dean Paula Krebs for their financial backing of this publication, as well as their assistance through ten course enhancement grants related to the research for this book. Assistance from members of the curriculum committee at Bridgewater State University Music Department, Jean Kreiling, Sarah McQuarrie, and Carol Nicholeris, was central to making the class that made this book possible. I would also like to acknowledge Salil Sachdev and Donald Running, department chairs at Bridgewater State, for their continued support.

I would like to express gratitude to my students, who helped me think this volume through by allowing me to test content on them. Claudine Griggs of the Writing Center of Rhode Island College provided support through three of the Center's Summer Faculty Writing Retreats, as well as through miscellaneous mentoring. Friends and former colleagues from Rhode Island College, Andrew Aziz, Paul Beaudoin, Samuel Breene, and Kathryn Kalinak, also provided advice and support. I also owe a debt to Stacy Grooters and the Center for Teaching and Learning at Stonehill College for their support through a writing boot camp. Bridget Meigs of Stonehill's Farmhouse aided in my work as a Farmhouse Writing Fellow.

Many individuals aided me in my research. Jonathan Heely and Rob Schneider at the Disney Music Group graciously provided the information included in the appendix of this volume. Steven Vagnini, Kevin Kerns, Ed Ovalle, Alesha Reyes, Dennis Emslie, Jennie Hendricksen, and Joanna Pratt were very helpful during my research trip to the Walt Disney Archives. Lisa Janacua from the Disney Music Group also aided me with research.

Jennifer Walsh and Mary Ellen West of the interlibrary loan department at Bridgewater State University were extremely helpful. Margaret Adamic and Maxine Hof at Disney Enterprises Incorporated provided answers to several questions, offered editorial advice, and were instrumental in getting clearance for research materials. Mark Palkovic, Kevin Grace, and Suzanne Maggard

Reller at the University of Cincinnati aided with access to the Leigh Harline Collection. Rachel Dreyer, Shaun Hayes, and Ginny Kilander from the University of Wyoming helped me with access to various collections from the American Heritage Center.

Paul Moulton of the College of Idaho provided information about Paul J. Smith and his family, and Jan Boles aided with access to the Robert E. Smylie Archives at the College of Idaho. Cindy Brightenburg, Norm Gillespie, and James D'Arc at Brigham Young University helped with access to the Ken Darby papers. Rachel Greer aided with access to the Buddy Baker papers at the Fales Library at New York University. Marcia Rodwin and Kay Peterson of the Archives Center of the National Museum of American History at the Smithsonian Institution helped with access to printed sheet music. Deanna Cronk at the National Library of Australia also provided access to materials.

Family members of individuals mentioned in this volume provided important information. Robert B. Sherman's sons Jeffrey and Robert helped out in this manner. Paul J. Smith's children Theresa Smith Powers and Jerome Smith aided in fleshing out a portrait of their father. I also received further information about Smith from his niece, Arlynn Anderson. Three relatives of Carl Stalling—Linda Britt, David Stalling, and Vanessa Stalling—provided valuable information about the composer. Actor and producer Tracey Birdsall (www.traceybirdsallsmith.biz) provided essential information about her great-grandfather Bert Lewis. I would also like to thank Marge Champion and Floyd Norman for taking the time to share their memories with me.

Several people have helped getting permission to print copyrighted materials for use in this volume. Of particular note in this regard is Jonathan Heely from Disney Music Publishing. Marco Berrocal and Keith Rudolph from the Bourne Company, and Eric Whelan from Alfred Music Publishing, were also helpful. Special thanks also go out to Kris Kinsey and Nicolette Bromberg of the Special Collections Division of the University of Washington Libraries. Buddy Baker's widow, Charlotte, gave her blessing for the inclusion of a couple of previously unpublished stories regarding Oliver Wallace. Several podcasts—*Mousetalgia* (www.mousetalgia.com), *The Sodajerker on Songwriting* (www.sodajerker.com/podcast), and *The Tiara Talk Show* (thetiaratalkshow.com)—were kind enough to grant permission to include extended quotations.

Special thanks to friends and colleagues for bits of information they have helped me out with, including Greg Austin, Jeffrey Baldwin-Bott, Keith Bernard, Kurt Doles, Joe Hillman, Jim Orheim, Eric Parks, and Trevor Teuscher. A number of online friends also helped provide bits of information, including Jeff Baham, author of *The Unauthorized Story of Walt Disney's "Haunted Mansion"*; Didier Ghez, editor of the *Walt's People* series of books (www.didierghez.com); David Lesjak, author of the book *Service with Character: The Disney Studio and World War II*; Ken Stigen of the website *Walt's Music* (www.waltsmusic.com);

David Tietyen, who wrote the 1990 book *The Musical World of Walt Disney*; Carol Calip; William Silvester; and Andrew Vickers. Stacia Martin, a Disney artist and historian provided helpful advice. My brother David furnished very useful information, as well as bits of trivia that contributed to the project.

I would also like to thank my proofreaders. My father and Walt Disney World steam enthusiast aided in the process. Former Walt Disney World monorail driver and talented sister Kristin Roling helped out, as did The Twilight Zone Tower of Terror fan and extremely patient wife, Melissa Freitas. Friends and former Bridgewater State University colleagues Sean Janson and Victoria Large also gave critical feedback. Additional editing advice came from Andrew Holman and Ellen Scheible from the *Bridgewater Review*. Finally, my sister-in-law and fan of Sadness (character from the Pixar film *Inside Out*), Rachel Freitas helped with editing.

I owe a great debt of gratitude to prolific author and filmmaker Jeff Kurtti, who not only wrote the foreword to this volume but also provided detailed feedback as well as editing suggestions. Likewise, Greg Ehrbar, the coauthor of *Mouse Tracks: The Story of Walt Disney Records*, was extremely generous in providing information, encouragement, and advice regarding research, editing, and revision. Garry Apgar (author of *Mickey Mouse: Emblem of the American Spirit*) and Brian Sibley (coauthor of Snow White and the Seven Dwarfs & the Making of the Classic Film) also provided feedback on the manuscript. My most sincere appreciation goes out to my editor, Craig Gill, as well as Emily Bandy, Cynthia Foster, Shane Gong Stewart, Katie Keene, Clint Kimberling, John Langston, Todd Lape, Courtney McCreary, Lisa McMurtray, and Leila W. Salisbury of the University Press of Mississippi. My gratitude also goes out to copy editor Lisa Williams. The cover of the book was designed by Sarah Adam (www.madsahara.com) and Pete Halverson (University Press of Mississippi).

I owe gratitude to my cats, Zooey and Marty, for sitting in my lap and reminding me that sometimes it is acceptable to not be working on something. Finally, I would also like to extend my thanks to my parents, Lawrence and Mary Bohn, for forty-some years of love and support. I lovingly dedicate this volume to them.

PERMISSIONS

Thanks to Alfred Music Publishing, the Bourne Company, and the Disney Music Group for providing permission to reprint excerpts of their music in this volume.

ALICE IN WONDERLAND SCORE from ALICE IN WONDERLAND
Music by Oliver Wallace
© 1951 Walt Disney Music Company

BAMBI SCORE from BAMBI
Frank Churchill and Ed Plumb
© 1942 Walt Disney Music Company

BELLA NOTTE (THIS IS THE NIGHT) from LADY AND THE TRAMP
Words and Music by Peggy Lee and Sonny Burke
© 1952 Walt Disney Music Company

CINDERELLA SCORE from CINDERELLA
Paul Smith and Oliver Wallace
© 1950 Walt Disney Music Company (ASCAP)

CRICKET THEME from PINOCCHIO
By Leigh Harline
© Copyright 1940 Bourne Co.
Copyright Renewed
All Rights Reserved International Copyright Secured
ASCAP

DOPEY'S THEME from SNOW WHITE AND THE SEVEN DWARFS
By Frank Churchill
© Copyright 1938 Bourne Co.
Copyright Renewed
All Rights Reserved International Copyright Secured
ASCAP

A DREAM IS A WISH YOUR HEART MAKES from CINDERELLA
Words and Music by Mack David,
Al Hoffman and Jerry Livingston
© 1948 Walt Disney Music Co. (ASCAP)

DUMBO SERENADE from DUMBO
By Oliver Wallace
© Copyright 1941 Bourne Co.
Copyright Renewed
All Rights Reserved International Copyright Secured
ASCAP

EGYPTIAN MELODIES from EGYPTIAN MELODIES
Frank Churchill
©1931 Walt Disney Company

FISHIN' AROUND SCORE from FISHIN' AROUND
Bert Lewis
©1931 Walt Disney Music Company

I'M WISHING from SNOW WHITE AND THE SEVEN DWARFS
Words by Larry Morey Music by Frank Churchill
© Copyright 1937 by Bourne Co.
Copyright Renewed

THAT'S WHAT MAKES THE WORLD GO AROUND from THE SWORD IN THE STONE
Words and Music by Richard M. Sherman and
Robert B. Sherman
© 1963 Wonderland Music Company, Inc.

THE THREE LITTLE PIGS from THREE LITTLE PIGS
By Frank Churchill
© Copyright 1933 by Bourne Co.
Copyright Renewed
All Rights Reserved International Copyright Secured
ASCAP

TRUST IN ME from THE JUNGLE BOOK
Words and Music by Richard M. Sherman and
Robert B. Sherman
© 1967 Wonderland Music Company, Inc.

THE UNBIRTHDAY SONG from ALICE IN WONDERLAND
Words by Jerry Livingston
Music by Mack David and Al Hoffman
©1948 Walt Disney Music Company

WHEN I SEE AN ELEPHANT FLY from DUMBO
Words by Ned Washington Music by Oliver Wallace
© Copyright 1941 by Walt Disney Productions
Copyright Renewed
World Rights Controlled by Bourne Co.
All Rights Reserved International Copyright Secured
ASCAP

WHEN YOU WISH UPON A STAR from PINOCCHIO
Words by Ned Washington Music by Leigh Harline
© Copyright 1940 by Bourne Co.
Copyright Renewed
All Rights Reserved International Copyright Secured
ASCAP

WHISTLE WHILE YOU WORK from SNOW WHITE AND THE SEVEN DWARFS
Words by Larry Morey Music by Frank Churchill
© Copyright 1937 by Bourne Co.
Copyright Renewed
All Rights Reserved International Copyright Secured
ASCAP

WHO'S AFRAID OF THE BIG BAD WOLF? from THREE LITTLE PIGS
By Frank Churchill Additional Lyric by Ann Ronell
© Copyright 1933 by Bourne Co.
Copyright Renewed
All Rights Reserved International Copyright Secured
ASCAP

MUSIC IN DISNEY'S ANIMATED FEATURES

INTRODUCTION

Animators were considered the stars of The Walt Disney Studios.[1] However, the composers, songwriters, lyricists, and orchestrators who worked on Disney films contributed greatly to the art and function of these pictures. Their work establishes character, relates the narrative, drives the pacing, indicates character motivations, and provides emotional underpinnings. Composers at The Walt Disney Studios function as story men and gag men. They provide as much motion as any animator, as much suspense as any effects animator, and as much color as ink and painters.

Two of the Studios' most prominent animators, Frank Thomas (1912–2004) and Ollie Johnston (1912–2008), expressed a similar sentiment in their 1981 book *Disney Animation: The Illusion of Life*:

> Music is undoubtedly the most important addition that will be made to the picture. It can do more to bring a production to life, to give it integrity, style, emphasis, meaning, and unity, than any other single ingredient. With the surge of a full orchestra, there will be bigness and majesty and soaring spirits: with a nervous, fluttering melody line on a single instrument, or pulsating drumbeats, there will be agitation, apprehension, suspicion. Music can build tension in commonplace scenes or ease it in ones that have become visually too frightening.[2]

This assessment carries significant weight, given that the duo were two of Walt's "nine old men" who worked with Walt for more than three decades apiece, both as animators and directors.

Animated films are the backbone of Walt Disney Pictures. The Company did not start releasing fully live action movies until nearly three decades after the Studios' founding. The body of animated features created by the Studios over the years has helped sustain the Company through some of its leanest times. Audiences assess animated features as being timeless in a way that live-action films are not. This allows these movies to be rereleased on a regular basis in a manner that is typically unavailable to live-action features.

Furthermore, family entertainment has a transgenerational appeal that other movies do not. Parents often want their children to see the same films they enjoyed in their youth. As children grow up, they begin to make their own choices concerning ticket purchases; thus, this sort of generational bonding over movies is most commonly reserved for family entertainment. For this reason, each successive generation is exposed to animated Disney features, some of which are more than seventy years old.

Disney's catalog of animated films and shorts contributed to its early success on the small screen in the *Disneyland* television series (1954–1958) and *The Mickey Mouse Club* (1955–1959). The characters and stories from these movies have also formed the narrative foundation of Disney Parks and Resorts. The Company's founder expressed a similar sentiment with his statement "Our only hope is we never lose sight of one thing: that it was all started by a mouse."[3]

By the time Walt Disney (1901–1966) moved to Hollywood in 1923, most of the major film studios were already in existence, including Columbia Pictures (then called C. B. C. Film Sales), Fox Film Corporation, Metro Pictures, Samuel Goldwyn Productions, Paramount Pictures, United Artists, Universal Pictures, and Warner Bros. In contrast to these live-action studios, Walt founded the first independent animated movie studio in Hollywood. In the already heavily competitive environment of the movie business, part of Disney's success was due to a unique and relatively narrow focus on animation and family enter-tainment. At that time, most animation studios were located in New York City, and no other Hollywood studio at that time had such a particular focus.

From the first Mickey Mouse cartoon that was released, music played a crucial part. The Silly Symphonies (1929–1939) elevated the role of music in the Studios' shorts. In Disney's first feature, *Snow White and the Seven Dwarfs* (1937), the music is so integral to the film that it is essentially an animated operetta.

Disney animated features, particularly earlier ones, were created using a system that put music at the center of the filmmaking process. In a typical movie, music is the last component added. In order to get a feature into theaters in a timely manner, composers are rushed through the process. Half a century ago, composers usually had about ten weeks in which to produce a score.[4] More recently, this timeline has shrunk to a mere three to six weeks.[5] Given such constraints, there is a limit on how intricate a score can be. However, Disney's classic animated features, that is, those made before *Cinderella* (1950), were all prescored. This afforded the Studios' composers nearly the entire time from early production planning to the final mixdown to compose, fine-tune, and perfect their work.

Furthermore, early Disney animated films integrate the evolution of the score with the progression of the film through the use of bar sheets. Creat-ed by Wilfred Jackson for *Steamboat Willie*, bar sheets required music to be developed before the animation began. The music then served as the backbone of the film. That is, the movie was essentially animated to fit the music, though animation-centric minds may wish to characterize the music as pre-written to support animation.

Bar sheets can be thought of as providing a similar function in the creation of the film as Ludwig van Beethoven's (1770–1827) continuity drafts. Glenn Stanley described the composer's use of continuity drafts in *The Cambridge Companion to Beethoven*:

> He appears here to have been trying to establish the overall flow of the music, and a sense of the proportions between one passage and the next. Such drafts are normally written with the texture compressed on to a single stave—whether the work was a symphony or a piano sonata—with only the main melodic outline shown.[6]

While bar sheets also include details such as sound effects, dialog, mixing information, camera moves, and action, what Stanley is describing here could certainly be the musical lines of a bar sheet.

The development of the bar sheet parallels The Walt Disney Studios' innovation of the storyboard. While storyboarding quickly expanded to be used throughout the movie industry, the bar sheet, while used somewhat commonly in animation, has unfortunately failed to catch on in film. Certainly such an involved process comes with a hefty price tag, one that Disney has been willing to pay, while others have not.

Over the decades The Walt Disney Company has expanded into live-action films, television, and theme parks, as well as other merchandise, media, and entertainment ventures. The Company's leading position among the world's largest, most successful media, entertainment, and resort conglomerates has been undisputed for nearly thirty years. The Company controls a diverse set of holdings, including: Disney/ABC Television Group, ESPN Inc., Hollywood Records, Hyperion Books, Lucasfilm Limited, Marvel Studios, Pixar Animation Studios, and The Muppets. This massive empire is built on the film industry, and the foundation of Disney's success in this arena is family entertainment, in particular, animated features.

Not only is music a central component to the Studios' animated features, it is also important to the image of the Company as a whole. Perhaps more than any other media company, The Walt Disney Company's branding is tied to its intellectual property. Cartoon characters serve as ambassadors for the Company, and the iconic mouse ears are as recognizable as any corporate logo.

Many Disney products strategically promote other projects and initiatives of the Company. Theme parks support film releases with parades, costumed characters, events, and advertising. Broadcast entities such as ABC, ESPN, and

The Disney Channel support both theme parks and the film division through thematic and interstitial programming. Disney Consumer Products utilizes all the characters and brands in a diverse array of products, both created by Disney and licensed to outside organizations and manufacturers. The former head of Disneyland Records, Jimmy Johnson (1917–1976), described this manner of cross promotion as the basket-weave concept, stating: "The basket-weave concept of Disney marketing works just as well with some Theme Park attractions as it does with films. Records and books help sell the ride, and the attraction sells the merchandise."[7] While we typically think of branding material as being visual in nature, music plays an important role in this arena as well, particularly in Disney media.

The iconic image of Mickey Mouse seen on a T-shirt may persist for a brief moment in the mind of the viewer after the visual stimulus is no longer there. However, the melody to "it's a small world (after all)" can stay in an individual's mind for minutes, if not hours, after even the briefest exposure to the song. Furthermore, songs in Disney films are not merely consumed as passive entertainment. These songs are often created to be singable by most amateurs. For nearly thirty years, the Company has repackaged individual songs in the video series *Disney's Sing Along Songs.* Likewise, most parents will recognize the practice of children singing along with their favorite songs while watching Disney films at home.

When a person listens to a given piece of music enough such that she or he internalizes it (can mentally "hear" it accurately without listening to it), that music becomes a part of that person. When someone sings a song aloud, an opportunity for self-identification with the onscreen protagonist is created. This self-identification may also extend to the protagonist's emotions, triumphs, and woes. For this reason, when one sings a song aloud, it can become a part of oneself in a more active, personal way.

By design, most Disney songs are crafted to have a strong emotional impact that serves to support the dramatic tone of the scene the tune accompanies. This emotional content survives even when the song is stripped from the film for which it was created, allowing corporate properties to have a deep resonance with their audiences. Thus, Disney music serves as an important branding element for the Company, one that can connect with primal emotive factors, be internalized through participation, be a potential conduit for self-identification, and remain in the consciousness of individuals for long periods of time.

While there are numerous books that point to the visual artistry of Disney's animated films, comparatively little attention has been given to the role of music in the success of the Studios' oeuvre. Yet, throughout the Company's history, music has played a crucial, central role in these movies. In fact, it is fair to say that no other film studio's output has been so dependent upon music as Disney's.[8]

Music in Disney's Animated Features: Snow White and the Seven Dwarfs *to* The Jungle Book investigates the role of music in Disney's animated films, including musical techniques and applications that are used by the Studios to achieve its artistic, entertainment, and business goals. The scope of this volume is the first three decades of the Studios' animated films, finishing with *The Jungle Book* (1967), the last animated film that Walt personally supervised. The subject of the book is further narrowed by focusing on the Studios' single-story features, leaving out detailed discussion of package films such as *Saludos Amigos* (1942), *The Three Caballeros* (1944), and *Make Mine Music* (1946). *Fantasia* (1940) is also excluded for the same reason, combined with the fact that nearly no original music was composed for the movie.

This book profiles several composers, songwriters, arrangers, and orchestrators that have contributed to early Disney animated features. In a collaborative art form such as film, it can be difficult, if not impossible, to attribute individual contributions to the whole. A volume that credits these musical artisans and their work is well deserved and long overdue.

In addition, the focus of this volume is on music in the finished films. There is some coverage of history and background leading up to these features. There is also information about the musicians who contributed to these projects, as well as details concerning their work. Yet the ultimate measure of any movie is the finished product. Likewise, the value of any musical score is dependent upon how it interacts with, informs, complements, and serves the feature to which it is attached. Thus, the lion's share of *Music in Disney's Animated Features* is devoted to analyzing the use and function of music in these films.

Some of the techniques highlighted in the book include: Mickey Mousing, leitmotif, rhymed dialog to transition into a song, the use of ballerinas as animation models, theme and variations, and the use of opening and closing storybooks as ersatz curtain openings and closings. In addition, songs in Disney animated features are often used to establish characters, reveal plot points, further narrative, and reflect American culture. A final approach used in soundtracks to Disney animated features was the use of song archetypes, such as the magic song, the silly song, the wish/dream song, and the work song.

Several individuals from the Disney Music Group provided the author with cue sheets for the features covered in this volume, as well as some for various shorts. The cue sheets for the features are very instructive and are the primary source of the information in the appendix. The cue sheets for several of the early shorts contain some questionable material that most likely came from unverifiable internet sources. Thus, these latter sources did not have much influence on the research process.

Occasionally this volume will make use of music analysis approaches, particularly techniques that come from Heinrich Schenker (1868–1935) and Allen Forte (1926–). However, it should be noted that Schenker is largely applied in this book to examine the foreground and middleground levels, and no attempt is made to connect these melodies with a fundamental structure. Those who are unacquainted with set theory, Schenkerian analysis, and music theory in general should not be discouraged, as these approaches are used infrequently, and the text attempts to explain such figures.

Due to the larger-than-life persona of Walt Disney, there are those who identify him as the ultimate creative engine of The Walt Disney Company, as well as hold him responsible for all decisions of the Company during his lifetime. Some go further, citing his strong leadership that created a culture that survived him, thus continuing his influence to this very day. While the importance of Walt Disney is obvious, to attribute all creative aspects of The Walt Disney Company to him is infeasible and undesirable. Furthermore, such considerations minimize the important contributions of the thousands of people who have helped make the company what it is today.

Since The Walt Disney Company is a first-name organization, this book refers to Walt Disney and his brother Roy O. Disney (1893–1971) by their first names. The use of the term "Disney" therefore is reserved in this volume to refer to the organization as a whole. Finally, while music is the subject of the book, it is important to note that the music in question is an integral part of the film at hand. Due to this fact, this volume will consider music not only on its own merits, but also in relationship to the movie as a whole, as well as in relationship to culture at large. Finally, in this book music is defined broadly to include performance arts that are based in music, including dance and musical theater.

Chapter 1

MICKEYS

In the first episode of the *Disneyland* television series, Walt Disney stated: "During the last few years, we've ventured into a lot of different fields. We've had the opportunity to meet and work with a lot of wonderful people. Our only hope is we never lose sight of one thing: that it was all started by a mouse."[1]

This statement is not entirely accurate. It started with music. Prior to *Steamboat Willie,* the first distributed Mickey Mouse cartoon, two other shorts featuring the now iconic mouse had been produced. In an attempt to capitalize on the popularity of Charles Lindbergh (1902–1974), Walt produced *Plane Crazy* (1928). *The Gallopin' Gaucho* (1928), a parody of the Douglas Fairbanks (1883–1939) movie *The Gaucho* (1927), followed. Neither cartoon performed very well, failing to secure a distributor.[2] The mouse did not achieve his fame until he was paired with music in *Steamboat Willie.*

STEAMBOAT WILLIE

By animation historian Michael Barrier's estimation, Walt first proposed the idea of a sound cartoon at a gag meeting for *Gallopin' Gaucho* that was held on May 29, 1928.[3] This meeting occurred a full two weeks after *Plane Crazy* had been test screened. Walt felt that the new technology would bring much-needed attention to his studio.

While *Steamboat Willie* is often credited as being the first sound cartoon, other animated shorts had used synchronized music, most notably the Fleischer Studios' Song Car-Tunes series (1924–1927). Paul Terry's *Dinner Time,* which was released on September 1, 1928 (two and one half months earlier than *Steamboat Willie*), featured synchronized music, dialog, and sound effects. *Dinner Time,* which was part of the Van Beuren Studios' Aesop's Fables (1921–1929) series, failed to achieve the public success that *Steamboat Willie* had. Walt saw *Dinner Time* in September but was not impressed, noting that "it merely had an orchestra playing and add[ed] some noises."[4] That being said, Walt felt that he was in competition with the series, later stating that "even as late as 1930, [his] ambition was to be able to make cartoons as good as the Aesop's Fables series."[5]

Steamboat Willie opens with Mickey Mouse at the wheel of a steamboat. Spinning the wheel, Mickey merrily whistles (performed by the piccolo[6]) the tune "Steamboat Bill," a song chosen for the cartoon by Walt himself.[7] This tune was written by Ren Shields (1868–1913) and the Leighton Brothers in 1910. Both "Steamboat Bill" and a previous song that the Leightons performed, "The Ballad of Casey Jones" (1909), were significant hits that involved a brave man who meets his fate trying to break a speed record.

The film's most memorable moment occurs when Minnie, a passenger on the steamboat, drops her sheet music to the song "Turkey in the Straw," which is promptly eaten by a goat. Mickey then opens the goat's mouth, and Minnie cranks the animal's tail, at which point the animal begins to play the song like an impromptu gramophone. What ensues is an amusing musical sequence where Mickey proceeds to play music utilizing a variety of animals. Animator Wilfred Jackson (1906–1988) selected "Turkey in the Straw" for inclusion in the short.[8]

Some of the visual material in Steamboat Willie comes from other earlier Disney silent cartoons. The central gag of the short, using a goat that has eaten sheet music as a gramophone, was previously used in the Oswald cartoon Rival Romeos (1928). Other material comes from one of the last Alice Comedies (1923–1927) the Studios had produced: Alice the Whaler (1927). The whaling ship featured in the short has a cook that is somewhat similar in appearance and demeanor to Steamboat Willie's Captain Pete. Assisting in KP duty is a diminutive mouse, who performs the same potato-peeling gag that appears near the end of Steamboat Willie. Later in Alice the Whaler, the cook gruffly orders the mouse to procure eggs, at which point the mouse blows raspberries at his superior, much as in the opening of Steamboat Willie.

While the title of Steamboat Willie references the 1928 Buster Keaton film Steamboat Bill, Jr., in a more general sense the short is an homage to The Jazz Singer (1927). While The Jazz Singer is often remembered as the first sound motion picture, several others had preceded it, including D. W. Griffith's Dream Street (1921) and the Warner Bros. films Don Juan and The Better 'Ole (both 1926). What made The Jazz Singer more popular than these predecessors was the degree to which the film incorporated music as a central element. Likewise, what made Steamboat Willie unique and successful was not simply the strong personality of Mickey Mouse or the novelty of a sound cartoon, but rather the close synchronization of Mickey Mouse playing music on various animals during the "Turkey in the Straw" sequence. The unique, humorous nature of this musical synchronization entertained and fascinated the early sound-era audience.

This high degree of synchronization was so endemic to Disney cartoons that the practice became known as "Mickey Mousing." Jackson and Walt devised a technique allowing for this close synchronization.[9] The process centered on animating cue marks on the film that would indicate the musical beat. In order to have a more accurate portrayal of the tempo, the film had to be run at twenty-four frames per second as opposed to the eighteen frames per second that had been standard with silent movies.

As a test of concept, Walt invited the Studios' personnel and their wives one June evening to an eight o'clock private viewing of the then-silent version of a scene from *Steamboat Willie.* A quartet of animators—Walt, Jackson, Johnny Cannon (1907–1946), and Ub[10] Iwerks (1901–1971)—stood behind the screen and provided live, synchronized music, dialog, and sound effects for the short.[11] Jackson provided melodic material on a harmonica, while Iwerks accompanied on washboard and slide whistle.[12] Cannon provided sound effects, while Walt performed the dialog.[13] Jackson reported :

> Walt's office had a glass window in the door, so we could close the door, and look through it, and see the back of the screen. The screen was a bed sheet that was hung up in this long room where the backgrounds were painted. Roy Disney got outside the building with the projector, and projected through a window, so the sound of the projector wouldn't be too loud.
>
> When Roy started the projector up, I furnished the music with my mouth organ . . . and the other fellows hit things and made sound effects. We had spittoons everywhere then, and they made a wonderful gong if you hit them with a pencil. We practiced with it several times, and we got so we were hitting it off pretty well. We took turns going out there ourselves, and looking at the thing, and when I went out, there wasn't any music, but the noises and the voices seemed to come from it just fine. It was really pretty exciting, and it did prove to us that the sound coming from the drawing could be a convincing thing.[14]

After the demonstration, Iwerks remarked, "I never saw such a reaction from an audience in my life. The scheme worked perfectly. The sound system itself gave the illusion of something emanating directly from the screen."[15]

Equally excited, Walt exclaimed, "This is it, this is it! We've got it!"[16] The enthusiastic group continued repeating the demonstration until two in the morning.[17] By this point, several of the attendees who had seen the presentation numerous times began to congregate in the hallway, angering Walt, who noted, "You're out here talking about babies and we're in here making history."[18] Despite his enthusiasm, he knew that the cartoon still needed polish, remarking that "it was terrible, but it was wonderful."[19] Iwerks was equally exuberant, stating later in his career that "nothing since has ever equaled it."[20] Fueled with such zeal, the young animators reconvened at six in the morning to continue their work.[21]

Walt's father, Elias (1859–1941), was an amateur fiddler, and his mother, Flora (1868–1938), served as an organist for a time at St. Paul's Congregational Church in Chicago. Nevertheless, their son Walt had little experience with music, save for a failed venture at learning the violin, an experience he recalled later in life:

> I was only fifteen then but I already knew I wanted to draw. But when I told my father, he just scoffed at me and said if I was foolish enough to want to become an artist, I should learn the violin; and then I could always get a job in a band if I was in need of money. He tore up my drawings, brought out his own violin, and forced me to saw and scrape at it for hours every day, although he must have known from the squawks I was making I was tone-deaf and would never be any good at music.[22]

In addition to not having any ability with music, Walt lacked some basic understanding regarding the fundamentals of music, particularly during the Studios' early years. As Wilfred Jackson noted, "When he thought a piece of action should be extended or shortened somewhat beyond what would fit with some certain part of a piece of music, he expected his musician to just simply find some way or other to expand or shorten that part of his music."[23] While Walt filled in many gaps in his knowledge over the years, as he collaborated closely with the talented composers who would join his studio, at this point the filmmaker needed help from a professional musician with this mission of a sound cartoon.

There is considerable disagreement in various sources over who wrote the soundtrack to *Steamboat Willie*. The only known paper document that could be used to support authorship is an eleven-page manuscript "score" held in the Walt Disney Archives. This manuscript, which features two staves per system, was clearly written by an amateur who borders on being a non-musician. System brackets, when they occur, are a simple arc. Clefs in the manuscript are consistently put in the wrong staff position. Eighth notes, as well as smaller subdivisions, are rarely beamed together to indicate beats. Note heads occasionally appear on the wrong side of a stem, and stems often point in the wrong direction.

Musically speaking, this "score" consists primarily of indications where "Steamboat Bill" and "Turkey in the Straw" appear in the short's timeline. When these tunes appear, they are presented solely as a melody with no accompaniment. The majority of the rest of this "score" involves rhythmic indications of where dialog and various actions occur, often written using a single repeated note. Thus, this manuscript really functions more as bar sheet than as a musical score.

Figure 1.1. Melody that accompanies Pete's entrance in *Steamboat Willie*

This bar sheet was almost certainly written by Wilfred Jackson. The animator worked out the timing, tempo, and locations of "Steamboat Bill" and "Turkey in the Straw" within the short. Such simple elements do not constitute composition. Furthermore, while Jackson's mother was a piano teacher, no evidence exists that he had any musical skills other than being able to play the harmonica, and a basic general knowledge of music. In fact, Disney composer Carl Stalling (1891–1972) once said of Jackson, "This man's no musician."[24] Walt later commented on Stalling's assessment of Jackson, stating, "Carl was right."[25] Jackson himself noted, "My contributions to sound cartoons were that I knew what a metronome was, and I worked out what was first called a dope sheet and later a bar sheet."[26] Clearly, Jackson made no claim that he wrote the score.

Before completely dismissing Jackson as not contributing to the score for *Steamboat Willie*, the bar sheet merits more consideration. Not only do the melodies for "Steamboat Bill" and "Turkey in the Straw" occur where Jackson notes, but they also appear in the keys (G and C major respectively) that the animator denoted. However, the rhythms noted in the bar sheet where Mickey plays drums on the trashcan are not similar to those that are heard in the final soundtrack.

Jackson specifies a gag of using the "Shave and a Haircut" tune both as the sound of the steamboat's whistles and as the end of his mallet performance on the bull's teeth. Only the latter instance of this tune is used in the short, and it appears in a different key than denoted in the bar sheet. Of all the other melodic fragments Jackson includes in his bar sheet, only one of them (Figure 1.1) is used in the final soundtrack. These five notes accompany the unseen steps of Pete, who is referred to in the document as "cat,"[27] as he makes his first entrance into the wheelhouse. It is also worth noticing that Minnie is also unnamed in the document and is referred to as "girl."[28] The five notes from Jackson's bar sheet into the final soundtrack qualify him as being a minor, contributing composer for the score to the short.

The amateur nature of Jackson's bar sheet indicates that the animator did not possess any knowledge of counterpoint, harmony, or orchestration that would be required to complete the final score. Thus, a primary composer for the short was necessary. Bob Thomas (1922–2014), in his book *Walt Disney: An American Original*, says that Walt hired former Kansas City area theater organist Stalling to write the score.[29] A list of shorts scored by Stalling prepared at the Walt Disney Archives during Dave Smith's tenure as chief archivist includes *Steamboat Willie*. Unfortunately, this document is not dated, does not indicate who created the list, and does not note what sources were used to establish authorship. It is plausible that Thomas's book may have been used to support the claim. However, in a 1971 interview Stalling claims, "I had nothing to do with that [the soundtrack to *Steamboat Willie*]."[30]

Michael Barrier, in his book *The Animated Man: A Life of Walt Disney*, uses Stalling's 1971 statement to posit that a different, as yet unidentified person wrote the score.[31] The Disney Music Group's cue sheets indicate that the score was composed by Bert Lewis (1879–1948), who had been a theater organist in Kansas City, and later in Los Angeles. Tracey Birdsall, Lewis's great-grand-daughter, confirms that family legend has it that Lewis composed the score for *Steamboat Willie*.[32]

Birdsall also notes that she had been told that her great-grandfather knew Walt in Kansas City, but that Lewis moved to California to follow Walt.[33] However, the musician was already living in Los Angeles by 1920.[34] If Lewis knew the young animator in Kansas City, they would have had to have met in 1919, when Walt was working at the Pesmen-Rubin commercial art studio. During his time at Pesmen-Rubin, Walt did some art for the Newman Theater Magazine, but it is unlikely that would have been an opportunity for the artist to meet Lewis.[35] However, the Gray Advertising Building, which housed Pesmen-Rubin, was only blocks from the Regent Theatre, so perhaps Lewis knew the young artist as a patron of the theater.

Even if Walt and Lewis never met in Kansas City, it is likely that the musician got the job scoring *Steamboat Willie* through Carl Stalling. When Walt took a trip to New York City to look into sound recording options, he stopped in Kansas City to consult with Stalling and asked the musician to score the cartoon.[36] At this meeting it is possible that Stalling suggested his former colleague Bert Lewis, who was already working in Los Angeles, to score the short. Thus, while definitive proof that Lewis scored *Steamboat Willie* is absent, not only is this primary authorship plausible, it is also supported by the recollections of his descendants.

The score for *Steamboat Willie* called for some twenty performers, who were each paid ten dollars an hour for the recording session.[37] The first musician to arrive for the first session, held on September 15, was a bassist.[38] This bassist, who kept a whiskey bottle in his case, overpowered the recording equipment and blew a vacuum tube when he played.[39] While this amplitude problem was solved by moving the performer out of the room, more problems continued.[40] Walt, who provided the voices for both Mickey and the parrot, ruined a take by coughing into the microphone. However, worst of all, the conductor, Carl Edouarde (1876–1932), was not able to stay in synch with the film.

Since the September 15 session resulted in no usable recordings, a second session was necessary. Committed to quality, Walt instructed Roy to get a loan from a bank, adding, "Slap as big a mortgage on everything we got."[41] Walt even gave Roy permission to sell his Moon Roadster in order to finance the second recording session.[42]

For the second session, which occurred on September 30, Walt managed to reduce the size of the orchestra to fifteen performers. According to Ub Iwerks, the synchronization was coordinated by having a copy of the film with a visual cue that followed the beat of the music projected onto a piece of sheet music on Edouarde's stand.[43] The three-hour recording session was a success, with Walt stating, "As a whole I would say that it was damn near perfect."[44]

During this time a nervous Walt expressed doubt about the project in letters to his wife, Lillian.[45] However, the young filmmaker wrote optimistically to his brother, already planning to produce fifty-two Mickey Mouse cartoons per year.[46] It is unclear whether the Studios were paid for *Steamboat Willie*'s run at the Colony Theater.[47] Later in life Walt claimed to have been paid five hundred dollars a week for the run, but it is also likely that he was so anxious to get the cartoon in front of the public that he may have let the Colony use it for free.[48] Regardless, the cartoon, and its integrated soundtrack, propelled Mickey Mouse, and Walt, to success.

Walt recognized the value of this achievement. Dave Smith found a copy of the script to *Steamboat Willie* in the bottom of a desk drawer in Walt's desk when he cataloged the contents of the filmmaker's office as one of his first tasks when starting the Disney Archives.[49] The script's presence in Walt's desk is almost certainly an indication of how important he regarded the short in terms of his career.

BERT LEWIS

Elbert (Bert) Clifford Lewis was born in Saint Louis, Missouri, on July 16, 1879.[50] His parents were salesman Charles Lee Lewis and his wife, Ellen (Holt) Lewis, who were born in New Hampshire and New York respectively.[51] Bert was the youngest of five surviving children that the couple had.[52]

Bert entered the workforce after high school.[53] By the time he was twenty, and the family was living in Topeka, he was working as a musician and was most likely supporting his parents.[54] On June 14, 1905, Lewis married Maud L. Shinkle in Kansas City.[55] The couple had two children, Harold Elbert (born 1906) and Miriam Ellen (born 1914). In the mid-teens Lewis was working as a theater organist at the Tenth Street Theatre in Kansas City.[56] A few years later he was working at the Regent Theatre, which at the time was part of the Newman Theater chain. The Regent was only a couple of blocks from the Royal Theatre, another Newman theater, where Carl Stalling worked during the same years.

Lewis moved with his family to California sometime between 1918 and 1920. Upon first moving out to California, he supported his family by accompanying silent films on the organ at the Wilshire Ebell Theatre.[57]

After his probable scoring of *Steamboat Willie*, during the time when Stalling was the music director at the Studios, Lewis would occasionally conduct some of the Studios' recording sessions.[58] He was officially hired by Disney in December of 1929 and was quickly promoted to music director when Stalling left the Studios in early 1930. Between 1930 and 1935, Lewis scored more than two dozen shorts for The Walt Disney Studios. The majority of these were Mickey shorts: *Pioneer Days* (1930), *The Barnyard Broadcast* (1931), *Fishin' Around* (1931), *Mickey Cuts Up* (1931), *Mickey Steps Out* (1931), *The Moose Hunt* (1931), *The Mad Dog* (1932), *Mickey's Good Deed* (1932), *Trader Mickey* (1932), *The Wayward Canary* (1932), *The Mad Doctor* (1933), *The Mail Pilot* (1933), *Mickey's Steam Roller* (1934), *Mickey's Fire Brigade* (1935), *Mickey's Kangaroo* (1935), *Mickey's Man Friday* (1935), and *On Ice* (1935). He also co-scored several shorts with Frank Churchill (1901–1942), including: *Birds in Spring* (1933), *Old King Cole* (1933), *Camping Out* (1934), *The Dognapper* (1934), *The Flying Mouse* (1934), and *Mickey Plays Papa* (1934). He scored several Silly Symphonies, including *Playful Pan* (1930), *Babes in the Woods* (1932), *Flowers and Trees* (1932), *Just Dogs* (1932), and *King Neptune* (1932).

Lewis stopped working for Disney in or after 1935. A couple of years later, in 1937, the composer became the first music director at MGM's fledgling cartoon studio.[59] At MGM Lewis scored at least sixteen shorts, including *A Day at the Beach* (1938), *Petunia Natural Park* (1939), and *Jitterbug Follies* (1939). By 1940 Lewis was largely out of work, indicating that he had not worked in a year, and that he had been fully employed for only thirteen weeks of 1939, on the 1940 census.[60] During this time the household was largely supported by Maud, who at that time was a cafeteria manager at a school.[61] The composer died some eight years later in Ventura, California, on November 30, 1948.

LESSONS LEARNED FROM STEAMBOAT WILLIE

On November 18, 1928, *Steamboat Willie* opened at the Colony Theater in New York City.[62] That day Stalling saw the film, reporting, "I was with Walt when *Steamboat Willie* was previewed at the Colony Theater, down on Broadway, and we got the audience reaction. The reaction was very good. We sat on almost the last row and heard laughs and snickers all around us."[63] The short preceded a movie called *Gang War* (1928), but the hit of the day was the cartoon.

At the center of the success of *Steamboat Willie* was sound. A review from the *New York Times* reported, "It growls, whines, squeaks, and makes various other sounds that add to its mirthful quality."[64] *Steamboat Willie* changed the field of animation overnight. Hal Walker, an animator for the popular Felix the Cat shorts, noted, "Disney put us out of business with his sound."[65]

The high degree of synchronization between image and music exhibited in *Steamboat Willie* not only was effective from an aesthetic point of view but also made economical sense. After the disastrous recording session of September 15, Walt noted that sound effects could be incorporated into a musical score. This inclusion would allow for the Studios to hire fewer sound effects performers and could cut down on rehearsal time. Thus, in a letter dated October 6, the young filmmaker encouraged the use of music to embody sound effects.[66]

Walt was interested in new technology and new approaches to filmmaking. For example, in his Alice Comedies, live-action film was combined with animation. Previous attempts at this mixture of techniques by other studios placed the cartoon beings in the real world, while Walt placed the human in a cartoon world. Being a successful early adopter of synchronized sound animation encouraged him to remain at the leading edge of entertainment technology throughout his career.

Walt was also a believer in creating the highest-quality product possible. For example, his early cartoon *Puss in Boots* (1922), during his Kansas City Laugh-O-gram era, featured a rich palette of gray tones in an era when most black-and-white cartoons were strictly black and white.[67] While *Steamboat Willie* may not have been the first sound cartoon, it was treated as such, as it was the first quality sound cartoon.

Perhaps the most important lesson learned from *Steamboat Willie* was the potential for music to play a primary role in the success of an animated film. The fact that Walt learned this lesson is self-evident, given that Mickey Mouse was quickly recast as a versatile musician. In *The Opry House* (1929), our hero plays piano, with Carl Stalling performing the part for the soundtrack.[68] In *The Karnival Kid* (1929), the mouse plays guitar, as well as hot dogs by poking them with a fork, causing them to bark. In 1931's *The Birthday Party*, Mickey performs a spirited piano duet with Minnie and later plays a xylophone while Minnie accompanies on the ivories. Mickey plays a piano that fortuitously washes up on the shore in *The Castaway* (1931). He plays a short arrangement of "Silent Night" on Christmas tree ornaments in *Mickey's Orphans* (1931). Mickey conducts the house orchestra in 1932's *Mickey's Revue*. Later in the revue, he performs a lively version of "Tiger Rag," playing percussion, xylophone, trombone, and tuba, again accompanied by Minnie on piano.

MICKEY MOUSE NOVELTY SONGS

One of the most important songs included in early Mickey Mouse cartoons is "Minnie's Yoo Hoo," which first appeared in the cartoon *Mickey's Follies* (1929).

The song, which was written by Carl Stalling with lyrics by Walt and Stalling, became Mickey's first theme song and was the first official Disney song to appear on sheet music and record. Leo Zollo and his Orchestra recorded the song and released it on Melotone records in 1931.

The song would also play an important role in a significant publicity campaign. On January 11, 1929, theater owner Harry Woodin started the first Mickey Mouse Club, in Ocean Park, California. The club was an incentive to get kids to come to Saturday matinees to watch Mickey Mouse cartoons.

Walt liked Woodin's idea and hired him to spread the concept around the world. By 1932 there were one million members worldwide, with a single movie theater chain in England boasting 160 local chapters. In 1930 the Studio put out a cartoon short where Mickey would lead a chorus of "Minnie's Yoo Hoo," which was used to lead local chapters in a sing-along of the club's official theme. Other chapters featured live music. In fact, future Disney animator Ward Kimball (1914–2002) worked his way through school playing in a Mickey Mouse Club band at a local theater.[69] Disney oversaw these clubs until 1935, but local chapters continued to exist through the Second World War.

Mickey Mouse mania had spread throughout the United States, and several musicians attempted to cash in on the trend. The first notable attempt to do so was by Harry Carlton. In 1930 the songwriter penned the tune "Mickey Mouse." In addition to its being released in the United Kingdom, lyricist Bert Reisfeld (1906–1991) created a German-language version. In England the song was recorded by the Rhythmic Eight on Zonophone Records, in 1930. The German version was recorded by Max Mensing (1886–1945) and the Saxophon Orchester Dobbri on Parlophon Records, as well as by a dance band called Dajos Béla on Odeon Records.

One of the first officially Disney-licensed songs, "What! No Mickey Mouse? What Kind of a Party Is This?" (1932), was by Irving Caesar (1895–1996). The song's title came from a cartoon in *Life* magazine that had gone on to be catchphrase expressing disappointment.[70] "What! No Mickey Mouse?" was recorded in 1932 by Ben Bernie and All the Lads on the Vocalion label. Bernie (1891–1943) was a popular bandleader in the twenties and thirties. In fact, he popularized one of the most iconic catchphrases of the twenties, "Yowsah, yowsah, yowsah." Furthermore, Bernie and his orchestra had provided live entertainment in the Colony Theater on the day of *Steamboat Willie's* premiere.[71]

Another notable Mickey Mouse novelty song, which was licensed by Disney, is 1936's "Mickey Mouse's Birthday Party." Written by Charlie Tobias (1898–1970), Bob Rothberg (1901–1938), and Joseph Meyer (1894–1987), the song was recorded by George Hall and His Orchestra, Billy Murray (1877–1954) with the American Novelty Orchestra, and Jack Shilkret (1896–1964) and the American Novelty Orchestra. The Bill Murray recording features several musical quotations, including "Happy Birthday to You," "Who's Afraid of the Big Bad Wolf?" (1933) and "The World Owes Me a Living" (1934). The latter two of these songs were both written for Silly Symphony cartoons.

On the fifth anniversary of Mickey Mouse, the Studios wanted to commemorate the event with a birthday song for the iconic mouse. To this end, Ann Ronell (1905–1993) submitted to Disney a song she had written for the occasion, "Mickey Mouse and Minnie's in Town."[72] The tune was accepted by the Studios as Mickey's official birthday song.[73] In the second half of 1933, some 3,768 copies of the sheet music sold, as well as 262 copies of an orchestral arrangement.[74] "Mickey Mouse and Minnie's in Town" was also recorded by Ben Bernie and All the Lads, Don Bestor and His Orchestra, and Frank Luther (1899–1980).

There were several other Mickey Mouse novelty songs of the era. "I'd Rather Stay Home with Mickey Mouse (Than Go out with a Rat Like You)" was written in 1932 by Jack Meskille (1897–1973) and David Lee. Licensed by Walt Disney Productions, "The Wedding Party of Mickey Mouse" was written in 1931 by Robert Bagar, with lyrics by Milt Coleman and James Cavanaugh (1892–1967). Cavanaugh was also known for cowriting "Mississippi Mud" (1927) and later cowrote "You're Nobody 'til Somebody Loves You" (1944). Written by C. Franz Koehler, "A March for Mickey Mouse" was published by the Boston Music Company in 1932.

In addition to Mickey Mouse–themed songs, the iconic character made cameos in lyrics to other songs from the era. One such song, Harry Revel (1905–1958) and Mack Gordon's (1904–1959) "It's the Animal in Me," was sung by Ethel Merman (1908–1984) in the film *The Big Broadcast of 1936* (1935). While this lyric may not have appeared in the movie, on the Brunswick recording of the song, Merman sings, "Look at Mickey Mouse, look at Minnie Mouse, they just live on love and cheese."[75]

Perhaps the most enduring non-Disney musical salute to the mouse was Cole Porter's (1891–1964) lyric from "You're the Top." Written for the 1934 musical *Anything Goes*, the lyrics relate, "You're the top! You're the Coliseum, You're the top! You're the Louvre Museum. You're a melody from a symphony by Strauss. You're a Bendel bonnet, a Shakespeare's sonnet, You're Mickey Mouse."[76] While "You're the Top" does not qualify as a Mickey Mouse novelty song, it does date from the same general era and indicates the degree to which the mouse had pervaded popular culture, particularly song.

This trend of Mickey Mouse novelty songs served two functions for Disney. First, they amounted to free advertising for their primary product line, and, second, they reinforced the potential for music to play a central role in terms of publicity. One piece of material evidence of the growing importance of music to Disney's product in the early sound era is the addition of a piano to Walt's office.[77] This space became known as the Music Room, which was shared by the animation director and the music director.[78] However, for the time being, the Studios would stay out of the music publishing and record business, choosing instead to license various songs to established publishers and record companies.

MICKEY STEPS OUT, MICKEY CUTS UP, AND FISHIN' AROUND

There are three manuscript scores of Mickey Mouse shorts resident in the Carl W. Stalling papers at the American Heritage Center at the University of Wyoming. All of these, *Mickey Steps Out, Fishin' Around,* and *Mickey Cuts Up,* were released well after Stalling quit the Studios on January 22, 1930. To complicate matters, the Disney Music Legacy Libraries contain different manuscript scores of the same soundtracks. The Disney Music Legacy Libraries contain two manuscript versions of each of the Mickey shorts, one in two staves, and the other in three staves.

The three-stave scores appear to be early, possibly first, drafts of the music. These versions contain numerous indications of visual action with multiple staff musical sketches. The two-stave scores, which are written in a different hand from the three-stave scores, are relatively complete piano drafts of the scores, which feature no indications of visual action. It is likely that these two-stave versions are later second drafts. The three manuscripts held at the American Heritage Center are all multiple-stave short scores (six to eight staves), which were probably one version away from a final draft.

The American Heritage Center manuscripts and the two-stave piano scores seem to be in the same handwriting. Stalling contains his page numbers in arcs (see Photo 1.1). His cut-time signatures contain an ornamental curl at the top of the C. Likewise, the curl at the top of his bass clefs forms a nearly complete loop, looking somewhat like the number nine.

The three-stave manuscripts are in a different handwriting that is self-consistent, suggesting a single author. These tend to feature page numbers contained in full circles. The curls featured in Stalling's cut-time signatures and bass clefs are nonexistent in these versions. While there are no markings that establish these drafts as being by Bert Lewis, given the small number of full-time musicians employed by the Studios at the time, along with Lewis's position as musical director, it is reasonable to assume that these three-stave scores were written by Lewis. The first page of the score to *Mickey Cuts Up* contains evidence of collaboration between Stalling and Lewis, with the note "Bert: is Bar #396 out?" crossed out in red pencil.[79] Further support of this comes from the fact that these three Mickeys in question were directed by Burt Gillett (1891–1971), who

Photo 1.1. Page 8 of manuscript score to *Fishin' Around*. Image courtesy of the American Heritage Center at the University of Wyoming (Carl Stalling Papers, #5725, Box 2A)—FISHIN' AROUND SCORE from FISHIN' AROUND—Bert Lewis—©1931 Walt Disney Music Company

at the time tended to work with Lewis. Ultimately, one can characterize these three scores as being composed by Bert Lewis and arranged by Carl Stalling.

Each page of the score to *Mickey Steps Out* held in the Carl W. Stalling Papers features three systems of seven staves each. Written in concert pitch, the first two staves feature alto (doubling flute) and tenor (doubling oboe and clarinet) saxophones. The following two contain trumpet and trombone parts. The final four present first violin, second violin, cello, and bass. The bass part is marked "tuba."[80]

The manuscript features thirty rehearsal numbers (Figure 1.2), which correspond to various animated sequences. The score for *Mickey Steps Out* essentially comprises five songs that are strung together. The first tune (rehearsals 1–4) is in binary form. The second, (rehearsals 6–8) has a distinct ragtime flavor. Minnie introduces a brisk waltz on the piano at rehearsal 10, which then continues through rehearsal 15 in orchestrated and solo piano versions.

Minnie also introduces "Sweet Georgia Brown" (SGB) on the piano at rehearsal 17. This performance lasts through rehearsal 22, with of "The Streets of Cairo, or the Poor Little Country Maid" (1895) at rehearsal 19. This tune, which is often referred to as "The Snake Charmer's Song" (SCS), accompanies Mickey as he balances his cane and hat on his nose. The final tune of the short is a brisk gallop (rehearsals 24–29) that emerges as Pluto begins to chase a cat through Minnie's house. Not included in the list of tunes that make up the score is the outro of "Minnie's Yoo Hoo" that occurs in rehearsal 30.

The Carl W. Stalling Papers contain a thirty-two-page manuscript to the composer's score for *Mickey Cuts Up*. The short score is written in concert pitch on six staves per system. The top stave contains woodwind parts (alto and tenor sax doubling piccolo, flute, clarinet, and baritone sax). The next two staves feature trumpet and trombone. First and second violins are contained on one stave, followed by the cellos and basses, each on their own staves.

The manuscript for *Mickey Cuts Up* features twenty-three rehearsal numbers (Figure 1.3) corresponding to various animated sequences of the cartoon. While nearly the entire short is in simple duple or quadruple, in rehearsal 4 there are three measures in compound duple where the tempo remains the same. This change of pulse portrays Mickey's skipping.

Ultimately, the soundtrack to *Mickey Cuts Up* consists of four tunes in sequence. The first three of these songs are all in variants of ternary form, where the center sections are trio-esque. The first song consists of rehearsal numbers 1 through 4, the second is rehearsals 6 and 7, and the last starts on rehearsal 10 and lasts through the end of rehearsal 12. This last song consists of Mickey and Minnie performing the song "Ain't We Got Fun" (1920). The trio-like section for this song (rehearsal 11) is adapted from the verse of "Ain't We Got Fun." The independence of each of these three songs is reflected in the key signatures to each section. The emphasis of ternary form with a trio-like center section in

#	ACTION	MUSIC
1	Mickey shaves	tune A, Bb Major, cut time
2	Mickey sings	tune B, Bb Major, cut time
3	Soap slides out of Mickey's hands	tune A, D Major, cut time
4	Mickey puts on his hat	Repeat rehearsal 2
5	Pluto sneaks	Scalar material capturing Pluto's motion
6	Mickey walks away from Pluto	tune C, G Major, cut time
7	Mickey on xylophone sidewalk	tune C, C Major, cut time
8	Mickey jumps from path	tune C, Ab Major, cut time
9	Mickey hears Minnie's piano	Arpeggiations, Marked as eight measure (un-notated) piano solo, in 3
10	Minnie at the piano	tune D, Marked as sixteen measure (un-noted) piano solo, in C, in 3
11	Bird in birdcage	tune D (orchestrated), in C, in 3
12	Bird in birdcage	tune D, in C in 3
13	Mickey whistling at bird	end of tune D, in C, in 3
14	Minnie at the piano	tune D, Marked as sixteen measure (un-noted piano solo, in 3
15	Mickey peering in the window	repeat of rehearsals 12 and 13
16	Mickey's head caught in window	no music, just dialog
17	Mickey enters room	Minnie plays "ta-da" chords and first four measures of SGB on piano, in G, cut time
18	Minnie at the piano	SGB orchestrated, G Major, cut time
19	Mickey spins hat on cane	4 measures of SCS interruption, then return to SGB, G Major, cut time,
20	Minnie at the piano	SGB, 4 measures piano, then orchestrated, in Bb Major, cut time
21	Mickey balances 2 plates and fish bowl	SGB in Bb Major, cut time
22	Mickey's head in fish bowl	End of SGB in Bb Major, cut time followed by piano chaos from Pluto and cat in the piano
23	Pluto runs out of piano	Orchestrated chromatics scale, in 2
24	Cat runs under Mickey	tune E, Gallop in F, in 2
25	Pluto chases cat in circles	tune F. Gallop dogfight, in A minor, in 2
26	Cat runs under Mickey near globe	tune G, Gallop trio, in F, in 2
27	Pluto looks under the bed	tune H, Gallop in F on the V, in 2
28	Mickey and Minnie riding cat and dog	tune E, moving on to new material Gallop under the rug in F, in 2
29	Pluto cuts through the rug	chromatic / diminished seventh material leading to punctuating falling fifths progression chords in F, in 2 with one measure of 3.
30	End title	MYH outro in F in cut time

Figure 1.2. Rehearsal numbers in the manuscript to *Mickey Steps Out*

#	ACTION	MUSIC
1	Mickey whistles while mowing	tune A, Eb Major, in cut time
2	Minnie sings while watering	tune A, Eb Major, in cut time
3	Mickey dances on top of handle of mower	tune B, C Major, in cut time
4	Mickey moves from under tree to shrub	tune A, Eb Major, in cut time, with a 3 measure interruption of compound duple
5	Bird emerges from shrub moves to tree	modulating passage
6	Minnie whistles with bird	tune C, G Major, in 4
7	Mickey whistles from inside birdhouse Minnie whistles with Mickey Ends with commotion music as cat attacks Mickey	tune D, C Major, in 4 tune C, G Major, in 4
8	silence for dialog	
9	Mickey as turtle	tune E, d minor, in 4, changes to cut time
10	Mickey as turtle, "Ain't We Got Fun" Minnie plays "Ain't We Got Fun"	AWGFC, F Major, in cut time AWGFC, F Major, in cut time
11	Harmonica duet "Ain't We Got Fun" (verse)	AWGFV, F Major, in cut time
12	Harmonica duet on "Ain't We Got Fun"	AWGFC, F Major, in cut to,e
13	Cat fights with Pluto	Interrupts with transitional chromatic lines double time, gallop in 2
14	Pluto chases cat	tune F, F Major, in 2
15	Pluto mows over tree	tune G, F Major on the V, in 2
16	Minnie falls on pump handle	repeat of rehearsal 15, in 2
17	Pluto runs through long underwear	tune H, Bb Major, in 2
18	Pluto mows over log	tune H, Bb Major, in 2
19	Skeleton fish jump out of pond	dogfight, D Major, in 2
20	Pluto mows the roof	repeat of rehearsal 14, in 2
21	Pluto gets caught on the clothes line	tune I, F Major, in 2
22	Cat continues to run down the hill	rehearsal 21 repeats, in 2
23	Pluto under dishes	tune J, F Major, in 2

Figure 1.3. Rehearsal numbers in the manuscript to *Mickey Cuts Up*

Mickey Cuts Up is similar to the first dance number of Stalling's score for *The Skeleton Dance* (1929).

The final number commences at rehearsal 14, after the transitional material of the previous section, which cuts short the last chorus of "Ain't We Got Fun" with double-time chromatic lines. This last number is a brisk gallop that is in a modified march form. A dogfight-like section occurs in rehearsal 19, which is followed by the first melody of the gallop. The final section, rehearsal 23, is coda-like in nature.

The scores to both *Mickey Steps Out* and *Mickey Cuts Up* share many structural elements. Firstly, both are composed from a number of short songs that

#	ACTION	MUSIC
1	Mickey and Pluto in a row boat	tune A, Eb Major, cut-time
2	Mickey looks at "No Fishing" sign	tune B, Ab Major, cut-time
3	Pluto barks	four measures of isolated chords
3.5	Fish walks on bottom of pond	tune C, c minor, cut-time
4	Mickey's pants go into the pond	tune B, Ab Major, cut-time
5	Pluto fishes with his tail	tune A, Eb Major, cut-time
6	Fish swims around Pluto	tune D, C Major, cut-time
7	Mickey whistling in row boat	tune E, G Major, cut-time
8	Fish dances with worm	tune E, G Major, cut-time
9	Pluto sniffs under the water	tune D, C Major, cut-time, last measure shifts to quadruple compound, with the beat being the same
10	Pluto chases fish into a cave	tune F, e minor, quadruple compound
11	Pluto jumps into the boat	tune D, C Major, cut-time
12	Mickey snares Pluto's tail on hook	tune E, G Major, cut-time
13	Policeman looks out from behind sign	tune G, F Major, cut-time
14	Mickey uses Pluto to bring in a fish	tune G variation, F Major, cut-time
15	16 mm. of music not used in short	
16	Policeman talks to Mickey	tune H, F Major, cut-time, two measures not used
17	Policeman changes his hat	Sound effects, written as 13 beats of rest
18	Similar to rehearsal 19, not used in short	
19	Policeman says, "Hands up."	Walking music and stinger, g minor, cut-time
20	Mickey paddles row boat	tune I, F Major, switches to fast simple duple gallop
21	Pluto gets into row boat	tune J, C Major, simple duple
22	End title	Music not written, marked tag ("Minnie's Yoo Hoo")

Figure 1.4. Rehearsal numbers in the manuscript to *Fishin' Around*

are strung together. Both cartoons are centered on a musical number containing a well-known popular tune. Each ends with a spirited gallop in a modified march form.

Both scores exhibit a similar approach to orchestration. Specifically, neither piece utilizes timbral variety to any significant degree. Rather, all the instruments play continuously throughout the majority of each score. While such an approach might not receive much more than a passing grade in a college orchestration course, it can be argued that Stalling's arrangement is appropriate, given the recording technology at the time. Namely, such tutti orchestration helps ensure that all the respective parts will be audible on the recording.

The scores to *Mickey Steps Out* and *Mickey Cuts Up* are very similar in form, style, and execution. While *Fishin' Around* also bears a strong relationship with the two aforementioned scores, it is the most unique of the three. Each page of the score to *Fishin' Around*, held in the Carl W. Stalling Papers, contains three systems each composed of eight staves. Written in concert pitch, the top three staves contains woodwind parts: flute (doubling piccolo), clarinet (doubling sax), and bassoon. The next two staves feature trumpet and trombone. First and second violins are contained on one stave, followed by the cellos and basses, each on their own staves.

The manuscript for *Fishin' Around* features twenty-two rehearsal numbers (Figure 1.4) corresponding to various animated sequences of the cartoon. Some of this material was not used in the finished short (rehearsals 15 and 18). The majority of the music is relatively consistent, with all but the end of the score (rehearsals 20–22) working somewhat like a modified rondo form at a moderate tempo. The conclusion of the short switches over to a fast gallop (rehearsals 20 and 21). The brevity of this gallop prevents it from modeling march form, as is done at the ends of *Mickey Steps Out* and *Mickey Cuts Up*.

Fishin' Around is somewhat unique in relation to other early Mickey cartoons in its apparent lack of quotation and paraphrase of preexisting music. Furthermore, the relative continuity of the score for *Fishin' Around* suggests that it is somewhat more advanced, musically speaking, than the scores for *Mickey Steps Out* and *Mickey Cuts Up*. *Fishin' Around* is even more advanced orchestrationally. While all the instruments are utilized nearly constantly in the score, there is a greater independence of the parts. Melodic material is even given to bass instruments such as the cello (rehearsal 1) and the trombone (rehearsal 13). Furthermore, a square-dance tuning motive is utilized in the last couple of bars in rehearsal 13. Meant to be evocative of a country-bumpkin manner, the orchestration aids in the establishment of character of the policeman. Stalling even instructs the violins in this section to play in a "hick style" (Photo 1.1).[81]

FROM SILENT TO SOUND

The transition from silent film to live-action sound motion pictures matured with the works of Hollywood composers Max Steiner (1888–1971), Erich Wolfgang Korngold (1897–1957), and Franz Waxman (1906–1967). They were Austrian (Steiner and Korngold) and German (Waxman). All three formally studied music and composition. In fact, not only did Steiner study under Gustav Mahler (1860–1911), but his godfather was Richard Strauss (1864–1949). Both Steiner and Korngold had experience in composing for theater or for the concert hall before scoring their first picture. Waxman had had experience as a pianist and an arranger for popular music before working as an orchestrator in the German film industry. Understandably, the classic Hollywood film score evolved to be symphonic in nature with a Germanic sound.

The composers who initiated the transition from silent cartoons to sound shorts at Disney had a decidedly different pedigree. Both Carl Stalling and Bert

Lewis were theater organists who cut their teeth accompanying silent films in Kansas City. As theater organists, Stalling and Lewis were used to cobbling together their cinematic accompaniments from classical music, traditional songs, and cue sheets.

Carl Stalling collected cue sheets that film studios distributed to accompanists during the silent era. The Carl W. Stalling Papers at the University of Wyoming's American Heritage Center contain cue sheets that the composer had collected from over one hundred movies. Stalling had also amassed a significant collection of cue anthologies that accompanists during the silent era would also use as potential tunes for their live, improvised scores. In particular, the composer's collection included material from *Berg's Incidental Series*, *Bosworth's Loose Leaf Cinema Incidentals*, *Hawkes Photo-Play Series*, the *Kinothek* series, and the *Lafleur Motion Picture Edition*. The fact that the composer saved these cue sheets through to the end of his career is an indication of how influential such an assemblage was to his career as a film composer.

Keyboard accompanists were not the only ones who assembled music for silent films in such a manner. Orchestral scores for many silent movies were compiled from classical excerpts. The D. W. Griffith (1875–1948) film *The Clansman* (1915) utilized a score by Carli Elinor (1890–1958). This score was assembled from excerpts of pieces by Wolfgang Amadeus Mozart (1756–1791), Ludwig van Beethoven, Gioachino Rossini (1792–1868), Franz Schubert (1797–1828), Friedrich von Flotow (1812–1883), Richard Wagner (1813–1883), Giuseppe Verdi (1813–1901), Jacques Offenbach (1819–1880), Franz von Suppé (1819–1895), Georges Bizet (1838–1875), and Jules Massenet (1842–1912).[82] Other such compilation scores include the Joseph Breil (1870–1926) score for *Birth of a Nation*, as well as a 1922 score put together by Frank Adams and Hugo Riesenfeld (1879–1939) for *Dr. Jekyll and Mr. Hyde* (1920).[83]

Stalling would utilize excerpts, fragments, and quotations from preexisting classical pieces, popular melodies, and traditional tunes throughout his career. During his career at Warner Brothers, the composer would refine this assemblage approach to cartoon scoring, creating a sort of a proto-postmodern interplay of quotations, where the music supplies wry commentary on the action. However, Stalling's earlier application of the technique, particularly during his years at The Walt Disney Studios, could be haphazard, sometimes to the point of confusion. For instance, the score to *The Gallopin' Gaucho* commences with a quotation of the abolitionist Civil War era tune "Kingdom Coming" (1862), which is also called "The Year of Jubilo." This connection is particularly perplexing, as neither the chronological nor geographical setting has anything to do with the War Between the States. Utilizing such a well-known song with such strong cultural associations in such a context seems to pit the short against its soundtrack.

In order to advance the art of animation synchronized with music, Disney would have to look beyond composers like Stalling and Lewis, who assembled their scores from preexisting musical material and short tunes. Fortunately, the success of the early Mickeys and Silly Symphonies permitted the Studios to expand their personnel. The next two composers to join Disney, Frank Churchill and Leigh Harline (1907–1969), would play instrumental roles in elevating the music used in the Studios' shorts. While these two composers had dramatically different musical backgrounds from each other, neither came predominantly from the world of accompanying silent films.

In 1933 Max Steiner wrote the score for *King Kong*. Steiner's music for this blockbuster film became one of the early models for the classic Hollywood soundtrack. Coincidentally, the same year featured Frank Churchill's score for *Three Little Pigs*. The huge success of this short's featured song, "Who's Afraid of the Big Bad Wolf?," caused the score to become a model, not only for Disney's animated shorts (and later features), but for animated shorts by a variety of studios from the era as well.

Chapter 2

THE SILLY SYMPHONIES

Music was an essential component of Walt's next major project, the Silly Symphonies. According to Carl Stalling, the Studios' first musical director, he and Walt Disney argued over whether music should be written to fit the animation or vice versa.[1] Stalling later related the conversation he had with Walt Disney:

> After two or three of the Mickeys had been completed and were being run in theaters, Walt talked with me on getting started on the musical series that I had in mind. He thought I meant illustrated songs, but I didn't have that in mind at all. When I told him I was thinking of inanimate figures, like skeletons, trees or flowers coming to life and dancing and doing other animated actions fitted to music in a more or less humorous and rhythmic mood. He became very interested.[2]

Wilfred Jackson remembers the start of the series a little differently:

> A lot of times Walt would want more time or less time for the action than could fit the musical phrase. So, there would be a pretty good argument going on in there. We'd sit out there, in the next room, and enjoy it. Walt could be pretty stiff when he got in an argument, and we'd be glad we weren't on the other end of it. But, finally, Walt worked out a thing with Carl. He said, "Look, let's work it out this way. We'll make two series. On the Mickey Mouse pictures you make your music fit my action the best you can, but we'll make another series, and they'll be musical shorts, and in them music will take precedence and we'll adjust our action the best we can to what you think is the right music."[3]

The name for the series, Silly Symphonies, was a joint effort between Walt and Stalling, as the later suggested the term "symphony," while Walt provided the adjective.[4] In the end the series reflected the interests of both individuals and became a collaboration of music and animation, both as an approach to match images to music and as an experiment with the potential of the medium.

THE SKELETON DANCE

The Silly Symphonies consisted of seventy-five cartoon shorts produced between 1929 and 1939, the first of which was *The Skeleton Dance* (1929). Carl Stalling explained the origin of the idea for the piece during an interview in 1971:

> *The Skeleton Dance* goes way back to my kid days. When I was eight or ten years old, I saw an ad in *The American Boy* magazine of a dancing skeleton, and I got my dad to give me a quarter so I could send for it. It turned out to be a pasteboard cut-out of a loose-jointed skeleton, slung over a six-foot cord under the arm pits. It would "dance" when kids pulled and jerked at each end of the string.[5]

Stalling went on to note, "I suggested the first subject, *The Skeleton Dance*, because ever since I was a kid I had wanted to *see* real skeletons dancing and had always enjoyed seeing skeleton dancing acts in vaudeville. As kids, we all like spooky pictures and stories I think."[6]

Ultimately, the first Silly Symphony became a graveyard fete, which incorporated *March of the Dwarfs*, op. 54, no. 3 (1889–1891) by Edvard Grieg (1843–1907).[7] Grieg's march, which was originally scored for solo piano, occurs near the end of the short in a sequence where one skeleton uses another's ribcage as a xylophone, while yet another skeleton dances a parody of the Charleston. A second prominent melody occurs earlier in the cartoon, a foxtrot in ternary form, which was penned by Stalling.

It is likely that the original plan for the short was to use *Danse Macabre*, op. 40 (1874) by Camille Saint-Saëns (1835–1921). In his article "Symphonists for the Sillies," Ross Care points out that the cartoon follows the same plot outlined by the poem by Henri Cazalis (1840–1909), which was used in the art song (1872) precursor to the iconic tone poem.[8] In addition, the use of the xylophone to sonically portray the rattling of the skeletons' bones is common to both *Danse Macabre* and Stalling's score for *The Skeleton Dance*. However, Stalling most likely used Grieg's *March of the Dwarfs* because it may have been too difficult to obtain permission to use *Danse Macabre*.

Walt expressed his interest in Stalling's idea in a letter to Roy dated September 28, 1928: "Carl's idea of the *Skeleton Dance* for a Musical Novelty has been growing on me ... I think it has dandy possibilities."[9] Later, when work on the short was well into production, Walt expressed his enthusiasm for the project in a letter to Ub Iwerks from February 9, 1929: "I am glad the spook dance is

"Mysterioso Pizzicato"

melody from *The Skeleton Dance*

Figure 2.1—"Mysterioso Pizzicato" and Melody from *The Skeleton Dance*—SKELETON DANCE from THE
SKELETON DANCE—Music by Carl Stalling—© 1930 Walt Disney Music Company

progressing so nicely—give her Hell Ubbe—make it funny and I am sure we
will be able to place it in a good way . . . we have a wonderful score to it. The
music sounds like a symphony. I feel positive everything will fit the picture
properly."[10] Clearly the animator felt that Stalling's music was intrinsic to the
effectiveness of the short.

An additional melody (Figure 2.1) occurs in *The Skeleton Dance*, which
betrays Stalling's earlier career as a silent film accompanist. The melody in
question occurs after the first skeleton comes out from behind a gravestone and
begins to sneak about the graveyard. This melody is very similar to one from
the first volume of the *Remick Folio of Moving Picture Music* (1914). This tune,
"Mysterioso Pizzicato," was likely written by Jens Bodewalt Lampe (1869–1929),
though this tune bears some similarity to a melody from a like collection from
the previous year. "Mysterious—Burglar Music," from the first volume of the
Sam Fox Moving Picture Music, was written by John Stepan Zamecnik (1872–
1953) and has a comparable contour and emphasis of a raised scale degree four.

Collectively, these tunes are sometimes referred to as the "Villain's Theme"
and would later be tagged with the lyrics "We Are Here to Scare You." This melody is often misattributed to a song from a Max Fleischer cartoon titled *Mysterious Mose*. The title song of the short was written by Walter Doyle (1899–1930).
Variants of Lampe's and Zamecnik's melodies became common during the
silent film era, being used by an army of accompanists throughout the country,
and it is these melodies that are the likely common ancestors to both Stalling's
melody from *The Skeleton Dance* and Doyle's "Mysterious Mose."

The synchronization of music and action of *The Skeleton Dance* was so me-
thodically planned out that Ub Iwerks animated the short while the soundtrack
was being recorded in New York.[11] In fact, the continuity script for the cartoon
closes with the direction, "Every frame of this is timed to music and all action
must be made as per [exposure] sheets."[12] The score to *The Skeleton Dance* was
recorded in February 1929.[13] During this time the soundtrack to *The Opry House*

was also recorded.[14] Stalling's musical contribution to *The Skeleton Dance* was noted in the opening credits, a fairly rare occurrence in the Studios' output of the time. Perhaps this credit was an acknowledgment of the composer's part in the origin of the Silly Symphonies.

Premiering at the Carthay Circle Theatre in Los Angeles on August 22, 1929, *The Skeleton Dance* was the first cartoon ever presented at that theater.[15] The film was frequently shown at theaters for more than a week at a time, which was uncommon for animated shorts. The cartoon, which had no dialog, little plot, and a narrative provided almost exclusively by the accompanying music, was heavily dependent upon its soundtrack for its success, much like *Steamboat Willie*. In 1994 members of the New York, Hollywood, Portland, and San Francisco chapters of the Association Internationale du Film d'Animation voted the short as the eighteenth-greatest cartoon of all time.[16] One testimony to its impact on animation came from Joseph Barbera (1911–2006), cofounder of the Hanna-Barbera animation studio, who later reported that the film's "impact on me was tremendous."[17]

CARL STALLING

Carl William Stalling (Photo 2.1), the third of three sons, was born to Ernest and Sophia Stalling in Lexington, Missouri, on November 10, 1891. Carl showed an early interest in music. His father, a carpenter, brought home a broken toy piano when Carl was only six.[18] After his father fixed the instrument, the young boy began to pick out melodies on it, leading his parents to have him study piano formally.[19] His first music lessons were from a pianist named Carrie Loomis.[20] He began to play church organs as well by the time he was eight or ten years old.[21]

Around 1903 Carl Stalling saw his first movie, *The Great Train Robbery*.[22] The experience had such a profound effect on the boy that he felt "from that day on [he] had only one desire in life: to be connected with movies in some way."[23] By 1904 he began to work in a theater in Lexington, playing piano between movies while the projectionist switched reels.[24] Six years later Stalling started playing piano at a theater in Independence.[25]

Stalling studied organ under Pietro Yon (1886–1943), who at one time was an organist at the Vatican.[26] Stalling also played classical piano and taught piano at the Kansas City Conservatory of Music.[27] At one concert given at the conservatory, he performed music by Johannes Brahms (1833–1897), Frederic Chopin (1810–1849), Christoph Willibald Ritter von Gluck (1714–1787), Felix Mendelssohn (1809–1847), and Moriz Rosenthal (1862–1946).[28] Not surprisingly, Stalling also performed the Second Hungarian Rhapsody (1847) by Franz Liszt (1811–1886).[29]

Photo 2.1. Carl Stalling; Image courtesy of Linda Britt

Stalling worked at a variety of theaters in Kansas City, including the Crescent, the Isis, and the Royal. For several years the musician also made extra income by working at the Walkenhorst Printing Company. Less than two weeks before getting married, Stalling listed on his draft registration card that he was supporting his parents as well as his older brother Fred, who was paralyzed.[30]

Stalling met violinist Gladys Baldwin (1889–1981), a fellow teacher at the conservatory.[31] The two married on June 16, 1917.[32] Gladys taught out of the home for several years, as well as at the Cranston School of Music and Dramatic Art in Kansas City in the mid-twenties.[33]

Stalling met Walt during the animator's Kansas City days. The composer recalled their early encounters :

I first met Walt Disney in the early twenties. He used to come to the Isis Theater, where I played the organ and had my own orchestra . . . Walt was making short commercials at the time, and he'd have us run them for him. We got acquainted, and I had him make several song films . . . this was before sound of course.[34]

After sound films came into being, the musician and the animator wrote to each other, resulting in Stalling being hired as the Studios' first musical director.[35] While adept at improvising, Stalling did his first formal composing when he scored his first cartoon for The Walt Disney Studios.[36] The musician related his scoring approach to his experience as a film accompanist, noting, "I just imagined myself playing for a cartoon in the theater, improvising, and it came easier."[37]

While Stalling was essentially self-taught as a composer, he did have some guidance from a variety of books on music. Stalling had at least three books on orchestration, including the 1929 edition of Cecil Forsyth's (1870–1941) book on the topic, as well as of Arthur Lange's (1889–1956) *Arranging for the Modern Dance Orchestra* (1927), and Frank Patterson's *Practical Instrumentation* (1923). Later he added film composer Frank Skinner's (1897–1968) *New Method for Orchestra Scoring* (1935). He also added to his collection a favorite of George Gershwin (1898–1937), Joseph Schillinger's (1895–1943) *The Schillinger System of Musical Composition* (1946). In addition to these resources, Stalling also had the help of an arranger when he worked for Disney.[38]

Stalling was close to his coworkers at The Walt Disney Studios, noting, "We were all very good friends, Walt and Roy and Ub and I."[39] Walt and Stalling worked together very closely in the early days of the Studios. On a trip to New York on October 26, 1928, the composer and animator shared a two-room suite, where they worked together on the scores to *Plane Crazy*, *The Gallopin' Gaucho*, and *The Barn Dance* (1929).[40] Walt wrote home to his wife about the experience, mentioning, "It sure seems nice to have someone near me that I know."[41] Late in life the composer stated that Walt's genius was "inspiring people who worked for him to come up with new ideas."[42] Stalling also observed, "I owe everything to Walt Disney; he gave me that first break in Hollywood."[43]

Stalling recalled that he often would consult with Walt before exposure sheets were prepared, in order to prevent the rhythm from becoming too monotonous.[44] He also related that sometimes Walt would have specific ideas in mind for music, and other times he was very open to differing opinions.[45] However, Wilfred Jackson recalled that Stalling could be assertive with his boss: "Both of those people [Walt and Stalling] could be pretty obstinate when they felt like it. Carl could stand up to Walt and give him what for and when it came to the music, if you pushed him a little too far he could put up a pretty good argument."[46] This confident, decisive attitude was most likely the result of Stalling being older than Walt, and the fact that the composer knew the filmmaker in Kansas City, well before the success of Mickey Mouse.

The close collaboration between the two was also financial in nature. One of Walt's early animation jobs, a Jenkins Music Company Song-O-Reel film of the song "Martha: Just a Plain Old-Fashioned Name," was procured through Stalling.[47] Furthermore, the musician had lent the Disney brothers $275 back in 1923 around the time when they had just moved to Hollywood.[48] In 1929, after joining the Studios, Stalling invested $2,000 in the Disney Film Recording Company.[49] This company was the sound recording division of the Studios, utilizing the Cinephone system. In addition to recording the Studios' early soundtracks, the Disney Film Recording Company also did sound recording for other films, including some made by Mascot Pictures (1927–1935). Stalling also had a one-third interest in the Silly Symphonies series while he worked at the Studios.[50] Walt repaid Stalling's generosity by loaning money to the composer after he had quit The Walt Disney Studios.[51]

Stalling scored numerous Mickey Mouse cartoons, including: *The Gallopin' Gaucho, Plane Crazy, The Barn Dance, The Op'ry House* (1929), *When the Cat's Away* (1929), *The Barnyard Battle* (1929), *The Plow Boy* (1929), *The Karnival Kid, Mickey's Choo-Choo* (1929), *Mickey's Follies, The Jazz Fool* (1929), *Jungle Rhythm* (1929), *The Haunted House* (1929), *Wild Waves* (1929), and *Minnie's Yoo Hoo* (1930). After leaving the Studios, Stalling arranged scores by Bert Lewis for at least three other Mickeys: *Mickey Steps Out, Fishin' Around,* and *Mickey Cuts Up.* Stalling not only came up with the initial idea for the Silly Symphonies, as well as the idea for its first short, but also had other ideas for the series. He suggested creating a cartoon for each of the four seasons.[52] Stalling himself was able to score three of the seasons, *Autumn* (1930), *Springtime* (1930), and *Summer* (1930), before he left the Studios.

Stalling scored other Silly Symphonies, including: *El Terrible Toreador* (1929), *Hell's Bells* (1929), and *Merry Dwarfs* (1929). After leaving the Studios, Stalling arranged Churchill's scores to *Egyptian Melodies* (1931) and *Three Little Pigs.* Stalling also played piano for several Disney shorts, including *The Op'ry House* and *Three Little Pigs.* The composer even performed the voice of Mickey Mouse for one of the early cartoons (most likely *Wild Waves*), as well as the voice of a cartoon walrus in (also in *Wild Waves*).[53]

While at Disney, Stalling devised what he called the tick system for synchronizing recordings with film:[54]'

> We made recordings of "tick" sounds at different beats—a tick every eight frames, or ten frames, or twelve frames—and played this on a phonograph connected to the recording machine and to earphones. Each member of the orchestra had a single earphone, and listened to the clicks through that.[55]

Stalling believes the first film that used this system was *The Skeleton Dance.*[56] Before that, images were drawn on the film to act as conducting cues.[57]

Typically, the music was completely scored before the animation was completed, though the score was not recorded until they were relatively certain that there would be no further changes in terms of timing.[58] During Stalling's time at the Studios, multitrack recording had not yet been developed, so music,

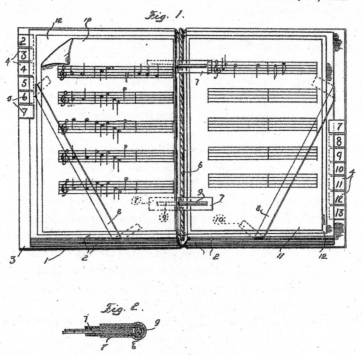

Photo 2.2. Carl Stalling's Portfolio for Sheet Music Patent

sound effects, and dialog had to be recorded all at once in a single take, usually with Stalling conducting the house orchestra of eight to ten players.

The composer worked for Disney for two years, leaving on January 22, 1930, the day after Iwerks left the Studios. Stalling cited personal problems with Walt and complained of unpaid back wages. Adding to the composer's incentives to leave were rumors that the Studios were in financial hot water. Stalling saw Ub's departure as an ominous sign and took a job with the Aesop's Fables Studio, which paid three times as much as he had been paid at Disney.[59]

The defection of Iwerks and Stalling was a personal blow to Walt. However, Roy pointed out to his brother, their desertion had a silver lining:

> If we had deliberately planned to use [Ub] and Carl over the period of time [when] we really needed them, and when they were essential to the success of the pictures, and had planned and plotted to throw them over at the first opportunity for selfish motives . . . the whole affair could not have worked out prettier.[60]

While it is likely that this message was simply Roy's attempt to cheer his brother up, it was essentially true.

In the short run, Stalling felt that he was used as a pawn in an attempt to destroy The Walt Disney Studios.[61] Once he started work at Aesop's Fables Studios, he realized that they did not have anything for him to do.[62] Simply speaking, they did not want him helping Walt.[63]

Stalling stayed at Aesop's Fables for only a few months and began to free-lance, working for Disney as well as for the short-lived Iwerks Studio (1930–1936). The composer was hired by Warner Bros. in 1936, a bit before Iwerks joined the same studio. At that time the head of Warner Bros. was Leo Forbstein (1892–1948), whom Stalling had performed with during his Kansas City days.[64] Stalling called Walt in 1953 when Warner closed for six months to see if The Walt Disney Studios had any work for him. While there was no work for the composer at the Studios, the two had an amiable conversation.[65]

In the long run, Stalling felt that leaving Disney was the right course for everyone involved .

> My leaving turned out better for Walt and it turned out better for me. At Warner Brothers, I could use a lot more popular songs; they didn't mind paying for them, as they had their own music publishing firm. . . . That opened up a new field so far as the kind of music we could use. At Disney's we had to go back to the Nineteenth Century, to classical music, to "My Old Kentucky Home."[66]

This access to a large library of popular song enabled Stalling to evolve into the proto-postmodern composer of highly referential music for which he became known.

In noting the importance of popular songs to his music at Warner Brothers, Stalling also acknowledges the way in which his scores are dependent upon external music and references. In fact, director Chuck Jones (1912–2002) said, "Stalling was good at writing his own music, but he seldom did."[67] Aesthetically speaking, Stalling never progressed far from his roots as a silent film accompanist.

While living in California, Stalling remained fond of Missouri and his family. In a 1940 letter to his cousin R. F. Stalling, the composer wrote:

> If I can ever find the time before it's too late I am coming back to old Lexington for a nice long visit. I have an almost constant yearning to see the old friends and relations of happy days gone by, and to walk the streets I used to walk and feel again the hopes and fears of childhood. Of course I know everyone has grown to manhood and a lot of the old folks have gone on, and too, the old town has changed a lot, but one thing I know; I wouldn't have any trouble feeling at home there.[68]

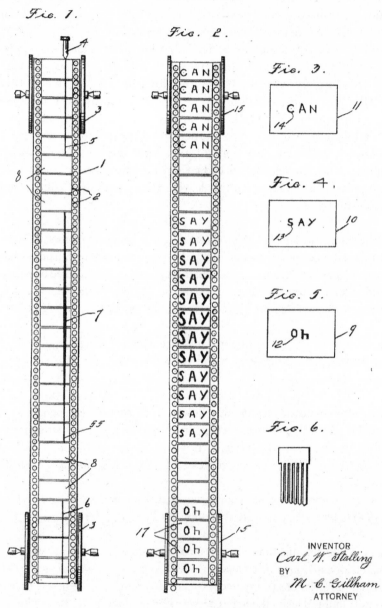

April 8, 1924.

C. W. STALLING

METHOD OF RECORDING AND DEPICTING MOTION PICTURES

Filed May 4, 1923

1,489,794

INVENTOR
Carl W. Stalling
BY
M. C. Gillham
ATTORNEY

Photo 2.3. Stalling's Patent for Synchronizing Motion Pictures and Live Music

In fact, Carl Stalling would visit for two weeks every summer to spend time with his brother Fred, who had been cared for by their Uncle George and Aunt Edith since at least 1930.[69] In their later years George and Edith moved in with their son Laurence.[70]

During Carl's visits he would teach Laurence's daughter Linda piano, by teaching her how to harmonize a melody.[71] Linda noted, "Carl was patient and lots of fun to be around. He was just family with us."[72] In Los Angeles, Carl and Gladys lived at 2644 Hollyridge Drive, a 1,750-square-foot house near the Griffith Observatory. By the late forties, the couple owned a citrus ranch near Upland, where they often spent their weekends.[73]

Stalling was arguably the most important founding father of the cartoon short score. His innovation in the field can also be seen through a couple of patents he obtained over the years. The first (1,416,903), filed April 3, 1920, was for a portfolio for sheet music (Photo 2.2). On April 8, 1924, the composer obtained a patent (1,489,794A) for a means of synchronizing motion pictures with live music (Photo 2.3).

During his time at Warner Bros., Stalling often churned out one score a week, each of which was recorded in only three hours. Warner Bros. became the studio that Stalling was most associated with, and he scored some six hundred cartoons for it, the last of which was completed in 1958, a Chuck Jones short (*To Itch His Own*). After retiring in the same year, he wrote music for the Neighborhood Music Settlement Program, where Gladys worked as a teacher.[74]

Stalling was enthusiastic in regard to his career as a film composer, stating in the late forties, "There's no business like show business, and I get just as much of a kick out of hearing my latest score as I did when I heard my first one, twenty years ago!"[75] The pioneering composer never scored a feature. However, scoring features was never a goal of his, according to a 1940 letter, in which he wrote, "I don't have any desire or ambition to do feature pictures; the cartoons are more interesting to me, and much more fun."[76]

The composer died on November 29, 1972, at the Hollywood Presbyterian Hospital, and was buried three days later at Hollywood Memorial Park.[77] Stalling was honored posthumously, in 1978, with a Winsor McCay Award, and remains one of the few composers to be honored with that distinction.

EGYPTIAN MELODIES

An eight-staves-per-system manuscript score for *Egyptian Melodies* (Photo 2.4), a Silly Symphony, is preserved in the Carl W. Stalling Papers at the American Heritage Center at the University of Wyoming. This short was released well after Stalling quit Disney. A three-staves-per-system manuscript for the score is held in the Disney Music Legacy Library.

Photo 2.4. First page of manuscript score to *Egyptian Melodies*—Image courtesy of the American Heritage Center at the University of Wyoming (Carl Stalling Papers, #5725, Box 2A)—EGYPTIAN MELODIES from EGYPTIAN MELODIES—Frank Churchill—©1931 Walt Disney Music Company

The three-staves score appears to be an early, possibly first, draft of the music. This version contains numerous indications of visual action with multiple-staff musical sketches. The manuscript held in the Carl W. Stalling Papers was likely only one version away from a final draft.

The two drafts appear to be in different handwriting. While the eight-staves-per-system version is in Stalling's handwriting, the three-stave version matches neither Stalling nor Lewis. In the latter draft, page numbers are enclosed in arcs, just as in Stalling's drafts of *Mickey Steps Out, Fishin' Around*, and *Mickey Cuts Up*. However, the curls featured in Stalling's cut-time signatures and bass clefs are missing in the three-stave draft. A further difference between the three-stave manuscript and the three-stave manuscripts for *Mickey Steps Out, Fishin' Around*, and *Mickey Cuts Up* is how cuts are marked. In the former, cuts are indicated using multiple cross-outs, while in the three Mickeys, they are indicated using a single large X.

Given that this handwriting for this three-stave manuscript matches neither Stalling's nor Lewis's, it is most likely that this handwriting is Churchill's. This is further supported by the fact that the director for the short is Wilfred Jackson, who at the time frequently worked with Churchill.[78] Accordingly, the score for *Egyptian Melodies* can be characterized as being composed by Churchill but arranged by Stalling.

Each page of the manuscript score to *Egyptian Melodies* held in the Carl W. Stalling Papers features three systems of eight staves each (see Photo 2.4). Written in C, the top two staves are for flute and clarinet, with the former doubling piccolo and the latter doubling oboe. The next two staves are for trumpet and trombone. The final four staves are for first violins, second violins, cello, and bass. The staff for the bass part is occasionally marked tuba. The entire piece is in simple duple meters.

The score features some twenty-four rehearsal numbers corresponding to various animated sequences of the short (Figure 2.2). The music for *Egyptian Melodies* is reminiscent of Stalling's soundtracks for both *Mickey Steps Out* and *Mickey Cuts Up*, in that it ends with a spirited gallop-like march. However, this Silly Symphony lacks the prominent melodic material featured in the first halves of the two aforementioned Mickeys.

Much of the material from *Egyptian Melodies* comes from *Ballet Egyptien* (1875) by Alexandre Luigini (1850–1906). Luigini's ballet became popular as a concert suite in the early twentieth century. An earlier Silly Symphony, *Arctic Antics* (1930), also used material from *Ballet Egyptien*.

There is scarcely any plot to *Egyptian Melodies*. A spider enters a pyramid, encounters dancing mummies, and witnesses hieroglyphs coming alive, staging a chariot race, and waging war against one another. The short is essentially a succession of gags. This virtual lack of plot suggests that the initial idea for the cartoon may have come from the music. Whether the idea of using Luigini's *Ballet Egyptien* came from Churchill, Stalling, or Lewis is unknown.

At the beginning of the short, only the opening fanfare (rehearsal 1) and introduction (rehearsal 2) feature prominent melodies. Rehearsals 3 through 6 focus on sustained suspense chords accompanied by a walking bass. The arpeggiated announcement motif (Figure 2.3), which begins rehearsal 7, comes from rehearsal B of the first movement of the suite from Luigini's ballet. This arpeggiated announcement recurs at the beginning of rehearsals 10 and 14.

#	ACTION	MUSIC
1	Opening title sequence	tune A, fanfare, c minor
2	Sphynx	tune B, g minor
3	Spider looks at door	Mickey Mousing fragments followed by transitional material
4	black (spider enters catacombs)	vamp, g minor
5	spider turns down hallway	vamps and Mickey Mousing fragments, G Major
6	spider turns down hallway	vamp, tic-toc, and Mickey Mousing as spider leaves coffin, G Major
7	four coffins	BEB, g minor
8	mummies dance out of coffins	BED, g minor
9	mummies dance to the left	repeat rehearsal 8
10	mummies begin to dance back	BEB, g minor
11	hieroglyphs play trumpets	bugle call followed by BEH, Eb Major
12	pharaoh yawns	tune C (trio-like), c minor
13	cymbal dancers	BEK, c minor
14	trumpets blow at pharaoh	BEB, g minor
15	chariot race begins	double time, BED, g minor
16	gray hieroglyphs with spears cheer	dogfight like, g minor
17	gray chariot in lead	repeat rehearsal 15 (starting on third measure in)
18	black hieroglyphs with spears cheer	repeat rehearsal 16, then mm. 3-6 and 15-18 of rehearsal 15
19	gray hieroglyphs with spears cheer	variant of rehearsal 16
20	hieroglyph battle	falling fifths progression, minor ninths in brass, g minor
21	hieroglyphs chase around column	falling fifths progression, modulating
22	long shot on chasing hieroglyphs	BEH (in double time), Eb Major
23	long shot on chasing hieroglyphs	repeat rehearsal 22
24	spider races through the catacombs	tune D (dogfight), missing 8 mm. cadential material, then coda (BEH), Eb Major

Figure 2.2. Rehearsal numbers in the manuscript to *Egyptian Melodies*

The tune that occurs at rehearsal 8 accompanies a mummy dance, which recalls *The Skeleton Dance*. This melody comes from rehearsal D of the first movement of Luigini's ballet suite (Figure 2.4). The tune also returns at rehearsal 15 in a relatively clever double time variation during the chariot race.

Rehearsal 11 introduces a march (Figure 2.5) that comes from rehearsal H of the first movement of the suite from *Ballet Egyptian*. When this melody recurs in double time at rehearsal 22, it actually recalls an occurrence of the tune in the finale of the last movement of the suite, in terms of tempo, register, and orchestration. Another second march strain is heard at rehearsal 13. This tune (Figure 2.6) is also from Luigini's ballet, appearing at rehearsal K in the first movement of the suite.

Figure 2.3. Arpeggiated Announcement motif from *Ballet Egyptien* by Luigini

Figure 2.4. Luigini theme from *Ballet Egyptien* adapted for Mummy Dance

Figure 2.5. March theme appropriated from Luigini's *Ballet Egyptien*

Figure 2.6. Second strain March adapted from Luigini's *Ballet Egyptien*

Three-quarters of *Egyptian Melodies* is derived from Luigini's ballet. Churchill even sets the melodies from *Ballet Egyptien* in the same keys as they were in the original. That being said, Churchill adapted Luigini's material effectively for an animated short, adding transitions and filling out the march to fit a more involved march form.

Mickey Steps Out and *Mickey Cuts Up* are both assembled from four or five songs that are strung together. By contrast, *Egyptian Melodies* has only three large-scale sections, an introduction (rehearsals 1–6), the mummy dance (rehearsals 7–10), and a march (rehearsals 11–24). This three-part form is even slightly more involved by having the main melody of the mummy dance recur in double time in the march. Furthermore, *Egyptian Melodies* is somewhat more orchestrationally advanced than *Mickey Steps Out* and *Mickey Cuts Up*, particularly in terms of textural variety and its use of soloistic material.

FLOWERS AND TREES

Another notable Silly Symphony is the 1932 release *Flowers and Trees*. The short was well into production in black-and-white when Walt saw a demonstration of a three-strip (cyan/magenta/yellow) Technicolor process, which offered much better results than the previous (red/green) two-strip process. The young filmmaker was sufficiently impressed that he scrapped the work that had been done in black-and-white, so the short could be made using this new color process. The black-and-white cels were washed on the back to remove the white and gray paints, leaving the ink and black paints on the front.[79] Thus, the backs were be repainted in color, and the cels were reshot at Technicolor's facilities.[80] In fact, Walt was so impressed with the process that he purchased an exclusive contract, allowing his studio to be the only that could utilize the process until September 1935. Furthermore, any non-Disney films created using the three-strip process could not be shown until 1936.

The plot of *Flowers and Trees* centers on the courtship of two young trees, as well as a conflict between a young male tree and a mean, gnarly-looking old tree who attempts to abduct a young female tree. The soundtrack for the short, written by Bert Lewis, is a pastiche of classical music. Given the composer's background as a silent film accompanist, such an approach is hardly surprising.

The opening scene of *Flowers and Trees* is set to a piece by Anton Grigor-evich Rubinstein (1829–1894), *Kamennoi-Ostrow,* no. 17. Early in the cartoon, the young male tree begins to play an improvised harp. The music (Figure 2.7) accompanying this sequence is from *Valse Bleu* (1900) by Alfred Margis. Later in the short, when the old tree appears to have been mortally wounded in a sword fight with the young male tree, a quote appears from Frédéric Chopin's *Funeral March*, the third movement of his Piano Sonata no. 2 in B-flat Minor, op. 35 (1839).

Another quote in the short is from Franz Schubert's (1797–1828) lied *Erlkönig* (1815). This quote occurs after the old tree starts a forest fire in an attempt to retaliate against the young male tree. *Erlkönig* presents a Johann Wolfgang von Goethe (1749–1832) narrative poem of a father who carries his sick son while

Figure 2.7. Theme from *Valse Bleu* by Alfred Margis used in *Flowers and Trees*

riding on horseback through the night to bring the child to a doctor. During the ride the son has delusions that the Alder King is coming to take him away. Schubert's music portrays the galloping of the horse in the rhythm of the piano. This piece was often used by silent film accompanists to portray villainous characters.

There are three quotes from Gioachino Rossini's (1792–1868) *William Tell Overture* (1829), two of which come from the storm section of the piece. The first occurrence is from the beginning of Rossini's storm section, and it directly precedes the Schubert quote. The second quote is from well into the storm section of the Rossini, and it is heard when the flames attack the old gnarled tree. The third quote comes from the "Ranz des Vaches" section of the overture. This excerpt accompanies the moment of peace after the forest fire in the cartoon short.

The short ends with an excerpt from the "Wedding March" from Felix Mendelssohn's *Incidental Music to a Midsummer Night's Dream*, op. 61 (1842). Here the orchestration is changed to have the melody played by bells. This reflects the action of flowers who play this melody on other flowers for the benefit of the two young trees, who have just become married. Birds, who are conducted by another tree, join in a bit later.

While the additional cost of Technicolor made Roy nervous, the expense paid off. *Flowers and Trees*, which was the first three-color Technicolor film, premiered at Grauman's Chinese Theater in Los Angeles on July 30, 1932. The cartoon won the first Academy Award for Animated Short Subjects, an award that the Studios won for the first eight years that the award existed.

THREE LITTLE PIGS

Arguably most important amongst the Silly Symphonies in terms of music and the Disney entertainment model was *Three Little Pigs*. Walt was particularly interested in the project, noting of the main characters, "We should be able to develop quite a bit of personality in them."[81] Animator Ben Sharpsteen (1895–1980) mentioned, "Walt practically lived in the music room while the director was working on it . . . he spent more of his time on it than he had on any picture up to that time."[82] The young filmmaker also specified that the dialog should be approached in a musical manner, stating that "anything they would say would be handled either in singing, or in rhyme."[83]

The short's three sibling porcine protagonists and their moral fable are portrayed in the film's signature tune, "Who's Afraid of the Big Bad Wolf?" Frank Churchill claimed to have written the tune in a mere five minutes.[84] Storyman Ted Sears (1900–1958) wrote lyrics for some of the verses.[85] Pinto Colvig (1892–1967), who is best known as the original voice of Goofy, provided the melody for the end of the chorus.[86] Carl Stalling also worked on the short as a freelancer, arranging the score and playing the piano part for the soundtrack.[87] In fact, the project was the last time Stalling worked for The Walt Disney Studios.[88]

The song is a composed taunt. The "tra-la-la-la-la's" that end the chorus function as jeering "nyah, nyah, nyahs." In his book *Walt Disney: An American Original*, Bob Thomas mentions a similarity between "Who's Afraid of the Big Bad Wolf?" and "Happy Birthday to You" (Figure 2.8), a claim that is repeated in David Tietyen's book *The Musical World of Walt Disney*. Both songs utilize large upward leaps, a descending triad, and a descending second motif. However, the similarity between the two seems to be more coincidental than derivative in nature.

The choice of instrument played by each of the siblings in the short furthers the establishment of character. Practical Pig's piano stands sturdily, reflecting the stalwart nature of its owner. In contrast, the frivolous Fifer and Fiddler Pigs play instruments that allow them to dance and cavort while they perform, reflecting their improvident disposition. Furthermore, the size of each instrument mirrors the sturdiness of each character's home.

Three Little Pigs demonstrates great improvement over the previous year's release of *Flowers and Trees*, not to mention *The Skeleton Dance*. The animation in the 1933 short is more mature than the rubbery style exhibited in *Flowers and Trees*. The narrative of *Three Little Pigs* is stronger than that of *The Skeleton Dance* and *Flowers and Trees*. Even the Mickey Mousing exhibited in *Three Little Pigs* is better integrated to the action of the narrative than the heavy synchronization utilized in *The Skeleton Dance*, which is closer in style in such a regard to *Steamboat Willie*.

Musically, *Three Little Pigs* is far more advanced than *The Skeleton Dance*, which is essentially a presentation of two comparatively unrelated musical

Figure 2.8. "Who's Afraid of the Big Bad Wolf?" WHO'S AFRAID OF THE BIG BAD WOLF? from THREE LITTLE PIGS—By Frank Churchill Additional Lyric By Ann Ronell—© Copyright 1933 by Bourne Co.—Copyright Renewed—All Rights Reserved International Copyright Secured—ASCAP

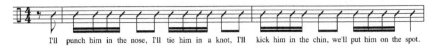

I'll punch him in the nose, I'll tie him in a knot, I'll kick him in the chin, we'll put him on the spot.

Figure 2.9. Example of rhymed, metered dialog from *Three Little Pigs*—THE THREE LITTLE PIGS from THREE LITTLE PIGS—By Frank Churchill—© Copyright 1933 by Bourne Co.—Copyright Renewed—All Rights Reserved International Copyright Secured—ASCAP

numbers, and *Flowers and Trees*, which is a classical pastiche. *Three Little Pigs* is a unified piece based primarily on a single theme, where each porcine sibling is introduced in his own verse, much as in an ensemble number from an operetta. Nearly all the dialog delivered by the pigs and wolf is rhymed (Figure 2.9), metered, and synchronized to the accompanying music. Furthermore, near the end of the short, the practical pig's piano answers to the Big Bad Wolf's attempts to blow down his house of bricks are evocative of a classical piano concerto.

Produced for $15,719.62, and released on May 27, 1933, *Three Little Pigs* was a resounding success. The short ran for a long time in theaters. In fact, one New York theater manager began to draw progressively lengthy beards on the pigs in the lobby's movie poster.[89] A small riot broke out in Dallas when the Majestic Theatre neglected to run *Three Little Pigs* before the feature as advertised.[90] To appease the crowd, they had to interrupt the feature, which had already been playing for ten minutes, to play the short.[91] By the end of the year, the short had grossed an unprecedented $125,000.[92] Sir Laurence Olivier (1907–1989) even noted that he based his film portrayal of Richard III on the Big Bad Wolf as he appeared in the short.[93] *Three Little Pigs* was awarded an Academy Award for Animated Short Subjects in 1933, and in 1994 the film was voted the eleventh-greatest cartoon of all time.[94]

Animator Chuck Jones (1912–2002) considered the short to be revolutionary:

"I realized something was happening there that hadn't happened before ... it wasn't how a character looked but how he moved that determined his personality. All we animators were dealing with after *Three Pigs* was acting."[95] In addition to this industry-wide influence on the technique of animation, the short is arguably just as important in terms of showing the potential for music and song in an animated film.

Likewise, future Disney staff composer Charles Wolcott (1906–1987) was spellbound by the short:

Of course I was fascinated by *Three Little Pigs* when it hit Broadway. Everybody was, whether it was Ed Sullivan, Winchell, all of them were raving about this fantastic animated cartoon. And the lines on Broadway were something, waiting for the little theater to open. Well, I didn't know the first thing about animation or cartoons, but as I say, I was fascinated by this thing.[96]

Wolcott even suggested that the short played a role in his desire to get started in the business of scoring films.[97]

After viewing *Three Little Pigs* with his wife, music publisher Saul Bourne contacted Roy to secure the rights to "Who's Afraid of the Big Bad Wolf?" for the company he had started with songwriter Irving Berlin (1888–1989) in 1919, the Irving Berlin Music Company, which would later be known as the Bourne Music Company. The Studios and the publisher entered into a contract whereby they would share profits on the music rights to songs from Mickey Mouse cartoons as well as songs from Silly Symphonies.[98] George Joy, who was then general manager at the Irving Berlin Music Company, recalled in 1934 his selection of Ann Ronell to adapt the song for popular release :

> I do definitely remember that we all decided it would have to be altered and lengthened because it was no good as a popular song in its original form. I thought of Ann Ronell to do the job because we had a pretty big hit of hers right about then in "Willow Weep for Me," which I had taken from her about a year back ... She was a bit puzzled as to how it could be done and Johnny Burke, who was under contract to the firm at the time, offered, as a friendly gesture to help her with it, though he did not want payment or credit for anything he contributed to it. He worked with Ann on it, though what part was his and what part was hers, I do not know.[99]

In 1955 Ronell recalled the incident differently; the songwriter stated that it was her idea to adapt the song for popular release, and she brought the idea to Joy.[100]

Regardless of the scenario, Ronell adapted "Who's Afraid of the Big Bad Wolf?" months after the short was released. By that point the cartoon and its affiliated song were already quite popular in the public sphere. Ronell's work on the song consisted of rewriting the lyrics for the verses and refitting preexisting melodic material from the short's score into a conventional song.

By decision of the Irving Berlin Music Company, the original credits on the printed music were listed as "words and music by Frank E. Churchill and Ann Ronell."[101] Churchill was furious, as Walt later testified:

> It was damn near a calamity ... I can't remember the incident in any detail, but it was a very unpleasant thing. Churchill was terrifically disturbed, and we were never consulted by Berlin or Bourne when the music was put out. In fact ... I didn't know about it until after it was out. I just can't recall the thing but Churchill was very disturbed.[102]

Walt pressured Bourne to change the credits of the song to list Churchill as the composer and to note "additional lyrics by Ann Ronell."[103] In 1955 Ronell attempted to sue Walt and the Studios over the credits for "Who's Afraid of the Big Bad Wolf?" (*Ann Ronell vs. Walt Disney Productions and Walt Disney*).[104] A little more than three years later, Ronell's complaint was dismissed by Judge John Clancy.[105]

The lyrics of "Who's Afraid of the Big Bad Wolf?" differ greatly between the version in the short and the adaptation for popular release. This is due to a change in narrative from the porcine protagonists telling their own tale in the short to a musical narrator relating their story in a popular song format. Furthermore, the version for popular release features more verses, since this format requires that the story be told entirely through lyrics, while the short tells much of the story visually.

Walt reportedly split his share of the published music with Churchill.[106] In its first three days of publication, the sheet music to "Who's Afraid of the Big Bad Wolf?" sold 39,000 copies in New York City alone.[107] In the second half of 1933, a grand total of 201,508 copies of the sheet music sold, as well as 9,177 orchestral arrangements of the tune.[108]

The tune made a cameo appearance in the Marx Brothers classic film *Duck Soup* (1933). The melody also appeared in the 1934 Stan Laurel (1890–1965) and Oliver Hardy (1892–1957) film *Babes in Toyland*, complete with three live-action costumed pigs that are clear references to the fifer, fiddler, and practical pigs.[109] Furthermore, *Time* magazine named "Who's Afraid of the Big Bad Wolf?" as one of the catchiest songs of 1933.[110]

Several recordings of the song began to appear in stores, including ones by Ben Bernie and All the Lads, Don Bestor and His Orchestra, Harry Reser and His Eskimos, and Victor Young [1899–1956] and His Brunswick Orchestra. Outside of the film, the public considered the song as an anthem against the Great Depression.[111] The song echoed a sentiment that was uttered less than three months earlier by newly elected President Franklin Delano Roosevelt (1882–1945) in his first inaugural speech, of March 4, 1933: "The only thing we have to fear is fear itself."[112]

Ann Ronell later reported her own evidence of the ubiquity of the song. In 1963 the songwriter noted that she "was thrilled to receive copies of the lyrics translated into numerous, different languages, including Latin."[113] "Who's Afraid of the Big Bad Wolf?" seemed to have international appeal. When Ronell traveled to the Soviet Union, a musicologist there told her that the theme of laughing in the face of fear "endeared the song to his countrymen as well."[114] Just as the tune had done with Americans during the Great Depression, "the song's story and humor had provided the Russian people with a warm note of comfort at a time when it was badly needed."[115]

MUSIC LAND

By the early to mid-thirties, recording processes for cartoon soundtracks became much more intricate at The Walt Disney Studios. A typical score would involve multiple takes that were recorded separately and then edited and dubbed together. What made this different from earlier approaches is that separate takes could be recorded at the same time and then later overlapped, or superimposed. During the thirties and forties, Disney was the only studio that utilized such complex techniques for its soundtracks.

The most-involved score of the era, and arguably one of the most involved of all time, was 1935's *Music Land*. This short presents a Romeo and Juliet–styled romance between a female violin from the Land of Symphony and a male saxophone from the Isle of Jazz. However, unlike the Shakespeare play, the cartoon has a happy ending. The story's plot necessitates a score that superimposes jazz on classical music.

The Leigh Harline Papers at the University of Cincinnati holds the composer's piano-conductor score to *Music Land* (1935). This score exists in twenty takes (Figure 2.10) that, as described, were recorded separately and assembled together for the final soundtrack. Many of these takes are played simultaneously or elided.

Take 1 accompanied the title sequence for the Silly Symphony. As was common practice for the Studios at the time, each measure was "numbered" with a letter, as measure number one was reserved for the music that accompanied the beginning of the short (past the title sequence). This first take contains several musical quotations. The very beginning utilizes the opening theme to the first movement of Ludwig van Beethoven's Third Symphony (1804), the *Eroica*. After a prominent cadence, the music continues with a quote from the same composer's Minuet in G (WoO 10, No. 2).

The second take continues with Beethoven's Minuet in G. Measures were numbered consecutively starting with this cue, allowing for clarity in relationship to the synchronization of each cue. The Isle of Jazz is introduced in take 3. Takes 4 through 7 feature symphonic music and cover the action from the violin descending the stairway through the saxophone being marched to prison. The fourth take begins with a quote from François-Joseph Gossec's (1734–1829) Gavotte in D Major.

Jazz returns in take 8 when the saxophone is locked in the metronome. This short clip of only four measures consists of several melodic tritones. The ninth take features the saxophone writing a note. The tune featured, both graphically and musically, is "The Prisoner's Song" (1924) by Vernon Dalhart (1883–1948). Take 10 introduces the King of Jazz, who is based on a caricature of Paul Whiteman (1890–1967). The take lasts through the brass arrangement of the trumpet call for assembly.

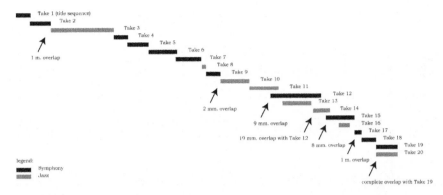

Figure 2.10. Synchronization of takes in *Music Land*

The eleventh take through the end of the short becomes much more complicated. Take 11 starts with the King of Jazz conducting his musical assault on the Land of Symphony. Take 12, which portrays return fire from the Land of Symphony, overlaps with the eleventh take by nine measures. The twelfth take is an extended quotation of Richard Wagner's "Ride of the Valkyries."

Take 13, performed by jazz band, begins after take 12 begins but ends before it is over. This superimposition is complicated by having the two settings utilizing the same beat in different meters. The "Ride of the Valkyries" quote is in triple compound, while the jazz band is predominantly in cut time. The difference in the number of beats per measures causes most of the barlines between the two takes to not line up. Namely, for every two measures of the Wagner quote, the jazz band plays three measures. In order to get the measure numbers to correspond with each other, Harline numbers every third measure in take 13 as a half.

Beginning when the prison explodes, the fourteenth take continues the jazz band music from the previous take in an attacca manner. Take 14, like the twelfth take with which it overlaps by nineteen measures, is in a triple meter, though it uses a simple subdivision unlike the compound subdivision of take 12. The superimposition with jazz band on top of "Ride of the Valkyries" in takes 13 and 14 is furthered by having bits of the jazz tune liberally paraphrase the Wagner (Figure 2.11). The copyright notice from the Bourne Company lists this excerpt as being arranged by J. H. Wood. Wood was a Brititsh composer who was commonly listed on American cue sheets in the 1930s to enable the collection of royalties from Europe.[116]

Four measures after the end of the twelfth take, symphonic music reenters in take 15. Jazz returns with the sixteenth take, which accompanies the King of Jazz riding his motorboat to help rescue the violin and saxophone. This take is completely superimposed with take 15.

Figure 2.11. *Music Land* takes 12 & 14 "Ride of the Valkyries" quote—RIDE OF VALKYRIES from MUSIC LAND—By Richard Wagner—Arranged by J. H. Wood—© Copyright 1935 by Bourne Co.—Copyright Renewed—All Rights Reserved International Copyright Secured—ASCAP

The symphonic seventeenth take overlaps with take 15 by a single measure. After a two-measure transition, the seventeenth take features a quotation of Wagner's "Wedding March." This quote continues, attacca, in take 18. The final two takes, 19 and 20, present a symphonic rendition of the "Wedding March," and a jazz paraphrase of the same tune respectively, with both takes ending on a jazzy add six harmony.

THE OLD MILL

Impressionism in music is conventionally linked to the idea of musical depiction, often of nature. For instance, in his book Introduction to Contemporary Music, Joseph Machlis characterized Claude Debussy's (1862–1918) approach to impressionism as "a pictorial art that wove a web of sensuous allure and conjured up the evanescent loveliness of the world."[117] Given such associations, it is not surprising that Leigh Harline utilized several impressionistic techniques in his score for *The Old Mill* (1937). This short contains no dialog. Rather, it depicts the animals that live in and around a dilapidated mill. The timeline for the story is twilight, moving into night, and finally into morning. This flow of time coincides with a prelude to a storm, the storm itself, and its aftermath.

Figure 2.12. Parallel motion and composed rubato in *The Old Mill*—MAIN THEME from THE OLD MILL—By Leigh Harline—© Copyright 1937 by Bourne Co.—Copyright Renewed—All Rights Reserved International Copyright Secured—ASCAP

Figure 2.13. Whole tone scale and composed rubato in *The Old Mill*—MAIN THEME from THE OLD MILL—By Leigh Harline—© Copyright 1937 by Bourne Co.—Copyright Renewed—All Rights Reserved International Copyright Secured—ASCAP

In a debate with his former teacher, Ernest Guiraud (1837–1892), Debussy spoke out against the rigidity of rhythm:

> "Rhythms are stifling. Rhythms cannot be contained within bars. It is nonsense to speak of 'simple' and ;compound' time. There should be an interminable flow of both."[118]

Not only does Harline frequently switch between subdivisions of two and three in his score for *The Old Mill*, but he even ventures into quintuplets. The overall effect of this generous rhythmic switching is that of a composed rubato, which offers the music an ebb and flow while still satisfying the rigid restraints of synchronization with animation.

Another trait of impressionism is the use of sonorities in parallel motion. Such planing harmonies not only work against conventional valuation of contrary motion but deny the functionality of harmony. Take 2 (Figure 2.12) from the short features melodic chords in parallel motion that also demonstrate composed rubato.

Impressionism also saw composers broadening their palettes through the use of novel scales. One of these, the whole tone scale, is unique in its lack of a tonal center. Harline makes protracted use of this scale in his score to *The Old Mill*. In particular, take 9 of the score (Figure 2.13) utilizes the scale's lack of a tonal center to build tension during the storm sequence. Again, this excerpt makes use of a written-out rubato.

SUMMARY

On May 19, 1937, the Studios released *Academy Award Review of Walt Disney Cartoons* in order to promote the upcoming feature *Snow White and the Seven Dwarfs* (1937). The package film was composed of five Silly Symphony shorts, all of which had been awarded Oscars. Thus, *Flowers and Trees* and *Three Little Pigs* were shown along with *The Tortoise and the Hare* (1934), *Three Orphan Kittens* (1935), and *The Country Cousin* (1936). In 1966 this package film was rereleased with the additions *The Old Mill* (1937), *Ferdinand the Bull* (1938), *The Ugly Duckling* (1939), and *The Reluctant Dragon* (1941).

As Tim Hollis and Greg Ehrbar note in their book *Mouse Tracks: The Story of Walt Disney Records*, Music from the Silly Symphonies was the first true soundtrack recording released.[119] The 1936 release on RCA's HMV label in England included music from: *Three Little Pigs*, *The Grasshopper and the Ants*, *The Pied Piper*, *Lullaby Land*, *Three Little Wolves*, and *Who Killed Cock Robin?*, as well as music from various Mickey Mouse cartoons, including *Mickey's Grand Opera* and *The Orphan's Benefit*.[120] Previous to this release, musical selections from films were rerecorded.[121]

By design, music played a central role in the Silly Symphonies. In fact, when speaking about the early days at The Walt Disney Studios, Ward Kimball remarked:

> "All of our pictures started out as musicals. You look at all the Mickey Mouse pictures, all the Silly Symphonies. They're musicals. Everyone's dancing and singing."[122]

Operationally, the importance of music is seen through the close collaboration between director and composer.

In the early years at The Walt Disney Studios, this collaboration was somewhat formalized, as the same duos tended to work together consistently. When Leigh Harline joined the Studios in late 1932, he was the third staff composer.[123] Harline began to work with Wilfred Jackson, who had previously worked with Frank Churchill.[124] Churchill began to collaborate with Burt Gillett (1891–1971) around the time of *Three Little Pigs*.[125] The final duo consisted of Bert Lewis, who tended to work with David Hand (1900–1986).[126]

In the late thirties, Jackson described the approach of creating cartoons from the early era in terms of stringing together gags that could be moved around:[127] "When you get in trouble with your timing you can play checkers with your gags. The music will give you the flow of continuity that you need."[128] Clearly, Jackson considered music to be the structural backbone of these shorts.

Another advantage of having music play an organizational role in animated cartoons is that when characters sing, animators can coordinate the mouth movements to the musical beat. Thus, it is not surprising that a number of the Silly Symphonies, such as *Father Noah's Ark* (1933), *The Pied Piper* (1933), and *Three Little Pigs*, feature rhymed, sung dialog.[129] Michael Barrier noted that little dialog was featured in the Silly Symphonies for the first couple of years of the series.[130]

The success of the Silly Symphonies reinforced the importance of music to the Disney product line. In the four short years from *The Skeleton Dance* to *Three Little Pigs*, the series matured from black-and-white shorts with loose narratives, rubbery animation, and scores that were reliant on public domain classical music, into cartoons where visual artistry was second to none. Furthermore, the Silly Symphonies evolved into shorts featuring rich storytelling, character-driven animation, and original music that featured iconic songs that both served the narrative and promoted the cartoon beyond the theater. In particular, the overwhelming success of *Three Little Pigs*, which was fueled in large part by "Who's Afraid of the Big Bad Wolf?," indicated the potential of original songs to lead toward commercial success.

However, music was only one stream of experimentation in the Silly Symphonies. Walt had learned just as much about storytelling, pacing, and character development, as well as technological approaches to animation. Given what he had learned, the young filmmaker felt he was willing to take a huge risk.

Chapter 3

SNOW WHITE AND THE SEVEN DWARFS

Walt Disney had planned for years to make an animated feature-length film. The young filmmaker felt that making animated shorts was a dead end financially speaking, while features were where the serious money was. The first plan Walt had for a feature harked back to his Alice Comedies days. The movie was to be an animated version of *Alice in Wonderland* starring a live-action Mary Pickford (1892–1979).[1] Furthermore, Walt reported that the actress had planned on financing the project.[2] The Studios did a screen test in 1933, but Paramount Pictures released a version of *Alice* later that year, causing the plan to be abandoned.

Pickford's husband, Douglas Fairbanks (1883–1939), had even discussed the possibility of collaborating on *Gulliver's Travels*.[3] Yet another plan for a feature that would mix animation and live action would have starred Will Rogers (1879–1935) in a version of *Rip Van Winkle*.[4] Walt secured the rights to the sequels to L Frank Baum's (1856–1919) *The Wonderful Wizard of Oz* (1900) during 1933–1934, but MGM had already procured the rights to the first book in the series.

SNOW WHITE AND THE SEVEN DWARFS

In May 1933, just as *Three Little Pigs* was released, Walt settled on *Snow White and the Seven Dwarfs* as the Studios' first feature-length film, and work on the project commenced the following year. During July 1933 Walt told the trade press that he was planning on making an animated feature.[5] A declaration to the popular press came a full year later.[6]

The story the young filmmaker chose for the project was one he saw in Kansas City when he was a teenager. Walt, who had been a newsboy since age ten, had been invited along with the rest of the city's newsboys to see a screening of *Snow White* (1916), a film starring Marguerite Clark (1883–1940) in the title role. The movie had made a significant impression on the teen, and it offered widespread appeal for a feature. Besides having the fairy-tale appeal of a hero, a heroine, and a villain, the story offered the sympathetic dwarfs, along with their comic potential.

The Silly Symphonies were a great testing ground for techniques and technology that would be used in *Snow White and the Seven Dwarfs*. In particular, *The Goddess of Spring* (1934) was an attempt to animate realistic-looking human figures. The attempt, however, was a somewhat failed one, as the movement of the protagonist (Persephone) was rubbery. An undeterred Walt remarked, "We'll get it next time."[7] Another important Silly Symphony that led to improvements utilized in *Snow White and the Seven Dwarfs* was the Academy Award–winning short *The Old Mill* (1937), which was the first cartoon to use a multiplane camera, a device that made use of depth of field.

Musically speaking, *The Goddess of Spring* was also a model for *Snow White and the Seven Dwarfs*. While several of the Silly Symphonies utilized sung dialog, *The Goddess of Spring* was intended as a burlesque of grand opera.[8] Ultimately, the satire was too understated for it to connect with audiences. However, the short is essentially a brief animated opera, which anticipates the operatic approaches intrinsic to *Snow White and the Seven Dwarfs*.

Work on *Snow White and the Seven Dwarfs* began on August 9, 1934.[9] At this time staff writer Richard Creedon (1890–1974) prepared a twenty-one-page document that indicated numerous ideas for characters, situations, and songs.[10] This document contains the suggestion of a song to be titled, "Some Day My Prince Will Come," which was approved by Walt.[11] Churchill would write the song only a few months later, in November 1934.[12]

As was the case with the Silly Symphonies, music would play an important part in the feature. In fact, it is clear from the beginning that Walt conceived of *Snow White and the Seven Dwarfs* as a film with several songs.[13] Following the success of *Three Little Pigs*, Frank Churchill would cowrite the songs with lyricist Larry Morey (1905–1971). Work on the songs for the feature started in late October 1934, with the first recordings made in January 1936. The first orchestral recordings of the score were made in late August 1937.[14]

Walt met personally with Creedon and Morey on three occasions during October 1934, indicating the importance of music to the formative stage of the movie.[15] By contrast, the first pencil tests for animation did not appear until February 19, 1936.[16] Additional music for the film was written by Churchill, Leigh Harline, and Paul J. Smith (1906–1985). According to Smith-family legend, Paul J. Smith conducted the orchestra for the recording sessions.[17] The soundtrack for the eighty-three-minute movie is composed of some eighty-nine musical sequences (see appendix).

Music is featured very prominently in *Snow White and the Seven Dwarfs*. There are very few moments in the movie that are not underscored. The longest of these is only twenty-two seconds long.[18] Leigh Harline estimated the complete conductor's score for the film to be twelve to fourteen hundred pages long.[19] The score featured a forty-piece orchestra, which was more than twice as large as the ensembles utilized for Disney's early shorts.[20] The choir used in the title sequence and close of the film was conducted by the vocal music director of Paramount Pictures, Max Terr (1890–1951).[21]

FRANK CHURCHILL

Frank Edwin Churchill was born in Rumford, Maine, on October 20, 1901. His father, Andrew J. Churchill, was a chemist,[22] who toward the end of his career sold real estate.[23] Andrew married Clara E. Curtis, and the couple had two sons, Frank and his elder brother, Warren.

When Frank was four, his family moved to Southern California. He began playing piano at theaters in Ventura, California, when he was fifteen years old. Later, the young musician dropped out of UCLA, where he was in a premed program, in order to pursue a career in music. While enrolled in college he did manage to take two semesters of music theory.[24]

For a while Churchill played piano in the bars of Tijuana and Juarez, and he performed with an orchestra in Tucson. The musician's time in Tijuana was somewhat adventure-filled:

> I went to Tijuana and played for honky-tonks, a very colorful experience for a kid out to see the world. This was in 1922, when I was 19 and had some pretty exciting times. There were many brawls and gunfights, augmented on one occasion by the sudden intrusion of a party of U.S. Marines on pleasure bent. Several times I found that dodging bullets would at least keep a person active, if nothing else.[25]

In 1924 Churchill became a staff accompanist and soloist for KNX radio in Los Angeles. During this time he also recorded with RKO Pictures.

Churchill related the importance of his piano playing skills to his early career in music:

> I'll never regret the eight months I spent in Tijuana and the six in Juarez. From there I jumped to Tucson, where our orchestra opened the Trilby Café. Because of the big overhead, the management started cutting salaries, and we shortly found ourselves broke and out of a job. Returning to Los Angeles, I now went into picture work, playing atmosphere parts.
>
> When talkies came in, I went into recording work and was radio broadcasting for Station KNX, Hollywood, for five years, as staff accompanist and

soloist. Finally, I quit radio work and went into piano recording for the studios, working at RKO-Pictures before coming here to Walt Disney. I guess it must have been just one of those things that happen, because I got a call one morning to report to The Walt Disney Studios, as they needed a man to play. I wasn't hired on the strength of my ability as a composer, but soon was engaged in making the arrangements for synchronized pictures.[26]

During his time as pianist providing atmosphere music for silent films, Churchill appeared in at least one film, *Beau Brummel* (1924).[27]

The fact that Churchill was hired by Disney as a pianist, and not as a composer, helped establish the view that the musician's strengths were as a pianist and a tunesmith. Wilfred Jackson's opinion was a summary of how the composer was seen at the Studios:

> Frank Churchill was primarily an accomplished pianist. Before he came to Disney, he had been playing "mood music" on the set to help the actors get the feeling of the scene while silent pictures were being filmed. To have Frank play anything at all on the piano, in person, was a delightful thing. He made everything he played sound great, and he seemed to have an endless variety of numbers, both classical and popular, in his repertoire. When he really got wound up and going good, he seemed to have an equally endless number of his own tunes.
>
> Frank's music was melodic . . . I mean the *melody* was the thing. His music was uncomplicated, and you could whistle or hum his music easily.[28]

Due to this reputation, Churchill's tunes were usually orchestrated by others, most often Harline and Smith.

That being said, Jackson also felt that Churchill's simplistic approach is what yielded success at the box office:

> Frank's music hit the mark . . . that is, appealed more to the tastes of the audience we were aiming for . . . and, in that way, I think Frank's cartoon scores were perhaps a bit more successful in accomplishing what Walt set out to achieve in that time period.[29]

Accordingly, Jackson felt that simple melodic songs, such as those written by Churchill, were an important contribution to the cartoons the Studio created in the early years.

Churchill composed at the piano, often working closely with a film's director, as Jackson related:

When Frank Churchill began to score a cartoon with me, he started right out playing pieces on the piano, suggesting one tune after another for whatever action we were starting to time. Usually, it didn't seem to make much difference to Frank which one of them I would pick to use, and if the one we chose didn't seem to be working out well, he was quick to suggest some different piece of music to try.[30]

Thus, Churchill used his improvisation skills as his modus operandi for composing a score.

Churchill joined the staff at Disney in 1931. It is likely that the first short that he scored was *The Castaway* (1931).[31] After writing the songs for *Snow White and the Seven Dwarfs*, he was promoted to supervisor of music. He worked on nearly sixty-five shorts, including *Egyptian Melodies*, *The Whoopee Party* (1932), *Mickey's Gala Premiere* (1933), *Camping Out* (1934), *The Orphan's Benefit* (1934), and *Playful Pluto* (1934). He wrote "Who's Afraid of the Big Bad Wolf?," "Lullaby Land of Nowhere," "Funny Little Bunnies," "You're Nothin' but a Nothin'," and "Who Killed Cock Robin?" for the Silly Symphonies series. He wrote songs for *Snow White and the Seven Dwarfs*, *Dumbo* (1941), and *Bambi* (1942), "Merrily on Our Way" for *The Adventures of Ichabod and Mr. Toad* (1949), and "Never Smile at a Crocodile" for *Peter Pan* (1953). He appeared at the piano in a promotional short entitled, *A Trip through Walt Disney Studios* (1937), and also appeared in a documentary segment of the film *The Reluctant Dragon* (1941), for which he also wrote the music.

Outside of Disney, Churchill served as musical director for the animated sequence in the Twentieth Century Fox feature *Servants' Entrance* (1934). The composer also wrote the songs "Happy as a Lark," "Put Your Heart in a Song," and "The Sunny Side of Things" for the RKO picture *Breaking the Ice* (1938), as well as two songs ("Blue Italian Waters" and "Song of Italy") that appear in another RKO film, *Fisherman's Wharf* (1939). In the late thirties, several of Churchill's songs made the hit parade, and the composer was one of ASCAP's highest-rated tunesmiths of the era.[32] He was twice nominated for best song in a motion picture, for "Baby Mine" and "Love Is a Song." He was also nominated for best music in a motion picture, for both *Snow White and the Seven Dwarfs* and *Bambi*, and he received an Academy Award for the music for *Dumbo*.

Animator Jack Kinney (1909–1992) was a friend of Churchill's at the Studios. The animator described the tunesmith in his 1988 book *Walt Disney and Assorted Other Characters*:

"Frank Churchill was a very fine musician with a wonderfully droll sense of humor. He was a fastidious dresser and a deeply motivated guy, who would never step on an ant or kill a fly."[33] Kinney described Churchill's work as "foot-tappin' and whistling' music."[34]

Jimmy Johnson echoed many of Kinney's assessments about the musician:

"Frank Churchill was one of a kind. He wrote simple, direct melodies that were just what Walt wanted. He would always appear at the Studio immaculately dressed, complete with bow tie."[35] Johnson added that the composer "drank a little, but it never interfered with his work."[36]

Churchill married Leona Milligan on the sixth of July, 1922.[37] The couple had a child, Corrine, who was born the following year. The marriage was Churchill's first and Milligan's second, but it did not last, as they divorced sometime before 1930.[38] Corrine continued to live with her father at least through 1930.[39] On June 10, 1933, Churchill married Carolyn Catherine Shafer (1905–1977), who was personal secretary to Walt Disney. As part of her job, Shafer answered the 30,000 monthly letters to Mickey Mouse. By 1939 the couple moved into a house at 4220 Parva Avenue,[40] which was about one block away from Walt Disney's home at 4053 Woking Way.

Churchill appeared to be a cheery individual but suffered from a nervous condition, dark thoughts, and alcoholism.[41] He underwent a nervous collapse in early 1937, leaving the Studios for several weeks.[42] Even after returning, the composer was not prepared to deal with the anxiety, causing him to take leave from the Studios in August 1937, leaving Harline and Smith to complete the score to *Snow White and the Seven Dwarfs*.[43] Churchill would periodically return to the Studios starting in 1938, despite his emotional problems.[44] By late 1941 the musician's health had declined significantly, leading him to visit a sanitarium on several occasions.[45] In December of 1941, Churchill bought Paradise Ranch near Castaic, California, where he would relax on weekends.

On May 14, 1942, Carolyn awoke to the sound of a gunshot, only to find her husband dead of a self-inflicted bullet wound. Churchill was found at the piano with a rifle, a rosary, and a note reading, "Dear Carolyn: My nerves have completely left me. Please forgive me for this awful act. It seems the only way I can cure myself. Frank."[46] Despite his problems, the composer had been to work at the Studio the previous day.[47]

Churchill had been depressed due to the recent deaths of two of his friends in the Disney orchestra.[48] The composer's last request had been that "Love Is a Song" from the then-forthcoming film *Bambi* be dedicated to his wife.[49] However, since the song had already been sent to the publisher, the request was denied.[50] Churchill's widow married the Paradise Ranch foreman Donald Durnford a year and a half later, on November 20, 1943.[51] Carolyn Shafer and Durnford divorced in 1972; according to Shafer's great-niece, Durnford "stole" the assets Shafer had inherited from Churchill.[52]

SNOW WHITE AND THE SEVEN DWARFS AS OPERETTA

The songs in Disney's first feature-length animated film were crucial to establishing character and communicating narrative. Paul J. Smith related that the songs were created in this vein well in advance of any animation: "In preparing *Snow White*, for instance, our composers were trying out effects to express Snow White's romantic interest, and the antics of the Dwarfs, long before the actual drawings were completed."[53]

These songs were a key part of the development of the picture, and some twenty-five songs were written for *Snow White and the Seven Dwarfs*, despite the fact that only eight appear in the film.[54] Walt could be very picky about music in his films, as he disliked it when characters broke into song and dance out of the blue, as often happens in Hollywood musicals. The young filmmaker stated, "We should set a new pattern . . . a new way to use music; weave it into the story so somebody doesn't just bust [*sic*] into song."[55]

The most prominent technique used in *Snow White and the Seven Dwarfs* to smooth the transition into the songs was the use of rhymed, metered dialog preceding the songs. This approach to dialog had been suggested by Walt himself, who stated that the dialog should "have meter, and at the right time, tie in with the music, so the whole thing has musical pattern . . . phrasing and fitting the mood."[56] While the Studios had used the technique before in shorts, most notably throughout *Three Little Pigs*, in *Snow White and the Seven Dwarfs* it is used mainly to transition in and out of songs.

In such a context, rhymed, metered dialog serves the same function as recitative in opera. Three-quarters of the songs in *Snow White and the Seven Dwarfs* are preceded by either rhymed, metered dialog or actual recitative, while only "Heigh-Ho" and the "Dwarfs' Yodel Song (The Silly Song)" lack such an introduction. The former is introduced by the rhythmic sound of the Dwarfs' digging, while the latter fades in.

Perhaps the most extensive application of rhymed, metered dialog as a transition into song is the introduction to "With a Smile and a Song." Snow White cries with her face to the ground in the forest after her scary nighttime flight from the Huntsman. Animals begin to surround her curiously, and she is startled by a rabbit that has come to sniff her. She begins, "Please don't run away. I won't hurt you."[57] The dialog then continues with six rhyming lines, ending with an interchange with a baby bird, where the princess queries, "What do you do when things go wrong? [bird sings] Oh! You sing a song!"[58] At this point the protagonist vocalizes in imitation of the bird in question, resulting in a short question-and-answer dialog with the bird that leads into "With a Smile and a Song."

At the end of "With a Smile and a Song" the birds join in twittering approval. This avian applause is followed by rhymed dialog. Snow White tells the animals,

"I really feel quite happy now. I'm sure I'll get along somehow."[59] She continues with another six lines of rhymed dialog, which lead into an instrumental version of "With a Smile and a Song," which functions like scene change music in a staged musical or operetta, covering her journey from the wooded glade to the Dwarfs' cottage. The animals that pull back the tree limbs at the end of this segment provide an ersatz curtain opening to the next scene.

The rhymed dialog, which leads out of the song, also functions to solve the problem of how Snow White finds the Dwarfs' cottage. One early concept had the protagonist asking the animals, "Maybe you know of someone who needs a housekeeper."[60] Ted Sears came up with a much more elegant solution, "It is not necessary to say anything more than her only worry is where she would sleep at night and do they know of any place and they say yes."[61]

The first written record we have of Churchill's "With a Smile and a Song" is from June 1935.[62] This time period coincides with Walt's absence from the Studios due to a European trip, as well as an accompanying hiatus in progress on the film.[63] This timing has caused Leslie Smith of The Walt Disney Studios music department to theorize that the song was composed by Churchill separate from his work on *Snow White and the Seven Dwarfs*.[64] The lyrics of the song function to boost the spirits of those who are facing adversity in much the same way as "Who's Afraid of the Big Bad Wolf?"

"I'm Wishing," which was one of the last songs developed for the film,[65] is prepared by having the protagonist hum the melody as she scrubs the steps of the castle. The song itself is led into with metered dialog, "Want to know a secret? Promise not to tell?"[66] She provides the rhyme to that line in accompanied recitative, "We are standing by a wishing well. Make a wish into the well. That's all you have to do. And if you hear it echoing, your wish will soon come true."[67] Landing on a strong half cadence, the music then continues with the iconic song.

"I'm Wishing" also features a clever hook, when some of Snow White's lines are echoed back to her by the wishing well.[68] Save for the end of the bridge, when Snow White vocalizes in thirds with her echo, the echo is an exact repetition of her voice. This melodic repetition also allows for the musical introduction of the Prince by having him sing "Today,"[69] at the end of the song in place of the echo. After this, the Prince leads into his only solo, "One Song," with recitative: "Now that I've found you, hear what I have to say."[70] Again, this line settles on a half cadence before continuing into "One Song." The two songs conclude with Snow White closing the curtains of the balcony doorway from where she watched the crooning prince. This closing curtain functions in a theatrical manner, signaling the end of a scene.

Formal recitative had previously been used in Disney cartoons. In particular, *The Goddess of Spring*, the Silly Symphony in which the Studios experimented with the animation of human figures, also featured this operatic technique.

However, in this short, the recitative has more of a flavor of full operatic singing, rather than the lighter operetta style exhibited in *Snow White and the Seven Dwarfs*.

Unfortunately, the movement of the human figures in *The Goddess of Spring* was significantly unrealistic. In order to correct this poor representation of human movement, Walt determined to use a live-action reference for the animators to consult when animating Snow White. Thus, Marjorie Belcher (1919–), was hired around November 1936, to be the live-action model for the film's title character.[71] Later known as Marge Champion, after marrying her second husband, Gower Champion (1919–1980), Belcher was daughter of Hollywood dance instructor Ernest Belcher (1882–1973). An accomplished dancer, she began to instruct ballet at her father's studio at the age of twelve. Her delicate, balletic movements provided another dimension to the classical flavor of the film. Her graceful motion also draws the audience in to admire the character.

While the Prince makes only two brief appearances in *Snow White and the Seven Dwarfs*, the live-action model hired to film those sequences was also a dancer. Louis Hightower, who was tragically killed in the Second World War, was another student from the Belcher studio. While Hightower's training is not as apparent in the Prince's movements, the choice of a dancer for the model is a clear indication that the Studios wanted musical movement in the characters.

Marjorie Belcher's filmed movements were the result of bits of suggestions from the animators, and a large part of improvisation on her part. The dancer recalled years later,

> "They showed me storyboards and then they would say, you know, why don't you try doing this or that or the other thing . . . That's all the guidance I had."[72] Ham Luske (1903–1968) was particularly involved in the process, as he worked as a director for these live-action reference films.[73] At one point Belcher even served as a live-action reference for Dopey, though it is unknown whether any of that footage was used.[74]

Another piece of the puzzle that helped provide the light-operetta flavor of *Snow White and the Seven Dwarfs* was the vocal casting of the title role. Some 150 actresses auditioned for the role.[75] Walt did not want to be influenced by seeing or knowing anything about the individual auditioning. Consequently, he listened to auditions through a speaker in his office that was connected to the Studios' sound stage. Through this process, he turned down Deanna Durbin (1921–2013), an operatically trained actress who was under contract at MGM. Walt felt that the then-fourteen-year old's voice sounded much too mature for the role. Another actress who was turned down for the role was Virginia Davis (1918–2009), who had been the first star of Walt's Alice Comedies.

Ultimately, the part was given to Adriana Caselotti (1916–1997). The eighteen-year-old operatically trained singer had a bel canto voice that suited the role admirably. Larry Morey noted of the young singer, "The girl does a good cadenza."[76] Caselotti started recording for the film on January 20, 1936, and was paid $970 for the entirety of her work for the movie. According to Marjorie Belcher, several of the Studios' artists began to refer to herself and Caselotti collectively as Mariana Belchalotti.[77]

The casting choice of Caselotti was complemented by the casting of Harry Stockwell (1902–1984) as the voice of the Prince. Stockwell had performed on Broadway, as well as in movies. His voice had a similar quality to the then popular Nelson Eddy (1901–1967), who later provided the voice for "The Whale Who Wanted to Sing at the Met" in *Make Mine Music*.

The finale of *Snow White and the Seven Dwarfs* also helps establish the film as an animated operetta by using the theatrical convention of a curtain call. When the Prince kisses the apparently dead Snow White, "Some Day My Prince Will Come" begins to play. The first two lines of the song are hummed, but as she stirs, a choir enters, singing the lyrics, "and away to his castle you'll go, to be happy forever we know."[78] Once it is clear that Snow White has awoken, the Prince lifts her onto his steed. The Prince then lifts the Dwarfs in turn so that Snow White may kiss them on the tops of their heads, much as she did when the Dwarfs went off to work. First he lifts Bashful, then Grumpy, then Doc, Happy, and Sneezy in a group, and finally Dopey is lifted so that he may receive a kiss. Absent from this process is Sleepy, who does appear in the crowd of Dwarfs directly following this sequence. Animator Frank Thomas confirmed that Sleepy's appearance was not possible, due to the musical timing of the scene. The score had already been locked in, and there just was not enough time for all Seven Dwarfs to say their good-byes.

After these good-byes are imparted, the Prince mounts the horse, and the couple ride off into the sunset, pausing briefly under the radiant clouds, which gradually cross-dissolve to a castle in the sky as the melody of the film's signature song builds to a choral climax. Even the castle in the clouds is evocative of representations of Valhalla in versions of Richard Wagner's (1813–1883) opera *Das Rheingold* (1854). This whole sequence, from celebrating the Dwarfs, to giving special recognition to Dopey, to the final acknowledgment of the principals, Snow White and the Prince, functions as the film's curtain call. The closing of the book that follows this scene acts as the final curtain coming down on a production.

LEITMOTIFS IN SNOW WHITE AND THE SEVEN DWARFS

In addition to the eight songs in *Snow White and the Seven Dwarfs*, there are other prominent, recurring melodies that are used in the soundtrack. These melodies are associated with characters in the manner of leitmotif, a technique utilized in the composition of operas, which was first defined by Richard Wagner. While use of leitmotif in a soundtrack is not uncommon, when *Snow White and the Seven Dwarfs* was first released in 1937, the use of the technique in film was still new.

Both the Magic Mirror and the Queen receive their own leitmotifs. While the Magic Mirror theme is heard both times the Magic Mirror is featured, the Queen's theme recurs fully only when she instructs the Huntsman to kill Snow White. The first three notes of the Queen's leitmotif occur as she attempts to convince Snow White to take a bite from the poisoned apple. The Magic Mirror's and the Queen's leitmotifs are related musically, as they are roughly inversions of each other (Figure 3.1).

The character with the most prominent leitmotif, which occurs four times in the film, is Dopey (Figure 3.2). Composed by Churchill in mid-1936,[79] this theme starts similarly, and has a rhythmic profile somewhat similar to Paul Dukas's (1865–1935) *The Sorcerer's Apprentice* (1896–1897). The score also identifies themes for Grumpy, and for the turtle that tries to climb the stairway in the Dwarfs' cottage. However, neither tune recurs, and Grumpy's theme, which appears when Snow White kisses his head as he leaves for work, lacks the clarity of Dopey's leitmotif.

Figure 3.1. Magic Mirror and Queen Leitmotifs—MIRROR THEME from SNOW WHITE AND THE SEVEN DWARFS—By Leigh Harline—© Copyright 1938 by Bourne Co.—Copyright Renewed—All Rights Reserved International Copyright Secured—ASCAP. QUEEN THEME from SNOW WHITE AND THE SEVEN DWARFS—By Leigh Harline—© Copyright 1938 by Bourne Co.—Copyright Renewed—All Rights Reserved International Copyright Secured—ASCAP

Figure 3.2. Dopey's leitmotif—DOPEY'S THEME from SNOW WHITE AND THE SEVEN DWARFS—By Frank Churchill—© Copyright 1938 by Bourne Co.—Copyright Renewed—All Rights Reserved International Copyright Secured—ASCAP

Figure 3.3. Thematic transformation of "One Song"—ONE SONG from SNOW WHITE AND THE SEVEN DWARFS—Words by Larry Morey Music By Frank Churchill—© Copyright 1937 by Bourne Co.—Copyright Renewed—All Rights Reserved International Copyright Secured—ASCAP

"Some Day My Prince Will Come," "One Song," and "Heigh-Ho" are treated as themes, as these melodies occur in the film outside their presentation as a song. A transformation of "Heigh-Ho" accompanies a disoriented Grumpy as he falls in a creek while leaving for work shortly after receiving a kiss on the head from Snow White. "Heigh-Ho" receives a heroic treatment when the Dwarfs race with the forest animals to try to reach Snow White before the Queen can harm her.

"Some Day My Prince Will Come" and "One Song" are featured prominently in the film. "One Song" opens the movie, directly followed by "Some Day My Prince Will Come." This order repeats at the end of the film, where "One Song" leads into the arrangement of "Some Day My Prince Will Come" that closes the film, forming a musical frame. A brief reference to "One Song" (Figure 3.3) occurs when Snow White wishes on the poisoned apple, believing that it is a magic wishing apple. This brief reference to "One Song" reinforces the Prince as the object of her affection.

A number of the techniques previously identified, such as use of leitmotif and accompanied recitative, are taken directly from opera. The use of rhymed dialog to serve as a transition into song is evocative of operatic recitative. Other strategies are more closely related to musical theater and theater in general, including scene change music, visual elements that represent the opening or closing of a curtain, and curtain calls. When taken as a whole, these approaches serve to establish *Snow White and the Seven Dwarfs* as an animated operetta.

MICKEY MOUSING IN *SNOW WHITE AND THE SEVEN DWARFS*

Mickey Mousing, close synchronization between image and music, is a prominent feature of *Snow White and the Seven Dwarfs*, contributing to the work's success. Leonard Maltin stated in *The Disney Films* that "the *entire film* was planned out to a musical beat."[80] This is certainly true, as made evident in the recent Disney Music Legacy Libraries release of *Walt Disney's* Snow White and the Seven Dwarfs *Master Score*. This edition is a color reproduction of the surviving bar sheets for the film. While the entire movie is laid out to musical beats, the tempo has frequent moments of rubato. That being said, this organization enabled the synchronization with any given action with music. The sequence that most prominently features this technique is the scene in which the animals help Snow White clean the Dwarfs' cottage.

"Whistle While You Work," written in December 1934, was one of the first songs developed for *Snow White and the Seven Dwarfs*.[81] It begins with rhymed dialog. "Now, you wash the dishes, you tidy up the room, you clean the fireplace, and I'll use the broom."[82] A trio of birds then whistles a bugle call ending on a half cadence, which then leads into the song.

All four key changes in the song are accompanied by Mickey Mousing. The first (from D to F major) occurs when a deer pumps water into the sink using its tail. The second (to B-flat major) is instigated by a mouse that kicks back some dust that has been swept into his hole by a pair of squirrels. A spider sliding down his web to scare a squirrel that is trying to sweep up the web accompanies the third modulation (to E-flat major). The fourth key change (returning to D major) occurs when a deer that is loaded down with laundry trips his way out the door en route to do the wash.

The laundry sequence in "Whistle While You Work" also has some effective instances of Mickey Mousing. After the raccoons scrub clothes in rhythm to the song, a chipmunk uses a turtle's belly as a washboard, causing the reptile to laugh. The chortle is presented musically with plunger-muted trombones playing glissandi. In the following sequence flutes accompany two birds wringing out a shirt and hanging it on a clothesline. These are but a tiny fraction of such examples of close synchronization between music and action in the film.

Walt devised an ending for the song in a story conference during which he suggested visual and orchestral elements:

> Get a way to finish the song that isn't just an end. Work in a shot trucking out of the house. Truck back and show animals shaking rugs out of the windows—little characters outside beating things out in the yard. Truck out and the melody of "Whistle While You Work" gets quieter and quieter. Leave them all working—birds scrubbing clothes. The last thing you see as you

truck away is little birds hanging clothes. Fade out on that and music would fade out—at the end all you would hear is the flute—before fading into the Dig, Dig song ("Heigh-Ho") and the hammering rhythm.[83]

The consecutive pairing of "Whistle While You Work" and "Heigh-Ho" are thematically linked as work songs, providing an aesthetically smooth transition.

"SOME DAY MY PRINCE WILL COME"

One of the most renowned melodies from *Snow White and the Seven Dwarfs*, the first feature film to come out of The Walt Disney Studios, is "Some Day My Prince Will Come." Part of the dreamy quality of the song comes from its emphasis of the dominant, the fifth note of the scale (or sol). The prominence of a tone most typically associated with the tension of a *Kopfton* lends the melody an unresolved nature. This unsettled nature can be interpreted as complementary to the idea of dreams, that is, the anticipation of an as-yet unachieved objective.

   "Some Day My Prince Will Come" begins and ends on the fifth scale degree (Figure 3.4). The first sub-phrase is an elaboration of the submediant chord. This motif is transposed up a fourth to create the second sub-phrase, which elaborates the supertonic. The first half of the phrase is an arpeggiation to the dominant. The second half of the antecedent consists of a sub-phrase that alternates between root and third of the dominant chord (scale degrees five and seven), which is repeated.

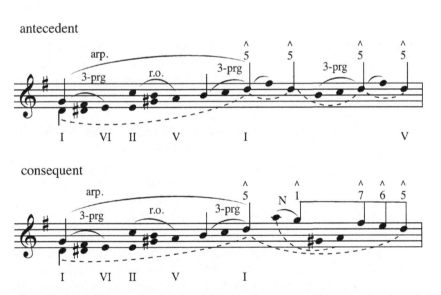

Figure 3.4. Melodic analysis of "Some Day My Prince Will Come"

The first half of the consequent is the same as the first half of the antecedent. The second half of the phrase features a linear descent from the tonic down to the dominant, sustaining the tension of the unresolved dominant. There is also an interruption of a register transfer of the supertonic down an octave, elaborated by a chromatic lower neighbor.

While "Some Day My Prince Will Come" features a harmonic resolution at the end of the song, the melody is unresolved, with both phrases beginning and ending on scale degree five. Furthermore, both feature a large-scale register transfer of the dominant up one octave. The second half of both phrases also emphasizes notes from the dominant, with the end of the first phrase alternating between the root and third of the dominant. This consistent melodic emphasis of the dominant leaves the song feeling unresolved in much the same way that a dream is open for resolution by its fulfillment.

The arrangement of "Some Day My Prince Will Come" that accompanies the conclusion of the film addresses the unresolved nature of the melody. The end of the song is appended with trombones playing a melodic fragment from "One Song" ending on the tonic. The choir further dissipates tension by having the sopranos move to the high tonic, and then upward to scale degree three. Ultimately, the score's resolution to this tension at the end of the film through the use of the Prince's melody, "One Song," serves as a fitting musical summary of the story's narrative.

"SILLY SONG," ENTERTAINMENT, AND UNUSED SONGS

One effective trick in drama involves the juxtaposition of emotionally contrasting scenes, causing the mood of each segment to be heightened. The prime example of this in *Snow White and the Seven Dwarfs* is "The Silly Song." This number is placed immediately after the transformation of the Queen into an old hag, which is one of the scariest segments of the movie. "The Silly Song" is easily the lightest, merriest scene in the feature.

It is also the most contemporary-sounding song of the film. Walt felt that using popular styles of music in the movie would work against what he wanted to accomplish: "I don't like the Cab Calloway idea . . . Audiences hear a lot of hot stuff. If we can keep this quaint, it will appeal more than the hot stuff."[84] In fact, "The Silly Song" seems to lightly lampoon popular stylings. When Dopey rides on Sneezy's shoulders to dance with Snow White, his long, baggy coat and finger-snapping stride could be considered a parody of a hepcat.

The sort of popular styling used in "The Silly Song" is much more conservative than Calloway's (1907–1994) flair, embodying the sweet jazz style practiced by band leaders like Paul Whiteman. While the yodeling is clearly intended to lend a European folk element to the song, the use of this vocal technique in this context is also reminiscent of Jimmie Rodgers (1897–1933), who introduced yodeling to popular music a decade earlier, in the late twenties.

The approach of avoiding popular music in general, and applying only conservative strains of such material when used, became a modus operandi for the Studios. For later Disney films that featured scores with music performed by popular artists, the Company selected non-controversial artists, such as Peggy Lee (1920–2002), Roger Miller (1936–1992), Billy Joel (1949–), Phil Collins (1951–), Sting (1951–), and Michael Bolton (1953–). While Elton John (1947–) was considered to be somewhat controversial in the early seventies, due to his flamboyant dress, by the time the talented songwriter worked on *The Lion King* (1994), he had been considered mainstream for nearly two decades.

"The Silly Song" also features some great examples of Mickey Mousing during which the Dwarfs sing, yodel, dance, and play various unique instruments. Perhaps most notable is the design of the organ played by Grumpy. The unique organ sound for "The Silly Song" was the brainchild of sound effects artist Jimmy Macdonald (1906–1991).[85] To achieve the sound of the pipes, he had a variety of personnel blow into large jugs.[86]

Walt noted some of the details that would make up the organ's visual design, specifying that "the smaller pipes would be carved as birds, the larger ones squirrels, owls, and bullfrogs, all carved like totem poles."[87] These carved elements would reflect the homemade craftsmanship that is present throughout the Dwarfs' cottage.[88] In addition, the animated organ includes a bench that doubles as a bellows, which is pumped by posterior power, an idea suggested by sketch artist Albert Hurter (1883–1942).[89] Walt remained concerned about the visual design for the organ, ordering four backgrounds reworked; consequently, the organ pipes had to be repainted only eleven days before the film's premiere.[90]

Dopey's drum solo, which is initiated by the dwarf attempting to smash a fly using his drumsticks, is another notable example of close synchronization. Walt saw the nutty dance performed by Dopey, with the help of Sneezy, as an important means of establishing the character of the mute dwarf.[91] The young filmmaker encouraged the emphasis of identity in the sequence, suggesting, "Bashful could half talk and half sing. You can bring their personalities in there."[92] During the final instrumental chorus of the song, the visuals feature several relatively short clips of closeup shots of details like the various Dwarfs playing instruments, Grumpy's organ, and clapping, all functioning to build to the song's climatic ending, which appropriately dissolves into laughter.

The concept for the song originated with Pinto Colvig on June 10, 1937.[93] The voice actor submitted eleven verses of lyrics to a song he proposed, titled "Gee, Ain't This a Silly Song."[94] Not only did Colvig not supply a melody for his lyrics, none of his drafted lyrics made it into the final version of the song.[95] Thus, the voice actor did not receive any songwriter credit for the tune.

Walt wanted the instruments in "The Silly Song" to not only look unique but sound unique as well:

> Their instruments have got to be unique and unusual . . . If you get a regular jazz organization you've not taken advantage of the opportunity . . . I don't want a flute to sound like a flute; I want it to sound like something else—whatever we have got drawn . . . If you use clarinets, trick them so they don't sound legitimate.[96]

Visually speaking, most of the instruments were very unusual, while aurally, only the organ really stood out as being truly innovative.

Six other songs, "Bluddle-Uddle-Um-Dum (The Dwarfs' Washing Song)," "Eenie, Meenie, Miney, Mo," "The Lady in the Moon," "Music Everywhere," "Music in Your Soup," and "You're Never Too Old to Be Young," which offered nothing more than pure entertainment, had been planned for *Snow White and the Seven Dwarfs*. Two of these songs, "Bluddle-Uddle-Um-Dum (The Dwarfs' Washing Song)" and "Music in Your Soup," would have featured the Dwarfs. In fact, the two would have occurred back to back in the feature. The former of the two made the cut for the film, while the latter was cut after a pencil test was made. "Eenie, Meenie, Miney, Mo," "The Lady in the Moon," "Music Everywhere," and "You're Never Too Old to Be Young" were all contenders for the entertainment sequence, which ultimately became "The Silly Song."

The concept for "Music in Your Soup" originated as a "Soup Symphony" noted by Walt in a "Skeleton Continuity" from December 1934.[97] A more formal description of the idea specified:

> Make the sounds rhythmic . . . Work also for different registers in soup sounds . . . Pick up first with a vamp, then a melody . . . Like a waltz rhythm with prominent bass . . . Must be funny, but pleasant to listen to . . . Anything that will create an unconscious feeling that they are doing a musical symphony.[98]

Experiments toward this tall order were first attempted in February 1936.[99] The sound effects department experimented with slurping sounds that were created by slowing down and reversing recordings of a marimba and a vibraphone.[100]

The song that Churchill and Morey composed in December 1936 bore little resemblance to the aforementioned description, save for the use of human-produced slurping sounds as part of the accompanying vamp.[101] "Music in Your Soup" was written as more of a rhythmic recitation than an actual song. This was due to the fact that Roy Atwell (1878–1962), the actor voicing the role of Doc, was originally slated to perform the number, and Atwell lacked the vocal skills for a conventional song.[102] However, the song was reassigned to Happy, played by Otis Harlan (1865–1940), not only because Harlan could sing better, but also because having Doc always as the leader would result in the character having too much focus.[103]

The original concept for the entertainment sequence of *Snow White and the Seven Dwarfs* was a tune that was to be called "Eenie, Meenie, Miney, Mo."[104] The song would introduce each of the Dwarfs, as they sang, made fun of each other, and performed some sort of dance or stunt.[105] Potential lyrics for the song were submitted following a November 1934 personnel meeting.[106] It is doubtful that any melody was composed for the number, and it was sidelined for more than a year, until it was replaced by a different concept.[107]

The author of "The Lady in the Moon" is unknown, though it has been suggested that Paul Smith wrote the tune, as he served as conductor at a demo recording session, which Frank Churchill did not attend.[108] This recording from December 23, 1935, was made using a combination of professional musicians, and some of the Studios' more musical staff members (all of whom were later founding members of Firehouse Five Plus Two), including Ward Kimball, Ed Penner (1905–1956), and Frank Thomas.[109] In order to create a jug band sound, Kimball and Thomas blew across the tops of bottles, and Penner played ocarina and penny whistle.[110]

The concept for the song was a story sung by the Dwarfs about five animals—a cricket, a fish, a frog, a mockingbird, and an owl— who fall in love with the lady in the moon.[111] As the story progresses, the animals become jealous of one another and begin to fight.[112] However, after they discover the lady in the moon is actually the man in the moon, they stop their quarreling and become friends.[113]

"The Lady in the Moon," which had replaced the concept of "Eenie, Meenie, Miney, Mo," was discussed at a story meeting on December 13, 1935.[114] It was decided that a second song should be added. It would be a jug-band-type number that would lead into "The Lady in the Moon."[115] While preexisting tunes like "Little Brown Jug" (1869) and "Three Blind Mice" were considered, Walt tasked Pinto Colvig with supplying an original song.[116]

Colvig delivered "Music Everywhere" ten days later, when it was recorded at the same session as "The Lady in the Moon." Colvig and Jimmy MacDonald provided the vocals.[117] The song would feature the Dwarfs playing rhythms on various household objects.[118] These two tunes were rerecorded a little over a month later on January 29, this time using Otis Harlan on the vocals.[119]

"You're Never Too Old to Be Young" was introduced by Churchill and Morey on January 6, 1936, at a story conference.[120] The song was recorded as a demo shortly thereafter.[121] The tune replaced "The Lady in the Moon" and "Music Everywhere" as the top contender for the entertainment sequence but never made it past the stage of a demo recording.[122]

Walt started to lose confidence in "You're Never Too Old to Be Young" in early 1937.[123] He critiqued, "It's kind of cold trying to get anything from the way it is," and "It begins to sound cut and dried."[124] While "You're Never Too Old to Be Young" was ultimately cut from the film, the song's distinctive yodel chorus was incorporated into "The Silly Song."[125]

RECEPTION AND SUMMARY

One notable musical element of *Snow White and the Seven Dwarfs* is that all the songs in the film are sung exclusively by morally upstanding characters. The Queen gets no song of her own. This restriction helps polarize good versus evil by withholding the levity of song from the Queen. Denying the antagonist the use of song is a model that is followed to one degree or another in many Disney animated features.

A total of 750 individuals contributed to the creation of the movie, which took three years and included some two and a half million pieces of art.[126] The cost of the film, $1,488,422.74,[127] was four times that of the average feature of 1937.[128] The last animation was not shot until December 1, only six days before a sneak preview, and less than three weeks before the premiere.[129]

Given the scope and cost of the project, Walt and Roy wanted the film to be distributed under the best terms possible. United Artists had previously distributed the Studios' pictures, but the brothers had become dissatisfied with the terms, so a new contract was drawn up for them to sign.[130] However, they noticed a clause requiring them to grant the distributor television rights to the films.[131] Walt would later state, "I don't know what television is, and I'm not going to sign away anything I don't know about."[132] Thus, they changed distributors and signed with RKO.

On December 21, 1937, *Snow White and the Seven Dwarfs* premiered at the Carthay Circle Theatre in Los Angeles. The film received a standing ovation from the audience of Hollywood elites, including Charlie Chaplin (1889–1977), Paulette Goddard (1910–1990), Shirley Temple (1928–2014), Mary Pickford, Douglas Fairbanks, Jr. (1909–2000), Marlene Dietrich (1901–1992), John Barrymore (1882–1942), Judy Garland (1922–1969), Ginger Rogers (1911–1995), Jack Benny (1894–1974), Fred MacMurray (1908–1991), Clark Gable (1901–1960), Carole Lombard (1908–1942), George Burns (1896–1996), Gracie Allen (1895–1964), Ed Sullivan (1901–1974), and Milton Berle (1908–2002). Animator Bill Peet (1915–2002) reported that audience members "were carried away by the picture from the very beginning, and as it went along everyone was bubbling over with enthusiasm and frequently bursting into spontaneous applause."[133] Layout artist Kendall O'Connor (1908–1998) noted, "They even applauded the background and layouts when no animation was on the screen."[134] O'Connor, who was seated near John Barrymore, noticed the actor's excitement as the Queen, disguised as the crone, poled her boat through the fog in front of the castle.[135]

Arguably the most significant observation of the premiere came from animator Ward Kimball:

> Clark Gable and Carole Lombard were sitting close, and when Snow White was poisoned, stretched out on that slab, they started blowing their noses. I could hear it—crying—that was the big surprise. We worried whether they would feel for this girl, and when they did, I knew it was in the bag.[136]

Such reactions from Tinseltown royalty were personally satisfying to Walt, who had founded his studio on poverty row, a section of Hollywood peppered with small, struggling studios, only a decade and a half earlier. The premiere had such an impact that Walt and figures of the Seven Dwarfs were featured on the cover of the next issue of *Time* magazine.

Snow White and the Seven Dwarfs ran for ten weeks at the Carthay Circle Theatre, grossing nearly $180,000.[137] At Radio City Music Hall in New York City, the movie ran for five weeks, which was a full two weeks longer than any other film shown previously at that venue.[138] The box office receipts rose from $108,000 the first week to $110,000 the second.[139] Lines at the theater frequently spilled down the block.[140] Reserved seat tickets that sold for $1.65 were being scalped for upward of five dollars apiece.[141] The theater's management estimated that 800,000 patrons saw the feature during its run at the Music Hall.[142] In London the movie ran for twenty-eight weeks, grossing over half a million dollars at just one theater.[143] By the end of 1939, the film had been dubbed into ten languages and seen in forty-nine countries.[144]

The animated feature was the most successful film in history until *Gone With the Wind* was released in 1939. In its first release *Snow White and the Seven Dwarfs* earned eight million dollars, and that was during a time when the average movie ticket was 23 cents.[145] During its general release in 1938, the feature made four times more than any other movie released that same year. After the film's seventh rerelease in 1993, the lifetime earnings of the movie had grown to eighty million dollars.[146] It has been estimated that if ticket sales were adjusted for inflation, *Snow White and the Seven Dwarfs* would have brought in over 868 million dollars, making it the tenth-most-profitable film of all time.[147]

Snow White and the Seven Dwarfs was the first feature to have a soundtrack album released.[148] The release was a set of three 78 rpm records on the Victor label. All three records became top ten hits in February 1938.

Several other recordings of songs from the film were released contemporaneously. Freddie Rich [1898–1956] and His Orchestra released versions of "Whistle While You Work," "I'm Wishing," "Some Day My Prince Will Come," "Heigh-Ho," "With a Smile and a Song," and "One Song" on Decca Records. Vocalion released Bobby Snyder's Collegians performing "Some Day My Prince Will Come" and "Heigh-Ho." Norman Cloutier's Madcaps released "Some Day

My Prince Will Come" on Conqueror Records. Both "Heigh-Ho" and "Whistle While You Work" were Top Ten hits for months on *Your Hit Parade* (1935–1959).[149] The film's music resonated well enough with audiences that during the 1944 re-release of *Snow White and the Seven Dwarfs*, Lyn Murray (1909–1989) released "Some Day My Prince Will Come," "Snow White Overture," "With a Smile and a Song," "Heigh-Ho," "Bluddle-Uddle-Um-Dum," "Whistle While You Work," "I'm Wishing," and "One Song" on Decca.

Several jazz artists would go on to record covers of "Some Day My Prince Will Come," including Dave Brubeck (1920–2012), Bill Evans (1929–1980), Miles Davis (1926–1991), Oscar Peterson (1925–2007), Herbie Hancock (1940–), Lena Horne (1917–2010), and Chet Baker (1929–1988). Sun Ra [1914–1993] and His Arkestra recorded "Some Day My Prince Will Come," "I'm Wishing," "Heigh-Ho," and "Whistle While You Work." Dave Brubeck (1920–2012–) recorded covers of "Some Day My Prince Will Come" and "Heigh-Ho." Louis Armstrong (1901–1971) and Brother Jack McDuff (1926–2001) recorded covers of "Whistle While You Work."

Other groups also recorded songs from *Snow White and the Seven Dwarfs*. Lawrence Welk (1903–1992) recorded covers of "Whistle While You Work," "Some Day My Prince Will Come," and "Heigh-Ho." A British pop group called Freddie and the Dreamers recorded covers of "Heigh-Ho" and "Whistle While You Work" for Columbia Records in 1966. Diana Ross (1944–) and the Supremes recorded "Whistle While You Work," "Heigh-Ho," and "Some Day My Prince Will Come" in 1967. The Mormon Tabernacle Choir recorded a medley of "Whistle While You Work" and "Heigh-Ho." A medley comprising "Some Day My Prince Will Come" and "One Song" was recorded by the female R & B group En Vogue. A disco version of "Some Day My Prince Will Come" surfaced in 1976, thanks to Dutch singer Patricia Paay (1949–).

"Whistle While You Work" is the first of several work songs to come out of The Walt Disney Studios. The most notable of these is "A Spoonful of Sugar" from *Mary Poppins* (1964). One of the more recent songs of this archetype is "Happy Working Song" by Alan Menken (1949–), with lyrics by Stephen Schwartz (1948–). The song, which is featured in the 2007 release *Enchanted*, is a tribute to "Whistle While You Work," as is the scene in which it occurs.

Another notable homage to a song from *Snow White and the Seven Dwarfs* was written by John Lennon (1940–1980). When asked by an interviewer about the Beatles tune "Do You Want to Know a Secret?" the esteemed songwriter noted:

> The idea came from this thing my mother used to sing to me when I was one or two years old, when she was still living with me. It was from a Disney movie: "Do you want to know a Secret? Promise not to tell? You [sic] are standing by a wishing well." So, with that in my head, I wrote the song and just gave it to George to sing.[150]

The number two hit was released on the album *Please Please Me* (1963), as well as on a single with "Thank You Girl" (1963).

All eight songs from *Snow White and the Seven Dwarfs*, plus one additional song titled "Snow White,"[151] were released as sheet music, published by Irving Berlin Music Publishers. Both "One Song" and "Some Day My Prince Will Come" have vocal introductions that do not appear in the film. The sheet music for "Heigh-Ho" features a second verse that does not appear in the movie. "Some Day My Prince Will Come" has a set of alternate lyrics to be used when the song is being sung about a woman.

Snow White and the Seven Dwarfs was critically acclaimed as well. That being said, the only Academy Award nomination the film received was for Best Score, and it lost to Universal's *One Hundred Men and a Girl* (1937). However, the following year at the eleventh annual Academy Awards, Shirley Temple presented Walt with an Honorary Oscar for his work on *Snow White and the Seven Dwarfs*. The award itself featured one full-sized Oscar, accompanied by seven other smaller Oscars.

More accolades followed. In 1938 Walt Disney, who had never completed high school, received honorary degrees from Harvard, Yale, and the University of Southern California. The degree from Harvard was the first honorary degree from that institution given to someone working in film.[152] Years later the American Film Institute named *Snow White and the Seven Dwarfs* as the number one animated film of all time, as well the thirty-fourth-best American film of all time.[153] "Some Day My Prince Will Come" was listed by AFI as the nineteenth-best song in a movie, and the Queen was listed by AFI as the tenth-best villain of all time in an American film. On a personal level, Ward Kimball stated of the film in the year 2000, "I still think it's the best thing we ever did."[154]

In 1938 William G. King of the *New York Sun* referred to *Snow White and the Seven Dwarfs* as "the nearest approach to true 'film-opera' yet created."[155] In a 1993 review of a compact disc release of the movie's soundtrack, composer and scholar Ross Care stated that "musically, *Snow White and the Seven Dwarfs* is fairly conventional in format, being basically an animated operetta."[156] In the review Care would go on to note *The Goddess of Spring* as a precursor for *Snow White and the Seven Dwarfs* and cite the use of "rhymed and metered dialogue lead-ins," though he did not connect that technique explicitly to recitative.[157]

Walt invested the financial success of *Snow White and the Seven Dwarfs* into building a larger studio on a fifty-one-acre plot in Burbank on Buena Vista Street.[158] Such a studio was increasingly a necessity, as the size of Disney's staff had doubled to over six hundred people in the four-year period from 1934 to 1938.[159] Perhaps more importantly, the success of his first feature film permitted Walt to work on new ideas without having to expend as much energy convincing financiers of the project's viability.

In terms of music, the influence of *Snow White and the Seven Dwarfs* is difficult to overrate. The overwhelming success of the movie caused the Studios to adopt the approaches to joining image and music in animated features as their gold standard. While no single animated film from The Walt Disney Studios utilizes all these techniques to the same degree, the influence of this movie's score is apparent in nearly all of the Studios' animated features. Moreover, given that *Snow White and the Seven Dwarfs* was the first movie of its kind, its influence as a progenitor of a genre is stronger than any other film's. Seventy-five years after the movie's premiere, the overwhelming majority of animated features produced in the United States are children's or family movies. Furthermore, many of these films continue to be reliant upon songs to establish character, provide emotional support, and aid in narrative.

Chapter 4

PINOCCHIO

Work on what would be the Studios' second feature-length film, *Pinocchio*, started shortly before the first was completed. The songs for the film were written by Leigh Harline, with lyrics by Ned Washington (1901–1976). Additional score development was provided by Paul J. Smith, while Edward Plumb (1907–1958), Frederick Stark, and Charles Wolcott served as orchestrators.[1] Hal Rees, a percussionist and composer who was at that time the head of the sound effects department, was credited with co-composing the "Clock Theme" with Harline.[2] Moreover, Harline conducted the orchestra for many of the scoring sections.[3] The composer also selected the singers for the choir and led rehearsals for the forty-voice group.[4] The eighty-seven-minute film is composed of some 106 musical sequences (see appendix).

LEIGH HARLINE

Born on March 26, 1901, Leigh Adrian Harline was the youngest of thirteen children. His parents, Charles Härlin and Johanna Matilda, converted to the Mormon faith in 1888. The couple moved from the village of Härfsta, Sweden, to Salt Lake City, Utah, three years later. Härlin, who had earlier been a soldier by trade, anglicized the family name upon moving to the United States. During his time in Utah, Charles worked as a farmer.[5]

Leigh graduated with a degree in music from the University of Utah, where he studied piano and organ under J. Spencer Cornwall (1888–1983), who later directed the Mormon Tabernacle Choir. Harline moved to Los Angeles in 1928, where he worked at a number of radio stations as a composer, conductor, performer, vocalist, and announcer. In 1931 the young musician wrote music for the first transcontinental broadcast to originate from the West Coast. Walt became aware of Harline from this broadcast, leading the animator to recruit the composer. Joining the Studios on December 10, 1932,[6] the following issue of the *Mickey Mouse Melodeon* made note of Harline's addition to the Studio : It seems that KHJ is thumbing its nose at us these days ... first Ted Osborne and now Leigh Harline. Welcome Leigh! We hope you like us half as much as we like you![7]

The blurb notes that Harline and writer Ted Osborne (1901–1968) both previously worked for radio station KHJ.

Harline scored more than fifty shorts for Disney, including *Father Noah's Ark* (1933), *Lullaby Land* (1933), *Mickey's Mechanical Man* (1933), *The Pet Store* (1933), *The Pied Piper* (1933), *Funny Little Bunnies* (1934), *The Goddess of Spring*, *The Grasshopper and the Ants* (1934), *The Wise Little Hen* (1934), *Peculiar Penguins* (1934), *The Band Concert* (1935), *Music Land*, *Elmer Elephant* (1936), *Hawaiian Holiday* (1937), and *The Old Mill*. The young composer worked with Frank Churchill and Paul J. Smith on the score to *Snow White and the Seven Dwarfs*. Harline wrote both the songs and a majority of the background score for *Pinocchio*, making it the largest contribution of a single composer to a feature-length Disney animated film during Walt's lifetime. Harline was also the first composer assigned to *Fantasia*, though the project was later reassigned to Ed Plumb. Harline appears conducting the Studios' orchestra in the promotional short *A Trip Through Walt Disney Studios*.

Director Wilfred Jackson described the process by which he and Harline would collaborate on films :

Leigh would more often just sit and think about it while he and I talked over the action for a fairly good-sized section of the cartoon. From time to time he would swivel around in his chair to face the piano and play an accompaniment while humming a little fragment of melody to himself, but the tune would not usually get very far before he stopped and turned around to talk some more. Finally, after sketching out with a pencil several of these fragments of tunes on a music staff, Leigh would go right through the entire section on the piano, though not really playing it non-stop ... Leigh "talked" his music as much as he "played" it—that is, he would stop to explain that " ... in this part violins will carry the melody with a deep countermelody on trombone, like this ..." and he would play the trombone part while humming or singing out the violin part, then continue with: " ... then when we come to this theme" and he would play it, " ... it will be carried by muted trumpet" and so on, right through the entire section we were discussing.

If I thought some part wasn't appropriate for the action, Leigh was quite flexible about re-working it, but he wasn't at all inclined to just discard some part of it completely and simply substitute a different piece of music ... Leigh more often found an alternative way to construct and perform the question-able material, working this way and that to give it a different feeling, trying to satisfy my requirements for the action. He would keep at it this way for a long time before deciding to actually discard the music in question and substitute something new.[8]

Thus, Harline utilized his skill as a formally trained composer by thinking in terms of orchestration and variation when he collaborated on a film.

Harline felt that scoring animation was more difficult than writing for a typical film:

Ordinarily I have about three seconds in which to set the mood for a cartoon (compared to about thirty seconds for an ordinary dramatic picture). That imposes a task not always easy to do. In a [sic] ordinary cartoon short we have to fit the music into very close limitations, for the whole character of a cartoon is based upon the coordination of musical rhythm and photographic frequency in addition to synchronizing music with action.[9]

The task was further challenged by such close collaboration between director and composer as practiced in The Walt Disney Studios. Conventionally speaking, composers for typical live-action films have the freedom of working much more independently.

In a 1937 interview Harline expressed the relative freedom of scoring an animated feature:

In the case of our feature-length cartoons there are many sequences where we are allowed the same liberty of composition and scoring as is the case in any major production. While we have a great deal more music to do than is customary with any other type of picture, the fact that we can get out of the strait-jacket put around us by ordinary cartoon requirements is a decidedly agreeable occasion for us. In fact, there are many sequences where the action of the picture gets quite dramatic. For these we have prepared music that is more or less symphonic—at least in instrumentation—and of a serious form ... We will use an orchestra of from thirty-six to forty men, whereas, ordinarily we use from sixteen to twenty ... The leading characters are treated as natural folks and not as caricatures. This, too, allows for more freedom in our musical treatment.[10]

While Harline felt a lack of restraint in some ways when composing music for animated features, he was challenged by having to write from themes composed by others. Here, Harline comments on taking over work on *Snow White and the Seven Dwarfs* from Frank Churchill during the latter's leave from the Studios due to anxiety :

There is one aspect of the thing that is not as easy as I should like to have it. Owing to a recent change in our personnel here, a part of the thematic material for the picture was written by another composer. I now have to write additional thematic material to complete the picture and, of course, must try to maintain the general atmosphere of what already has been composed. The latter has been recorded and naturally, we cannot discard it. So, fitting my ideas into those of the previous composer and escaping any hint of "patchwork" is not easy. Don't misunderstand me!—the other composer's work is not being criticized—it quite likely is as good as what I might have done; but, you understand, it isn't mine and I have to make other music which must be kept in character.[11]

While Harline stayed at The Walt Disney Studios for less than a decade, given the challenges of the variety of scoring he had done during this time, he was well prepared to take on any assignment Hollywood could offer.

Harline left Disney in 1941 after completing the score for a Pluto short, *The Sleepwalker* (1942). He had already been freelancing for Columbia Pictures, composing music for the Blondie film series. He went on to score for other studios, including MGM, Paramount, and RKO, working on films that included *The Pride of the Yankees* (1942), *Johnny Come Lately* (1943), *Isle of the Dead* (1945), *They Live By Night* (1949), *The Wonderful World of the Brothers Grimm* (1962), and *7 Faces of Dr. Lao* (1964). During this time Harline was music director for two Fred Astaire (1899–1987) musicals, *You Were Never Lovelier* (1942) and *The Sky's the Limit* (1943). The composer even wrote the score for a non-Disney animated feature, the Fleischer Studios' 1941 film *Mr. Bug Goes to Town*. In 1947 he returned to radio for a while as music director of *The Ford Summer Theater*.[12] Starting in the late fifties, Harline broadened his palette to work on various television series, including *Shirley Temple's Storybook* (1958–1961), *Ben Casey* (1961–1966), *Gunsmoke* (1955–1975), and *Daniel Boone* (1964–1970).

As a member of the Church of Jesus Christ of Latter-Day Saints, he composed scores for the LDS production films *Man's Search for Happiness* (1964) and *In This Holy Place* (1968), the former of which was used for the Mormon pavilion at the 1964 World's Fair. The church also commissioned him to write an orchestral piece, *Centennial Suite* (1947), for the one hundredth anniversary of the settlement of Utah. The composer belonged to numerous organizations, including: AFM, ASCAP, Beta Theta Pi, the Bohemian Club, the Composer and Lyricists Guild of America, the Motion Picture Academy of Arts and Sciences, and the Screen Composer's Association.[13] He was also involved in civic and cultural matters, serving on the Municipal Arts Commission and as a member of the Mayor's Music Advisory Board.[14]

Harline and his wife Catherine (Palmer) had two daughters, Karen (born 1931) and Gretchen (1932–2011), and six grandchildren. The composer died from throat cancer on December 10, 1969, in Long Beach, California. Harline received eight Academy Award nominations over the course of his career and won two Academy Awards, one for Best Score (for *Pinocchio*) and one for Best Song ("When You Wish Upon a Star").

PINOCCHIO

The score for *Pinocchio* includes significantly fewer songs than *Snow White and the Seven Dwarfs*. Only five are featured in *Pinocchio*: "When You Wish Upon a Star," "Little Wooden Head," "Give a Little Whistle," "Hi-Diddle-Dee-Dee," and "I've Got No Strings." All of these tunes, with the exception of "I've Got No Strings," appear at least twice in the movie.

In a 1940 interview with Rose Heylbut, Paul J. Smith related the use of leitmotif in the score to *Pinocchio*:

> The songs are the first basis of the complete score. We like to use them as leitmotifs, to suggest both characters and situations throughout the picture. Take, for instance, the little theme with the hippity-hop rhythm that symbolizes Jiminy Cricket. It is stated as the Cricket's tune, and appears as the inner voice of a more important theme, or merely as a rhythmic suggestion, in every scene in which Jiminy is about to assume the center of the stage. The star song is sung but twice in the picture, but it appears (in free variation, parallel chords, and so on) in every sequence where Jiminy and the Fairy combine their powers in working out Pinocchio's destiny. The development of the theme requires the most detailed care. The spectator must be aware of the theme and of its slightly altered form, but neither theme, nor variation may at any time rise to the point of occupying his conscious attention.[15]

This sort of treatment, where song melodies are treated as leitmotifs for characters, is typical not only of *Pinocchio*, but of many other Disney animated features that follow.

Perhaps the musical element of *Pinocchio* that shows the most development since *Snow White and the Seven Dwarfs* is the orchestration. Paul Smith's scoring for *Pinocchio* is colorful in a picturesque manner that not only reflects the visual elements of the film but also provides an innovative, musical variety that contributes to a highly compelling score. That being said, Smith's work came with some advice from Walt, who suggested, "vibra harps [vibraphones]" and "soft temple blocks" for the undersea cues.[16]

Like *Snow White and the Seven Dwarfs*, the film begins with a storybook centered in frame. Above the book is Jiminy Cricket, who had been singing "When You Wish Upon a Star" over the beginning credits. After finishing the song, he speaks directly to the audience: "I'll bet a lot of you folks don't believe that . . . about a wish coming true . . . do you?"[17] He then opens the storybook and begins to tell the story of Pinocchio while an instrumental version of "When You Wish Upon a Star" plays in the background.

Jiminy Cricket is the only being in the film that is aware of, and speaks directly to, the audience. He is also a character within the story he tells. The role was voiced by Cliff Edwards (1895–1971), who was a singer in the twenties and thirties known as "Ukulele Ike." The crooner had had a number one hit with "Singin' in the Rain" in 1929.

Jiminy Cricket's leitmotif (Figure 4.1) first appears when the cricket approaches Geppetto's fire at the beginning of the film. The tune also appears prominently during the Blue Fairy's first scene in the film, after Jiminy descends from a shelf to chide Pinocchio for not knowing what a conscience is. Figaro and Cleo share a leitmotif (Figure 4.2) that occurs frequently in the score. While the tune is referred to as the "Kitten Theme" in the cue sheets for the film, the theme appears in the flute accompanying a scene where Geppetto says goodnight to Cleo well before the toy maker instructs Figaro to say good-night to the fish. The melody is also associated with Cleo when the fish blows smoke rings after Geppetto extinguishes Pinocchio's burning finger in Cleo's bowl. The theme recurs in the clarinet when Figaro opens the window (Figure 4.2).

The most recognizable theme in the film is "When You Wish Upon a Star." The melody occurs not only at the beginning of the film, but anytime the Blue Fairy appears. It also recurs when Geppetto, before going to sleep, wishes that

Figure 4.1. Jiminy Cricket leitmotif—CRICKET THEME from PINOCCHIO—By Leigh Harline—© Copyright 1940 by Bourne Co.—Copyright Renewed—All Rights Reserved International Copyright Secured—ASCAP

Figure 4.2. Figaro and Cleo's leitmotif—KITTEN THEME from PINOCCHIO—By Leigh Harline—© Copyright 1940 Bourne Co.—Copyright Renewed—All Rights Reserved International Copyright Secured—ASCAP

Figure 4.3. "When You Wish Upon a Star"—WHEN YOU WISH UPON A STAR from PINOCCHIO—Words By Ned Washington Music By Leigh Harline—© Copyright 1940 by Bourne Co.—Copyright Renewed—All Rights Reserved International Copyright Secured—ASCAP

Pinocchio were a real boy. In the first scene that the fairy appears, she fully materializes before the tune begins. In all, the song is heard in four noncontinuous instances during the Blue Fairy's first scene in *Pinocchio*, being interrupted for the music that accompanies the puppet's awakening, as well as Jiminy's leitmotif.

The melody (Figure 4.3) for this song is fairly dramatic in terms of contour. The first four measures are built from a two-measure sub-phrase that is sequenced upward. This sub-phrase starts with an octave leap upward. This motion is further accentuated by a smaller ascending leap at the end of the sub-phrase. The following two measures balance this upward contour by having a stepwise melody that brings the range down an octave. The last two measures of the phrase feature a leap down of a seventh, then a leap back up a sixth to the dominant. When this eight-bar phrase is repeated as a consequent phrase, the leap down to the leading tone steps up to the tonic, resolving the leap.

All of these leaps not only function to produce a dramatic contour but fashion a vehicle for showcasing Cliff Edwards's range and abilities. In fact, at the end of the song (Figure 4.4), Edwards leaps from the submediant up to the mediant and finally rests on the dominant, a full two octaves above the song's first note.

Another subtle, yet effective, element of the song is the accented upper neighbor tone on the first note of the line "Everything your heart desires,"[18] which gives a strong nine to eight resolution. This motion is reflected in two following accented passing tones, seven to six and five moving down to four. It is notable that the same portion of the melody in the consequent phrase

dreams come true.

Figure 4.4. Ending of "When You Wish Upon a Star"—WHEN YOU WISH UPON A STAR from PINOCCHIO—Words By Ned Washington Music By Leigh Harline—© Copyright 1940 by Bourne Co.—Copyright Renewed—All Rights Reserved International Copyright Secured—ASCAP

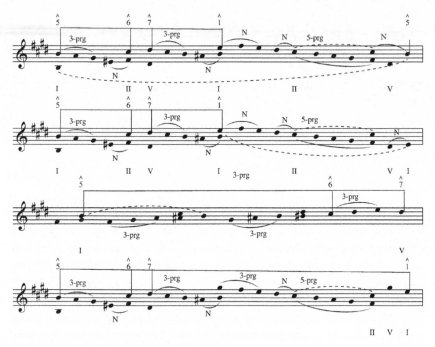

Figure 4.5. Melodic analysis of "When You Wish Upon a Star"

accompanies the song's title line. This accented dissonance helps to contribute a sort of bittersweet mood to the song.

"When You Wish Upon a Star" is composed of four phrases (Figure 4.5) in thirty-two-bar form. The first features a register transfer of the dominant from the first note up an octave to the half cadence that ends the phrase. The first sub-phrase consists of a linear ascent from scale degree five to the tonic. The second phrase is identical to the first, save for the end, which is altered to accommodate an authentic cadence. While this resolution is harmonically satisfying, the lower register tonic leaves the phrase unresolved in the obligatory register. The bridge features a linear ascent from scale degree five to the leading tone, elaborating the dominant, and furthering the tension of the song.

The final phrase of "When You Wish Upon a Star" resolves the melodic tension of the bridge with an ascent from scale degree five to the tonic resolution at the cadence. The end of the first sub-phrase ends here on scale degree three, while the authentic cadence resolves the tonic in the obligatory register, coinciding with the lyrical resolution "Your dreams come true."[19] The version of the final phrase presented here is the version sung by Cliff Edwards and the chorus at the close of the film. The final phrase ends differently in the version of the song from the beginning of the feature.

The opening version of "When You Wish Upon a Star," sung by Jiminy Cricket, concludes by changing the final note to a dominant two octaves above the first note of the song. This ending is doubly unresolved due to settling on an unstable note, as well as the high register of the tone. This lack of resolution allows for a large-scale closure of the melody at the end of the movie. While the melody of the song at the film's conclusion lands on the tonic, a short tag line sung by the chorus is appended with the lyrics "you'll find your dreams come true,"[20] settling on scale degree three.

This large-scale resolution of the melody over the course of the movie is aided by having both the opening and concluding arrangements in the same key. Thus, the ends of both *Pinocchio* and *Snow White and the Seven Dwarfs* are musically similar in the sense that the melodic resolution of the song in question coincides with the fulfillment of the protagonist's dream. Furthermore, both endings land on a high register mediant, voiced by a choir.

"Little Wooden Head" is utilized in the film as a leitmotif for Pinocchio. The melody appears at the very beginning of the opening credits, directly before "When You Wish Upon a Star" enters. The only time the tune occurs with lyrics is when Geppetto marches Pinocchio about his workshop.

Just as Snow White introduces "I'm Wishing" by humming the song as she works, Geppetto's singing of this song is prepared by his vocalizing the same melody as he paints a mouth on the wooden puppet. The words express the toy maker's affection for his creation, "Little wooden head go play your part. / Bring a little joy to every heart. / Little do you know and yet it's true / That I'm mighty proud of you."[21] The orchestration of this version is very vibrant, with its use of bells and high whistles to evoke the sound of Geppetto's music boxes. In addition, the end of this sequence runs down in tempo, again in imitation of a music box. Paul J. Smith cites this orchestration as helping establish the toy maker's character: "The old worldliness of Geppetto's life was caught by the tinkle of the music boxes."[22]

"TURN ON THE OLD MUSIC BOX" AND THE BLUE FAIRY'S MUSIC

"Turn on the Old Music Box" is a song that was written for *Pinocchio* that appeared in the film without its lyrics. The melody of the song is first heard as a waltz in a sequence when Geppetto dances with the newly live Pinocchio. The tune later appears in four when Pinocchio sets out for school. It also occurs near the end of the film, again in four, when the toy maker and Pinocchio dance in celebration of the puppet's transformation into a live boy.

The tick-tock sequence that disturbs Jiminy Cricket's sleep is scored solely for wood blocks and metallic percussion. While some might consider the audio for the segment to be a sound effect; it is in reality a very cleverly arranged cue that gradually layers individual ostinati on top of each other, culminating in a complex rhythmic tapestry.

The scene leading up to the first appearance of the Blue Fairy is vividly orchestrated with an electric organ sound that evokes an otherworldly sense of spirituality. Pitch-wise, the segment starts by moving out chromatically from a central pitch. Paul J. Smith said of this passage, "One of the means we used to embellish the fairy effect was to add half-tones, in both directions to one of the higher, flutier tones of the Novachord [an electric organ manufactured by Hammond Organs], combining them in tonal clusters of rather free fantasy, resolving them always in consonance, and with great care for musical phrasing."[23] In fact, *Pinocchio* was the second film to use a Novachord in its soundtrack, after *Gone With the Wind*.

This materialization sequence ends with a series of rapid celesta arpeggios, which recur in the same scene when the fairy uses her wand to imbue Pinocchio with life, and again when she confers the title of conscience on Jiminy. These arpeggiations also end the scene as the Blue Fairy disappears.

The Blue Fairy has a bit in common with Glinda the Good Witch from the previous year's *The Wizard of Oz*. The bright light of the Blue Fairy traveling through the sky is similar in design to the bubble that brings Glinda to Munchkin Land. The fairy's materialization is accompanied by celesta, while Glinda's bubble is introduced with similar orchestration as it glides through the air. While each character's gown is significantly different from the other's, both are designed in soft pastels, rich with sparkles, and equipped with the ability to float.

"GIVE A LITTLE WHISTLE," "I'VE GOT NO STRINGS," AND UNUSED SONGS

"Give a Little Whistle" is more closely related to the songs in *Snow White and the Seven Dwarfs* than any other song in the film. In fact, "With a Smile and a Song," "Whistle While You Work," and "Give a Little Whistle" are all led into by whistling. "Give a Little Whistle" also utilizes a musical echo, just as "I'm Wishing" does, though the echo of the whistling in the former echoes back as a musical sequence as opposed to pure repetition. Such similarities indicate that the Studio reused effective elements of *Snow White and the Seven Dwarfs* in the design of *Pinocchio*.

The reuse of ideas is accomplished in a way that does not diminish the individuality of "Give a Little Whistle." While this song and "The Silly Song" from *Snow White and the Seven Dwarfs* both use elements of popular music of the era, the style of "Give a Little Whistle" seems a bit more contemporary, as evidenced by the relatively progressive-sounding woodwind flourish that leads into the first verse, as well as the syncopation that accompanies Jiminy's reaction to smelling Geppetto's pipe. The orchestration of the song is also related to other sequences of the movie by the inclusion of a countermelody to the bridge played on shaken handbells. In the film, these bells are played by mechanical figures from one of the toy maker's clocks.

"I've Got No Strings" is a unique sequence in *Pinocchio*, as it presents the protagonist performing within the reality of the film. The animated audience claps for and laughs at the wooden boy's antics, which encourages moviegoers to appreciate the character. After Pinocchio's solo, the song features a short set of international variations, an aesthetic precursor to "it's a small world (after all)." The first variation features a Dutch clog dance in three. The second is a brightly orchestrated imitation of a can-can. The final variation invokes the sounds of Russian folk music, including a slower vocal section with balalaika accompaniment, and a fast trepak dance section. An African variation had been considered but was not used in the film.[24]

While "I've Got No Strings" contains some of the strongest instances of Mickey Mousing, the technique is used throughout the movie. One particularly clever instance of this technique occurs after Pinocchio first encounters John Worthington Foulfellow and Gideon. As the two con artists follow the puppet in amazement, Gideon's leaps to peer over a fence are musically represented by flutes, which rhythmically form a hemiola in relationship to the instrumental version of "Turn On the Old Music Box," which accompanies Pinocchio's skipping.

Leigh Harline and Ned Washington penned several other songs for *Pinocchio*, but they were not utilized in the film. One of these, "No Strings," was to serve as an introduction to "I've Got No Strings."[25] In this song, the puppets would have introduced the title character of the movie to Stromboli's audience.[26] "Rolling Along to Pleasure Island" would have been sung by boys traveling to the hedonistic fair.[27] J. Worthington Foulfellow would have had a solo in the song "As I Was Say'n to the Duchess."[28]

Harline and Washington also wrote a song called "Figaro and Cleo." The lyrics of the song relate a tale of how Figaro cannot bring himself to eat Cleo, and because of this, Figaro is ostracized by the cat community.[29] Harline had intended on using the tune, which is unrelated to the previously mentioned "Kitten Theme," from this song as a leitmotif for Figaro. Three unused score sketches resident in the Leigh Harline Papers at the University of Cincinnati make use of the melody in scenes featuring the animated cat. The tune appears in a sketch for the scene where Figaro displays his jealousy of Pinocchio following the music box sequence.[30] Shortly afterward, the melody is used in two different sketches, the first of which would have accompanied Figaro saying good night to Cleo,[31] and the second of which would have underscored Figaro opening the window.[32]

SUMMARY AND RECEPTION

While *Pinocchio* took three years to make, Paul Smith noted that "the preparation of the complete score—from the first sketching out of the songs, the roughing in of the blue print to set synchronization and special accents, to the drafting of the score and its orchestral arrangement—took a little over a year."[33] The film premiered on February 5, 1940, at the Center Theatre in New York City. The premiere was bolstered by an exhibition at the New York Museum of Science and Industry of artwork demonstrating the development of the film.[34]

An additional promotional device was used not as successfully. Eleven dwarves were hired to don Pinocchio costumes at the premiere, and to cavort and wave to passersby from the theater's marquee. This attempt at adding atmosphere was not continued past the first attempt, as the eleven imbibed significantly during their lunch break and returned to their posts naked, interested mainly in playing a game of craps and belching.[35]

While *Pinocchio* received generally positive reviews, the film had not performed as well at the box office as Walt had hoped. The filmmaker perhaps had a premonition of what was coming when he stated shortly before *Pinocchio's* premiere, "I'd rather have an artistic flop than a box-office smash hit any day."[36] The movie had cost around 2.6 million dollars to make, over a million dollars beyond what *Snow White and the Seven Dwarfs* had cost only three years earlier.[37] Only 1.4 million dollars of that cost had been recouped by 1947.

The meager ticket sales have been blamed in part on the fact that the film could not be released in a large part of Europe due to the war. In fact, the movie was initially dubbed only in Portuguese and Spanish.[38] Others blame the poor sales on the feature's dark imagery. The movie has become very profitable over the long term, earning over 537 million dollars when adjusted for inflation, making it the thirty-eighth-most-profitable film of all time.[39]

Despite its initial mediocre reception at the box office, *Pinocchio* has been critically well received. The film won Academy Awards for both Best Song ("When You Wish Upon a Star") and Best Scoring of a Soundtrack. In fact, the American Film Institute lists "When You Wish Upon a Star" as the seventh-best song in a movie. ASCAP gave the song an award in 1989 for the most-performed feature film standard. In 2005 Time.com named the movie as one of the hundred best films of the past eighty years. The American Film Institute listed *Pinocchio* as the second-best animated movie, and the thirty-eighth-most-inspirational film of all time.

The Academy Award for Best Scoring of a Soundtrack was given to Leigh Harline and Ned Washington. Washington's credit for this award annoyed Charles Wolcott : "The Academy awarded the Best Scoring of a Musical Picture to *Pinocchio*, and gave it to Leigh and Ned Washington. Ned Washington was a lyric writer and had nothing to do with scoring the picture!"[40] Accordingly, in an attempt to give credit to his colleagues, Harline took out a full-page ad in the trades, which gave credit for the Best Scoring award to Leigh Harline, Paul Smith, Ed Plumb, and Charles Wolcott.[41]

Jiminy Cricket's ability to speak directly to the audience enabled him to appear in numerous other Disney media products. The crooning cricket appeared in the 1947 film *Fun & Fancy Free* and *Mickey's Christmas Carol* (1983). His moral authority and singing voice made him the perfect match for the musical "E-N-C-Y-C-L-O-P-E-D-I-A," "I'm No Fool," and "You, the Human Animal" sequences on the 1950s-era *Mickey Mouse Club*. Furthermore, Jiminy also appeared in numerous episodes of *Disneyland*, as well as later versions of the Disney anthology series.

The music from *Pinocchio* was strongly promoted and widely recorded. Decca Records released recordings of "When You Wish Upon a Star," "I've Got No Strings," "Turn On the Old Music Box," "Little Wooden Head," "Jiminy Cricket," "Three Cheers for Anything," "Give a Little Whistle," and "Hi-Diddle-Dee-Dee" in December of 1939, more than two months before the film's February 23 premiere.[42] These recordings feature vocals by Cliff Edwards, Julietta Novis (1909–1994), and the Ken Darby [1909–1992] Singers with the Victor Young Orchestra. A set of soundtrack recordings, including "When You Wish Upon a Star," "Little Wooden Head," "Give a Little Whistle," "Hi-Diddle-Dee-Dee," "I've Got No Strings," and "Turn On the Old Music Box" appeared in January 1940 on Victor Records, which was available as a set for $2.75.

Other unofficial versions of songs from *Pinocchio* appeared rapidly on the market. Buddy Clark [1911–1949] and His Orchestra recorded "When You Wish Upon a Star," "I've Got No Strings," "Give A Little Whistle," "Hi-Diddle-Dee-Dee," and "Turn On the Old Music Box" on Varsity Records. Glenn Miller [1904–1944] and His Orchestra released recordings of "Give a Little Whistle" and "When You Wish Upon a Star." Horace Heidt [1901–1986] & His Musical Knights released versions of the same two songs on Columbia Records. Bob Chester and His Orchestra released "I've Got No Strings" and "Turn On the Old Music Box" for Bluebird Records in January 1940. Hal Kemp [1904–1940] and His Orchestra released "I've Got No Strings" and "Give a Little Whistle" on Victor Records. Gene Krupa [1909–1973] and His Orchestra released "I've Got No Strings" on Columbia Records. Dick Jurgens [1910–1995] and His Orchestra released a version of "Give a Little Whistle" on Conqueror Records.

By far, the most popular song from *Pinocchio* was "When You Wish Upon a Star." Louis Armstrong said of the melody, "This goldarned 'When You Wish

Upon a Star' is so beautiful and more than that, man—I listen to that tune three or four times a night."[43] Coming from Armstrong, who recorded several Disney songs over the course of his career, the statement is high praise indeed.

RCA Records released a version of "When You Wish Upon a Star" by David Rose [1910–1990] & His Orchestra. Columbia Records released a version of the tune by Kate Smith (1907–1986) with the Jack Miller Orchestra (35412). Covers of the tune were recorded by Red Nichols (1905–1965) and his Five Pennies on Capitol Records (40062). The song has also been recorded by a variety of artists, such as Fred Waring [1900–1984] & His Orchestra, Louis Armstrong, Lawrence Welk, Chet Atkins (1924–2001), Tony Bennett (1926–), Billy Joel, and Gene Simmons (1949–), as well as groups, including Little Anthony and the Imperials, Dion and the Belmonts, the Mike Curb [1944–] Congregation, the Manhattan Transfer, and Diana Ross and the Supremes.

"When You Wish Upon a Star" was also re-orchestrated by John Williams (1932–), and included in the last scene of *Close Encounters of the Third Kind* (1977) at the request of Steven Spielberg (1946–). In fact, the filmmaker suggested the first seven notes of the melody as a model for the iconic tune that is used to communicate with the aliens.[44] Spielberg used the song to associate the movie's protagonist with Pinocchio.[45]

Broadway singer Barbara Cook (1927–) recorded both "When You Wish Upon a Star" and "Give a Little Whistle." Freddie and the Dreamers recorded the same two songs on Columbia Records. Glenn Miller (1904–1944) and the Dave Brubeck Quartet recorded "Give a Little Whistle." Bill Frisell (1951–) and Wayne Horvitz (1955–) collaborated on a recording of "Little Wooden Head." A cover of "I've Got No Strings" was recorded by the Gypsy Kings.

Brian Wilson's (1942–) melody for "Surfer Girl" (1963) owes a debt to "When You Wish Upon a Star." Both tunes are in 32-bar form, and feature a melody that starts with a large leap upward from scale degree five. In fact, the rhythm of melody for the first four measures is identical, and the contour of the first four notes of each two-measure sub-phrase is identical. The harmonic motion of the first measure of both tunes moves from the tonic to a chord built on scale degree six. Finally, the first couple of two-measure sub-phrases of both melodies sequence up a third. Wilson admitted that "Surfer Girl" was inspired by the Dion and the Belmonts 1960 cover of "When You Wish Upon a Star," which, like Wilson's song, was accompanied in a quadruple compound meter.

The movie *Tangled* (2010) contains an homage to *Pinocchio*. The wooden puppet appears in the rafters of the Snuggly Duckling pub. This discreet tribute is perhaps in reference to the song in the scene, Alan Menken (1949–) and Glenn Slater's (1968–) "I've Got a Dream," which invokes the Disney dream theme that was born out of "When You Wish Upon a Star."[46]

Understandably, a film that depicts an inanimate puppet coming to life would be dear to the heart of a company known for bringing inanimate drawings to life. "When You Wish Upon a Star" was the theme for the Studios' first weekly television series, *Disneyland*, and has served as somewhat of an anthem for The Walt Disney Company. The song has been used in a variety of Walt Disney Pictures opening logos for films, videos, and DVDs. It has also been used in opening medleys for *The Wonderful World of Disney*. The tune is used in the annual Super Bowl "I'm Going to Disneyland" commercial. The song is also used in a number of shows in the company's theme parks, including parades and fireworks.

The connection between *Pinocchio* and the concept of animation as the inanimate being brought to life was also reflected in the *Magic of Disney Animation* preshow at Disney's Hollywood Studios in Walt Disney World Resort, where the animation process was demonstrated. Walter Cronkite (1916–2009) and Robin Williams (1951–2014) star in this show, which ran from 1989 through 2003. In the video, Williams was to star as a lost boy in a *Peter Pan*–themed animated short. When his character is brought to life, the soundtrack uses music similar to that which is used in *Pinocchio* when the Blue Fairy imbues the wooden puppet with life.

The story of the wooden puppet that was imbued with life is distinct from the fairy-tale princess of *Snow White and the Seven Dwarfs*. The Studios would follow these two films with a string of three features, *Fantasia*, *Dumbo*, and *Bambi*, each of which was unique in story, musical approach, and visual style. This rich variety is characteristic of the salad days of the Studios, when high-minded artistry was enthusiastically embraced throughout Disney.

Chapter 5

DUMBO AND BAMBI

After *Pinocchio*, *Fantasia*, and the mixed live-action and animated film *The Reluctant Dragon* all failed to sell more than their respective costs, the Studio really needed a hit. Walt invested most of the profits from *Snow White and the Seven Dwarfs* into building a new studio. Walt and Roy placed their father, Elias, in charge of supervising the carpenters building the studio in the hope that it would keep him distracted from his wife, Flora's, recent death.[1] Elias had confided in his son, "Walter, how on earth are you going to support this big place with those cartoons of yours? Aren't you afraid you'll go broke?"[2] Though Walt reassured his father that he could always sell the studio for a hospital, the fact is that the Studios did come dangerously close to financial ruin.

While *Bambi* had been planned as a feature as early as 1937, the next film that the Studios released was *Dumbo*. The idea for the movie first came about in early 1939.[3] In January of the following year, a structured chronology for the plot was laid out by Joe Grant (1908–2005) and Dick Huemer (1898–1979).[4] By February, Walt was clear about his intention to make the film.[5]

Based on a story by Helen Aberson (1907–1999) and Harold Pearl, *Dumbo* features songs by Oliver Wallace (1887–1963) and Frank Churchill, with lyrics by Ned Washington (1901–1976). Edward Plumb was the orchestrator for the soundtrack. Ken Darby (1909–1992) and Charles Henderson (1907–1970) provided vocal arrangements for the score.[6] The soundtrack for this sixty-four-minute film is composed of some eighty individual musical sequences (see appendix).

DUMBO

Unlike the soundtracks for *Snow White and the Seven Dwarfs* and *Pinocchio*, very few of the songs in *Dumbo* are sung by characters in the film. In fact, the only tunes sung by onscreen characters are "Song of the Roustabouts," "Clown

Song," and "When I See an Elephant Fly," not counting the stork's singing of unconventional lyrics to Effie Canning's (1857–1940) "Rock-a-Bye Baby" (1887), and his crooning version of "Happy Birthday to You." The majority of the songs in the movie are sung by offscreen voices. In contrast, *Snow White and the Seven Dwarfs* and *Pinocchio* use offscreen vocals only during the choral arrangements of each film's signature song that accompany the end of each respective feature.

Two of the three songs that are sung by onscreen characters in *Dumbo* are sung by men, which is incongruous, given the limited role people play in the film. The movie avoids showing human faces whenever possible. People are often seen in silhouette, or covered in clown makeup. This helps emphasize the humanness of the animal protagonists. Both songs sung by people, "Song of the Roustabouts" and "Clown Song," are centered on issues of work and labor. The lack of significant emotional content in these songs functions to further distance the audience from the humans in the film.

The general lack of songs sung by onscreen characters is complemented by the fact that the protagonist never speaks, though he does trumpet a few times. In fact, *Dumbo* is the only Disney animated feature in which the title character never talks. Furthermore, Mrs. Jumbo speaks very little in the movie.

One of the most prominent leitmotifs in the film is one that represents the protagonist, expressing his innocence and joy (Figure 5.1). In cue sheets this melody is referred to as "Dumbo Serenade." This theme first appears when the elephants initially admire Dumbo, before he sneezes and reveals the size of his ears. The most complete version of the melody occurs when Mrs. Jumbo gives him a bath, which is followed by a loving game of hide-and-seek. A version of the leitmotif in minor (Figure 5.2) occurs when we see the baby elephant crying next to a water barrel after he has been separated from his mother. The leitmotif also occurs when Dumbo approaches the water barrel shortly before "Pink Elephants on Parade."

Figure 5.1. Dumbo's leitmotif—DUMBO SERENADE from DUMBO—By Oliver Wallace—© Copyright 1941 Bourne Co.—Copyright Renewed—All Rights Reserved International Copyright Secured—ASCAP

tempo rubato

Figure 5.2. Dumbo's leitmotif in minor—DUMBO SERENADE from DUMBO—By Oliver Wallace—© Copyright 1941 Bourne Co.—Copyright Renewed—All Rights Reserved International Copyright Secured—ASCAP

The two tonalities of this melody are used expressively when Dumbo approaches the other elephants, hoping for contact. As he draws near, we hear the theme in major. After the elephant matriarchs turn their backs on him and close him out, we hear a brief snippet of the tune in minor, portraying his sorrow over his rejection. Likewise, when Timothy washes Dumbo with a toothbrush after the elephant's first humiliating performance as a clown, his theme appears in minor. The overall visual and aural mood is a stark contrast to the joyful bath scene featuring Mrs. Jumbo and her baby. However, when Timothy proceeds to cheer the baby elephant up by telling him he is going to take him to visit his mother, the theme modulates to its parallel major as a smile appears and the elephant's blue eyes begin to light up.

Another prominent leitmotif in the movie is "Casey Junior," which was written by Frank Churchill, with lyrics by Ned Washington. The song occurs when the circus train is in motion. A percussive arrangement of the melody appears when the train passes a sunset over a bridge and rounds the corner out of a tunnel. This segment features xylophone and thick piano chords in a somewhat discordant arrangement, with driving sixteenths provided by brushes on a snare drum. Following a subsequent scene where the train travels up and down a particularly steep mountain, the final approach of the train is accompanied by chromatically moving sixteenth notes presented in parallel motion in the piano. Another colorful arrangement accompanies the train traveling through the rain after the collapse of the pyramid of pachyderms. The minor key choral vocalization in this arrangement lends it a mournful tone.

The emotional center of the film is provided by the song "Baby Mine," which was penned by the duo of Churchill and Washington. After the first verse of the song is presented, the animation moves from the elephant mother and son to images of mothers from the circus menagerie slumbering with their offspring. The final image from the song—Dumbo reaching up with his trunk to prolong contact with his mother as he leaves her—is easily one of the most touching moments in the history of animation. This image is followed by the music seguing into a major key presentation of Dumbo's leitmotif, reflecting the title character's joy at having just visited his mother.

One of the most innovatively animated sequences in the film, or indeed any animated feature, is accompanied by the song "Pink Elephants on Parade." The music, written by Oliver Wallace, appears as a theme and variations. The theme is presented initially as an instrumental, brass-heavy march in a compound duple meter. The second section of the theme features a bass line ostinato in natural minor moving stepwise downward from tonic to dominant (Figure 5.3). This portion of the melody presents a chromatic upper neighbor figure, which is later sung with the lyric "Pink Elephants." After the discordant fanfare from the beginning repeats, vocals are added, and the accompaniment changes to electric organ.

Figure 5.3. Bass Line Ostinato in "Pink Elephants on Parade"—PINK ELEPHANTS ON PARADE from DUM-BO—Words By Ned Washington Music By Oliver Wallace—© Copyright 1941 By Walt Disney Productions—Copyright Renewed—World Rights Controlled by Bourne Co.—All Rights Reserved International Copyright Secured—ASCAP

Figure 5.4. Variation 4 of "Pink Elephants on Parade"—PINK ELEPHANTS ON PARADE from DUMBO—Words By Ned Washington Music By Oliver Wallace—© Copyright 1941 By Walt Disney Productions—Copyright Renewed—World Rights Controlled by Bourne Co.—All Rights Reserved International Copyright Secured—ASCAP

Subsequent variations of "Pink Elephants on Parade" are all instrumental. The first is an exotic evocation of Middle Eastern music. The second variation is a waltz featuring harp and strings that accompanies a duo of ice-skating elephants, while the third is an upbeat Latin dance number. The final variation is an accelerando that builds to the climactic ending of the song as the elephants appear as various forms of transportation racing wildly about the screen. This final variation, which functions like a coda, reduces the theme to its first two pitches (Figure 5.4).

The stylistic breadth of variations within "Pink Elephants on Parade" helps establish the atypical temperament of the song. The discordant fanfare that begins the segment functions as a statement of oddness. However, the most salient feature that contributes to the unusual nature of the piece is Ned Washington's eccentric lyrics.

Perhaps the most subtle, yet most effective, means of establishing the character of the song is the rhythmic instability of the ten-measure main theme (Figure 5.5). Initially, what appears to be beat one is out of sync between the

Figure 5.5. Rhythmic instability in "Pink Elephants on Parade"—PINK ELEPHANTS ON PARADE from DUM-BO—Words By Ned Washington Music By Oliver Wallace—© Copyright 1941 By Walt Disney Productions—Copyright Renewed—World Rights Controlled by Bourne Co.—All Rights Reserved International Copyright Secured—ASCAP

melody and accompaniment. The first statement of "Pink Elephants on Parade" forms a pattern of three beats, causing melody and accompaniment to align rhythmically. However, when the melody returns to the initial minor second motif on the lyric "They're here," it rejoins one beat off from the accompaniment.[7] This requires another pattern of three to realign the two accent patterns, which is provided by the lyric, "there, pink elephants ev'rywhere."[8]

This rhythmic instability is reflected in the tonal ambiguity of the piece. The most emphasized tone in the melody is actually scale degree six, not the tonic. There are tonal, agogic, and dynamic accents on both the high dominant as well as the leading tone to the dominant (sharp scale degree four). While they are displaced by an octave, together these three prominent melodic tones form a chromatic cluster. It is only the last note of the melody that firmly establishes the tonic.

There are some wonderful moments of Mickey Mousing in "Pink Elephants on Parade," many of which have a psychedelic flavor to them. During the march theme two elephants march in line with each other. The two alternate rhythmically between growing and shrinking, such that one would step over the head of the other one, only to have their sizes reverse in the next step. The following shot in the sequence features a large elephant playing cowbells, led by a short elephant who plays his trunk like a horn. Every other step of the large elephant lands on the small one, causing him to toot his horn. In the second variation, an elephant that had recently appeared as a statue runs across the surface of the water, accompanied by scalar woodblocks.

The cymbal crashes in the instrumental portion of the theme feature some effective Mickey Mousing. The first cymbal crash that follows the initial fanfare portrays the explosion of a large bell of a brass instrument, out of which comes the initial hallucinatory parade. The next major cymbal crash accompanies the aforementioned small elephant kicking the large cowbell-playing elephant in retaliation. The kick results in the large elephant changing into three smaller elephants, who blow their trunks, which appear as horns, at the original elephant while their sizes change. As the small elephant becomes larger than the other three, he smashes the three in a cymbal crash, causing them to turn into a dozen or so smaller elephants. These smaller elephants march around all four sides of the screen while Dumbo looks on. As these elephants begin to fill the entire screen, they explode, again accompanied by a cymbal crash.

During the vocal portion of the theme, two light gray elephants look at each other, one from above and one from below. They pull their heads rapidly out of frame when a cymbal crashes, following the line "what an unusual view."[9] The following scene features a vertical-striped and a horizontal-striped elephant, who pass each other and get caught, forming a single two-headed plaid elephant. A cymbal crash accompanies the explosion that occurs as they pull apart, which is the final instance of cymbal-oriented Mickey Mousing in "Pink Elephants on Parade."

The visual spectacle of "Pink Elephants on Parade" is completely unprecedented in the history of cinema. That being said, one potential aesthetic ancestor of the sequence can be seen in the elaborate staged numbers in Busby Berkeley (1895–1976) musicals. In particular, two numbers from *Dames* (1934), "I Only Have Eyes for You" and "Dames," feature constantly shifting perspectives where people and graphic images merge together in a geometric fashion.

As "Pink Elephants on Parade" ends, the pink elephants visually morph into pink clouds in the morning sky. This is accompanied by a soft musical sequence that is reminiscent of the morning music melody from Rossini's *William Tell Overture*. While the film has moved on, it is not quite through with the melody for "Pink Elephants on Parade." A bit later in the sequence, the song is used as a leitmotif while Timothy considers how he and Dumbo came to be up in the tree.

"When I See an Elephant Fly," penned by Wallace and Washington, is the only song in *Dumbo* that is sung by significant onscreen characters. The most prominent elements of the song are Washington's lyrical puns. Several of these puns take the format of a multi-word noun, where the last word can also function as a verb, such as "I saw a front porch swing, heard a diamond ring."[10] The humorous nature of the lyrics lends it a similarity to "The Silly Song" from *Snow White and the Seven Dwarfs*.

The crows that sing "When I See an Elephant Fly" are clearly cast as African Americans, a fact that is evident in their manner of speech, singing, dress, and dance. This can be seen near the end of the sequence where the lead crow, referred to as Jim Crow in the script, and the crow with round glasses scat and strut about. The apparel worn by the crows is sort of a mixture of several styles, including pachuco and hepcat.

The last line of each verse illustrates this relation with the lyric, "I be done seen about everything, when I see an elephant fly,"[11] an imitation of black vernacular. Other bits of period black slang can be heard in dialog such as "looky here" and "well, hush my beak," as well as the way in which the crows refer to each other as "boy" or "brother."[12] Further imitation of black-vernacular elements appear in the manner in which Jim Crow often mispronounces words and puts unusual emphases on the syllables of longer words, such as "ROOkus" (instead of ruckus), "EEregular," and "ADdress."[13]

The vocal style of "When I See an Elephant Fly" is similar to that of black male gospel quartets that rose to prominence in the thirties, such as the Dixie Hummingbirds, the Swan Silvertones, and the Spirit of Memphis. However, the voice of Jim Crow was sung by Cliff Edwards, who had also sung the part of Jiminy Cricket in *Pinocchio*. Other parts of the song were sung by James Baskett

(1904–1948) and Jim Carmichael (1909–1988), with backup by the Hall Johnson Choir, a gospel group in Los Angeles.

The performance of the music was central to the design of the sequence, as animator Ward Kimball noted :

> The development and differentiation of the characters really began on the night that we started recording. After listening to the voices, I decided that maybe the squeaky, high voice might be the little crow with the kid's cap and pink glasses, and Jim Crow would be the big, dominating boss crow with the derby. Later, I began to graphically re-design the characters to make them emphatically different types.[14]

In fact, Kimball went on to mention that this method was somewhat common in the animation process at Disney: "In the beginning you'd only have a miscellaneous set of characters, but by the time the voices were set, you have a pretty good idea how they would individually look, react, and even function in the sequence."[15]

Although "When I See an Elephant Fly" is the last song of the film to be introduced, it quickly becomes the most prominent song of the film, appearing in nearly every subsequent scene of the movie. The crows sing one chorus of the song at the end of the scene where Timothy and the crows first convince the elephant to fly. A choral version accompanies the finale of the film where Casey Junior rides off over the countryside; we see Mrs. Jumbo in Dumbo's private railroad car, as the baby elephant comes in for a landing into his mother's arms.

Several other songs were written for *Dumbo* but were unused. "It's Spring Again," penned by Churchill and Washington, was originally intended for the spot in the film where "Look Out for Mister Stork" appears.[16] While "It's Spring Again" was cut from the movie, the lyrics of the first verse were used as for the opening narration of the feature.[17]

While Ned Washington's lyrics for "It's Circus Day Again" were not used, Churchill's melody is used in the circus parade sequence of the film. "Sing a Song of Cheese," which would have been sung by Timothy Mouse, was written by Churchill with lyrics by Joe Grant and Dick Huemer. Since the number did not serve the narrative of the picture, it was cut.[18]

An early concept for the Pink Elephant sequence was dated May 5, 1940.[19] This song, "The Pink Elephant Polka," was written by Churchill with lyrics by Grant and Huemer. Ultimately, this tune was replaced with Wallace's "Pink Elephants on Parade." A lead sheet for another song, "Spread Your Wings," indicates that the tune was completed by June 13, 1940.[20] Churchill's melody for "Spread Your Wings" is used in the scene portraying Dumbo's flight, while the lyrics that Washington had written for the song remained unused.[21]

RECEPTION

Walt had originally planned on releasing *Dumbo* as a half-hour featurette. Ultimately, the film clocked in at sixty-four minutes, a duration that RKO felt was too short for a feature. The filmmaker refused to lengthen the movie, citing that the story was stretched out enough as it was, and noted that adding an additional ten minutes could potentially cost an additional half million dollars.[22]

Despite its brevity, *Dumbo* has a tight, effective narrative. In fact, the film is a favorite of Ward Kimball :

> Sure, we've done things that have had a lot more finish, frosting, and tricky footwork, but basically, I think the Disney cartoon reached its zenith with *Dumbo*. To me, it is the one feature cartoon that has a foolproof plot. Every story element meshes into place, held together with the great fantasy of a flying elephant. The first time I heard Walt outline the plot I knew that the picture had great simplicity and cartoon heart.[23]

Thus, the baby elephant proves that good things come in small packages.

After a year and a half in production, *Dumbo* was ready for release. The movie was created with a modest budget of $800,000, which was half the cost of *Snow White and the Seven Dwarfs*, and less than a third of the cost of *Pinocchio*. Walt later noted, "It wasn't an easy job to get on the screen something that had the same entertainment value at almost one-third the cost."[24]

The premiere of the film was in New York City on October 23, 1941. The movie not only was received well but also performed well at the box office, earning $1.3 million in its first release.[25] While this is more than half a million dollars less than *Pinocchio* earned, the relatively low cost of *Dumbo* resulted in this being a healthy profit.[26] In fact, it was the first Disney feature since *Snow White* to turn a profit at the box office. While becoming a publicly traded company with a stock sale alleviated some of the Studios' financial problems, having a profitable hit came at a good time, not only in terms of investor confidence but also in terms of studio morale.

Dumbo won an Academy Award for Best Original Music Score and was nominated for Best Song ("Baby Mine"). The feature was also awarded best animation design at the 1947 Cannes Film Festival. A unique homage to *Dumbo* appears in the 1979 film *1941*. Director Steven Spielberg included a scene where General Joseph W. Stilwell (1883–1946) appears at the Hollywood Boulevard premiere of *Dumbo*, an event that the real-life general actually attended. Spielberg's movie shows the general shedding a tear during the song "Baby Mine."

Several recordings of songs from *Dumbo* were released within two weeks of the premiere of the film. Singer Jane Froman (1907–1980) released recordings of

"Baby Mine" and "When I See an Elephant Fly" on Columbia Records. Johnny Messner [1909–1986] and His Orchestra released recordings of the same two songs on Decca Records. A recording of "When I See an Elephant Fly" was released on OKeh records by trumpeter Charlie Spivak [1905–1982] and His Orchestra.

The two songs from the film that have had the strongest presence outside of Disney media products are "Baby Mine" and "Pink Elephants on Parade." Broadway singer Barbara Cook (1927–) sang both songs and "When I See an Elephant Fly" on a 1991 compact disc. "Baby Mine" has been recorded by Art Garfunkel (1941–), Bonnie Raitt (1949–), and Was (Not Was), as well as by Alison Krauss (1971–). "Pink Elephants on Parade" has been recorded by Sun Ra and His Arkestra. Freddie and the Dreamers recorded "When I See an Elephant Fly" on Columbia Records. Furthermore, the "Pink Elephants on Parade" sequence of the film had a strong influence on "Hefalumps and Woozles" from *Winnie the Pooh and the Blustery Day* (1968). It can also be argued that the surreal, disorienting animation style that pervades *Uncle Grandpa* (2010–) descends directly from "Pink Elephants on Parade."

BAMBI

Despite the fact that *Bambi* was not released until after *Dumbo*, the story of the iconic fawn had been considered for the Studios' first feature.[27] In 1933 MGM director Sidney Franklin (1893–1972) bought the rights to Felix Salten's (1869–1945) novel *Bambi: A Life in the Woods* (1923).[28] Franklin quickly realized that the story would be sufficiently difficult to film as a live-action movie and approached Walt, offering to transfer the rights to Disney.[29] Ultimately, the rights were transferred to Disney in April 1937.[30]

Even in August 1937, as the Studios raced to finish *Snow White and the Seven Dwarfs* in time for a December premiere, work on the story and structure for *Bambi* took place.[31] Although *Bambi* had been considered for the Studios' second animated feature as late as October 1937, within two months *Pinocchio* was moved in line in front of *Bambi*.[32] Salten's story proved to be a strong enough narrative and artistic challenge that Walt appointed a small team of animators to work on the film on the side.

At first they worked in an annex across from the main Hyperion Avenue studio but were moved in October 1938 to Hollywood's Harman-Ising building on Seward Street.[33] Finally, members of the *Bambi* team were among the first Disney staff members to move to the new facility that was being built in Burbank.[34] This physical separation allowed them to work relatively independent from Walt. In fact, story writer Perce Pearce (1900–1955) would warn, "Man is in the Forest!" whenever their boss would approach.[35]

While *Bambi* and *Dumbo* were made concurrently at The Walt Disney Studios, there is very little in common between the films, save for three factors that are true for both, though each factor is more intense in *Bambi*. Both have little dependence on dialog, both vilify humans, and both feature young protagonists who are separated from their mothers. Furthermore, the movement away from songs sung by onscreen characters is continued in *Bambi*.

The visuals in *Dumbo* are comparatively simple and evoke an illustrative style reminiscent of images used in children's books of the time. The visual style of *Bambi* is a cultivated amalgam of realism, impressionism, and expressionism. The expressionistic elements can perhaps best be seen in sequences like the forest fire.

Leigh Harline was the musician in attendance at the first story conference for *Bambi* in August 1937.[36] However, Harline was reassigned to *Pinocchio*, and Frank Churchill took over the project. The songs in *Bambi* were cowritten by Churchill and lyricist Larry Morey. Although the two had worked together before on *Snow White and the Seven Dwarfs*, this collaboration occurred near the end of Churchill's life. Because the composer suffered from emotional issues and alcoholism, Morey pushed the increasingly unreliable musician to produce for the film.[37] In October 1940 Walt assigned Edward Plumb (1907–1958) to *Bambi* as an associate composer, arranger, score developer, and co-orchestrator.[38] Ultimately, a full third of the score to the film would be attributable to Plumb.[39]

Perhaps Plumb's October assignment to *Bambi* was due in part to Walt's reaction to a viewing of the running reel of the film: "I hate to see us taking the risk of being subtle. The music is inclined to be a little too different and new. We've got to take this thing out and make it appeal to a very broad audience."[40]

Up to that point, Plumb's major contribution to the Studios was the work he had done as music director for *Fantasia*. One might question whether such a change would lead toward an "appeal to a very broad audience."[41] However, the import of the change from well-established, seasoned Disney composers to a relatively fresh face within the Studios was significant.

The score for the film *Bambi* was written by Frank Churchill and Edward Plumb, with orchestrations by Charles Wolcott and Paul J. Smith, and choral arrangements by Charles Henderson. Alexander Steinert (1888–1977) served as a conductor for the film and contributed to some of the orchestration. Sid Fine, who later freelanced as an orchestrator at Republic Pictures, arranged the "Gallop of the Stags."[42] The score to the sixty-nine-minute film is composed of 157 musical sequences (see appendix).

Conductor John Mauceri (1945–) has described the soundtrack of *Bambi* as a "pastoral symphony for children." The musician went on to indicate that *Fantasia*, which was in production at the same time as *Bambi*, featured

Beethoven's *Pastoral Symphony*.[43] In fact, Walt himself made this connection at a sweatbox meeting. As Frank Thomas and Ollie Johnston related:

> One day [Walt] was called into a meeting on the forest fire sequence in *Bambi*, just as he finished viewing the work reels on Beethoven's *Pastoral Symphony*. The *Bambi* picture reel was only half completed, but the intent was clear and the musician, Ed Plumb, was eager to present his ideas on the score he was writing. Halfway through his presentation, Walt stopped him and asked the projectionist if the *Fantasia* reels were still up in the booth. They were, so he asked to hear the storm music from the *Pastoral Symphony* run in sync with the *Bambi* reel. We were stunned by the power of the music and the excitement it gave to the drawings. When it was over, Walt turned and said, "There Ed. That's what I want. Something big."[44]

Given Mauceri's astute assessment, the contribution of Edward Plumb was critical.

EDWARD PLUMB

Ed Plumb came from a wealthy and prominent family. Most eminent among his ancestry is his grandfather's brother Colonel Ralph Plumb (1816–1903), a dedicated abolitionist who was involved in the Underground Railroad and spent three months in prison for helping a fugitive slave escape.[45] As a colonel Ralph Plumb served as quartermaster for General James Garfield during the Civil War.[46]

After settling in Unionville, Illinois, later renamed Streator, Ralph worked for the Vermillion Coal Company and eventually established his own coal company.[47] The colonel's other business ventures included a drain tile factory, the Streator Paving Brick Company, and the Plumb Opera House.[48] In the political arena, the colonel was Streator's first mayor and later served two terms as Congressman.[49]

Edward's grandfather Samuel Levancia Plumb (1812–1882) was a brother to Colonel Plumb. Samuel was the first president of the Bank of Streator, which later became the Union National Bank.[50] Like his brother, Samuel was a community leader, serving as president of the Streator Library Association and president of Streator's Board of Trustees.[51] Samuel and his wife had four children, including Samuel Walter Plumb, who followed in his father's footsteps as a banker.[52]

Edward Holcomb Plumb was born in Streator on June 6, 1907. He was the youngest of three sons born of Samuel Walter Plumb and Anna (Dresser) Plumb. Edward's domestic music studies were at Dartmouth College, where he was awarded a scholarship, and the David Mannes School of Music, where he earned a fellowship.[53] He later studied in Vienna at the Universität Wien.[54] While in Austria, he had private composition lessons with Josef Marx (1882–1964) and Hans Weisse (1892–1940).[55]

Plumb moved to Hollywood in the 1930s to work as a composer and orchestrator. He freelanced for such bandleaders as Paul Whiteman, Andre Kostelanetz (1901–1980), Rudy Vallee (1901–1986), Vincent Lopez (1895–1975), and Johnny Green (1908–1989).[56] The composer joined the staff at The Walt Disney Studios in 1937. The first work he did for the Studios was scoring *Mother Goose Goes Hollywood*, a 1938 Silly Symphony. During this time period, the composer also freelanced for other studios, such as Columbia Pictures and Twentieth Century Fox. He left the Studios in 1945 but rejoined Disney in 1951. During this six-year period away from Disney, Plumb worked at other studios, including Paramount, Republic, Universal, and MGM.[57]

Charles Wolcott praised Plumb's work as music director on *Fantasia*, noting:

"Ed had the darn hard, tough job of making sure that those things which were useful for animation came out, which means adding an oboe here, a bassoon there, or whatever, to bring the line out."[58] This estimation is even more meaningful given that many attribute most of the credit for the film's music to Leopold Stokowski (1882–1977).

Plumb married Louise Mason, and the two had three daughters, Susan, Anne, and Elisabeth. In the early forties, the Plumb family moved to Laurel Terrace in Studio City, where they lived near two other Disney composers, Wolcott and Joseph Dubin (1900–1961).[59] Wolcott characterized Plumb as "a very shy, unassuming person" who "was a fine musician," with "good taste."[60] The last film Plumb orchestrated was *Johnny Tremain* (1957). Unfortunately, Plumb suffered from alcoholism[61] and died on April 18, 1958, in North Hollywood.

Besides his work on *Fantasia*, *Dumbo*, and *Bambi*, Plumb worked on numerous other Disney films, including *Song of the South* (1946), *So Dear to My Heart* (1948), *Cinderella* (1950), *Peter Pan* (1953), and *Lady and the Tramp* (1955). He also served as an orchestrator on *The Living Desert* (1953), *The Vanishing Prairie* (1954), and *Secrets of Life* (1956) from the True-Life Adventure series (1948–1960). Plumb also orchestrated cues from *Davy Crockett, King of the Wild Frontier* (1955), *Davy Crockett and the River Pirates* (1956), and *Westward Ho the Wagons!* (1956). Over the course of his career, Plumb was nominated for four Academy Awards: 1943's Best Music for a Dramatic or Comedy picture for *Bambi*, 1944's Best Music for a Dramatic or Comedy picture for *Victory Through Air Power* (1943), 1944's Best Music for a Musical Picture for *Saludos Amigos*, and 1946's Best Music for a Musical Picture for *The Three Caballeros*.

THE SCORE TO *BAMBI*

In his article "Threads of Melody: The Evolution of a Major Film Score—Walt Disney's *Bambi*," Ross B. Care compares the soundtrack to *Bambi* to the opera *Wozzeck* (1919–1922) by Alban Berg (1888–1935), pointing out that every section of both the film (Figure 5.6) and the opera is constructed on a different musical form.[62] Care's points in the article help elucidate the classical flavor of the score. However, the assertion that each sequence of the film is in a different form is not as ironclad, as Care occasionally uses terms that generally denote style or genre rather than form: berceuse, gallop, mysterioso, nocturne, pastoral, tone poem, and waltz. Furthermore, other sequences in the film are glossed over or not identified in terms of form. That being said, Care's overall point that the score for *Bambi* has a strong classical character is well made.

Given the classical flavor of the soundtrack to *Bambi*, it is not surprising that the score is much less reliant upon songs than its predecessors were. The movie features only four songs: "Love Is a Song," "Little April Shower," "Let's Sing a Gay Little Spring Song," and "Looking for Romance (I Bring You a Song)," and none of these are sung by characters in the film. However, at an early story conference for the project Walt expressed skepticism about the use of offscreen voices: "If we start thinking of offstage voices we will get into difficulties. If the mother can talk I see no reason why she can't sing. It is natural for a mother to sing to her child."[63] Ultimately, the move to offscreen voices can be understood both in terms of a movement toward the illusion of life and as an aid in establishing a contemplative mood by leaving the levity of song out of the characters' nature.

SEQUENCE	FORM
Main Title and Pictorial Opening	Pastoral
From Pictorial Opening to the Thicket	Introduction and Scherzo
Interior of Thicket	Berceuse
Bambi Learns to Walk	Rondo
Raindrops, Little April Shower, and The Storm	Song and Tone Poem
Dawn on the Meadow	Free-form Mysterioso
Bambi Meets Faline	Scherzo
Galop of the Stags	Galop
Man in the Meadow	Passacaglia
Autumn	Waltz
On Ice or Winter Part I	Introduction and Waltz
Winter Part II and The Death of Bambi's Mother	Chorale and Passacaglia
Spring Again; Twitterpated	Theme and Variations
Buckfight and Nightwinds	Pas de Deux Agitato and Nocturne

Figure 5.6. Care's analysis of form in the score to *Bambi*

From the very beginning of the project, music was an important consideration. Walt directed from an early story meeting:

> We will shoot the sketches and make a music track all of which will make our story pretty tight. Our sound track will be a dummy track composed of a cello, a violin, a piano and an organ, which will be enough to give us an idea of the music. When we do that, we will have a chance to preview the thing before we go into layout and animation.[64]

Walt felt the music, not the dialog, should express the action.[65]

On October 24, 1940, Walt saw a cut of *Bambi* with Churchill's rough score, which consisted of sixteen major sections. While Walt was somewhat critical of the music as it was in that draft, he was positive about the role of music in the film:

> There's a terrific power to music. You can run any of these pictures and they'd be dragging and boring but the minute you put music behind them they have life and vitality they don't get in any other way. We have to do that with this picture. Put an emphasis on the music. Completely reconstruct the score, but not throwing away themes we have.[66]

However, this reconstruction was most likely done by orchestrators Plumb, Smith, and Wolcott.

Walt himself suggested Charles Henderson to do the choral arranging for the film:

> The guy that arranged *Ave Maria* . . . if we could get him to come in and arrange the voices. Not only the wind, but I wondered if it couldn't be used for relief and contrast to the orchestra playing through it. When the Stag comes in, the voices could swell up for the finale. I wish we could get him—Henderson's his name—because he sure knew voices. We borrowed him from Fox and could do it again.[67]

Walt also suggested orchestrational ideas in terms of size:

> The music has to supply something that would ordinarily be supplied with dialogue and a more gripping story maybe. The music has to supply that, and it can. I think at times you have to use 40 or 50 pieces for your peak dramatic points. There's a lot of places where a smaller orchestra, even down to the point of five instruments for some of the cuter, lighter stuff, will serve.[68]

In both examples, we see Walt play a guiding role in the music for the film.

In story conferences it is evident that Walt had been broadened by his experience with *Fantasia,* at one point wondering how "music like *The Rite of Spring*" would work behind a fight sequence.[69] A strong Stravinskian influence is heard in the score during the fire scene near the end of the movie. Ross Care points out that the music in this sequence bears a strong influence from the "Kaschei" portion of *The Firebird* (1910).[70]

In the first draft of the score, *Bambi* opened and closed with a "Pastoral."[71] This theme was replaced in a later draft with the Churchill-penned tune "Love Is a Song." Although Churchill's "Pastoral" was excised from *Bambi,* the theme was used for the opening credits sequence of *The Reluctant Dragon,* which was in production at the same time.[72]

"Love Is a Song" is sung in the opening by British-born tenor and actor Donald Novis (1906–1966), who would later cowrite the script for and act in Disneyland's *Golden Horseshoe Revue.* The tenor solo is accompanied by a choir and orchestra. After the credits finish, the song fades out, only to fade in again with an arrangement using orchestra and a choir singing vocables that accompanies the film's opening multiplane shot. As the camera centers on Friend Owl settling in for his morning rest, the melody to "Love Is a Song" is shortened and varied to become a leitmotif (Figure 5.7).

Shortly after this sequence, birds enter to announce the birth of the title character with a musical theme (Figure 5.8) that is very similar to the main

Figure 5.7. "Love Is a Song" and related leitmotif—LOVE IS A SONG from BAMBI—Words by Larry Morey—Music by Frank Churchill—© 1942 Walt Disney Music Company

Figure 5.8. Announcement leitmotif / *An American in Paris* motif—BAMBI SCORE from BAMBI—Frank Churchill and Ed Plumb—© 1942 Walt Disney Music Company

motive of *An American in Paris* (1928) by George Gershwin. This three-note cell in *Bambi* is based on Churchill's "Song of the Magpies" that was originally written for the film.[73] The announcement leitmotif recurs at the end of the movie when the forest animals go to visit Bambi and Faline's offspring. As the focus moves to the newborn twins, a wordless choir starts to sing "Love Is a Song," opening up to a full version of the song with lyrics when the camera focuses attention on Bambi and his father on the bluff overlooking the thicket. This choral arrangement of the movie's most prominent song at the film's finale recalls similar musical endings of *Snow White and the Seven Dwarfs* and *Pinocchio*.

The use of the protagonist's birth and the birth of the protagonist's offspring as framing devices paired with "Love Is a Song" suggests that the lyrics mean love is passed down from generation to generation and thus "is a song that never ends."[74] This natal bookend was later used in the Disney movie *The Lion King* (1994), expressed in song with Elton John and Tim Rice's (1944–) "Circle of Life." Likewise, the generational aspect of "Love Is a Song" is reflected in the "endless" themes in the "Circle of Life."[75]

The first scene in the thicket where the newborn protagonist is presented features the first occurrence of the "Walking" theme (Figure 5.9). The scene ends with an arrangement of "Love Is a Song" vocalized by a wordless chorus. The lyrics to the song are printed in the score, though an annotation in the margin notes that the lyrics should be deleted in favor of vocables.[76] A following scene where Bambi, Thumper, and Thumper's brothers and sisters walk through the forest not only includes the "Walking" theme but also contains the first instance of Flower's leitmotif (Figure 5.10). Flower is actually one of the few characters in the film to have his own distinct theme.

"Little April Shower" accompanies Bambi's experience with a light rainfall that becomes a storm. Like most film scores, the cue is the result of the collaboration of multiple individuals. Churchill's simple tune was developed

Figure 5.9. "Walking" theme—BAMBI SCORE from BAMBI—Frank Churchill and Ed Plumb—© 1942 Walt Disney Music Company

Figure 5.10. "Flower" leitmotif—BAMBI SCORE from BAMBI—Frank Churchill and Ed Plumb—© 1942 Walt Disney Music Company

and orchestrated by Alexander Steinert with vocal arrangements by Charles Henderson.[77] The melody goes through numerous variants, starting with a few notes on a clarinet, to a round, to an expressive passage that represents heavy wind, as well as the young fawn's fear of the storm. These three musicians collaborated in the same manner later in the film in "I Bring You a Song," which portrays Bambi and Faline's romance.[78]

As the sequence builds to a storm, the wind is portrayed by a choir singing vocables. The idea of musically depicting the wind goes back to an early story conference for the film from September 4, 1937. Walt suggested the idea in relationship to a lullaby that had been planned for an early part of the movie:

> I visualize Bambi's mother singing the lullaby with Bambi lying down, listening. We could show clouds in the sky and hear the wind start to blow. We could have an accompaniment with the wind blowing through the trees. We might have little shots of different things that the wind comes in contact with, and we could hear the voice of the wind.[79]

Besides appearing in "Little April Shower," the use of choir to represent wind also appears in the winter scenes.

The following scene, in which Bambi's mother brings the young fawn to the meadow, commences with the "Walking" theme but moves into some hesitant music consisting of dissonant bitonal harmonies set in slow shifting meters that accompany the mother's cautious motion into the open landscape. Once it is determined to be safe, Bambi joins his mother, cavorting in the meadow. The music that accompanies this cue, "Looking for Romance (I Bring You a Song)," is beautiful yet is perhaps poorly chosen, as Care points out the Oedipal overtones of using the same tune that later portrays Bambi and Faline's romance.[80]

Bambi and Faline meet for the first time in the scene that follows, and the music that accompanies the playful interaction includes a quote from "Love Is a Song" (Figure 5.11). The frolicking of the two fawns is interrupted by the spirited "Gallop of the Stags" (Figure 5.12). The use of an arpeggiated minor triad played by brass instruments gives it a heroic flavor, somewhat akin to the theme of the first movement of Beethoven's *Eroica* (1804), but with a more somber tone.

Conductor John Mauceri pointed out that two of the most powerful moments in the soundtrack are those where there is a lack of music.[81] The first of

Figure 5.11. "Love Is a Song" appearance with Bambi and Faline—LOVE IS A SONG from BAMBI—Words by Larry Morey—Music by Frank Churchill—© 1942 Walt Disney Music Company

Figure 5.12. "Gallop of the Stags"—BAMBI SCORE from BAMBI—Frank Churchill and Ed Plumb—© 1942 Walt Disney Music Company

Figure 5.13. "Man" leitmotif—BAMBI SCORE from BAMBI—Frank Churchill and Ed Plumb—© 1942 Walt Disney Music Company

Figure 5.14. Variation of "Man" leitmotif—BAMBI SCORE from BAMBI—Frank Churchill and Ed Plumb—© 1942 Walt Disney Music Company

these is when Bambi's mother states "Man was in the forest,"[82] while the other is after Bambi's mother dies. It is the absence of music that lends these moments the gravity they deserve.

Man is the villain in *Bambi*, and the scenes that are related to man are the film's most tense and dramatic. The first of these ends with Bambi's mother stating, "Man was in the forest."[83] That sequence begins with the Great Stag listening to a flock of crows rising from the thicket. This is followed by the first entrance of the Churchill-penned "Man" leitmotif (Figure 5.13), which builds incrementally and then dramatically cuts to silence pierced by the sound of the gunshot. The ensuing sequence, in which Bambi's mother reassures her fawn, features a variation on the "Man" leitmotif, which was written by Plumb and orchestrated by Wolcott (Figure 5.14). The simple, iconic, low-pitched upward chromaticism of the man motive was appropriated by John Williams more than three decades later for a similarly menacing villain, the shark from *Jaws* (1975).

Figure 5.15. Ice Skating Waltz—BAMBI SCORE from BAMBI—Frank Churchill and Ed Plumb—© 1942 Walt Disney Music Company

Figure 5.16. "Desolate Winter" chords—BAMBI SCORE from BAMBI—Frank Churchill and Ed Plumb—© 1942 Walt Disney Music Company

This tense scene is followed by the light and vibrant autumn sequence, which functions as a transition to the winter segment. The beginning of the winter scene contains some of the lightest, most charming material of the film as the protagonist has his first experience with snow—in particular, the sequence in which Thumper shows Bambi how to skate on the ice. The scene is accompanied by a spirited waltz (Figure 5.15), which is used in a Mickey Mouse fashion to contrast the fawn's awkwardness with the rabbit's ease.

The lead-up to the death of Bambi's mother is one of most memorable sequences in the film. A wintry scene in which the fawn and his mother looking for sustenance amid the bleak landscape is accompanied by oscillating quartal harmonies (Figure 5.16) presented in wordless choir and orchestra. The "Man" leitmotif enters when mother and son are in the meadow eating spring grass, and the theme appears as an ostinato that builds to the fatal gunshot.

The fawn's mournful crying for his mother is heightened by a chorus singing vocables. This is a re-orchestration of the music that is heard when Bambi and his mother look for food in the preceding scene. This choral writing has a dual function of being both representational and expressionistic. It serves as a musical analog to the bitter winter wind that accompanies the snow. At the same time it is dirgelike and expressionistic, much like the black, gray, and deep blues of the chilling, wintry scene.

Just as "The Silly Song" provides much-needed levity after one of the darkest sequences in *Snow White and the Seven Dwarfs*, "Let's Sing a Gay Little Spring Song" follows the aforementioned death scene. The song is easily the lightest song of the film. The animation provides stark contrast to the preceding scene in its bright, vibrant colors and presentation of avian pairs cavorting and frolicking.

Figure 5.17. Twitterpated march theme—BAMBI SCORE from BAMBI—Frank Churchill and Ed Plumb—© 1942 Walt Disney Music Company

Figure 5.18. Twitterpated waltz variation—BAMBI SCORE from BAMBI—Frank Churchill and Ed Plumb—© 1942 Walt Disney Music Company

A set of informal variations underscores the "twitterpated" sequence. Segments of the twitterpated theme arise while Friend Owl instructs Bambi, Thumper, and Flower about twitterpation. The first full statement of the theme is arranged as a march (Figure 5.17), which ensues as the three friends walk off into the woods. A first variation develops as a female skunk flirts with Flower, culminating with a drunken version played on the clarinet when Flower turns red after being kissed.

A second variation accompanies a girl rabbit who flirts with Thumper while casually vocalizing the theme. This rendition came from a first-take recording that was improvised off of Churchill's twitterpated melody by the actress who voiced the part of the female rabbit.[84] As with the first variation, an inebriate clarinet accompanies Thumper's stupefied reactions to his wooer. Another humorous bit happens at the end of Thumper's scene, where the girl bunny's trill on the supertonic coincides with Thumper's rapidly tapping foot, a reaction to the female rabbit's charms. Finally, when Bambi encounters Faline the music is used primarily as punctuation, though again, a drunk-sounding clarinet presents Bambi's reaction to being licked by Faline. Following this intimate encounter the theme, presented as a waltz (Figure 5.18), underscores a semidream sequence of the two deer prancing through a cloudscape together.

The "Man" leitmotif resurfaces when Bambi and Faline look for each other after man returns to the forest. While the theme once again builds as an ostinato, it does so with a bit more variation. The clearest presentations of the motif end with the gunshot that kills the quail. More remote variations of the theme occur until Bambi is attacked by a pack of dogs.

THE FIRE SEQUENCE AND UNUSED SONGS

Scored by Plumb, the fire sequence is likely the most daring, agitated sequence in the film. Accordingly, the music is much more modern, rousing, and strident. The musical denouement from the scene features an impressionistic, parallel

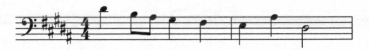

Figure 5.19. "Love Is a Song" in minor—LOVE IS A SONG from BAMBI—Words by Larry Morey—Music by Frank Churchill—© 1942 Walt Disney Music Company

motion, wordless choir doubled with tremoloed strings. As Faline stands at the edge of the lake looking for Bambi, we hear a mournful minor-key version of "Love Is a Song" in the cello (Figure 5.19). A bright orchestration of the melody follows when Bambi and his father emerge from the lake and mist; this version leads into the final scene, where Bambi and Faline's offspring are born. A choral rendition of "Love Is a Song" enters as the multiplane camera then trucks out from Bambi and his father, completing the framing device established at the beginning of the film.

One early concept for *Bambi* involved a repeating gag where the magpie would sing little songs throughout the film, aging as the story progressed. As Walt explained in a story conference on September 4, 1937:

> She [the magpie] could be a character who was always making up a song. Bambi's birth might remind her of a song. I thought she might start to sing, "What is his name?" The mother would say, "Bambi." She would say, "Bam-bi—Bambi—I got it! La, la, la," etc. The other animals standing around would look at her and go off. She would be singing away and Bambi's mother would say, "Please, I'm tired." The magpie would fluff up and say, "I'm busy too. Goodbye!" Later on in life when Bambi was in love she might meet him and come out with a silly song about love. Her voice would be growing worse all the time. It would be pretty broken at the end of the story.[85]

Walt also saw the potential for the magpie to be an intuitively wise character:

> "She could be making subtle and indirect remarks about Bambi and Faline being in love—something like the old maid in [the 1937 film] *Quality Street*, who was always way ahead of everyone. Bambi wouldn't know what she was talking about. Faline would become embarrassed."[86]

Leigh Harline added this idea: "The magpie should never finish any song she starts. There should always be some interruption."[87] David Hand envisioned using the character as a framing device, suggesting, "It would be good to bring her back for the ending sequence, when she would be pretty old, and she would be singing about spring."[88]

Two songs developed in 1938 by Churchill and Morey for *Bambi* were not used in the picture. Salten's original book featured a passage where two leaves discuss their own mortality as they cling to a branch near the end of autumn. The two anxiously muse on what will follow their inevitable fall from the tree. In writing the passage Salten personified members of the plant world. Churchill and Morey went one better by humanizing raindrops in "The Rain Song," which would have had the raindrops express their pleasure in fulfilling their duty by falling from the sky to make pastures and brooklets grow.[89] Ultimately "The Rain Song" was replaced by "Little April Shower," lending a third-person narrative to the rainstorm.

Another early song concept for *Bambi* was "Twitterpated." This jazzy number would have been sung by Friend Owl. However, it was ultimately decided that having one of the onscreen characters sing a song would have worked against the comparatively realistic approach of the film, and "Twitterpated" was cut from the project.[90]

RECEPTION

After five years of preparation and over $1.7 million dollars in production costs, *Bambi* was ready to meet the public. The world premiere of the film was on August 8, 1942, in London, with the US premiere five days later in New York City. The film failed to turn a profit by only sixty thousand dollars during its initial run,[91] and it began to make money for the Studios in 1947. Some have speculated that part of the film's initial failure may be due to the portrayal of man as an irresponsible, gun-wielding, heartless being, which was out of step with the patriotic militarism that pervaded the United States during the Second World War. The movie has become lucrative over time, earning over 507 million dollars when adjusted for inflation, making it the forty-seventh-most-profitable film of all time.[92]

The movie was nominated for three Academy Awards: Best Sound, Best Original Music Score, and Best Song. "Love Is a Song," the Best Song nominee, lost out to Irving Berlin's "White Christmas." *Bambi* was listed by the American Film Institute as the third-best animated film of all time. Man from *Bambi* was named the twentieth- greatest villain from a movie by the AFI. Due to the fact that many children are traumatized by the death of the title character's mother, the film was also listed as the twentieth-best horror film by *Time* magazine.

Starting in January 1941, more than three-quarters of the radio stations in the country signed with Broadcast Music Incorporated (BMI) in what amounted to a boycott of the American Society of Composers, Authors, and Publishers (ASCAP).[93] The National Association of Broadcasters had encouraged the formation of BMI two years earlier as an alternative to ASCAP, which had been raising its fees to radio stations.[94] Thus, for nearly the entire calendar year, virtually no ASCAP-licensed music was played on the radio. Accordingly, as *Bambi* neared completion, Roy assigned the copyrights for the music from the film to BMI.[95] Years later, Jimmy Johnson, then the head of the Walt Disney Music Company, was able to win back the rights to the songs from BMI in return for starting the Wonderland Music Company, a Disney-owned BMI music-publishing firm.[96]

The only song from *Bambi* that has been widely recorded is "Love Is a Song." It was recorded in 1942 by Teddy Powell [1905–1993] and His Orchestra for Bluebird Records. Decca Records released versions of the song by Guy Lombardo [1902–1977] and His Royal Canadians, and by Annunzio Paolo Mantovani (1905–1980) and his orchestra. Later, a recording of the song was made by the Mormon Tabernacle Choir. Several excerpts of the soundtrack to *Bambi* were used to accompany the 1942 film *South of the Border with Disney*.[97] Excerpts from the score to *Bambi* were also used in the educational shorts *Planning for Good Eating* (1946) and *Environmental Sanitation* (1946).[98]

The soundtrack to *Bambi* is unique among Disney's early animated features. Not only are none of the songs sung by onscreen characters, but the score, with the exception of *Fantasia*, is the most classically inspired. The use of wordless choir that recurs throughout the film establishes a somewhat modern tone, recalling pieces such as "Sirens" from Claude Debussy's *Nocturnes* (1899), Maurice Ravel's (1875–1937) *Daphnis et Chloé* (1912), and "Neptune" from *The Planets* (1914–1916) by Gustav Holst (1874–1934). Other modernistic elements include some relatively advanced harmonies, such as those that appear in the winter scene, and the music that accompanies the fire scene. Excluding *Fantasia*, the soundtrack to *Bambi* is arguably the furthest in style and approach from *Snow White and the Seven Dwarfs*. Nevertheless, the next single-story animated feature released by the Studios would return to the model established by *Snow White and the Seven Dwarfs*.

Chapter 6

CINDERELLA

The war years were a double-edged sword for The Walt Disney Studios. On December 8, 1941, part of the Studios was taken over by the United States Army for eight months, due to its proximity to the Lockheed plant. The government wanted to use the Studios as a base to defend against any potential attack of the plant. The war hurt the entire film industry, as a majority of European markets were completely inaccessible to American movies, or at least ticket sales were significantly diminished.

On the other hand, the Studios received numerous contracts to produce instructional cartoons for the military, such as *Aircraft Carrier Landing Signals* (1942) and *Aircraft Welding* (1943). Work on such training films allowed the Studios to demonstrate that they were doing work that was vital to the war effort, which enabled them to prevent many of their artists from being drafted into the armed services.[1] The Studios also produced propaganda shorts such as *The New Spirit* (1942) and *Der Fuehrer's Face* (1942). The State Department even commissioned the "package films"[2] *Saludos Amigos* (1942) and *The Three Caballeros* (1944), and while these government-sponsored projects helped sustain the Studios, they took time away from creating features.

The Studios also faced a strike in 1941, which, though resolved, affected Walt for years.[3] In addition, by the end of 1946, the company's debt had risen to 4.3 million dollars.[4] These problems led the Studios to look away from single-narrative animated features for years. From 1943 through the end of the decade, the Studios made six package films: *Saludos Amigos, The Three Caballeros, Make Mine Music, Fun and Fancy Free, Melody Time* (1948), and *The Adventures of Ichabod and Mr. Toad.*

In 1922 Walt produced a Laugh-O-gram short based on the story of *Cinderella*, and the story had been considered as a potential animated feature for the Studios as early as 1938.[5] By 1946 Charles Wolcott and Larry Morey created a score for *Cinderella*, but for an unknown reason, the music was never used for the film that was ultimately produced.[6] However, the music was not completely wasted, as Jimmie Dodd added lyrics to one of the tunes written by Wolcott for the film, and retitled it "Sleepy Time."[7]

By 1948 the company's financial situation was sufficiently dire. Clearly, the package films of the preceding years were not the route to firm financial foot-ing, so Walt felt the Studios had to return to making animated feature-length films.[8] However, it was decided that they should focus on producing a single animated feature-length film, despite the fact that *Cinderella, Peter Pan,* and *Alice in Wonderland* had all been in production since before the war.

In order to help decide whether to proceed with *Cinderella* or *Alice in Won-derland,* Walt set up meetings where the creative team for each project present-ed its work to noncreative employees, using storyboards and presenting some of the songs that had been written.[9] Although Walt made the final decision, the consensus seemed to be that *Cinderella* presented more "heart and warmth."[10] In addition, Walt felt that *Cinderella* had many features that had allowed *Snow White and the Seven Dwarfs* to hit.[11] In fact, in an attempt to capitalize on the success of his first feature, Walt considered reusing Snow White and the Prince as the main characters in *Cinderella.*[12] While Walt did not reuse Snow White or the Prince, he did choose to bet the Studios' future on the classic story of the girl with a glass slipper.

Accordingly, it was not until 1950 that the Studios released their first sin-gle-story animated feature-length film since *Bambi. Cinderella* marked a return to the fairy tale genre that worked so well in *Snow White and the Seven Dwarfs.* It also harked back to *Snow White* in the way that it features numerous songs, nearly all of which are sung by onscreen characters.

The songwriting team for *Cinderella* featured the talents of Mack David (1912–1993), Al Hoffman (1902–1960), and lyricist Jerry Livingston (1909–1987). The musical directors for the film were Paul J. Smith and Oliver Wallace, with Joseph Dubin serving as an orchestrator. The soundtrack to the seven-ty-four-minute film is composed of 150 individual musical sequences (see appendix).

PAUL J. SMITH

Born in Calumet, Michigan, on October 30, 1906, Paul Joseph Smith (Photo 6.1) was favored with perfect pitch. His parents, Joseph Smith (1875–1936) and Anna (Schmidt) were married about three years earlier. Joseph worked as a clerk in a mine office, and later as an accountant at a bank. Joseph was also a composer and musician who served in the Spanish-American War as a member of a regimental band and later performed as a flutist with the St. Paul Symphony.

In 1919 Joseph Smith and his family moved to Caldwell, Idaho, where he be-gan to teach at the College of Idaho in 1921, serving as a conductor of numerous

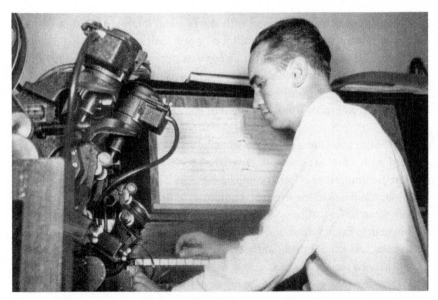

Photo 6.1. Paul Joseph Smith—n.d. Paul Smith working at the Disney Studios. B/w silver print, 5" X 7," given to the College of Idaho by Paul Smith in 1955. Photo courtesy of the Robert E. Smylie Archives at the College of Idaho

ensembles, including the College of Idaho Orchestra. As a teacher, Joseph was, "quite a task master."[13] After a particularly disappointing violin lesson, Smith told a student, "Wanda, you need to practice more so you have something to fall back on. You never know what kind of a bum you might marry."[14] As fate would have it, the student in question, Wanda Wilton, went on to marry Joseph's son Arthur (1913–1995).

Joseph Smith began to teach his son a variety of instruments, starting with piano at the age of four, followed by violin at the age of seven.[15] Trumpet, viola, and banjo followed, and by the age of twelve, the young prodigy was playing bass drum in the town band. While in Caldwell, Paul studied piano under Frederic Fleming Beale and violin with Raymond Pittinger.[16] As a teen the budding musician conducted his high school band.

Paul studied at the College of Idaho from 1923 through 1925, and at Chicago's Bush Conservatory of Music from 1925 through 1927.[17] There he earned the Julliard Scholarship in music theory, and taught violin and piano. After graduating he taught brass for two years at Elmhurst College and York High School, both in Elmhurst, Illinois. He moved to Los Angeles in 1932 to study English at UCLA, where he wrote four musical comedies and ran his own dance band, the Paul Smith Orchestra.[18]

Smith joined the staff at The Walt Disney Studios in 1934 on a temporary six-month contract,[19] persuaded to join by his friend Larry Morey. For his audition, he orchestrated some music Frank Churchill wrote for a Pluto cartoon called *Playful Pluto* (1934).[20]

The composer was impressed with the musical quality of Disney's shorts, noting of the first Mickey Mouse cartoon he saw, "Mickey was playing the piano and I noticed that the sound of the keys was perfectly matched to his finger action. But, what impressed me the most, he was playing the correct keys!"[21]

Within the Studios, Smith was considered a composer who trended toward the complex, as Frank Thomas observed:

> Paul Smith was young and eager when he arrived at Disney really tried too hard on his first assignments. He wanted to do so very well, and felt there were no limitations on what could be done. As a result, his music was complicated and lacked the sweep and simplicity of Frank Churchill's. Because of this, when he was called upon to write scores for the True-Life Adventures, he was able to catch sync in unexpected places, and to write novelties, unusual themes, and special material that no one else could match. In addition, he had learned simplicity and sweeping orchestration and emotional statements. He was never as good at cartoon music as he was at live-action, but he was outstanding . . . amazingly outstanding in that field.[22]

The Studios contained such experimental zeal early on by primarily using Smith as an orchestrator.

In his three decades with the Studios, Smith scored nearly 70 animated shorts, including *Thru the Mirror* (1936), *Clock Cleaners* (1937), *Hawaiian Holiday*, *The Practical Pig* (1939), *Goofy and Wilbur* (1939), *Johnny Appleseed* (1948), *Pecos Bill* (1948), *Susie the Little Blue Coupe* (1952), and *Trick or Treat* (1952). Smith worked on numerous animated features, including: *Snow White and the Seven Dwarfs*, *Pinocchio*, *Bambi*, *Saludos Amigos*, *The Three Caballeros*, *Fun & Fancy Free*, *Melody Time*, and *Cinderella*. Smith family legend has it that Paul also served as a representative for the Studios during Leopold Stokowski's (1882–1977) *Fantasia* recording sessions of the Philadelphia Orchestra that were made in the City of Brotherly Love.[23] Smith wrote music for a number of live-action features, including: *Victory Through Air Power*, *Song of the South*, *So Dear to My Heart*, *20,000 Leagues Under the Sea* (1954), *The Great Locomotive Chase* (1956), *Westward Ho the Wagons!*, *Perri* (1957), *The Shaggy Dog* (1959), *Pollyanna* (1960), *Swiss Family Robinson* (1960), *The Parent Trap* (1961), *Moon Pilot* (1962), *Bon Voyage!* (1962), *In Search of the Castaways* (1962), *Miracle of the White Stallions* (1963), and *The Nine Lives of Thomasina* (1964).

The composer made his most indelible mark through his work on the True-Life Adventure series, scoring *Beaver Valley* (1950), *Nature's Half Acre* (1951), *The Olympic Elk* (1952), *Water Birds* (1952), *Bear Country* (1953), *The Living Desert*, *Prowlers of the Everglades* (1953), *The Vanishing Prairie*, *The African Lion* (1955), and *Secrets of Life*. The composer himself noted that scoring these films was particularly enjoyable for him: "For some reason, I found animal and nature films a joy to work on. This was especially true with the True-Life series. Even though, as a child, I had no pets. I think it provided an opportunity and setting for me to use my classical training in new and imaginative ways."[24]

Smith pointed out that he used music as a means to try to humanize the animals in the series:

> In the True-Life series, music seeks to complement the pictorial scene by pacing the picture, by pointing up the action, and by making the emotional content more poignant. The music attempts, in a sympathetic way, to give the 'critters' seemingly human characteristics that will be recognized by a theater audience. The balance of the characters—the hero, the villain, the ingénue, etc.,—are described in musical terms. [25]

Smith's work on the True-Life Adventure series even resulted in the release of a 1957 soundtrack album on Disneyland Records (WDL-4011).

Paul J. Smith was not well known as a tunesmith. He was often aided in this arena by Hazel "Gil" George (1904–1996), who was both the studio nurse and Smith's domestic partner. George wrote lyrics for the theme he wrote for *The Vanishing Prairie*, resulting in "Pioneers' Prayer" from *Westward Ho the Wagons!* The duo of Smith and George also penned the song "From All of Us to All of You" and the "Jimmie Bean Song."

Songwriter Don Raye (1909–1985) wrote the lyrics to "Jing-a-Ling, Jing-a-Ling," which was based on a theme of Smith's from *Beaver Valley*. "Jing-a-Ling, Jing-a-Ling" was recorded by the Andrews Sisters for Decca Records, while Anne Lloyd (1923–1999) recorded the song for Golden Records. The song's melody was also used in the backing score for Disney's first foray into television, *One Hour in Wonderland* (1950).

Having grown up in Idaho, Smith was a nature lover and often dreamed of returning to the state.[26] The composer was an avid fisherman and liked to camp.[27] He even volunteered for the local Boy Scout troop when his son was young, serving as a treasurer.[28]

Richard Sherman (1928–), who worked with Smith on *The Parent Trap*, described Smith as a, "sweet, gentle quiet gentleman with great talent."[29] Sherman said of Smith's music, "He wrote so beautifully, but he wrote to service the film. He didn't write to service his own ego."[30] Sherman added that "it was wonderful because he made every scene come to life through his gentle magic."[31] Sherman went on to summarize Smith's contributions: "He wrote great music . . . Paul Smith's legacy to the world of film music is vast . . . he lives in his music, he'll always live."[32]

Disney staff composer Buddy Baker (1918–2002) said of Smith: "Paul was a very soft-spoken, very quiet type of guy. He was a super musician."[33] Baker went on to note:

"I would look at his scores and you knew how great it was going to sound by just looking at it. I looked at his score and it was like Ravel wrote it, for goodness sakes, you know? He was that concise with everything he put down. He was just marvelous.[34] Baker considered Smith's scores for the True-Life Adventure series to be the composer's finest work.[35] Baker praised him highly: "I learned so much from Paul Smith—possibly the greatest film composer I have ever known."[36]

Charles Wolcott also admired Smith's music for the True-Life Adventure series.

"The artistic taste that he brought to them [the True-Life Adventures] was fantastic. I'm not sure whether Hollywood, quotation marks, truly recognized what a contribution he made to scoring of that kind of a picture."[37]

George Bruns (1914–1983) noted, "Paul Smith was a good melody man."[38] Buddy Baker provided the greatest compliment to Smith, stating "You can't name anybody that was a better composer than Paul Smith."[39]

Two of Smith's three brothers were musicians, and both followed their older brother to Hollywood. Arthur Charles Smith worked as a Tinseltown studio musician. He performed the flute solo for Disney version of *Peter and the Wolf*, as well as the saxophone solo for the opening theme to *My Three Sons* (1960–1972).[40] He also appeared on Elmer Bernstein's (1922–2004) soundtrack for *To Kill a Mockingbird* (1962), and the Beach Boys' classic "Good Vibrations" (1966).[41] In addition, Art played numerous unconventional instruments, such as recorder, ocarina, tin flute, slide whistle, and jaw harp. Accordingly, he performed "Wilbur's Theme" on recorder from *Charlotte's Web* (1973), and the jaw harp part for *A Boy Named Charlie Brown* (1969).[42] Art played ocarina in the Hugo Montenegro (1925–1981) recording of the theme to *The Good, the Bad, and the Ugly* (1966)[43] and performed on several cues for the television show *Daktari* (1966–1969). George Warren Smith became a studio musician in Hollywood and later, for the last twenty-five years of his career, played in the Disneyland Band.

Smith had a friendly relationship with Ann Ronell. Shortly after signing a contract with The Walt Disney Studios, Smith wrote to Ronell.[44] The letter, which Smith set to music, seems to indicate that Ronell had suggested to him that he move out East, as Smith expressed regret at not being to make the move due to his recent employment with the Studios.[45] Years later Smith conducted Ronell's score for the film *Love Happy* (1949) and wrote an article about Ronell's use of Mickey Mousing in the soundtrack for *Film Music Notes*.[46]

Paul Smith married Theresa Allen in April 1935.[47] Allen was a professional dancer who had studied under Ernest Belcher, the father of Marjorie Belcher.[48]

Allen appeared as an onscreen dancer in *The Phantom of the Opera* (1925) when she was only sixteen.[49] Smith adopted Allen's daughter from a previous marriage, Theresa Louise, and the couple also had a son, Jerome.[50] The couple separated in 1947.[51]

After the separation, Paul Smith became close to Hazel George, the Studios' nurse. The two were also collaborators, as Hazel wrote lyrics for Smith under the pseudonym Gil George. Hazel was like a second mother to Jerome Smith and was a gentle, calming force in the household.[52]

Paul Smith and his family were friendly with both Frank Churchill and Oliver Wallace.[53] Their families would frequently socialize, and Churchill's wife, Carolyn Kay, was the confirmation sponsor of Smith's daughter, Theresa.[54] In fact, the Smiths were at Churchill's ranch on December 7, 1941, when Pearl Harbor was attacked.[55]

Animator Jack Kinney described the friendship between Smith and Churchill:

> "They hit it off immediately. They both liked wine, women, and song, and yet were gentlemen. Both were creative, both liked practical jokes. They would save empty champagne bottles and extra-good booze bottles and place them on top of their trashcans so the neighbors would know they were men of good taste."[56]

Kinney added, "I admired and respected both."[57]

Smith was moved by the Second World War and did what he could to help in the war effort. In addition to the scores he wrote for numerous training films, he would frequently visit the local USO and bring home a serviceman to enjoy a home-cooked meal.[58] One year he even used his vacation time to volunteer as a fieldhand at a vineyard, since farms were short of workers due to the war.[59]

Paul Joseph Smith was awarded an Academy Award for his work on the soundtrack to *Pinocchio*. According to David Tietyen, Smith used his Oscar later in life for propping a door open.[60] He was also nominated for Academy Awards for *Snow White and the Seven Dwarfs*, *Bambi*, *Saludos Amigos*, *Victory Through Air Power*, *The Three Caballeros*, *Song of the South*, *Cinderella*, and *Perri*. The composer also earned an honorary doctorate in music from the College of Idaho in May 1955 and appeared on camera as one of the onstage violinists in *Fantasia*.

While nearly all his career was spent at Disney, Smith did occasionally work for other studios. He served as the assistant musical director for the animated sequence in the Twentieth Century Fox film *Servants' Entrance* (1934). Near the end of his career, Smith wrote music for the last season of *Leave It to Beaver* (1957–1963). The last film that he worked on, in 1962, was *The Nine Lives of*

Thomasina (1964). In the mid-seventies the composer stopped playing instruments, due to an ailing shoulder.[61] Smith passed away on January 25, 1985, in Glendale, California, from complications of Alzheimer's disease.

CINDERELLA

Since the premiere of *Bambi*, Disney released several films that mix live action and animation, such as *Saludos Amigos*, *The Three Caballeros*, *Song of the South*, and *So Dear to My Heart*. This movement toward live action went hand in hand with movement away from music being used as the organizing principle for the timing of an animated feature. Wilfred Jackson, one of the directors of *Cinderella*, recalled, "*Cinderella* . . . was the first cartoon I worked on in which the musician, Ollie Wallace, composed his music for all the sequences I directed after the animation was finished and okayed for inking, with the exception, of course, of the musical sequences."[62]

Thus, with the move toward live-action films, the Studios began to treat music the way the rest of Hollywood did, creating the score after the film was shot and edited. Jackson looked sadly at this trend: "It seemed to me that the time and effort I spent in pre-timing the action, working closely with the musician as he pre-composed the musical interpretation of it, was not only the very most delightful part of directing a cartoon, but also one of the most significant for effectiveness."[63]

This trend may have resulted in less Mickey Mousing, a technique that various critics have found fault with in the Disney oeuvre, but it also decoupled the close link between image and music that was one of the unique traits of the Studios. Yet one of the hidden benefits of this relative dissociation between image and music is a score that features a more rubato approach to tempo.

Another manner in which *Cinderella* was conceived differently than preceding Disney films, is that the songs for the film were written by outside contractors. Walt approached the Tin Pan Alley songwriting trio of Al Hoffman, Mack David, and Jerry Livingston. The team had written the hit "Chi-Baba Chi-Baba" for Perry Como (1912–2001), and it seems that Walt felt that something similar to "Chi-Baba Chi-Baba" would work well for the Fairy Godmother sequence.[64]

The songwriting team worked for nine months on the project.[65] When they began to work, they were surprised to discover that there was no script, and that the story was changed regularly.[66] Sequences were even dropped after being scored and animated.[67]

Mack David and Jerry Livingston asked Ilene Woods (1929–2010) to sing on a demo recording including "Bibbidi-Bobbidi-Boo," "A Dream Is a Wish Your Heart Makes," and "So This Is Love." The songwriters knew Woods from her show, *The Ilene Woods Show*, on ABC radio's Blue Network. The show featured fifteen minutes of music, and David and Livingston had their music presented on it. Walt loved the resulting demo recording and asked Woods to voice the role of Cinderella.

Cinderella is the first Disney protagonist to have a title song named after her. The song, which is used during the opening credits, tells the story of the poor scullery maid who wears "an air of queenly grace."[68] The second verse of the song uses the prevalent Disney theme of dreams, stating that Cinderella will see her "dreams unfold."[69] While touched on in this song, dreams are the central theme to the most important song of the film, "A Dream Is a Wish Your Heart Makes."

Following the opening title sequence, the film features a storybook opening that is reminiscent of the start to *Snow White and the Seven Dwarfs*. However, unlike the 1937 release, the movie follows with backstory narration. This sequence is initially accompanied by an instrumental version of the song "Cinderella." Near the end of this scene, the camera tracks to the tower in which the protagonist lives, and as light begins to shine on it, the melody of "A Dream Is a Wish Your Heart Makes" plays in the underscoring. This theme is reinforced by the narrator who states that "with each dawn she found new hope that someday her dreams of happiness would come true."[70]

The end of this introductory scene is the beginning of the film's story. This is denoted by the two bluebirds that open the title character's curtains, functioning much like the raising of a curtain at the beginning of a theatrical production. When the scene cuts to an interior shot of the tower, light begins to shine in the room as the curtains open, placing the sleeping Cinderella in an ersatz spotlight.

A DREAM IS A WISH YOUR HEART MAKES

Just as the titular character's first song in *Snow White and the Seven Dwarfs* is an opportunity for her to express her wishes, Cinderella's first song also allows her to sing about wishes and dreams. This song, "A Dream Is a Wish Your Heart Makes," has an even greater relationship to "When You Wish Upon a Star" from *Pinocchio*. Both connect wishing to the heart, both equate wishing with dreaming, and both invoke celestial imagery. The two also convey the merits of wishes in general to the audience, rather than communicate the specific wish of the protagonist, as is the case with "I'm Wishing" from *Snow White and the Seven Dwarfs*.

There are also musical similarities between "A Dream Is a Wish Your Heart Makes" and "When You Wish Upon a Star" (Figure 6.1). Both songs feature melodic motion of an ascending minor second followed by a large ascending leap. Furthermore, the two feature prominent melodic motion of a ninth above

Figure 6.1. Comparison of "A Dream Is a Wish Your Heart Makes"—"A DREAM IS A WISH YOUR HEART MAKES" from CINDERELLA—Words and Music by Mack David, Al Hoffman and Jerry Livingston—©1948 Walt Disney Music Co. (ASCAP).—WHEN YOU WISH UPON A STAR from PINOCCHIO—Words By Ned Washington—Music By Leigh Harline—© Copyright 1940 by Bourne Co.—Copyright Renewed—All Rights Reserved International Copyright Secured—ASCAP

the tonic to an octave with the dissonance on the strong beat. Likewise, the downward scalar passage that accompanies "how your heart is"[71] from "A Dream Is a Wish Your Heart Makes" is similar in its emphasis of accented dissonance as the melody that supports the phrase "anything your"[72] from "When You Wish Upon a Star."

"A Dream Is a Wish Your Heart Makes" also bears some similarity to "Some Day My Prince Will Come." The melody that accompanies "when you're fast asleep," and "will lose your heartaches,"[73] is the same as the beginning of "Some Day My Prince Will Come." Furthermore, in each song the female protagonist wishes to be rescued by a prince, though in the song from *Cinderella*, this dream is expressed visually, rather than lyrically.

Despite these similarities, "A Dream Is a Wish Your Heart Makes" is a bit more tonally advanced than either "When You Wish Upon a Star" or "Some Day My Prince Will Come." The first phrase modulates, ending on a half cadence in the key of the supertonic. The melody moves to this key through chromatic motion from dominant to the submediant (the new dominant) on the strong beats. Having the second phrase begin in a minor key helps color the song as somewhat bittersweet.

The chromatic motion to the dominant, and the transposition of the beginning of first phrase to begin the second phrase, results in a melodic sequence

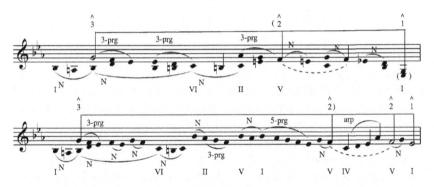

Figure 6.2. Melodic analysis of "A Dream Is a Wish Your Heart Makes"

of a descending diminished fourth, which moves up a minor third before having a delayed resolution of the melodic dissonance. The second of these two fragments has the last note functioning as a delayed resolution of the melodic dissonance as well as the resolution of a ninth to octave motion above the root. The second of these two ninth to octave motions accompanies the word "heartaches,"[74] which helps connect the voice-leading with a vaguely melancholy sentiment.

"A Dream Is a Wish Your Heart Makes" features two phrases (Figure 6.2). The *Kopfton* of each is a mediant approached by an upward leap from the dominant. Likewise, each phrase features a stepwise descent to the tonic, very much in line with Schenker's theory. However, the end of the first phrase actually lands on the mediant in the low register, with an implied tonic beneath. This resolution is doubly unsatisfying, due to both the use of a substitution (the tonic for the mediant) and the lower register of the tone. The second phrase, however, not only resolves in the obligatory register but does so coinciding with the lyric "The dream that you wish will come true."[75]

This song is important in establishing the character of Cinderella as a girl who despite adversity can remain optimistic. It also portrays her as an individual who takes refuge in an interior world. While she tells two of her avian friends, "Of course if you tell a wish, it won't come true,"[76] her internal dream is externalized to the audience. The castle is shown in view from her bedroom window during the line "In dreams you will lose your heartaches."[77] As the end of the first time through the song approaches, the camera pans over to the window, again showing the castle during the line, "The dreams that you wish will come true."[78] In fact, the castle is shown fully centered in the shot on the last word of the song. After a brief dialog interlude, the titular character again returns to the last line of the song, this time changing the pronoun: "The dreams that I wish will come true."[79] This line is sung while the protagonist embraces her pillow, looking at it longingly. After what sounds like the final cadence, the music changes to a brisk waltz, and Cinderella dances briefly with her pillow, then proceeds to make her bed, dress, and fix her hair, all the time waltzing merrily.

Although it does not rhyme, the use of the introductory line, "Of course if you tell a wish, it won't come true, and after all,"[80] functions like spoken recitative, in much the same manner as several songs from *Snow White and the Seven Dwarfs*. In fact, during the dialog interlude, there is one internal rhyme, "Get up you say, time to start another day,"[81] which points toward a pseudo-recitative treatment. This intermission ends with Cinderella stating, "And perhaps someday," leading directly into the lyric, "The dreams that I wish will come true."[82] While the dialog during these brief bits of verbal recitative is not as strongly underscored as in *Snow White and the Seven Dwarfs*, the similarity to this other fairy tale film is also established by the manner in which Cinderella sings to her animal friends.

"A Dream Is a Wish Your Heart Makes" is also used as a leitmotif. It occurs when Cinderella wakes the dog Bruno up from a dream, and when the protagonist plans to alter her mother's dress. It appears at the end of the Fairy Godmother scene when Cinderella first notices her glass slippers. The melody also accompanies the moment when Cinderella and Prince Charming first meet. A frightened version of the melody sounds when the protagonist's stepmother locks Cinderella in the tower. The melody also recurs when the protagonist sees mouse friends Jaq and Gus coming with the key when she is locked in the tower. After Lucifer the cat pounces on the duo, trapping them under a bowl, the theme modulates to minor, indicating Cinderella's belief that her situation is hopeless. Finally, the melody returns when she sits down in a chair to try on the glass slipper.

The most effective appearance of "A Dream Is a Wish Your Heart Makes" outside of the initial song occurs after Cinderella's dress is torn to shreds by her stepsisters. After a long twelve seconds of silence, which provides a somber mood allowing the weight of the stepsisters' violence to sink in, she runs out of the room with her dress in tatters as we hear a transformation (Figure 6.3) of the melody of "A Dream Is a Wish Your Heart Makes." Furthermore, the melody

Figure 6.3. Transformation of "A Dream Is a Wish Your Heart Makes"—"A DREAM IS A WISH YOUR HEART MAKES" from CINDERELLA—Words and Music by Mack David, Al Hoffman and Jerry Livingston—©1948 Walt Disney Music Co. (ASCAP)

continues as a transition to the Fairy Godmother scene. The tune is hummed by an offscreen choir, with lyrics entering appropriately on the line "you will lose your heartaches."[83] This lyric is scored with a reverberant solo female voice, lending it an ethereal quality. As the lyrics continue, the rest of choir joins in, creating a scored crescendo into a rubato, a cappella arrangement for full choir. Notes from an April 19, 1948, story meeting reveal that it had been Walt's idea to use the song to underscore this scene.[84]

The scene is made all the more poignant by having two visual callbacks to the film's exposition. Cinderella's location in the garden near the fountain recalls an earlier scene where she is seen happy with her father. Furthermore, she is crying in nearly the same position she was in when mourning her father's death in her bedroom.

While the song "Cinderella" is used to start the film, "A Dream Is a Wish Your Heart Makes" concludes the movie. The iconic song starts as Cinderella and Prince Charming enter the carriage. The lyrics sung by the choir end the feature with a message addressed to the audience, "No matter how your heart is grieving, if you keep on believing, the dream that you wish will come true."[85] As the couple rides away in the carriage, and the film cross-dissolves to an image of a storybook closing, it is easy to see the similarities to the ending of *Snow White and the Seven Dwarfs*.

Another commonality between *Snow White* and *Cinderella* is that both female protagonists were animated using live-action reference footage of a trained dancer. In the case of the latter, Helene Stanley (1929–1990) provided the model for the animated princess. Stanley was later used as the live-action model for Princess Aurora in *Sleeping Beauty* (1959). As was the case with Snow White, having Cinderella's motion modeled on that of a ballerina lends the film a classical flavor.

"OH, SING SWEET NIGHTINGALE" AND "THE WORK SONG"

"Oh, Sing Sweet Nightingale" functions to reinforce warm feelings for the protagonist. The beginning of the song features Cinderella's stepsisters performing miserably in a music lesson, singing and playing out of tune with horrible tone. The cacophony drives Lucifer from the room, to discover the titular character singing the same melody while she washes the floor of the main hall. Her effortlessly mellifluous singing stands in stark contrast to that of her stepsisters, reinforcing the good character/bad characters comparison that is firmly established in the visual realm.

The sequence turns into a dream sequence where Cinderella sings with herself in two-, three-, and four-part harmony, transcending her toilsome, mundane existence through song and a rich inner life (as alluded to in "A Dream

Is a Wish Your Heart Makes"). In his book *The Fairest One of All: The Making of Walt Disney's* Snow White and the Seven Dwarfs, J. B. Kaufman pointed out that having the protagonist sing in harmony with herself is an elaboration of Snow White's singing in "I'm Wishing."[86] This multivoice counterpoint is also part of the titular character's inner life, imaging her voice layered upon itself as she sings various inventive counterpoints to the simple melody. The number of vocal parts is indicated visually by the number of bubbles that feature images of the protagonist. The movement from a single vocal part to two-voice counterpoint is accompanied by a harp flourish that Mickey Mouses a rush of bubbles that form as Cinderella rinses her rag in the soap bucket.

A five-page memo from the mid-forties describes a "hurry" number for the sequence where Cinderella's gown is built.[87] This number, "The Work Song," serves an important function. In the song the mice object to the manner in which Drizella, Anastasia, and Lady Tremaine overwork the picture's title character. This expression of compassion permits Cinderella to not complain about her labor, which prevents the sympathetic character from appearing weakened with self-pity.[88]

"The Work Song" bears a basic similarity to "Whistle While You Work" from *Snow White and the Seven Dwarfs* in the utilization of animal labor as a story device. The song also uses rhymed dialog as an introduction, with Jaq declaring that "every time she find a minute, that's the time when they begin it."[89] "The Work Song" is also important in establishing empathy for the titular character, by having the sympathy of the mice promote similar sentiments from the audience.

The musical number has an interruption while Jaq and Gus go to get trimming for the dress the mice are making. This sequence is underscored primarily by snippets of "The Work Song." However, while Jaq removes buttons from an outfit, he hums the melody to "A Dream Is a Wish Your Heart Makes," which continues to appear in snippets in the accompaniment. When Jaq and Gus return to help make the dress, the mice sing "A Dream Is a Wish Your Heart Makes," connecting the effort of the mice to Cinderella's dreams.

"The Work Song" also functions like a leitmotif. It is actually heard before its formal presentation in the film, occurring when Cinderella uncovers Gus from under Lucifer's paw. Bits of the melody continue through to the point at which the titular character is called into her stepmother's room. The melody recurs as a theme when Jaq and Gus try to warn Cinderella that her stepmother is coming, and as they attempt to bring the key to their human friend after she is locked in the tower. The leitmotif continues as the protagonist's animal friends ward off Lucifer and go to get Bruno.

"BIBBIDI-BOBBIDI-BOO" AND "SO THIS IS LOVE"

As earlier stated, the songwriting trio of Al Hoffman, Mack David, and Jerry Livingston were hired due in large part to the song "Chi-Baba, Chi-Baba," which they wrote for Perry Como. Walt felt that something similar would work well for the Fairy Godmother scene, and the resulting song, "Bibbidi-Bobbidi-Boo," has the same lilting compound rhythm. While the contour of the first full beat of the melody is inverted, both songs share the same general contour. The compound rhythm of "Bibbidi-Bobbidi-Boo" is Mickey Moused in the bouncing, pulsating movement of the pumpkin as it transforms into the coach.

After the main song, where the pumpkin is transformed into a coach, the Fairy Godmother has bits of rhymed dialog associated with the transformation of the animals into horses, a coachman, and a footman, as well as the transformation of Cinderella's rags into a gown. For instance, when the dog is transformed into a footman, the Fairy Godmother says, "Yes, Bruno, that's right, you'll be footman tonight, Bibbidi-Bobbidi-Boo."[90] This rhymed dialog serves a dual function, as both recitative and as a magical incantation.

"So This Is Love" is the first love duet in a Disney animated feature. The melody is introduced as the waltz to which Cinderella and Prince Charming initially dance. While the audience hears the voices of both Cinderella and the Prince, neither character moves their lips to the song, indicating that the music is a mutual, internal fantasy of both characters. The melody ends right as the two are about to kiss, when the clock begins to strike twelve. Shortly after the pumpkin, the animals, and Cinderella's gown all transform back to their original states, the tune recurs as a leitmotif while the protagonist relates to her animal friends what a good time she had. Later, Cinderella sings "So This Is Love" absentmindedly while she prepares for the arrival of the Duke.

"THE KING'S PLAN"

Much of *Cinderella* is underscored like a cartoon short. Namely, brief melodic material is interspersed with a significant amount of Mickey Mousing. This is certainly true of the music for the chapter titled "Plans Afoot at the Palace" on the 2005 Platinum Edition DVD of *Cinderella*. This scene is underscored with five different musical sequences, each of which is presented one after the other in a segue-like manner. These five sequences are labeled in the Piano-Conductor score as M 34.96, M 35.20, M 36.02, M 36.14, and M 37.04 (Figure 6.4). The Walt Disney Music Publishing Cue Sheets (see appendix) for the film title those cues as "The Royal Palace," "The King's Plans," "A Silly Idea," "The King's Plan (Continued) / So This Is Love / It Cannot Fail," and "Strict Orders." In keeping with the fragmented character of this underscoring, the music frequently

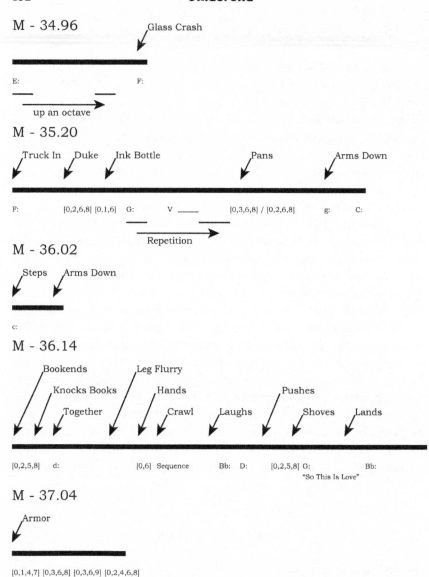

M - 34.96   Glass Crash

E: F:

up an octave

M - 35.20

Truck In   Duke   Ink Bottle   Pans   Arms Down

F: [0,2,6,8] [0,1,6]   G: V ____   [0,3,6,8] / [0,2,6,8]   g: C:

Repetition

M - 36.02

Steps   Arms Down

c:

M - 36.14

Bookends   Leg Flurry
      Knocks Books   Hands   Pushes
             Together   Crawl   Laughs   Shoves   Lands

[0,2,5,8]   d: [0,6] Sequence   Bb: D: [0,2,5,8] G: Bb:
                                                              "So This Is Love"

M - 37.04

Armor

[0,1,4,7] [0,3,6,8] [0,3,6,9] [0,2,4,6,8]

modulates, at times to distantly related keys. Furthermore, the music often drifts out of tonality for significant stretches.

Of the five musical sequences that underscore the scene, the first, "The Royal Palace," M 34.96 (Photo 6.2), is the most tonally straightforward. This cue accompanies the establishing shot of the palace. For all but the last measure of the sequence, the music remains in the same key (E major). Moreover, the opening motive returns an octave higher eight measures later. However, the

Photo 6.2. "The Royal Palace," M 34.96. Photo courtesy of the Robert E. Smylie Archives at the College of Idaho—CINDERELLA SCORE from CINDERELLA—Paul Smith and Oliver Wallace—© 1950 Walt Disney Music Co. (ASCAP)

very last chord of the cue is a loud F major triad, which captures the action of the king throwing his crown through a window. This F major harmony came from the dominant of E major, a tritone away, using the third of the F chord as a common tone with the seventh of the dominant.

The next cue, "The King's Plans" (M 35.20) starts out in F, emphasizing the dominant for four measures. However, when the Duke emerges from behind a shield, the sequence moves onto a five-measure atonal section that emphasizes tritones moving chromatically downward. This phrase introduces a pitch grouping, [0,2,6,8], that will recur later in the sequence. Others might classify this grouping as a dominant seventh chord with a lowered fifth, but Smith's chromatic setting for the chord, as well as his using of other less tonally oriented pitch groupings utilizing the tritone, suggests set theory as a more appropriate labeling system.

By measure 11 the harmony settles on a fully diminished seventh chord built on F-sharp, allowing the harmony to lead into an eleven-measure segment in G major, which contains some repetition of material within the section. The panning from one family portrait to another is accompanied by downward flourishes of tritone-laden harmonies, most typically the [0,2,6,8]. These flourishes transition the music back into a largely atonal context where tritone-oriented harmonies predominate with the occasional triad. The last line of dialog underscored by the cue is the king's exclamation, "Let him alone?"[91] This interjection is accompanied by an agitated upwards flourish ending on a C Major chord.

"A Silly Idea" (M 36.02) is the shortest cue of those that constitute the scene. The sequence suggests C minor and consists largely of a clarinet solo, which makes use of downward chromatics, portraying laughter.

"The King's Plan (Continued) / So This Is Love / It Cannot Fail" (M 36.14) presents tritone-oriented harmonies, many of which are half-diminished seventh chords [0,2,5,8], along with more conventional chords in a largely atonal context. There is one three-measure phrase in D major, which repeats material from "The King's Plan" (M 35.20). The cue concludes with two tonal segments, the first of which is a brief snippet of "So This Is Love" in G major, the second of which is a horn call in B-flat major.

The final sequence of the scene, "Strict Orders" (M 37.04), presents mostly tritone-oriented harmonies in an atonal context. It starts when the Duke asks, "Tonight?"[92] His exasperation is underscored with a whole-tone trill between parallel [0,1,4,7] harmonies in the woodwinds. These harmonies are voiced as a root position diminished triad with a major seventh above the root. The penultimate harmony of the cue is an [0,2,6,8], while the final harmony is a superset [0,2,4,6,8], which is only one note away from a whole-tone scale.

The long atonal segments, as well as a consistent emphasis of dissonant harmonies containing tritones, help establish the music that underscores the scene as being fairly progressive. This nature is all the more surprising given the lack of significant dramatic tension in the plot during the scene. It can be argued that the instability of the tritone, particularly when it is unresolved, helps to keep the music, and thus the scene, moving forward.

UNUSED SONGS

The songs written for *Cinderella* by Wolcott and Morey were all composed by September 18, 1946, when they were written out as lead sheets. One of these unused songs, "Mouse Song," came from a concept Walt introduced during a story meeting. In the tune Cinderella dresses up the mice as they sing about the finery of their wardrobe.[93]

The unused work song "Sing a Little—Dream a Little" was replaced by "Oh, Sing Sweet Nightingale," yet the basic concept of Wolcott and Morey's song found its way into the film.[94] In "Sing a Little—Dream a Little" Cinderella first imagines herself to be two people, and then four, in order to make her work seem manageable.[95] Likewise, "Oh, Sing Sweet Nightingale" has the protagonist following the advice of the title lyric of the 1946 number, namely, singing and dreaming in order to pass the time while working.[96]

"The Dress That My Mother Wore," another unused song, would have expressed how the dress helps keep the memory of her deceased parents alive in Cinderella's imagination. In his book Disney's Lost Chords, Russell Schroeder rightly intuits that using such a song in the film would have made the destruction of dress by her stepsisters too traumatic for the title character, as well as younger audience members.[97] "Dancing on a Cloud" would have had Cinderella and the Prince imagining a romantic celestial fantasy. A similar setting had originally been considered for the animation for "Some Day My Prince Will Come" in *Snow White and the Seven Dwarfs*. One like setting that did appear in a Disney animated feature is "Looking for Romance (I Bring You a Song)" from *Bambi*.[98]

In the Wolcott and Morey conception for *Cinderella*, both the title character and Prince Charming would have had songs that each would sing after the ball, relating their feelings after their night of romance. The title character's number, "I Lost My Heart at the Ball," was to be sung to the mice and a bluebird.[99] The Prince's song, "The Face That I See in the Night," was cut because the animators were having a difficult time creating a convincing depiction of a human male.[100]

There were also several unused songs from *Cinderella* that were written by the trio of David, Hoffman, and Livingston. One such song was "Raga-Da-ga-Day." Completed on January 30, 1948, this number would have functioned as a work song. Furthermore, like "Bibbidi-Bobbidi-Boo," the tune would have featured an invented word as its title.[101] Another unused song, "Horse-Sense," would have had the horse, Major, giving Bruno advice on how to deal with Lucifer.[102] Completed on March 23, 1948, the song was likely cut due to the fact that it did not serve to relate the narrative or to aid in the establishment of any of the film's major characters.

RECEPTION

Cinderella premiered in 1950, the day after Valentine's Day in Boston, Massachusetts. The film's 2.2 million-dollar price tag was only slightly higher than any one of the package films that had preceded it.[103] The movie grossed nearly eight million dollars and was the Studios' greatest financial success since *Snow White and the Seven Dwarfs*.[104]

Cinderella was a cover feature on the February 13 issue of *Newsweek* magazine. The film was nominated for three Academy Awards: Best Original Song ("Bibbidi-Bobbidi-Boo"), Best Music Scoring of a Musical Picture, and Best Sound. In June 2008 *Cinderella* was named the ninth-greatest animated film of all time by the American Film Institute.

Despite the fact that music formed the backbone of the Studios' output for the past two decades, publishing rights for this music had been assigned away to other companies, such as the Bourne Music Company. In October 1949 the Walt Disney Music Company was established to handle music-publishing rights for music from The Walt Disney Studios. Thus, finally, the Studios would maintain publishing and licensing control over one of their most valuable products, their music. In fact, the Walt Disney Music Company was formed in anticipation of what the Studios hoped would be a string of popular songs from *Cinderella*.[105]

The RCA Victor release of the story and songs from *Cinderella* sold 750,000 copies in its first release.[106] The album was also listed as a number one pop seller by *Billboard* magazine, a rarity for an album of so-called children's music.[107] Sy Oliver (1910–1988) and His Orchestra released a disc with "A Dream Is a Wish Your Heart Makes" backed with "Bibbidi-Bobbidi-Boo" on Decca Records, more than three months ahead of the release of the film. These two songs were also recorded by Lawrence Welk, and by Perry Como with the Mitchell Ayres [1909–1969] Orchestra. The latter recording hit number fourteen on the *Billboard* chart.

Mantovani released recordings of "A Dream Is a Wish Your Heart Makes" and "The Work Song" on Decca Records in December 1950. "A Dream Is a Wish Your Heart Makes" was also recorded by Marjorie Hughes (1925–) with the Frankie Carle (1903–2001) Orchestra for Columbia Records. Recordings of "Bibbidi-Bobbidi-Boo" were made by Jo Stafford (1917–2008) with Gordon MacRae (1921–1986), Bing Crosby (1903–1977), and Dinah Shore (1916–1994). The Jo Stafford recording spent seven weeks on the *Billboard* charts, reaching number nineteen. "So This Is Love" was recorded by Vera Lynn (1917–), Leroy Holmes [1913–1986] and His Orchestra, and Vaughn Monroe (1911–1973).

"A Dream Is a Wish Your Heart Makes" was also recorded by Johnny Mathis (1935–), the Mike Curb Congregation, Diana Ross and the Supremes, Bette Midler (1945–), Cher (1946–), and Michael Bolton. In an episode of *Full House* called "The House Meets the Mouse, part 2," the character Jesse and his band perform the song. "A Dream Is a Wish Your Heart Makes" is perhaps the most important anthem for The Walt Disney Company after "When You Wish Upon a Star." For this reason, it is not surprising that "A Dream Is a Wish Your Heart Makes" appeared in medleys used for the opening titles of *The Wonderful World of Disney* (1969–1979) and *The Magical World of Disney* (1988).

"Bibbidi-Bobbidi-Boo" has been recorded by the Mormon Tabernacle Choir, Fred Waring & the Pennsylvanians, Louis Armstrong, and Lawrence Welk. Three characters from Akira Toriyama's (1955–) franchise *Dragon Ball* are named Bibidi, Babidi, and Buu (sometimes spelled Boo). "Bibbidi-Bobbidi-Boo" was also parodied by Mickey Katz (1909–1985) as "The Bubbe, the Baby, and You." The song was again parodied in an episode of *Pinky, Elmyra, and the Brain* titled "Narfily Ever After." Moreover, the lyrics to "Bibbidi-Bobbidi-Boo" are analyzed by the character Mr. Garrison in an episode of *South Park* titled "Royal Pudding."

Clearly, music was a primary contributor to the success of *Cinderella*. Accordingly, one of the greatest tributes to the film came from Paul Smith, who stated, "Occasionally you really fall in love with a film. In my case, it was *Cinderella*."[108]

Chapter 7

ALICE IN WONDERLAND AND PETER PAN

Alice in Wonderland was one of the first features planned by Walt Disney. The initial idea to place a live-action Mary Pickford in an animated world was shelved when Paramount released its own live-action version of the story. Plans to use Ginger Rogers or Luana Patten (1938–1996), who starred as Ginny in *Song of the South*, were also scrapped after the Second World War. Frank Churchill was assigned to *Alice in Wonderland* in 1939, and his music was used to accompany a presentation reel featuring artwork by David Hall.[1] Although none of Churchill's music appears in the 1951 film, a melody he wrote for the "Lobster Quadrille" was reused as the tune for "Never Smile at a Crocodile" from *Peter Pan*.[2]

Walt considered putting *Alice in Wonderland* or *Peter Pan* into production in mid-1943.[3] A version of *Alice* that combined live action and animation was in production during the fall of 1945.[4] However, the plan to combine live action and animation with *Alice* was abandoned in spring 1947, after the Studios were disappointed with the box office tallies for *Song of the South*.[5] When work resumed on *Alice,* Mack David, Al Hoffman, and Jerry Livingston, who had written songs for *Cinderella*, were invited to work on *Alice*.[6] However, only one song by the trio, "The Unbirthday Song," made its way into the movie.

Alice in Wonderland is notable as the Disney film that features the most songs, although many of them last for only a few measures. Some of them utilize poetry from Carroll's original books, while others feature newly composed lyrics. Oliver Wallace wrote the score for the film, Joseph Dubin served as an orchestrator, and Jud Conlon (1910–1966) was responsible for some of the vocal arrangements.

The songs for *Alice in Wonderland* were written by a variety of individuals. "Very Good Advice," "In a World of My Own," "All in the Golden Afternoon," "Alice in Wonderland," "The Walrus and the Carpenter," "The Caucus Race,"

Photo 7.1. Ken Darby's Sketch for "A Mad Tea Party"—Courtesy, L. Tom Perry Special Collections, Harold B. Lee Library, Brigham Young University, Provo, UT . THE UNBIRTHDAY SONG from ALICE IN WONDERLAND—Words by Jerry Livingston—Music by Mack David and Al Hoffman—©1948 Walt Disney Music Company

"I'm Late," "Painting the Roses Red," and "March of the Cards" were written by Sammy Fain (1902–1989) and lyricist Bob Hilliard (1918–1971). Oliver Wallace and Ted Sears wrote "We'll Smoke the Blighter Out," "Old Father William," and "A E I O U." Wallace cowrote "How D'Ya Do and Shake Hands" with lyricist Cy Cobin (1919–2006), while Don Raye and Gene de Paul (1919–1988) wrote "'Twas Brillig."

Joseph Dubin made piano arrangements of "The Caucus Race," "I'm Late," "In a World of My Own," "Very Good Advice," "The Walrus and the Carpenter," and the unused song "Beyond the Laughing Sky" sometime around May 10, 1949.[7] Around May 25, 1950, Conlon wrote vocal arrangements of "The Caucus Race," and an unused song called "Beware the Jabberwock."[8] The score for this seventy-five-minute film comprises some 141 musical sequences (see appendix).

There is a sketch (Photo 7.1) housed in the Ken Darby Papers at Brigham Young University entitled "A Mad Tea Party: Walt Disney, Preliminary Notes for *Alice in Wonderland.*" The melody for the song in this document is the same as that penned by Mack David, Al Hoffman, and Jerry Livingston, and while it seems that none of Darby's work made its way into *Alice in Wonderland*, it confirms that the tune for this sequence was most likely set by 1948, when Darby left Disney for Twentieth Century Fox. Furthermore, the sketch suggests that Darby would have been assigned to *Alice in Wonderland* had he continued to work for Disney.

OLIVER WALLACE

Born in London on August 6, 1887, Oliver G. Wallace (Photo 7.2) moved to Canada in 1904 with his family. Having completed only middle school, Wallace's musical career started in 1906 when he began to play piano for vaudeville shows. In 1910 the young musician moved to Washington state, where he began to work as an accompanist for silent films. Wallace was most likely the first person to accompany silent movies on a pipe organ.[9]

While in Washington he collaborated with songwriter Harold Weeks (1893–1967) to write "Hindustan" (1918), a love song, which was Wallace's first large-scale success. Following this, he began a long-term collaboration with lyricist Arthur Freed (1894–1973). Freed would later be known for his work producing MGM musicals such as *Meet Me in St. Louis* (1944), *The Harvey Girls* (1946), *Easter Parade* (1948), *On the Town* (1949), and *Singin' in the Rain* (1952). The two wrote numerous songs together, including: "Dance It Again with Me" (1919), "Indiana Moon" (1919), "Rainbow of My Dreams" (1919), "Reaching for the Moon" (1919), "I've Got a Sentry" (1920), "Silks and Satins" (1920), "Louisiana" (1920), "Norse Maid" (1920), "That Colored Jazzboray" (1920), "When It's Honeysuckle Time Way Down in Georgia" (1920), "When Your Hand First Touched Mine" (1920), and "My Oriental Symphony" (1925). During this time Wallace wrote "Land of Allah" (1919) and "Other Lips" (1923), the latter of which he cowrote with Mort Harris.

Around 1933 Wallace moved to Hollywood to compose for motion pictures. He worked a variety of studios, including Jefferson Pictures Corporation, Paul Malvern Productions, and Universal Pictures, and among the early pictures

Photo 7.2. Oliver Wallace conducting the Disney Studio Orchestra—Photo Courtesy of the University of Washington Libraries, Special Collections, Negative no: UW 35670. © Disney

he scored was 1935's *Murder by Television*, staring Bela Lugosi (1882–1956). Additionally, his skills as an organist can be heard in the 1935 classic film *The Bride of Frankenstein*.

Roy approached Wallace with an offer to work for Disney on January 22, 1930, the day that Carl Stalling quit the Studios. Wallace turned down the offer due to the low salary but later joined the staff at Disney, in 1936. The first cartoon he scored for the Studios was *Mickey's Amateurs* (1937), and he continued writing for shorts until he was assigned to work on the feature film *Dumbo*. In fact, Wallace scored some 140 shorts for the Studios, including: *The Little Whirlwind* (1941), *The New Spirit, Chicken Little* (1943), *Der Fuehrer's Face, Duck Pimples* (1945), and *Tea for Two Hundred* (1953).

The composer worked on *Victory Through Air Power, Make Mine Music, Fun & Fancy Free, Seal Island* (1948), *The Adventures of Ichabod and Mr. Toad, Cinderella, Alice in Wonderland* (1951), *Peter Pan, Lady and the Tramp, Old Yeller* (1957), *Darby O'Gill and the Little People* (1959), and *Jungle Cat* (1959). He also wrote music for numerous episodes of *Disneyland* (1954–1990), as well as the successor anthology programs. He composed the music for the Main Street section of the record *A Musical Tour of Disneyland*,[10] while the final film the musician scored was *The Incredible Journey* (1963).

Wallace appeared as himself in three episodes of *Disneyland*: "Cavalcade of Songs," "The Story of the Animated Drawing," and "Where Do the Stories Come From?" In the latter episode the composer appears in the first segment of the show, dramatizing the creation of the song he wrote as a theme for Daisy Duck. That song, "Crazy Over Daisy," was first used in a Donald Duck cartoon of the same name, and Wallace reused the tune for the song "Meet Me Down on Main Street."

The composer acted as a saloon pianist in an episode of *Walt Disney's Wonderful World of Color* entitled "Texas John Slaughter: A Holster Full of Law" (1961). Wallace voiced the part of Mr. Winky in *The Adventures of Ichabod and Mr. Toad* and provided the whistling for Ichabod Crane in the same film. He performed Captain Hook's piano part in *Peter Pan* and also had a cameo as the bandleader in the movie *Toby Tyler, or Ten Weeks with a Circus* (1960).

In 1942, after Frank Churchill died and Leigh Harline left The Walt Disney Studios, Wallace's and Paul J. Smith's responsibilities increased markedly. Disney animator Frank Thomas considered Wallace a genius and cited his contributions as "responsible for so many unique musical moments in our pictures."[11] Thomas said of the musician:

> "Ollie Wallace was a madman, funny eccentric, unexpected and loved by everyone. He was caustic, satiric, looked like a little Bantam rooster, specialized in criticism, but usually funny and never let anyone get the best of him."[12]

While Thomas characterized Wallace as a hard worker, he noted that if the composer did sleep through a story meeting, "he would snore so loudly so everyone knew he was sleeping."[13]

Buddy Baker noted that Wallace "had a great sense of humor," and that he "liked to play jokes on people."[14] Baker recalled a time when he was able to play a prank on Wallace:

> I remember one time I could hear him working, playing something over and over on the piano. I just copied it down and kept it for a couple of weeks. Ollie said to me one day, "You know, kid, if you get any ideas, let me hear them because I'm running out of ideas." So I waited until he said that to me next time and I took this thing in and put it out there. I said, "Ollie, I came up with this. I thought it was okay." Then he played me some of the music. He got into it about six bars, then turned around to me and said, "You son of a bitch!"[15]

Baker added, "Ollie was a real character."[16]

On at least one occasion Walt noted that Wallace could be long-winded as a composer, stating, "Ollie gets slap happy on a theme."[17] George Bruns felt that "Ollie Wallace was a good melody writer, a damn good melody writer."[18] Robert

Sherman (1925–2012) characterized Wallace as, "a very warm person" but noted that the elder composer had a "façade" of a "crotchety old man."[19]

Certainly in the last decade of his career, Wallace was a bit cantankerous. Buddy Baker recalled a time during which he and Wallace were at Stage A of the Studios during lunch break when Walt came up to the duo and asked, "What are you guys doing?"[20] The elder composer responded, "I'm saving your goddamned picture."[21] Baker noted a similar story about Walt and Wallace. The two had offices across from each other, and they both tended to arrive to work early in the morning.[22] Walt asked, "Ollie, why don't you come over and have coffee with me, since you always come in early?"[23] Wallace responded, "Maybe you don't have anything to do, but I'm busy."[24]

Wallace married musician Claire Burch, who had been a faculty member of the University of Washington. Like Wallace, Claire had also worked as a theater organist.[25] The couple had two daughters, Martha and Mary. The composer worked for Disney right up until the end, finishing the score to *The Incredible Journey* before dying on September 15, 1963, after a short illness.

Wallace's work on *Dumbo* was rewarded with an Academy Award that he shared with Frank Churchill. His work on *Victory Through Air Power, Cinderella, Alice in Wonderland*, and *White Wilderness* (1958) earned him four more nominations from the Academy. In 1957 he was recognized with an Emmy nomination for his work on the *Disneyland* television series. Wallace was known for penning music for "Pink Elephants on Parade," "When I See an Elephant Fly," and "Pretty Irish Girl" (from *Darby O'Gill and the Little People*), as well as the music and lyrics to "Der Fuehrer's Face."

ALICE IN WONDERLAND

"Alice in Wonderland," the title song of the film, underscores the opening credits, with a choir singing Bob Hilliard's lyrics. The tune continues into the first scene, with the melody hummed by the choir. The lyrics contemplate the ephemeral, pondering, "Where do stars go?"[26] This emphasis of fleeting imagery subtly prepares the idea of Alice's wonderland being a dream.

The melody to "Alice in Wonderland" is used as a leitmotif associated with the protagonist. The tune appears instrumentally multiple times in the film. For instance, it occurs when Alice enters the multiple doors at the bottom of the rabbit hole. Another prominent appearance of the theme is right before she meets the Cheshire Cat. It also recurs in the Tulgey Wood sequence, where Alice believes she is being led home by the mome raths. Its final occurrence accompanies the end of the film, when she wakes from her dream.

Although the use of recitative-like dialog to lead into songs does occur in *Alice in Wonderland*, the use is not nearly as pronounced as it is in *Snow*

White and the Seven Dwarfs. Perhaps the strongest example of this in *Alice in Wonderland* is the lead into "In a World of My Own," where the protagonist addresses Dinah. The dialog neither rhymes nor is particularly metric in nature; it is underscored much like recitative. The song is sung by Kathryn Beaumont (1938–), a child actress who voiced the part of Alice after being cast by Walt, who saw her in the 1948 film *On an Island with You*. The young actress was also used for live-action reference footage that was shot for the animators.

"In a World of My Own" and the preceding dialog set up some of the aspects of topsy-turvydom that defines the wonderland that Alice will subsequently explore. Not only does this song help establish the premise of the film, it serves as a framing device when paired with Alice's awakening from her afternoon dream at the end of the feature.

"I'm Late" is introduced when the White Rabbit runs past Alice and Dinah in the real world, enticing the protagonist to follow the hare into its burrow. The melody of the song is also used as a leitmotif associated with the White Rabbit. The tune reappears as Alice sees the rabbit upside down when she completes her fall down the rabbit hole. It also occurs when she comes upon the house of the White Rabbit. The melody next serves to transition into the following scene, as Alice chases the White Rabbit when he runs away from his house.

Perhaps the most unusual feature of the soundtrack to *Alice in Wonderland* is that music which reflects some of the film's surreal aspects. Most notable among these is the scene where the protagonist falls down the rabbit hole. The accompanying montage is led into by downward harp glissandi, which is followed by a soundscape that bears a similarity to Henry Cowell's (1897–1965) *Aeolian Harp*. The sequence features slow chromatic glissandi on the high strings of a piano, as well as a middle-range piano string being struck by a mallet, which is used to portray the chiming of a clock. More rapid chromatic glissandi punctuate Alice's rapid falls. These accentuating sounds are clearly edited to have abrupt cutoffs, and the metallic sound of the scene is enhanced by the use of vibraphone with pronounced tremolo.

The song "All in the Golden Afternoon" features bouncy choral writing to represent the singing of the various flowers in the garden. The song is set in a key that is a bit too high for Beaumont, such that when Alice enters on the last verse her voice sounds strained, breaking on the high note near the end. The segment also reuses a visual gag that is reminiscent of *Flowers and Trees* where bellflowers are rung like chimes.

The transition from the garden to the scene with the caterpillar is bridged musically with an oboe underscoring Alice's complaints about the manner in which the flowers treated her. This oboe sets up the exotic tonality of "AEIOU," the song that introduces the Caterpillar. The melody continues throughout the scene, acting as a leitmotif for the insect.

"'Twas Brillig" features lyrics from Lewis Carroll's (1832–1898) poem "Jabberwocky." In the film the song is sung by the Cheshire Cat, performed by the talented Sterling Holloway (1905–1992). Mirroring the off-balance nature of the character, the first verse features an unconventional accompaniment of strings and vibraphone with a rapid tremolo. The tune is used as a leitmotif for the Cheshire Cat, recurring when he reappears after the Tulgey Wood sequence, and again when he materializes during the game of croquet.

Jerry Livingston recalled the genesis of the song for the Mad Tea Party scene:

> One day Walt asked us to give it some thought even though we weren't on the picture. Here was a ten-to-fifteen-minute major scene that they didn't know how to handle. Finally, Mack David came up with the "un-birthday" idea. Since there are 364 un-birthdays each year, it was a perfect reason for a mad tea party. And, it fit perfectly with the more-than-mad hatter.[27]

The woodwind-rich orchestration for the song lends it a calliope-like sound, which is reinforced by the frequently out-of-tune performance. "The Unbirthday Song" serves to bookend the Mad Tea Party sequence, as Alice hears the tune when she first approaches the scene. In addition to being performed after the March Hare attempts to explain the concept of unbirthdays, the song recurs at the end of the sequence, when the Mad Hatter and March Hare throw the White Rabbit out after they have ruined his watch.

As earlier mentioned, Ken Darby began to sketch an arrangement for this song, most likely before he left Disney in 1948. The primary melody is the same as that penned by David, Hoffman, and Livingston, but Darby includes instrumental passages, and additional tunes that did not make their way into the final score. Likewise, the plot of the scene is essentially the same, yet much of the lyrics and dialog are somewhat to quite different.

The Tulgey Wood sequence contains a melody (Figure 7.1), which is used as a theme and variations, musically representing many of the bizarre characters that Alice encounters. A faux-Chinese, fifth-rich variation occurs as the frog-cymbals leap from pad to pad. A spirited version of the melody occurs when the umbrella birds are bathing underneath the waterfall (Figure 7.2), while a shortened scherzo-esque variation follows, accompanying the birdcage (Figure 7.3).

Figure 7.1. The Tulgey Wood Theme—ALICE IN WONDERLAND SCORE from ALICE IN WONDERLAND—Music by Oliver Wallace—© 1951 Walt Disney Music Company

Figure 7.2. Umbrella birds variation—ALICE IN WONDERLAND SCORE from ALICE IN WONDERLAND—Music by Oliver Wallace—© 1951 Walt Disney Music Company

Figure 7.3. Birdcage variation—ALICE IN WONDERLAND SCORE from ALICE IN WONDERLAND—Music by Oliver Wallace—© 1951 Walt Disney Music Company

"Very Good Advice" is the emotional center of the film, where the protagonist begins to cry, realizing that her being lost is her own fault, and that she may not find her way home. The transition into song is softened by having Beaumont speak the first line in rhythm. This vocal approach recurs starting in the bridge, allowing the actress to intermittently sob and speak. Many of the surreal animals from the previous Tulgey Wood sequence look at Alice sympathetically, in a manner similar to scenes from *Snow White and the Seven Dwarfs* and *Cinderella*.

This emotive scene occurs much nearer to the end than the beginning. Thus, this attempt to establish an emotional connection between the protagonist and the audience occurs too late in the process for the viewer to retroactively care about Alice's journey up to this point. Walt cited this lack of an opportunity to connect emotionally with the protagonist as a failure of the film.

There is often a recitative-like quality to the underscoring of the dialog for the Queen of Hearts (Figure 7.4). This regal underscoring is heavy on brass, giving the brash Queen's words a fanfare-ish affectation. Many of the scenes that include the Queen utilize the melody for "March of Cards" in the score, indicating the monarch's martial power. There are other characters in the Queen of Hearts sequence who have their dialog punctuated in a recitative-like manner. For instance, when the White Rabbit announces the trial, not only is his dialog punctuated, but, when the White Rabbit acknowledges the King, the corresponding punctuation in the woodwinds is weak and feeble, reflecting the diminutive King's lack of power.

Figure 7.4. Recitative-like Underscoring of the Queen of Hearts' dialog (in rhythm with the line "Then let the games begin!")—ALICE IN WONDERLAND SCORE from ALICE IN WONDERLAND—Music by Oliver Wallace—© 1951 Walt Disney Music Company

The scene where Alice is being chased by the Queen and her army of cards functions both as a frantic medley of a variety of songs from the film and as a montage of the movie's characters. "March of the Cards," "The Caucus Race," and "The Unbirthday Song" are featured in turn, with the last song's orchestration being somewhat discordant. A soundscape featuring a tremoloed vibraphone, similar to the music that accompanies the protagonist's fall down the rabbit hole, reappears as Alice approaches the door.

Frank Churchill commenced his score for *Alice in Wonderland* with a bright instrumental in a simple triple meter that he sketched in August of 1939.[28] Another tune he set down on the second of that month was "Alice and the Bottle," a duet between the song's title characters featuring lyrics by Disney story man Ted Osborne.[29]

Churchill planned at least two songs for the film that utilize Lewis Carroll's poetry as lyrics. One of these was the "Pepper Lullaby" that would have featured the Duchess.[30] Churchill's lead sheet for the two-verse song was dated July 27, 1939.[31]

One of Carroll's characters that was originally planned for the film but not included was the Mock Turtle.[32] Four different versions of the turtle's soup song, using Carroll's original lyrics, were planned but later abandoned for the project.[33] One such plan had the words sung to the tune of the *Blue Danube Waltz* by Johann Strauss II.[34] Perhaps the earliest version of the song was the "Mock Turtle Soup Song," which was completed on June 15, 1939, by Frank Churchill.[35] Don Raye and Gene de Paul also attempted an adaptation of the poem in their song "Beautiful Soup," which was penned by the duo on July 16, 1947.[36]

Don Raye and Gene de Paul wrote at least one other unused song for *Alice in Wonderland*. Although the duo's arrangement of Carroll's "Jabberwocky" poem did appear in the film, an alternate, jazzier arrangement, "Beware the Jabberwock," did not.[37] Bob Hilliard and Sammy Fain wrote at least two unused songs for the film. One of these, "Beyond the Laughing Sky," which was written in 1949 on February 22, would find a second life in *Peter Pan*.[38] Another tune, written later in the year, on October 18, "I'm Odd," was to be a signature song for the Cheshire Cat.[39]

The trio of Mack David, Al Hoffman, and Jerry Livingston wrote at least two unused songs for *Alice*. "Curiosity," penned in 1948 on June 28, would have been sung by the film's title character.[40] The tune "Dream Caravan," written later that year, on August 4, would have featured the Caterpillar singing "Zoom Gollee, Gollee," alternating with a description of the ephemerality of his dreams.[41]

RECEPTION

Alice in Wonderland was promoted by the Studios in 1950 with a one-hour television special titled *One Hour in Wonderland*, aired on NBC at 4:00 PM Christmas Day. The special, which was Disney's first foray into the world of television, was sponsored by Coca-Cola for $125,000. Kathryn Beaumont starred in the special, along with Walt, his daughters, Bobby Driscoll (1937–1968), Edgar Bergen (1903–1978), and Charlie McCarthy. The special contained several cartoon segments, a performance by Firehouse Five Plus Two, a Dixieland jazz band made up of Disney animators, and a five-minute preview of the forthcoming film. Walt was pleased with the results:

> "I am a great believer in the TV medium to sell pictures and what we are doing here with *Alice* is sort of proving it. Gallup found that our Christmas show sent the penetration way up. We plan to use TV for point of sale."[42]

Less than four years later, the Studios premiered their first television series.

Alice in Wonderland was also promoted on the March 18, 1951, episode of *The Fred Waring Show* (1949–1954), a musical program that featured his band, the Pennsylvanians. The *Alice*-themed episode starred Kathryn Beaumont and Sterling Holloway (1905–1992) performing the roles they voiced for the film, with Mary Blair (1911–1978) designing the sets for the episode. After the movie's premiere *Alice in Wonderland* was adapted for a one-hour radio presentation on an episode of *Lux Radio Theater* (1934–1955) that aired on Christmas Eve, 1951. This radio performance included many of the film's songs, as well as performances by Kathryn Beaumont, Jerry Colonna (1904–1986), and Ed Wynn (1886–1966).

Five years in the making, *Alice in Wonderland* cost the Studios three million dollars. The movie premiered on July 26, 1951, in London and New York City. In the film's general release it was accompanied by *Nature's Half Acre* from the Studios' True-Life Adventures series. *Alice* did not perform as well at the box office as Disney had hoped. The movie drew criticism from fans of the book, in terms of the manner in which it deviated significantly from Carroll's narrative, as well as in the lack of visual reference to John Tenniel's (1820–1914) original illustrations. The film lost one million dollars in its first release.[43]

Walt never allowed *Alice in Wonderland* to be rereleased during his lifetime. It is one of the only Disney animated features that Walt permitted to be shown on television. To this end, the movie was edited down for presentation on television for the second episode of *Disneyland*.

Walt compared *Cinderella* to *Alice in Wonderland* in order to demonstrate one of his guiding principles of filmmaking:

Cinderella hit big, made a lot of money. *Alice in Wonderland* came out and just made a nosedive. You see, Cinderella, you pulled for Cinderella, you felt for Cinderella. Alice, there were millions of people who didn't care about Alice. There's no heart to it. Without that heart, you see, I don't think anyone will laugh. In other words, for every laugh, there must be a tear somewhere, and I believe in that.[44]

While Ward Kimball also cited a lack of warmth as being one of the shortcomings of *Alice in Wonderland*, he placed the blame on a management issue:

There's no denying that there are many charming bits in our *Alice*, but it lacks warmth and an overall story glue. *Alice* suffered from too many cooks—directors. Here was a case of five directors each trying to top the other guy and make his sequences the biggest and craziest in the show. This had a self-canceling effect on the final product. [45]

Regardless of the cause, the film was able to rebound only in the decades following Walt's death.

While the movie may have been considered a failure, the music did not disappoint. Decca Records had been contracted to produce a soundtrack album for the movie but declined when *Alice* performed poorly at the box office.[46] In 1956 Disney finally got around to recording a second cast album, [47] starring Mouseketeer Darlene Gillespie (1941–) in the title role. This album sold well into the eighties.

Numerous 78 rpm recordings from *Alice in Wonderland* were released in 1951. Rosemary Clooney (1928–2002) recorded an album called *Songs from "Alice in Wonderland"* with Percy Faith (1908–1976). The album was released on Columbia and contains the film's title song, "The Unbirthday Song," "All in the Golden Afternoon," and "I'm Late." Richard Hayes (1930–2014) recorded "The Unbirthday Song," "I'm Late," and "Caucus Race" on Mercury Records. Les Brown's (1912–2001) Band of Renown recorded "Very Good Advice" and "'Twas Brillig" on Coral Records. The Modernaires recorded "Alice in Wonderland" and "I'm Late" on Coral Records, while an all-star recording of "How Do You Do and Shake Hands" with Danny Kaye (1913–1987), Jimmy Durante (1893–1980), Jane Wyman (1917–2007), and Groucho Marx (1890–1977) with the Sonny Burke [1914–1980] Orchestra appeared on Decca Records. The Melodeons released a recording of "The Unbirthday Song" on MGM Records, and Anne Shelton (1923–1994) recorded "All in the Golden Afternoon" on Decca Records. "Very Good Advice" was recorded by the Dinning Sisters, Ralph Flanagan [1914–1995] and His Orchestra, and Doris Day.

Several artists recorded songs from *Alice in Wonderland* in years after the original release of the film. Erich Kunzel (1935–2009) and the Cincinnati Pops recorded a medley from *Alice in Wonderland*, containing the film's title song, "How Do You Do and Shake Hands," "All in the Golden Afternoon," "I'm Late," and "The Unbirthday Song." The same album contains a recording of "March of the Cards" by the same orchestra. Mary Martin (1913–1990) recorded "I'm Late" for Disneyland Records. "Alice in Wonderland" was covered by Dave Brubeck in 1957 and by Bill Evans in 1961, while Freddie and the Dreamers recorded "The Unbirthday Song." Barbara Hendricks (1948–) covered "All in the Golden Afternoon," "I'm Late," and "Very Good Advice," while Michael Feinstein (1956–) recorded "Alice in Wonderland" and "I'm Late." Certainly, the music of *Alice* helped usher the film to its eventual success.

PETER PAN

Walt had considered the J. M. Barrie (1860–1937) 1904 classic *Peter Pan* for a second animated feature. The Studios acquired the rights for the story in 1939, with David Hall producing some early concept art. Frank Churchill wrote eight pages of sketches including several songs for *Peter Pan* in the early forties,[48] while Charles Wolcott provided more songs for the project in 1941.[49]

As finances were grim, due to the war, the film was tabled for several years, with work on the project restarting in 1944. Jack Kinney acted as director for this iteration of the film.[50] In six months nearly 400,000 sketches were produced, and Eliot Daniel (1908–1997) wrote songs for the movie.[51] However, this version of the project was also abandoned so the Studios could focus on finishing *Cinderella*.[52] Work on *Peter Pan* resumed after the release of *Cinderella*. The score for this final, released version of the film was written by Oliver Wallace, with Edward Plumb acting as an orchestrator. Jud Conlon is credited with writing some of the vocal arrangements.

The songs in the film were created by a variety of individuals. "The Elegant Captain Hook," "The Second Star to the Right," "What Makes the Red Man Red?," "You Can Fly! You Can Fly! You Can Fly!" and "Your Mother and Mine" were written by Sammy Fain and Sammy Cahn (1913–1993). Oliver Wallace and screenwriter Erdman Penner wrote "A Pirate's Life." Screenwriter Winston Hibler (1910–1976) assisted Oliver Wallace and Ted Sears with writing "March of the Lost Boys (Tee Dum Tee Dee)." The movie even contains an instrumental song theme by Frank Churchill and Jack Lawrence (1912–2009), "Never Smile at a Crocodile," which was the last Churchill-penned melody to appear as an original song in a film. The seventy-six-minute film contains some 124 musical sequences (see appendix).

Peter Pan utilizes musical techniques similar to those used in many other Disney animated films. In particular, the score enlists many melodies from the songs in the film as leitmotifs. In addition, the title character has his own

Figure 7.5. First appearance of the Peter Pan leitmotif—PETER PAN SCORE from PETER PAN—Music by Oliver Wallace—© 1953 Walt Disney Music Company

Figure 7.6. Peter Pan leitmotif and "The Second Star to the Right"—PETER PAN SCORE from PETER PAN—Music by Oliver Wallace—© 1953 Walt Disney Music Company. "THE SECOND STAR TO THE RIGHT" from PETER PAN—Words by Sammy Cahn—Music by Sammy Fain—© 1951 Walt Disney Music Company

Figure 7.7. Variants of "The Second Star to the Right" with Peter Pan leitmotif—"THE SECOND STAR TO THE RIGHT" from PETER PAN—Words by Sammy Cahn—Music by Sammy Fain—© 1951 Walt Disney Music Company

instrumental motif (Figure 7.5), and the rhythm for the motif reflects the spoken rhythm of Never Land. When Peter tells Wendy of his plan to bring her to the fabled locale, the three-note motif sounds simultaneously with Wendy's excited reply, "Never Land?"[53] The pitch of the motif is also suggested by the beginning of the song "The Second Star to the Right" (Figure 7.6). The connection between Peter's theme and the song is furthered by having fragmented variants of "The Second Star to the Right" appear between iterations of the leitmotif in the scene where he first appears (Figure 7.7).

Peter Pan's leitmotif occurs prominently throughout the film, often being played by the flute, suggesting the mythological origins of Pan. In fact, Peter plays the motif on a pan flute when Peter and Wendy first meet in the Darling family nursery, as well as shortly after Wendy sings "Your Mother and Mine." A fanfare-ish version of the theme accompanies the scene where Peter has captured Captain Hook's ship.

Several times *Peter Pan* uses rhymed dialog to transition into a song. "You Can Fly! You Can Fly! You Can Fly!" is led into by the rhymed dialog of Peter, Wendy, and John discussing various happy thoughts. Likewise, the entire first verse of "Your Mother and Mine" is spoken. Mr. Darling's dialog is often underscored in a recitative-like manner (Figure 7.8), much like the Queen of Hearts' dialog in *Alice in Wonderland*, a choice of Oliver Wallace, who worked on both scores. Later in the nursery, scene Peter's lines receive a similar underscoring.

Figure 7.8. Recitative-like Underscoring of Mr. Darling's dialog (in rhythm with the line "Out! Out I say!")——
PETER PAN SCORE from PETER PAN—Music by Oliver Wallace—© 1953 Walt Disney Music Company

"The Second Star to the Right" plays over the opening credits of *Peter Pan*. Sung by the Jud Conlon Chorus and The Mellomen, the song asserts that "the dreams you plan really can come true."[54] While this message invokes similar sentiments to "When You Wish Upon a Star" and "A Dream Is a Wish Your Heart Makes," the song's single reference to dreams serves an additional function, namely, to suggest that the fantasy world of Never Land is one of imagination.

The lyrics of the song also reference "Twinkle, Twinkle, Little Star" (1806), the well-known nursery rhyme by Jane Taylor (1783–1824). This allusion plays off the prominent celestial imagery and helps establish the childlike quality of the narrative. The lyrics at the song's conclusion were rewritten for popular release. In this version the singer requests, "Lead me to the one who loves me, and when you bring him my way, each time we say 'goodnight,' we'll thank the second star that shines, the second from the right."[55]

The melody of "The Second Star to the Right" was originally written for the film *Alice in Wonderland*. This song, which was titled "Beyond the Laughing Sky," was deleted from the 1951 film. It was felt that having an opening ballad sung by a female character that longs to escape her reality would invite too much comparison with the MGM classic *The Wizard of Oz* (1939).

The lyrics of "You Can Fly" are spoken in rhythm by Peter, Wendy, Michael, and John while they are in the nursery. Once these characters are airborne and have left the Darling residence for the skies over London, the lyrics are first sung by an offscreen choir, not by the characters themselves.

The arrangement of the song features some effective Mickey Mousing, including a fast woodwind flourish that reinforces the rapid change of direction each character takes as they fly in front of the moon, as well as a fast descending scalar passage that accompanies the characters flying in a dramatic downward arc toward the Thames. The arrangement also features a couple of instances of Peter's leitmotif, the first of which is played by Peter himself when he swoops downward to a pond to land on two swans, and again when the sequence ends and Never Land emerges in the sky from a star.

The lyrics spoken by the Darling children in the nursery foreshadow their coming adventures. Wendy speaks "of a mermaid lagoon … underneath a magic moon."[56] John imagines "a pirate's cave,"[57] while Michael dreams of being "an

Indian brave."[58] Such foretelling suggests that Never Land is not a real locale, but rather is a collective fabrication of the trio's minds.

Pleasant thoughts are the central theme to "You Can Fly! You Can Fly! You Can Fly!" as the lyrics state: "Think of the happiest things, it's the same as having wings."[59] This statement further establishes that the fantastic world that follows is one of imagination, and it also serves as a moral lesson to the listener that optimism is a mind-set. The song also continues the dreamlike imagery that was introduced in "The Second Star to the Right," which declares, "Every dream that you dream will come true."[60] This, and lines such as "Think of all the joy you'll find when you leave the world behind,"[61] lend an escapist flavor to the song, which again suggests that Never Land is located within the mind. In addition, placing the idea of flying off to an imaginary world changes it from the literal to the metaphorical, thus imparting a lesson of believing in oneself.

A merry-go-round-esque version of the song occurs near the end of the film when Peter pilots Captain Hook's ship through the air on the way to London to return the Darling children to their home. The carousel sound is established by the metric change to waltz, along with utilizing rolled glockenspiel and dramatic harp glissandi. At the end of this rendition of the tune, it returns to common time and is decorated by several instances of Peter Pan's leitmotif.

The song makes its final appearance in the film at the very end, sung by an offscreen choir. The lyrics enter as Mr. and Mrs. Darling embrace Wendy at the nursery window, in a moment that also functions as a curtain call, and watch the celestial ship dissolve into the London sky. The verse sung is clearly directed at the escapist nature of the song: "Think of all the joy you'll find, when you leave the world behind, and bid your cares goodbye."[62]

"YOUR MOTHER AND MINE" AND UNUSED SONGS

The emotional center of the film is the song "Your Mother and Mine." This scene finds Wendy acting as an ersatz mother to her brothers and the Lost Boys. The song is an aesthetic complement to "Baby Mine" from *Dumbo*, as "Your Mother and Mine" is a lullaby sung by a child about the merits of a mother, while "Baby Mine" is a lullaby sung by a mother to a child.

Wendy's lullaby has a strong effect on her brothers and the boys, and is overheard by Captain Hook and his pirate crew, who are on the verge of a sneak attack on Peter Pan and the Lost Boys. The pirate crew tears up as they listen to Wendy's song. Having Wendy's brothers, the Lost Boys, and the pirate crew react so strongly to the song also functions to encourage a reflective reaction in the audience. Furthermore, the similar reaction of the pirate crew to the Lost

Boys indicates a parallel between the two groups, suggesting that the buccaneers share a common bond with Peter's followers.

Peter is disaffected by Wendy's song and storms off, breaking an arrow in frustration. This reaction reveals Peter to be a childishly vain leader who resents not being the center of attention. This reaction makes it easier for the more mature Wendy to resolve to leave her hero, and return home to her parents.

Being the emotional center of the movie, "Your Mother and Mine" is used somewhat like a leitmotif. A snippet of the melody for "Your Mother and Mine" occurs early in the film after Wendy retorts, "What would Mother say?"[63] during her first meeting with Peter in the nursery. This connection early in the film foreshadows Wendy's desire to return to the real world.

"Your Mother and Mine" was sung by Kathryn Beaumont, who voiced the role of Wendy Darling. The young actress had previously voiced the titular role in *Alice in Wonderland*. In the time between the two films, Beaumont's singing voice improved significantly, yielding a better performance than that heard in *Alice*.

Consistent with most stage productions of *Peter Pan*, Hans Conried (1917–1982) performs the roles of both Captain Hook and Mr. Darling. Whether the viewer interprets Never Land as a real place in the context of the film or as a figment of the Darling children's imagination, this double casting functions to establish the father as an antagonist. In the case of the latter interpretation, the children imagine the pirate captain with their father's voice, thus relating their own father to the notorious villain.

Another ramification of this dual casting concerns the similarity of the Lost Boys to Captain Hook's crew. Near the end of the film, Mr. Darling recognizes the celestial ship from when he was a child. If Mr. Darling had had adventures with Peter Pan when he was a child, his casting as Captain Hook reflects his own earlier experience as a Lost Boy and exemplifies the ramifications of growing up.

Numerous unused songs had been written for *Peter Pan*. One uncredited lyric sheet exists for a proposed song about Never Land, which was later set to music by Richard Sherman for the 2007 DVD release of *Peter Pan*.[64] Frank Churchill and Larry Morey penned "When the Bos'n Pipes a Tune" for Captain Hook's crew to sing.[65] Another song created by the duo for the film was the "Pirate Song," which was intended to be sung to introduce the pirates early in the film and would have been reprised near the end as the crew attempts to entice the captured Lost Boys to join their crew.[66]

RECEPTION AND SUMMARY

Four years in the making, and costing four million dollars, *Peter Pan* was pre-miered on February 5, 1953. Also on the bill was the True-Life Adventure film *Bear Country*. Jimmy Johnson recalled New York's Radio City Music Hall open-ing of *Peter Pan*:

> It was a raw and wintry day, but nevertheless the lines of people waiting to get in and see *Peter Pan* extended clear around that very long block. I saw all the red noses but I also saw the smiles of anticipation on the faces of adult and child alike. I knew for sure that the dark days at Disney were past and the Studio had no place to go but up. *Peter Pan* turned out to be a smashing success at the box office.[67]

While the animated feature received no Academy Award nominations, it was nominated for the Grand Prize of the Cannes Film Festival. Over the years, when adjusted for inflation, *Peter Pan* has brought in 362 million dollars for the Studios, making it the 111th-most-successful film of all time.[68]

Like *Alice in Wonderland*, *Peter Pan* was promoted on a Christmas Day tele-vision special in 1952. Likewise, *Peter Pan* appeared on an episode of *Lux Radio Theater*, which aired on December 21, 1953. This hour-long radio performance featured songs from the movie, and Bobby Driscoll reprising his role as the title character.

Hugo Winterhalter [1909–1973] and His Orchestra released recordings of "Second Star to the Right," "Your Mother and Mine," "Never Smile at a Croco-dile," and "You Can Fly! You Can Fly! You Can Fly!" on RCA Victor. Jerry Lewis (1926–) recorded "Following the Leader" and "Never Smile at a Crocodile" on Capitol, while the same two songs appeared on Columbia, recorded by the Paulette Sisters. "You Can Fly! You Can Fly! You Can Fly!" was released by Ernie Rudy on Coral Records and by Betty Clark on MGM Records. Eddy Howard [1914–1963] and His Orchestra recorded "Your Mother and Mine" on Mercury Records, while "The Second Star to the Right" was recorded by Doris Day on Columbia. In later years "The Second Star to the Right" has been recorded by Sun Ra and His Arkestra, Barbara Cook, and James Taylor (1948–).

"When You're Alone," from the 1991 film *Hook*, has a distant relationship to "Your Mother and Mine." While "When You're Alone," which was written by John Williams and Leslie Bricusse (1931–), bears no similarity to the song from *Peter Pan* either melodically or lyrically, both are lullabies sung by female visitors to Never Land. Furthermore, both songs elicit responses from their respective onscreen audiences of Lost Boys and pirates ranging from pensive to tearful. Finally, even though "When You're Alone" is not maternally themed, the song is led into with a discussion between Peter and Thud Butt about their mothers. The net effect of both is a nostalgia and longing for the familial world outside Never Land.

Alice in Wonderland and *Peter Pan* have much in common besides being produced consecutively, and being directed by the same individual. Both are based upon works by British authors and are centered on having children travel to a land within their imagination. While the former is explicitly clear that Wonderland is a figment of the protagonist's mind, the film *Peter Pan* is not clear whether Never Land is real or imagined. The time frame of less than three hours between the time Mr. and Mrs. Darling leave and when they return from their evening out advocates that the children's adventures were but a fantasy. Furthermore, as the Darling children leave Never Land, the islands cross-dissolve to the moon, then to Big Ben, and finally to a grandfather clock. These visual associations suggest that the children's adventures were contained within the walls of the Darling household. Finally, the evaporation of Captain Hook's ship into clouds at the end of the film suggests a thoughtlike ephemerality, which the music reinforces. Songs such as "The Second Star to the Right," which invoke dreams, and "You Can Fly! You Can Fly! You Can Fly!" which declares that happy thoughts are "the same as having wings,"[69] seem to imply that Never Land is a creation of the mind.

A final commonality between the two films is that, in both cases, the children in the center of the story feel a need to abandon the world of their imagination in order to return to the real world. Thus, Disney's enthusiastic endorsement of the realm of the imagination as a means of escapism, fulfillment, and empowerment is tempered by an adult's concern for a return to the pragmatism of reality. *Peter Pan*, however, softens this message by having Mr. Darling tell Wendy that she could grow up, "all in good time," reinforcing a common Disney message to stay in touch with one's inner child.[70]

Chapter 8

DISNEY ANIMATED FEATURES
1955–1961

The era following *Peter Pan* through *One Hundred and One Dalmatians* was a time of unprecedented expansion for Walt Disney Productions. The two years that followed the release of *Peter Pan* saw the Studios expand into television with their series *Disneyland* and *The Mickey Mouse Club*, as well as into theme parks, with the opening of Disneyland. This time period also saw a rapid increase in the number of the Studios' live-action movie releases, from two films a year in 1953 to five a year in 1961. With this expansion of business and increase of live-action movie production, animated features became a smaller part of the organization's output. Of the thirty-four films released by the Studios from 1954 through 1961, only three of them, fewer than 10 percent, were animated movies. These animated features, *Lady and the Tramp, Sleeping Beauty*, and *One Hundred and One Dalmatians*, are three of the most unique consecutively released Disney animated films.

LADY AND THE TRAMP

A plan for a movie called *Lady* surfaced at the Studios in the late thirties.[1] Ray Gilbert (1912–1976) and Eliot Daniel wrote at least one unused song for the project in the mid-forties. However, the only songs that appear in *Lady and the Tramp* were written by Peggy Lee and Sonny Burke (1914–1980). The score for the movie was composed by Oliver Wallace, with Edward Plumb and Sidney Fine (1904–2002) acting as orchestrators, and John Rarig (1912–1991) working on the vocal arrangements for the feature.

A comment Walt made during a sweatbox session on July 9, 1954, indicates an inclination away from the nearly wall-to-wall scores that accompanied the Studios' earlier features: "I think this business of trying to score under everything . . . is not good. Put music under business that needs it—then if there are vacant spots we can always go back and put music in. Once we get music we hate to take it out because we have the tracks."[2] This decrease in underscoring would affect the Studios' animated features in a pronounced manner starting with *One Hundred and One Dalmatians*, distancing these films significantly from Disney's early animated movies.

Despite the Studios' expansion into live-action films, Walt remained very involved in *Lady and the Tramp*. This involvement included the use of music. In a sweatbox session on March 24, 1953, Walt provided input on how the calendar montage should be underscored:

> I think this thing has to have a movement to music. When she gets that line there: "When a baby moves in, the dog moves out," carry her expression musically. It's an impact. It hits her. Then we go into the calendar and keep coming back to it. Is there any way we can build a thing that gives you the feeling of going thru the nine months?[3]

Not surprisingly, Walt's description of what he is looking for musically is really a dramatic description, not an inherently musical one. That being said, earlier in the same meeting he used a more musical description of the same scene: "It's one of those things like Beethoven's that builds and progresses with variations and finally comes to a big payoff."[4]

For the following scene, Walt not only was interested in establishing emotion but also specified instrumentation: "In cuts, show she [Lady] creeps in slowly. Jim comes in. When he comes in he'd come in very quietly. At the finish use the vibraharp—and Jim is scratching Lady ... He'd take her in his arms at the end. You can't be corny with this. Try to keep humor in it. Keep the pathos."[5] While the cue in question has little vibraphone in it, Wallace did focus primarily on celeste, which is certainly sonically similar. Shortly after this comment, the filmmaker returned to drama and pacing, noting, "Maybe in the routine the music should sweep a little more," and adding, "Speed Peggy up."[6]

One of the best-known songs from *Lady and the Tramp*, "The Siamese Cat Song," is strongly characterized by the orientalism that saturates the piece. The main melody is largely pentatonic, featuring harmonies in fourths. The orchestration of the song also imitates oriental music, utilizing a koto-like instrument at the beginning of the sequence, as well as plenty of percussion, including pitched gongs, finger cymbals, toms, and marimba. While the latter instrument has its roots in Mexico, for Americans such percussive music often represents the exotic. Even the use of oboe in the arrangement evokes the Chinese sheng. The orientalism of the song also pervades the lyrics, which are filled with instances of broken English. Furthermore, a percussive rhythm concludes each phrase. This rhythm is used in a similar manner at the end of the first phrase

Figure 8.1. Return from the bridge of "Bella Notte"—BELLA NOTTE (THIS IS THE NIGHT) from LADY AND THE TRAMP—Words and Music by Peggy Lee and Sonny Burke—© 1952 The Walt Disney Music Company

of "The March of the Siamese Children" from the 1951 musical *The King and I* by Richard Rodgers (1902–1979) and Oscar Hammerstein II (1895–1960).

Such imitations of oriental traits may not have aged well but were somewhat common in the fifties. Rodgers and Hammerstein wrote two musicals centered on orientalism in the fifties: *The King and I* and *Flower Drum Song* (1958). Films of the decade that featured exoticism include *Road to Bali* (1952), *The Rains of Ranchipur* (1955), *The Conqueror* (1956), *Teahouse of the August Moon* (1956), *The Bridge on the River Kwai* (1957), *Sayonara* (1957), and *The Barbarian and the Geisha* (1958).

One clue as to the source of interest in orientalism and exoticism in the fifties comes from the setting of yet another Rogers and Hammerstein collaboration, the 1949 musical *South Pacific*. Based on the book *Tales of the South Pacific* (1947) by James Michener (1907–1997), the story features a nurse at a naval base on a Polynesian island during World War II. Thousands of American veterans of the recent world war who had served in the Pacific theater brought home with them an interest in the Far East.

The opening title sequence of *Lady and the Trap* features a choral arrangement of "Bella Notte," the film's romantic ballad. The primary occurrence of the song in the movie is heard in an italianate orchestration featuring accordion, mandolin, and guitar. To help drive in the return of the main melody after the bridge, the half cadence that concludes the bridge moves to an augmented chord on the dominant, resulting in a raised scale degree two, leading into the first note of the main melody (Figure 8.1). When the scene changes from Tony's Restaurant to a romantic stroll in the park, the arrangement turns purely choral. One technique that appears in this portion of the song is the use of countermelodies that are voiced by wordless singing.

Voice actor and vocalist Thurl Ravenscroft (1914–2005) related the story of Walt's concept behind the inclusion of "Home Sweet Home" in *Lady and the Tramp*:

He said, "Every class B movie I've ever seen in my life has had a prison scene . . . In the background there's always a barbershop quartet singing some mournful song like 'If I Had the Wings of an Angel, Over These Prison Walls I Would Fly,' or something of that nature. Well . . . we're going to have a prison scene in *Lady and the Tramp*, but of course it's a dog pound, and there's

going to be conversation between Lady and Tramp . . . and some of the dogs."
And he said, "In the background we've gotta have four dogs howling 'Home
Sweet Home' in four part barbershop howling harmony. So do you think we
can make it?" He said, "It can't sound like humans sounding like dogs, it's
gotta sound like dogs howling." So we said, "ok" . . . We took an arrangement
we had of "Home Sweet Home" and we went out to the Studio—big sound
stage—and we were messing around howling . . . you know the four part
barbershop harmony . . . we finally thought we had a pretty good idea, so
they called Walt down from his office, and he listened. And he said, "That's
wonderful, but . . . it sounds like human beings howling instead of really dogs
. . . Is there anyway you can change it to make it really like dogs?" And we
said, "Let's break for lunch, and then we'll try something different."[7]

After breaking for lunch the quartet overdubbed sounds of whimpering and
dog howls.[8] This time when Walt listened to the results he was pleased, stating,
"That is absolutely perfect, it sounds like dogs, that's wonderful."[9]

"He's a Tramp" is sung by Peg, voiced by Peggy Lee, who also sang "La La Lu"
and "The Siamese Cat Song" in the film. The jazzy style of the song is incorporated into the cartoon in a number of entertaining ways. One dog performs
a cymbal fill by tapping his tail on a dog dish and a pail. Later a Chihuahua
scratches another fill, suggesting a snare drum played with brushes. A bulldog
vocalizes a countermelody punctuated by another dog's bark, a trio of howling
dogs provides harmonic changes, and a variety of barks and whimpers accen-
tuates the arrangement.

The character design of Peg presents her as a nightclub singer. The long
hair typical of a Lhasa apso on Peg appears to be wild and unkempt. Typically
only one of her eyes is visible, as her hair covers the other eye. The visible eye
appears baggy, suggesting a night owl or a lush. Peg even utilizes her bushy tail
at times in a manner that suggests a feather boa. These design elements not
only play well off the music but also help establish the character as a low-class
individual of questionable morals, contrasting heavily with Lady.

There is little use of leitmotif in Lady and the Tramp. That being said, a snippet of the melody of "La La Lu" occurs after Lady says, "But who'd watch over
the baby?"[10] to Tramp after their night of romance. This connection between
the melody and Lady's comment helps to express the character's desire to be a
part of a human family.

The predominant theme of Lady and the Tramp is that of belonging. Early
in the film Lady is clearly proud of her new collar and license, which serves as
a symbol of her domestication. Trusty states that a license is "the greatest honor
man can bestow," while Jock regards it as "a badge of faith and respectability."[11]
Accordingly, these two domesticated animals have a low opinion of Tramp. In

a film where different breeds of dogs are presented as representing various cultures, this preoccupation with licensure can be seen as symbolizing citizenship and assimilation in the diverse multiethnic society of America.[12] This is reflected in the songs in the film, which portray a variety of ethnic music: oriental, Italian, and American jazz, which is itself a blend of African and American traditions.

Of the several unused songs from *Lady and the Tramp*, one of them was written by Ray Gilbert and Eliot Daniel on August 5, 1946.[13] This tune, "I'm Free as the Breeze," was written for Tramp to sing.[14] Peggy Lee and Sonny Burke wrote a song with a similar sentiment on October 20, 1952, called "I'm Singing ('Cause I Want to Sing)."[15]

RECEPTION

Produced for around four million dollars, *Lady and the Tramp*, which was the first animated feature presented in CinemaScope, premiered on June 16, 1955, in Chicago. While critics initially felt that the film was subpar, it performed very well at the box office. The movie earned more in its first release than any Disney animated film since *Snow White and the Seven Dwarfs*. After adjusting for inflation, *Lady and the Tramp* is the sixty-eighth-most-successful movie of all time, bringing in the equivalent of 442 million dollars.[16]

Walt enlisted Ward Greene (1892–1969) to pave the way for the feature's release by writing a novelization of the movie, which was published in 1953. *Lady and the Tramp* was promoted on two episodes of *Disneyland*. One was a 1954 episode titled "A Story of Dogs"; the other was the episode "Cavalcade of Songs" (1955), which featured a segment on the music in *Lady and the Tramp*.

Lady and the Tramp was nominated for a British Academy of Film and Television Arts Award for Best Animated Film, and the film garnered a David di Donatello Award for Best Foreign Producer for Walt. Furthermore, the movie was named the ninety-fifth-greatest Love Story by the American Film Institute.

When the film was first released, several of the feature's songs were released on a variety of labels. Peggy Lee's recordings of "He's a Tramp" and "The Siamese Cat Song" appeared on Decca. MGM pressed recordings of the same two songs performed by the Marion Sisters with Joe Lipman. Lipman also conducted a recording of Kay Armen (1915–) singing "Bella Notte" and "La La Lu" on MGM. Lu Ann Simms recorded "The Siamese Cat Song" and "La La Lu" on Coronet and Columbia. Gordon MacRae (1921–1986) released a recording of "Bella Notte" on Capitol. The Lennon Sisters recorded "The Siamese Cat Song" on Coral. In later years Lawrence Welk, Bobby McFerrin (1950–), and Freddie and the Dreamers recorded covers of "The Siamese Cat Song." Bette Midler recorded a cover of "He's a Tramp" for a two-disc set of Peggy Lee songs.

Peggy Lee cowrote four more *Lady and the Tramp*–themed songs with Sonny Burke. "Jim Dear," "Old Trusty," "Singing ('Cause He Wants to Sing),"[17] and "That Fellow's a Friend of Mine" were recorded for a Decca album, *Songs from Walt Disney's "Lady and the Tramp"* nearly a year and a half after the movie was released. All four songs were published by the Walt Disney Music Company. With lyrics like "call him a tramp, call him a rover," "That Fellow's a Friend of Mine" functions like a theme song for Tramp.[18] Likewise, "Singing ('Cause He Wants to Sing)" references Tramp with lines like "wearing no man's collar except of course his own."[19]

Lady and the Tramp marks the first of several Disney films where the songs are contracted out to a popular artist. The Studios would not try this approach again until *Robin Hood* (1973), which features music by Roger Miller. Most notable amongst these pop collaborations is *The Lion King*, which includes music by Elton John and lyrics by Tim Rice (1944–). Elton John's fellow countryman Phil Collins wrote music for the 1999 release *Tarzan,* as well as for *Brother Bear* (2003). Yet another English pop star, Sting, cowrote songs for *The Emperor's New Groove* (2000) with Dave Hartley.

SLEEPING BEAUTY

Sleeping Beauty (1959) was considered for a feature in 1950. Sammy Fain and Jack Lawrence wrote half a dozen songs in 1952 for an early incarnation of the project.[20] In the following year, Walt decided that the score for the film should be based on Tchaikovsky's ballet score, making all but one of Fain and Lawrence's songs unusable for the movie. Only one of their creations, "Once Upon a Dream," had been based on music from the classic ballet, specifically the "Sleeping Beauty Waltz."[21]

During the early stages of work on *Sleeping Beauty,* Walter Schumann (1913–1958) was the composer assigned to the project. While work on the film had advanced by 1954, it was set aside for two years while the Studios focused on Disneyland and the television series *Disneyland* and *The Mickey Mouse Club,* with work resuming on *Sleeping Beauty* in 1956.[22]

Most of the music for the movie is a reduced-instrumentation adaptation of Tchaikovsky's ballet of the same name, with George Bruns acting as the arranger.[23] In order to convince Walt that he was up to the task, Bruns said, "I can rewrite it. I've been rewriting him for my songs for years."[24] The choral arrangements for *Sleeping Beauty* were made by John Rarig.

The songs in the film were products of a variety of tunesmiths. "Hail to the Princess Aurora," "One Gift," "Sing a Smiling Song," and "Sleeping Beauty Song" were created by Tom Adair (1913–1988) and George Bruns. "Skumps" was written by Adair, Bruns, and Ed Penner. "I Wonder" was written by Winston Hibler, Ted Sears, and Bruns.

GEORGE BRUNS

The son of a sawmill worker, George E. Bruns was born on the third of July, 1914, in Sandy, Oregon. He began studying piano at the age of six and was proficient at the trombone and tuba by high school. Over time he would add another dozen instruments to his repertoire. During this time he also began to study composition under a local pianist named Dent Morey.[25] While studying engineering at Oregon State Agricultural College, Bruns put himself through school by playing in the ROTC band. He left school in 1934 before completing his degree, in order to pursue a career in music. The musician summarized his own educational experience as being self-taught:

> As far as legitimate music education, I was really mostly all self-taught. I started writing for bands in 1932, in college. I wrote some for the college band and then I started taking private lessons from a very good teacher in Portland. But I learned very little from teachers. I learned from mainly just doing it, and copying the phonograph records and stuff like that.[26]

In addition to music, Bruns played basketball and football.[27] He also labored in his father's sawmill, and worked as a shipyard layout man during the Second World War.[28]

Bruns played in several popular bands of the day, including the Jim Dericks Orchestra, Jack Teagarden's (1905–1964) band, a Hawaiian band headed by Harry Owens (1902–1986), the Rose City Stompers, Turk Murphy's [1915–1987] Jazz Band, the Webfoot Jazz Band, and the Castle Jazz Band. He also formed his own band, which included Doc Severinsen (1927–) on trumpet. Later, he served as music director and arranger at a few Portland-area radio stations, including KOIN and KEX, and was music director at Westinghouse.

He moved to Los Angeles in 1950, where he worked for Capitol Records and later at UPA Studios as an arranger and conductor. Bruns got the job at UPA through Ward Kimball. The two knew each other through LA's jazz scene. UPA contacted Kimball asking for a suggestion for a jazz tubist they could use for a short titled *Little Boy with a Big Horn* (1953).[29] Kimball suggested Bruns, who composed the score for the short and stayed on at UPA, scoring a dozen shorts,[30] including *Magoo's Masterpiece* (1953) and *How Now Boing Boing* (1954). During this time he also ran his own band and wrote arrangements for his wife, Jeanne Gayle, a singer who appeared on Capitol Records.

Bruns also studied composition privately with Buddy Baker during the early fifties. Baker recalled:

I first met him [Bruns] when he was playing bass with a little band down at a ballroom in downtown L.A. George asked me if I gave any private lessons, and I told him that I would. So he studied with me for quite a while until he got a handle on how to do animation and all that kind of stuff.[31]

Once Bruns was working at Disney, he would be instrumental in getting his former teacher a job at the Studios.

Originally, the composer slated to work on *Sleeping Beauty* was Walter Schumann (1913–1958).[32] However, Schumann argued with Walt and was fired. Walt turned to Kimball for advice, and the animator replied, "Well, why don't we give George Bruns a try?"[33]

Bruns was initially hired in 1953 on a trial basis, working for 150 dollars a week.[34] The first scene he worked on for *Sleeping Beauty* was the bluebird sequence.[35] While at the Studios, he scored several animated features: *Sleeping Beauty, One Hundred and One Dalmatians* (1961), *The Sword in the Stone* (1963), *The Jungle Book, The Aristocats* (1970), and *Robin Hood*. He also worked on several live-action movies, including: *Davy Crockett: King of the Wild Frontier, Davy Crockett and the River Pirates, Westward Ho the Wagons! Johnny Tremain* (1957), *The Absent-Minded Professor* (1961), *Babes in Toyland* (1961), *Son of Flubber* (1963), *The Ugly Dachshund* (1966), *Follow Me, Boys!* (1966), *The Fighting Prince of Donegal* (1966), *The Adventures of Bullwhip Griffin* (1967), *The Horse in the Gray Flannel Suit* (1968), *The Love Bug* (1968), and *Herbie Rides Again* (1974).

The composer also worked on both the *Disneyland* television series and *Zorro* (1957–1959). In fact, a full third of the episodes of the *Disneyland* television series, as well as its later incarnations, feature music by Bruns.[36] Notably, the composer was able to collaborate with his friend and champion Ward Kimball with the episodes "Man in Space" (1955), "Man and the Moon" (1955), and "Mars and Beyond" (1957). He also scored an Emmy-winning episode about the film *20,000 Leagues Under the Sea*, titled "Operation Undersea" (1954).

Working on the *Disneyland* television series was demanding. The stress began to take a physical toll on Bruns: "I damn near killed myself. My blood pressure was just unbelievable. I had to slow down a little bit. There was so much pressure."[37] George was able to slow down by inviting Buddy Baker to work at Disney and take over some of the work.[38]

Bruns was also the original music director for *The Mickey Mouse Club* and provided numerous songs and cue music for the show, including: "Fun with Music Day," "I'm No Fool," "The Mickey Mouse Club Newsreel," the theme to the Hardy Boys serial, and the Boys of the Western Sea serial.[39] Bruns appeared as himself in an episode of *Walt Disney's Wonderful World of Color* titled "Back-stage Party" (1961) and also played tuba with Firehouse Five Plus Two on a second-season episode of *The Mickey Mouse Club*. Bruns joined Firehouse Five Plus Two, a Dixieland band composed of members of The Walt Disney Studios animation department, after tubaist Ed Penner died in 1956.

Bruns cowrote numerous songs for *The Mickey Mouse Club*, including "The Humphrey Hop," "I Want to Be a Fireman," "Nineteen Twenty-Five," and "Talent Round-Up." In terms of music for attractions, he wrote music for the Rainbow Caverns Mine Train and the Enchanted Tiki Room (1963–). For the 1964 World's Fair, Bruns wrote music for the Ford pavilion and played the tuba line for the German polka band in it's a small world.[40] Bruns cowrote "Yo Ho (A Pirate's Life for Me)" with Xavier Atencio (1919–) for the Pirates of the Caribbean (1967–) attraction. Bruns and Atencio also cowrote the songs for The Country Bear Jamboree. Bruns wrote the music for the Frontierland and Tomorrowland sections of the record *A Musical Tour of Disneyland*.[41]

Bruns was quite a tunesmith, having cowritten with Tom Blackburn (1913–1992) "The Ballad of Davy Crockett," as well as the theme to the show *Zorro*. The former sold over eight million copies and topped the Hit Parade for six months, while the latter sold a million copies.[42] The composer also played bass on the first recording of "The Ballad of Davy Crockett" that was released.[43] In what may have been an attempt to capitalize on Crockettmania, Bruns cowrote with Blackburn "The Ballad of John Colter" and the title song for *Westward Ho the Wagons!*

When Bruns first started working at Disney, Walt was heavily involved in approving the music to come out of the Studios:

> Walt was really in on the music, and the producer of the picture had nothing to say about it. It was all him. You dealt with him and that was it. After we got bigger and bigger, he kind of left it up to us because he just didn't have time to get in on these things, with Disneyland and all that.[44]

Bruns also noted that while Walt would give feedback, he would keep it general, noting to George, "You're the musician, you know what to do."[45] The composer also felt that Walt had "a knack for knowing what people like."[46] According to Buddy Baker, the admiration Bruns had for his boss was reciprocated in that Walt personally liked George.[47]

Baker felt that one of Bruns's gifts as a composer was his sense of humor:

> He had a strange sense of humor. He would see something funny or he would write some music and see it back with the picture, and it turned out to be as funny as he thought it would be and maybe more so, because he would sit there and laugh at his own music like he was the audience.[48]

In his assessment of Bruns, Baker compared him to Billy May (1916–2004), who composed music for numerous television shows, including *Batman* (1966–1968).[49]

During his time at The Walt Disney Studios, Bruns also worked for other studios. He worked on two Ivan Tors productions, including *Island of the Lost* (1967) and *Daring Game* (1968). He also wrote music for three non-Disney television series, including *Calvin and the Colonel* (1961–1962), *Beetle Bailey* (1963), and *Cowboy in Africa* (1967–1968).

Bruns was nominated for four Academy Awards, three for Best Score (*Sleeping Beauty*, *Babes in Toyland*, and *The Sword in the Stone*), and one for Best Original Song, for "Love" from *Robin Hood*. He was awarded a Golden Laurel for Top Musical Score for *Babes in Toyland*.

The composer retired from The Walt Disney Studios in 1975. He then returned to his native Oregon, where he recorded a jazz album and taught part-time at Lewis and Clark College. Bruns's hobby was woodworking, and he was especially adept at cabinetmaking.[50] The composer died of a heart attack on May 23, 1983, in a hospital in Portland, Oregon.

THE SCORE TO *SLEEPING BEAUTY*

Walt had not yet met Bruns when he approved the assigning of the composer to *Sleeping Beauty*.[51] The two first encountered each other during a meeting where Walt was shown a sequence from the film with some birds. Bruns had scored the scene using some of Tchaikovsky's music on the flute, and Walt approved of the scene's underscoring, stating, "Yeah, I think that's the idea of what we want to get ... that's going to work fine."[52] Afterward, Bill Peet introduced Walt to the composer, who happened to be a physically large person.[53] Walt noted, "God, I'm glad I didn't say anything bad about the music."[54]

Early on in Bruns's work on *Sleeping Beauty*, Walt instructed the composer to take a different approach than was typical with the Studios' scoring: "Now, we want to do *Sleeping Beauty* differently. Usually, you know, we catch everything. We 'Mickey Mouse' the action. In this we just want to play Tchaikovsky and let it feel the action."[55] However, closer to the film's release, Walt gave opposing feedback: "George, you know how we do things. Why didn't you catch all of that stuff? Why didn't you catch it? ... I think you're going to have to do that thing over again and catch all of that action."[56] In a desire to keep his job, the composer did not remind his boss that he had initially instructed him not to Mickey Mouse the score.[57]

Fortunately for the composer, Walt took the film home and watched it over and over for at least three nights.[58] After doing so the filmmaker told Bruns, "You know, after I've seen it, I think you're right. I just had not gotten used to it."[59] Bruns, recalling the experience years later, observed: "That's the way he was. He would tell you when he thought he was wrong. He was great to work with."[60] Ultimately, the score's use of classical music and comparative lack of Mickey Mousing edged the film stylistically toward *Fantasia* and away from their other animated features.

According to Bruns, he was able to adapt Tchaikovsky's music for about two-thirds of *Sleeping Beauty*.[61] For the other third, he wrote original music in the style of Tchaikovsky.[62] When Bruns reflected on the project later in his career, he noted that it was "a heck of a job to do."[63]

In a 2002 article, Ross Care pointed out that some of the music that Bruns adapted from Tchaikovsky was used for similar functions in the ballet, while some was not.[64] For instance, some of the music in the ballet for Carabosse was used to represent Maleficent, her counterpart in the film.[65] The opening for the movie came from the prologue of the ballet, in particular "March: Entrance of King Florestan."[66] However, Tchaikovsky's Lilac Fairy theme is used in the film as a love theme.[67] A variation from the "Pas de Six" in the ballet's prologue became a motif representing the movie's three fairies.[68] The music accompanying Maleficent's metamorphosis into the dragon comes from the first scene in the ballet from a passage representing the King's anger at the villagers.[69]

Sweatbox notes from early in the planning stages, February 11, 1953, when Walter Schumann was the musical director, record Walt's evolving concept for how the fairies theme and their gifts should be treated in the film. The initial impetus came from his criticism of the dialog: "It's long in dialog. I wonder if we need 'How do you do. Your Majesties,' etc. 'It's a nice day' and all that . . . Nothing is more boring than dialog that doesn't get anywhere . . . can't we do it with music?"[70] At first he was concerned with the greetings, noting that "the arriving stuff never sounds as good spoken as put to music."[71] He then turned to the gifts bestowed by the fairies: "We're bringing in the sprites and things representing their powers. Why can't we let that be it?"[72]

Walt then became concerned with musical themes, and the time it would take for them to unfold. He turned to Schumann and suggested, "But look, Walter, I don't know. Maybe I'm on the lowbrow side, but I feel we should have one theme for all the fairies. Can't you take the one and use different orchestrations for it?"[73] Schumann responded, "We have a time limit. Actually each of these takes seven seconds, like establishing a melody."[74] Walt countered:

> That's what's wrong. Have something that's just them, not try to break it into three. The "Good Fairies Theme," instead of a theme for each one of them, because that gets complicated and too intellectual, so you have to send a pamphlet along with the picture. I think it has to be right there. They work as a team all the time. We have one for Maleficent and one for the good fairies so we don't get into the complicated type of thing. I think each one, when

you single out an individual fairy, you can find a different way to carry the orchestration.[75]

This excerpt clearly demonstrates Walt's evident frustration with Schumann. Bruns, who would take over from Schumann, closely followed Walt's description of how the music should unfold for the scene.

Later, when discussing Schumann's realization of "Hail to the Princess Aurora," Walt criticized the arrangement for being too heavy:

It parallels so close the *Pomp and Circumstance* thing. I thought we could get something more in the fairy tale theme. Is there any trick you can do to get more tempo? . . . What if there was a big, powerful voice, "Hail to the Princess, Aurora," and the chorus came in with an echo? Would that keep it from being ponderous?[76]

Moments later, while Schumann demonstrated on the piano, Walt compared the music to "'Onward Christian Soldiers.' Oh, maybe it's just me. I feel like I'd like to have it all just singing out—joyous."[77]

Two of the best-known songs from *Sleeping Beauty* are "I Wonder" and "Once Upon a Dream." Presented consecutively in the film, both numbers utilize melodies that are adapted from Tchaikovsky's ballet. These two sequences also help connect the film to *Snow White and the Seven Dwarfs* and *Cinderella*. Both songs feature Princess Aurora interacting with the forest animals, much as Snow White does in "With a Smile and a Song" and "Whistle While You Work." The rapport that the protagonist has with the animals is similar to that which Cinderella has with her mouse friends.

Helene Stanley served as the live-action model for the title character of *Sleeping Beauty*. Stanley, a trained dancer, had fulfilled the same function for *Cinderella*. Marjorie Belcher, who had been the live-action model for Snow White, had been a ballerina. Having all three protagonists modeled on dancers lends the visual motion of the characters continuity from film to film.

When the protagonist first sings the second verse of "I Wonder," she enters a clearing as she reaches the lyrics "Will my song go winging to someone who'll find me?"[78] A castle is prominently visible on the horizon, and as the song concludes, the film cuts to a medium shot of the palace. The reveal of the castle coinciding with the lyric "someone who'll find me"[79] is similar to the visual framing of the palace in *Cinderella* during the song "A Dream Is a Wish Your Heart Makes." The connection between these scenes is strengthened by Princess Aurora's dialog with the forest animals that follows: "Yes, it's only in my dreams, but they say if you dream a thing more than once, it's sure to come true."[80] This statement of dreams coming true mirrors the lyrics of "A Dream Is a Wish Your Heart Makes."

While "Once Upon a Dream" may not be introduced with rhymed dialog, the dialog does serve as a transition into the lyrics, with Princess Aurora stating, "No, I'm really not supposed to speak to strangers, but we've met before."[81] The music that accompanies this dialog lands on a dominant chord, leading into the song musically in the same manner that recitative does. Prince Phillip joins in with Princess Aurora's song while she is distracted in her daydream in much the same manner that the prince joins in at the end of "I'm Wishing." After a brief interlude of dialog, Prince Phillip sings the first half of the song, with the choir singing the second half. The dancing that accompanies this portion of the sequence is reminiscent of "So This Is Love" from *Cinderella*.

There were several unused songs created for *Sleeping Beauty*. A title song for the film was written on August 13, 1952, by Jack Lawrence and Victor Young.[82] The citizens of King Stefan's kingdom would have been profiled in "Holiday," a song written by Sammy Fain and Jack Lawrence on September 26, of the same year.[83] This duo also wrote a song on May 14, 1952, that would have been sung by Kings Stefan and Hubert, "It Happens I Have a Picture."[84] "Sunbeams (Bestowal of Gifts)" was written by Fain and Lawrence and would have featured Flora, Fauna, Merryweather, and Maleficent.[85] "Mirage (Follow Your Heart)," a song written by Fain and Lawrence, would have lured Princess Aurora to her fateful encounter with the spinning wheel.[86] Fain and Lawrence also wrote "Where in the World," a song that is similar in concept to "I Wonder."[87] Like this latter song, "Where in the World" was written to lead into "Once Upon a Dream."[88]

Walter Schumann wrote "Berries to Pick," which would have been sung by Briar Rose.[89] Winston Hibler described the number during a sweatbox session on February 11, 1953:

> Our plan is to change this in a small way and introduce a heigh-ho type of gay song with the girl dancing thru the forest with animals and waking others who join the party. Start-the-day-in-the-happy-way thought. They finally reach a point where the girl sees an opening in the trees and her mood changes. The outside world.[90]

However, Walt was concerned with the idea of recycling an idea from *Snow White and the Seven Dwarfs*: "I worry about the Heigh-Heigh-Derry-Do, now. If we could work on it, and keep it from being too much like *Snow White*—Even the girl's voice sounds like it. I remember some of our early tests and one thing we liked was she wasn't so high-pitched."[91]

That being said, Walt followed it up with a concept for the number that was similar to "Oh, Sing Sweet Nightingale":

> I think it's a thought set to music rather than a song. One of those things that's about as simple—if they keep doing it—no more to it than that—"Berries to

pick—berries to pick today." They fly over, pick them, some of them are eating them. She's over there with it going on, but sort of going off into a daydream. She has a chore to do but can't help daydreaming.[92]

It is likely that the difficulty in finding an original approach to this work song doomed the concept.

Several abandoned songs for *Sleeping Beauty* came from later stages of the project, when George Bruns was serving as music director, adapting the music from Tchaikovsky. One such tune, "Go to Sleep," featured lyrics by an unidentified individual, while a separate tune, which was a proposed prolog to the film, featured lyrics by Tom Adair.[93] Adair and Ed Penner wrote the lyrics for "Evil-Evil." Set down on paper on September 14, 1955, this song would have been sung by Maleficent and her Goons.[94] "Riddle Diddle One, Two, Three" had been written for Flora, Fauna, and Merryweather to sing. The song features lyrics by Winston Hibler and Ted Sears that relate the fairies' preparations for Briar Rose's birthday.[95]

RECEPTION

The score to *Sleeping Beauty* was recorded in Germany, due to a musicians strike.[96] The movie cost some six million dollars to make, resulting in the most expensive animated film up to that time. The feature premiered on January 29, 1959, in Los Angeles. The movie was a visual spectacle, having been produced in Technirama. This wide-gauge format complemented the stereo score.

Sleeping Beauty was one of the top-grossing films of 1959.[97] However, the high cost of the movie translated into a loss for the Studios. Moreover, the feature was met with a somewhat lukewarm reception from critics.

In order to offset high production costs, ticket prices were put at double than normal rates that are more typical of road show releases.[98] To alleviate criticism of these ticket prices for a seventy-five-minute cartoon, the feature was paired with a twenty-nine-minute CinemaScope film, *Grand Canyon* (1958), which features imagery of Arizona's most famous travel destination paired with music from *Grand Canyon Suite* (1931) by Ferde Grofé (1892–1972). Ultimately, the visual virtuosity offered by *Sleeping Beauty* did little to attract an audience that was more interested in a compelling narrative, sympathetic characters, and comic relief.

Sleeping Beauty was promoted on television in an episode of *Disneyland* titled "The Peter Tchaikovsky Story" (1959). To promote the stereophonic audio of the film, the episode was simulcast on ABC affiliate radio stations (both AM and FM), allowing the soundtrack of the episode to be heard in stereo. This simulcast stereo technique for television broadcast had been used only a handful of times before. The technique was used as late as 1984 for the broadcast of George Lucas's (1944–) *The Ewok Adventure.* "The Peter Tchaikovsky Story" included some footage from *Sleeping Beauty* in letterbox format that Disney dubbed "The Magic Mural Screen."

Not surprisingly, critical reception of *Sleeping Beauty* tended to compare the film to *Snow White and the Seven Dwarfs* and *Cinderella.* Such connections did not favor the 1959 film. *Sleeping Beauty* had little of the comedic release that its predecessors had. In addition, while *Sleeping Beauty* had an intense action sequence in Prince Phillip's battle with the dragon, the film had little else to occupy the attention of most boys.

In a humorous moment in his review of the film, Bosley Crowther (1905–1981) noted that "the princess looks so much like Snow White they could be a couple of Miss Rheingolds separated by three or four years."[99] The same review was critical of the soundtrack:

> There are other things about *Sleeping Beauty* that compare less favorably with *Snow White.* The musical score is sorely lacking in notable melodies. Even though it is liberally adapted from Tchaikovsky's *Sleeping Beauty Ballet* and does afford effective background music, it is shy on singable songs. Only one stands out. That is lifted from the waltz number in the original ballet and is equipped with lyrics that tag it "Once Upon a Dream." The other two songs, "One Gift" and "I Wonder," are virtually thrown away.[100]

This judgment of the soundtrack points to the film's nature as a somewhat ineffectual union of fairy tale films like *Snow White and the Seven Dwarfs* and the high-minded *Fantasia.* While Crowther feels that the adaptation of Tchaikovsky's music does afford "effective background music," its lack of "singable songs"[101] is a problem for a film like *Snow White and the Seven Dwarfs* or *Cinderella,* while such an observation would be irrelevant for a movie like *Fantasia.* Thus, this problem with the music in *Sleeping Beauty* is not related to the execution of score so much as to the concept behind it. Or, to put it another way, the high-art pretenses of the film work against the popular reception of it.

Walt himself was even somewhat critical of the movie, acknowledging that it held too much in common with *Snow White and the Seven Dwarfs* and *Cinderella*: "It had many of the elements we had already used in *Snow White* and *Cinderella.* You've got to give the creators new things to work with so they'll be able to keep their enthusiasm up. You're in trouble if they start saying, 'Haven't we done this before?'"[102] This admission indicates the filmmaker's opinion that *Sleeping Beauty* suffered from a lack of originality.

The feature was a net loss for Disney, earning only 5.3 million dollars at the box office during its first release.[103] However, the Studios interpreted the initial failure of *Sleeping Beauty* as an indication that the public was no longer interested in fairy tales. It would be three full decades before Disney released another animated feature based upon a fairy tale, *The Little Mermaid* (1989). Despite the film's slow start, rereleases of *Sleeping Beauty* have been very successful, giving the movie a lifetime gross of 579 million dollars when adjusted for inflation, making the feature the thirtieth-most-profitable movie of all time.[104]

The music to *Sleeping Beauty* performed fairly well, being nominated for a Best Music Academy Award and a Best Soundtrack Album Grammy. A storybook album containing several songs from the movie with Mary Martin singing and narrating was released on Disneyland Records in 1958. A separate release, a 1959 official Mickey Mouse Club album, featured Mouseketeer Darlene Gillespie singing the part of Briar Rose. Years later, the Mike Curb Congregation recorded "Once Upon a Dream" for their album *Walt Disney's Greatest Hits*.

ONE HUNDRED AND ONE DALMATIANS

The score for *One Hundred and One Dalmatians* was written by George Bruns, with Franklyn Marks (1911–1976) acting as an orchestrator. The songs for the movie were written by Mel Leven (1914–2007). The human protagonist of the feature, Roger, is a songwriter. In order to reflect this occupation, the score at times has somewhat of a more commercial flavor to it. However, ironically, the film features the fewest songs in any Disney animated feature up to that point. Likewise, there are relatively long stretches of the movie that feature no underscoring.

The most compelling musical segment of the film is the opening credits, which features a visually inventive sequence with brightly orchestrated music that travels through a variety of musical vignettes. These segments are stylistically diverse, though several of them are arranged in a big-band style. The best-known song from the film, "Cruella De Vil," is featured twice in the opening title sequence. The leitmotif that represents the Dalmatians also appears in the medley. The sequence also features a large degree of Mickey Mousing, including musical punctuations of the title of the film, and the credit for Dodie Smith's (1896–1990) original book.

One Hundred and One Dalmatians uses only a single non-song leitmotif, which is itself a false sequence, down a fourth. This theme, which represents the Dalmatians (Figure 8.2), is used when Pongo first searches for Anita and Perdita in the park, as well as when Anita and Perdita emerge from the pond. The tune recurs when Perdita gives birth to the pups, and when Roger sends Cruella De Vil away without the pups. The melody also appears when Pongo and the pups roll in soot in order to escape from Cruella, and when the Dalmatians arrive safely at Roger and Anita's house after their escape. William

false sequence down a fourth

Figure 8.2. Dalmatian leitmotif—ONE HUNDRED AND ONE DALMATIANS SCORE—From ONE HUNDRED AND ONE DALMATIANS—Music by George Bruns—© 1961 The Walt Disney Music Company

Dunham (1910–2001) added lyrics to this melody, resulting in the song "Playful Melody," which was included on the Disneyland Storyteller record titled *Walt Disney's* 101 Dalmatians *in Story and Song.*

There were several songs that were developed for *One Hundred and One Dalmatians* but not used. Mel Leven wrote an earlier concept for "Cruella De Vil," titled "Cruella De Vil (Wicked Ole Thing)." In contrast to the bluesy version that made its way into the film, this song was sort of a minor-key schoolyard taunt.[105] An earlier concept for "Dalmatian Plantation" that Leven had written in August of 1958 was abandoned when Bill Peet asked for a new song that emphasized words that ended with "tion."[106]

"The March of the One Hundred and One" would have occurred in the moving van that the dogs used to escape from Cruella De Vil. Leven wrote "Cheerio, Good-Bye, Toodle-oo, Hip Hip!" on October 27, 1958, for the pups to sing as they left their captors.[107] "Don't Buy a Parrot from a Sailor" was written to sound like a pub song for Cruella's henchmen to sing to amuse themselves.

RECEPTION AND SUMMARY

Costing some four million dollars, *One Hundred and One Dalmatians* premiered on January 25, 1961, at Radio City Music Hall in New York. The movie performed well at the box office and was the highest-grossing film of 1961. The feature performed so well during its initial and subsequent releases that it has been listed as the eleventh-most-successful movie of all time, with a gross of over 796 million dollars when adjusted for inflation.[108]

The film also pleased critics. *One Hundred and One Dalmatians* was awarded a British Academy of Film and Television Arts Award for best animated movie of 1962. Cruella De Vil has also been listed as the thirty-ninth-greatest villain in movie history by the American Film Institute.

One Hundred and One Dalmatians features the most memorable song about a villain, "Cruella De Vil," in any Disney movie. The 1996 live-action film version of *101 Dalmatians* also includes the song "Cruella De Vil." The song's title character has become prominent in popular culture. The song "Let Me Entertain You" by the rock group Queen contains a reference to De Vil. The bands Children 18:3 and Deadsy have both written songs about the infamous diva ("The

Cruel One" and "Cruella" respectively). *The Simpsons* (1989–) had an episode ("Two Dozen and One Greyhounds") that parodies *One Hundred and One Dalmatians*. The episode features a version of "Be Our Guest" from *Beauty and the Beast* (1991) with rewritten lyrics ("See My Vest"). The 2000 film *Rugrats in Paris* contains a character (Coco LaBouche) who is a parody of Cruella De Vil.

In the six-year period from 1955 to 1961, the Studios were able to release three very different animated films. *Lady and the Tramp,* with its collaboration with popular songwriter Peggy Lee, would set the stage for such future Disney productions as *Robin Hood, The Lion King, Tarzan,* and *Brother Bear. One Hundred and One Dalmatians,* which ironically features a songwriter as a protagonist, distanced itself from what had become a tradition of songs being central to the narrative of Disney animated films. This approach was later used in such films as *The Black Cauldron* (1985), *The Rescuers Down Under* (1990), and *Atlantis: The Lost Empire* (2001).

Of the three animated movies produced by the Studios from 1955 to 1961, *Sleeping Beauty* was the one that looked back the most. The 1959 classic not only looks back to the model of fairy-tale princess stories like those of *Snow White and the Seven Dwarfs* and *Cinderella* but also owes a great deal to *Fantasia,* not only in its adaptation of a classical ballet, but also in the manner in which it pushed the envelope for artistry in animated features. While the Studios would return to the genre of fairy tales in 1989 with *The Little Mermaid,* it would be hard to make a strong comparison between relatively recent princess films such as *Beauty and the Beast* (1991), *Aladdin* (1992), and *The Princess and the Frog* (2009) and *Sleeping Beauty,* with its classically minded score and emphasis of visual artistry. Thus, the animated films of this time period, 1955–1961, find the Studios starting a new era, while making a final acknowledgment of a previous one.

Chapter 9

THE SWORD IN THE STONE AND THE JUNGLE BOOK

T. H. White (1906–1964) published his book *The Sword in the Stone* in 1938. This was the first in what would become a series of four books on the legend of King Arthur. The final installment in The Once and Future King series was published in 1958. The popular series became the basis for Alan Jay Lerner (1918–1986) and Frederick Loewe's (1901–1988) musical *Camelot* (1960).

Disney decided to adapt the first book in the series for their eighteenth animated feature. The songs for the movie were written by brothers Richard and Robert Sherman. The score for the film was composed by George Bruns, with Franklyn Marks acting as an orchestrator.

ROBERT AND RICHARD SHERMAN

Robert and Richard Sherman (Photo 9.1) were born into a musical family. Their paternal grandfather, Samuel Sherman, was a concertmaster, first violinist, and composer at the court of Emperor Franz Josef (1830–1916) in Prague. Samuel brought his family to America in 1909, settling in New York City. Samuel left his wife Lena and their children due to stress over not being able to find work.

Despite having a musician as a father, Samuel's son (and Robert and Richard's father) Al Sherman (1897–1973) was self-taught as a pianist. Al worked as pianist providing improvised mood music on the sets of silent films, and was signed by Universal Studios in 1916, appearing in several movies alongside stars such as Mary Pickford, Mary Fuller (1888–1973), and William Powell (1892–1984). Al has had his songs performed by a variety of artists, including: Al Jolson (1886–1950), Eddie Cantor (1892–1964), Duke Ellington (1899–1974), Louis Armstrong, Rudy Vallee, Bing Crosby, Lawrence Welk, Tommy Dorsey (1905–1956), Ozzie Nelson (1906–1975), Benny Goodman (1909–1987), Billie

Photo 9.1: Richard M. Sherman and Robert B. Sherman in 1964—Photo courtesy of Robert J. Sherman, Trustee of the Robert B. Sherman Administrative Trust created under the Sherman Family Trust.—© Disney

Holiday (1915–1959), Frank Sinatra (1915–1998), Ella Fitzgerald (1917–1996), Peggy Lee, Patti Page (1927–), and Cyndi Lauper (1953–).

Al Sherman never formally worked with animation. However, a 1933 song that he cowrote with Buddy Fields (1889–1965) and Al Lewis (1901–1967), "You've Got to be a Football Hero," became the topic for a 1935 Popeye cartoon of the same name. Likewise, a 1934 song cowritten with Abner Silver (1899–1966) and Al Lewis called "No! No! A Thousand Times No!" was used in a 1935 Betty Boop cartoon of the same name.

Born in New York City on December 19, 1925, Robert Bernard Sherman was the first born of Al and Rosa (Dancis) Sherman. Al paid for the hospital bill with a royalty check for a song of his titled "Save Your Sorrow" (1925). As a child, Robert played violin, piano, and ukulele, and enjoyed painting and writing poetry. He attended PS 241 and the Ethical Culture Fieldston School.

Richard Morton Sherman was born nearly three years later on June 12, 1928. The life of a professional songwriter caused the Sherman family to move frequently, from hotel to hotel, from apartment to apartment.[1] In 1937 the family moved to Beverly Hills, California, and as fate would have it, one of the first memories the brothers had of California related to their future employer, as Robert related: "Our first impression of Hollywood when we arrived as youngsters in 1937 had been the street in front of the Carthay Circle Theater. It was resplendent with Disney characters from the premiere of *Snow White*. What a way to see Hollywood for the first time."[2]

After the move Robert attended El Rodeo School, where he wrote scripts for radio and stage productions. One of these, *Armistice and Dedication Day*, earned the then sixteen-year-old a citation from the War Department, as well as a prize of several thousand dollars in war bonds. During high school, Richard became interested in music, learning to play piccolo, flute, clarinet, and piano.

At seventeen Robert received permission from his parents to enlist in the army. In April of 1945, he and his squadron were the first Allied troops to enter Dachau, only hours after the concentration camp had been abandoned by the German military. On Thursday, April 12, 1945, the day that President Franklin D. Roosevelt died, Robert was shot in the knee, resulting in the songwriter having to walk with a cane for the remainder of his life. Furthermore, due to a snafu, Robert's parents received a telegram the following day notifying them that their son had been killed in action.[3] Richard spent the weekend trying to convince his parents that it was a mistake.[4] On Monday the Shermans thankfully received a second telegram, letting them know that Robert was alive.[5]

Sherman was sent to Taunton and Bournemouth, England, to recover from his injury. During this time he developed a fascination with British culture. A decorated soldier, Robert earned two Battle Stars, a World War II Victory Medal, a Good Conduct Medal, and a Purple Heart, as well as American and European-African-Middle Eastern Campaign Medals. He also earned several badges: Combat Infantry, Marksman (carbine), and Expert (rifle and grenade). One coincidence that foreshadowed Robert's future career was that the hospital ship that brought him home to the states from England was the *A. A. Milne*.[6]

While Robert was in the service, Richard studied briefly at the University of Southern California. During a rehearsal with the marching band, he began to improvise a countermelody. After being scolded by the conductor, he decided he did not want to be a performing musician, "playing the same notes over and over."[7]

After Robert returned to the States, both Sherman brothers attended Bard College, starting their studies in January 1946. Robert's two years in the army allowed Richard to catch up to his older brother scholastically. At Bard, Richard studied music, while Robert majored in English literature and painting. Meanwhile, Robert studied literature under Dr. Irma Brandeis (1905–1990). Robert kept very busy during his college years: "I began seriously painting during my years at Bard, and I've continued to dabble in oils ever since. In those busy days at Bard, I also wrote two novels, four plays, and 75 short stories—all while acting as the editor, frequent contributor, and sometimes cover artist for *The Bardian*, our college newspaper."[8] Both Sherman brothers valued their experience at

Bard, from which they graduated in June of 1949. During the Korean conflict, Richard was drafted into the army, serving from 1953 to 1955, and conducting a band and a glee club.

After graduating from Bard, the brothers moved to Los Angeles, where they shared a fifty-dollar-a-month apartment.[9] Their songwriting father challenged the two of them to "write a song that a kid would spend his lunch money on."[10] As Robert put it, "Dad felt that we were gifted guys, but that we should work together. So we gave it a try."[11] The first significant hit by the duo was "Gold Can Buy You Anything But Love" (1951), which was recorded by Gene Autry (1907–1998). Another early song to come from the brothers was "Things I Might Have Been" (1953), which was recorded by Kitty Wells (1919–2012).

Jeff Kurtti, who collaborated on their book *Walt's Music: From Before to Beyond*, asked the brothers how they begin work on a song, and Robert looked at Richard, and stated, "We start with a story."[12] Such an approach would have endeared the songwriters to Walt. Furthermore, the brothers elaborated on their approach to songwriting in *Walt's Time*: "We call our system 'Shermanizing.' It's a sort of verbal ping-pong, with ideas and phrases and snatches of melody bouncing back and forth between us. Once one of us hits on an inspired phrase, then that inspires the song."[13] Thus, according to this summary, the brothers wrote the songs together, neither specializing in music or lyrics.

Richard elaborated on the unique give-and-take inherent to their collaboration process:

> "We read each other's mind . . . I'll start it, and then he'll finish it. I can say one word and that will trigger something in Bob and he'll know what I'm talking about. He'll say, 'Oh, that was 1937,' and I'll know exactly what he means."[14] Clearly, their cooperative efforts were well served by their siblinghood. When discussing their creative process, Robert emphasized the intellectual component, adding, "It's not like just sitting there banging on the piano throwing lines in the air. It's reasoning something through, discussing."[15]

The duo received further advice from their father, who told them that a successful song must "resolve the three s's: simple, singable and sincere."[16] The two expanded on the last of these three in *Walt's Time*: "It's so easy to rub our noses in the crud of the world, but it's a great deal harder to look on the bright side. We believe that a glass of water is always half-filled, never empty. This world is what we've got, so let's look for the best part!"[17] It is likely that this optimistic viewpoint is one of the major reasons for the success of the Sherman brothers at the Studios, as well as one of the contributing factors of the close relationship that developed between the two and their notoriously optimistic boss.

Richard went into greater detail about their dedication to simplistic melodic writing:

We're not ultra-sophisticated writers, but there's sophistication in our simplicity . . . So many times people don't know how difficult it is to get a clean,
original line. There is a lot of craft in getting it simple, and if the statement
is made right, it's that little pebble dropped in a clear pool, and all the ripples
start floating out around it.[18]

Richard elaborated on the deceptive simplicity of songwriting: "Dad was a
great songwriter . . . in the beginning, we sort of said, 'Well that's what Dad
does; he writes popular songs.' But later, we began to realize what an art it is to
write that stuff. You really have to know how to get the world on the head of a
pin."[19] Richard also commented that writing cheery music is much more of a
challenge than writing sad music: "You know it's very difficult to write happy.
You can compose a minor melody in two minutes, it's nothing, but a happy
tune, a really originally happy tune, that's vibrant and full of joy, you gotta dig
for that. Major chords, oh, that's a big wall."[20]

Composing jubilant music with an elegant simplicity would become the
hallmark of their years at The Walt Disney Studios and would continue into
their post-Disney careers.

While the Sherman brothers are well known for writing happy music, many
of their songs have melancholy moments in them. These occasions provide
contrast to the overall mood of the song. As Richard Sherman noted, "Unless
you have shades of gray and blackness, the sun doesn't shine as brightly."[21]

The dedication that the Sherman brothers had to a cheery, optimistic worldview exists in part due to Robert's experiences in the Second World War. As
Richard put it in *Walt's Time*:

Bob had some pretty horrible experiences. On April 12th, 1945, the day that
Franklin Roosevelt died, Bob was seriously wounded in the knee. He would
never again participate in the sports and physical activities that he loved.
In the war, he saw terrible, tragic things. He came back changed. War has
that kind of effect. Bob had seen enough ugliness for a lifetime, and forever
turned away from it. He embraced the beautiful things of life with a renewed
fervor, and his desire to create beauty—whether it be through stories, songs,
paintings or sculpture—became his primary motivation.[22]

Not only does the experience explain Robert's devotion to beauty, it may also
explain in part his productivity as an artist.

Robert's youngest son, Robert Jason Sherman, lived with his father for the
last decade of the senior songwriter's life.[23] The son, who is also a composer,
received a lot of advice from his father on the art of songwriting during this
period.[24] While the father did not play musical instruments much during his
adult years and was "very famous for his lyric writing," his son considers him

to have been "very much a musician."[25] Robert J. Sherman said of his father's mentorship: "Most of his critiques were not really about the lyrics of my songs. They tended to be more about the music, the structure, the chord progressions, and melody lines."[26] Thus, while Robert B. Sherman specialized in lyrics, he certainly had detailed knowledge of music, and a strong regard about how musical elements serve the art of songwriting.[27]

Richard was influenced by several classic songwriters: Cole Porter, Noel Coward (1899–1973), Richard Rodgers, Lorenz Hart (1895–1943), Oscar Hammerstein II, and Harold Arlen (1905–1986).[28] He stated, "All of these great writers who wrote in the past were part of my life, part of my childhood."[29] In terms of rock and roll, Richard admired the work of Jerry Leiber (1933–2011) and Mike Stoller (1933–).[30]

Richard routinely brought his work home, as his son Gregg recalled in an interview from 2012: "My dad never was done working. We had five pianos in the house. At any given moment when we'd be sitting at a dinner table or whatever, he would just bolt out of his chair without saying a word to anybody and continue to work on the song . . . there was music all the time."[31] Certainly such dedication contributed to the brothers' success as songwriters.

Richard and Robert cowrote a song called "Tall Paul" (1958) with Bob Roberts. The song featured a twist on a trend of the time to write songs with female names in the title.[32] The brothers believed in the song enough to personally finance three thousand single records, which they sent to DJs across the country.[33] This version of the song was recorded by Mouseketeer Judy Harriet (1942–). Eventually, a representative of Disney's record company encountered the song while visiting a disc jockey.[34] The representative felt "Tall Paul" would be a good match for Mouseketeer Annette Funicello (1942–2013).[35] Funicello's recording sold 700,000 copies and hit number seven on the *Billboard* chart, becoming the first top ten hit for both the brothers and Annette.[36] The collaboration between the brothers and Funicello continued, resulting in some three dozen songs written for the singer by the duo between 1958 and 1965.[37]

STAFF SONGWRITERS AT DISNEY

Walt was looking for songwriters to add to his full-time staff.[38] He approached Jimmy Johnson, who was the general manager of the Walt Disney Music Company, and asked, "These Sherman boys that you have writing songs for Annette—are they any good?"[39] The Studios' head added, "I'm going to make a film in England with Annette. There's a spot for a song. Do you think the Shermans would be interested?"[40] The brothers jumped at the opportunity and wrote "The Strumming Song" for *The Horsemasters* (1961).

The songwriters brought the song to Johnson on a Monday, and Johnson in turn called Walt's secretary to see if they could play the song for him. When they arrived at his office, Walt was preoccupied with *The Parent Trap*. He launched into a description of *The Parent Trap*. Johnson interrupted, explaining they were there to play the song for *The Horsemasters*.[41] While Walt seemed put out by the situation, Johnson convinced him to listen to the song.[42] Walt was satisfied, so Johnson pressed his luck, suggesting, "As long as the boys are here, maybe you'd like to give them a crack at the songs for the Hayley Mills picture."[43] Walt consented, and the brothers left with an additional assignment: to write a title song for *The Parent Trap*.

After their having written a total of six songs for the Studios, Walt handed a copy of the Pamela L. Travers (1899–1996) book *Mary Poppins* (1934) to the Shermans, asking them to read the book and tell him what they thought of it.[44] For the next two weeks, the brothers read the book, selected what they felt was the best material, linked the ideas together as a plot, and wrote three sample songs.[45] The songwriting duo set up a half-hour meeting with Walt, which turned into an hour-and-a-half meeting when the studio head cancelled his lunch and sent out for sandwiches.[46] Impressed with their work, Walt offered the brothers full-time jobs, saying, "You guys really like to work. How'd you like to work for me?"[47] Needless to say, the brothers accepted.

Following the meeting, Walt called Johnson to negotiate how the brothers would be paid, stating:

> I like these boys. I think I can work with them. I'd like to put them on the payroll, but they want too damn much money for staff songwriters. Your music company is going to benefit from all these great song copyrights they are sure to produce, so I think you should bear half their salaries.[48]

Thus, the filmmaker made their jobs a joint appointment between the Studios and the music company, where each division paid half the brothers' salaries.[49] Richard and Robert each received a weekly salary, mechanical royalties, and performance royalties.[50] The first two contracts the brothers had with the Studios were for six months, while the next two contracts each had a one-year term, and the final two had three-year terms.[51]

Adjoining the brothers' office (3C-11) in the Animation Building, was 3C-12, then occupied by Roy Williams (1907–1976).[52] Williams, who became known as one of the adult hosts of the *Mickey Mouse Club*, worked in the Studios as an artist and a storyman. He was best known for the gags he wrote for cartoon shorts. The brothers developed a close relationship with the jovial Williams, who frequently would sketch caricatures of the Shermans and slip the drawings under the door to amuse the brothers.[53]

Early in their days at the Studios, the duo was thought of as "the rock-and-roll guys."[54] The Shermans reflected that they "were politely tolerated but felt like outsiders."[55] They had a talent, though, for pleasing the boss, which caused Johnson to dub the duo "the come-through boys."[56] As their assignments became increasingly varied, they earned the respect of their more straitlaced colleagues.[57] Accordingly, their status at the Studios grew, and the brothers began to lunch with Johnson at the "Writers' Table" in the Coral Room, the Studios' executive dining room.[58]

While Walt often had clear ideas about what he was looking for in music, the brothers did not feel constrained by such directives: "When we worked with Walt, we did what we liked to do, rather than what we thought he wanted us to do. After all, he hired us for our creative ability. You couldn't try to pigeonhole him, you just did your best and waited for his response."[59]

The brothers enjoyed working for the filmmaker, as Richard stated: "Walt would throw us things, and we would catch them and run with them . . . he was very inspiring, and we were very much on his wavelength."[60] Over time the duo formed a close relationship with the filmmaker, who took a personal interest in the hardworking brothers. Furthermore, Walt suggested that they formalize their names from Bob and Dick Sherman to Robert and Richard Sherman in order to lend an air of "dignity."[61] The brothers went one step further by adding their middle initials.[62]

Their boss notoriously slight on praise, the brothers got used to the stock phrase that Walt would use when he was pleased with their music: "That'll work."[63] Notwithstanding, the duo treasured their time working for Walt. As Richard stated, "I know our work was inspired by Walt Disney and it's been a real gift."[64] Robert added: "There's a line in *Mary Poppins* that goes, ;A man has dreams of walking with giants. To carve his niche in the edifice of time.' At Disney, we've walked with giants."[65] The use of the plural here denotes that the songwriter considered other unnamed collaborators in his high praise.

The brothers had special admiration for their boss. Robert appreciatively stated . . . I don't think any songwriters were ever more honored by the public through a man with the stature of Walt Disney. He gave us an opportunity to become songwriters of stature.[66] Despite the humility of the duo, it is hard to argue with Robert's assertion.

Ultimately, the brothers earned the respect of their colleagues. Buddy Baker reflected, "The Sherman brothers were just marvelous young guys. They were easy to work with and we understood each other. We never had a cross word, ever."[67] Given the high-stakes environment of a major film studio, such an assessment is particularly meaningful.

The Sherman brothers' collaboration with Disney bore rich fruit, yielding over two hundred songs, many of which are both memorable and popular. The large size of this catalog is not surprising, given how hard Walt worked them.

The filmmaker often had them laboring on several projects at a time. As Walt quipped, "You're not really working unless you're doing five or six things at the same time."[68]

While many of these songs became hits, Richard knew that mere popularity was not the goal: "The songs you write for a production are not necessarily meant to be hit songs. They're meant to work for a scene, they're meant to work for a situation or character."[69] Despite this critical self-assessment, the strong catalog of songs written by the brothers places them amongst the most successful songwriters of all time.

They felt that their songs had to reinforce the characters. As Richard related:

> Everything had to feel right for the character, and those characters are as real as a live action actor. Like when we were working on "The Wonderful Thing About Tiggers" for Tigger, the character. He's a bouncy little guy. It had to just bounce like him ... There's no other way to write for Tigger than what we wrote, and that's the way we feel about it ... Winnie the Pooh was a gentle sweet personality. He had to have a sweet gentleness about him.[70]

Thus, the brothers were primarily concerned with narrative and character development.

While such an approach may sound difficult, Richard enjoys working from a story. He found working outside the context of a film to be a challenge. In a 2013 interview he stated, "The hardest thing in the world is to sit in a room with no story, no characters, no problem, just say write a song, and make it a hit."[71]

MUSIC FOR FILM, TELEVISION, AND THEME PARKS

The Sherman brothers wrote songs for numerous Disney films, including: *The Absent-Minded Professor, In Search of the Castaways, Moon Pilot, Big Red* (1962), *The Legend of Lobo* (1962), *The Miracle of the White Stallions, Summer Magic* (1963), *The Sword in the Stone, Mary Poppins, Those Calloways* (1965), *The Monkey's Uncle* (1965), *That Darn Cat!* (1965), *Follow Me, Boys!, The Adventures of Bullwhip Griffin, Monkeys, Go Home!* (1967), *The Gnome-Mobile* (1967), *The Happiest Millionaire* (1967), *The Jungle Book, The One and Only, Genuine, Original Family Band* (1968), *The Aristocats*, and *Bedknobs and Broomsticks* (1971). The duo composed several songs for the nineteen-minute short *A Symposium on Popular Songs* (1962), which lampooned popular music stylings from a variety of eras. The brothers also penned songs for several *Winnie the Pooh* shorts that were later assembled into *The Many Adventures of Winnie the Pooh* (1977). After an almost thirty-year break from The Walt Disney Studios, the Sherman brothers reunited to create songs for *The Tigger Movie* (2000).

The songwriting siblings wrote the "Swiss Family Robinson Calypso" for an episode of *Walt Disney Presents* entitled "Escape to Paradise" (1960). They wrote two songs, "Como Esta Usted?" and "Amo Que Paso?" for Annette Funicello for her appearance on a one-hour episode of *Zorro* called "The Postponed Wedding" on *Walt Disney Presents* (1961). Another episode, "Texas John Slaughter: A Holster Full of Law," contains a song by the brothers called "Come Light the Lovelight." The brothers also wrote two songs for the first episode of *Walt Disney's Wonderful World of Color*: "The Green with Envy Blues" (1961) and "The Spectrum Song" (1961). They also composed the theme song for the show *The Wonderful World of Color* (1961) and the song "Disneyland '61" for an episode of the same name. The duo penned "The Strumming Song" for season eight's "The Horsemasters" (episodes 2 and 3),[72] and "Hang a Lantern in Your Window" and "Mr. Piano Man" for the first episode of season nine, "The Golden Horseshoe Revue" (1962). The brothers wrote three songs that appeared on the two-part movie *Escapade in Florence* (1962). They also penned the theme song for several other two-episode movies, including: *The Mooncussers* (1962), *Johnny Shiloh* (1963), and *The Ballad of Hector the Stowaway Dog* (1964).

The Sherman brothers wrote numerous songs for Disney theme parks, such as "The Tiki, Tiki, Tiki Room" (1963), "it's a small world" (1964), "There's a Great Big Beautiful Tomorrow" (1964), "Miracles from Molecules" (1967), "The Glorious Fourth" (1974), and "The Best Time of Your Life" (1974) for Disneyland and the Magic Kingdom at the Walt Disney World Resort. They also created six songs themed on the Orange Bird character that was designed for the Walt Disney World Resort's Sunshine Pavilion, home of the Enchanted Tiki Birds. The melody for one of these songs, "I'll Fly the Sky-Way," was originally written for *The Aristocats*.[73] "The Computer Song" (1982), "Magic Journeys" (1982), "Makin' Memories" (1982), "One Little Spark" (1982), and "The World Showcase March" (1982) were created for EPCOT Center. The siblings originally wrote "Meet the World" (1983) for an attraction originally designed for the Japan Pavilion in EPCOT Center. Ultimately, the attraction in question was featured in Tokyo Disneyland.

FILMED APPEARANCES, PERFORMANCES, AND POST-DISNEY CAREER

Richard Sherman occasionally worked as a performer, playing the kazoo part for the spirited version of "Entrance of the Gladiators" that accompanies the animated penguins in *Mary Poppins*. He also sang the part of Uncle Albert for the Disneyland Records recording of "I Love to Laugh."[74] In addition, the brothers have appeared in numerous shorts about their work as songwriters and their contributions to Disney films. They also collaborated on a book about their work with Walt Disney, titled *Walt's Time: From Before to Beyond* (1998). *The Boys: The Sherman Brothers' Story*, a documentary about the siblings, was released by Walt Disney Pictures in 2009. This documentary was directed by Robert's son Jeffrey and Richard's son, Gregory.

After leaving Disney, the Sherman brothers worked on their collaborations in a studio in West Hollywood,[75] writing music for such non-Disney films as *Chitty Chitty Bang Bang* (1968), *Snoopy, Come Home* (1972), *Charlotte's Web* (1973), *Tom Sawyer* (1973), *Huckleberry Finn* (1974), *The Slipper and the Rose: The Story of Cinderella* (1976), *The Magic of Lassie* (1978), *Little Nemo: Adventures in Slumberland* (1989), and *The Mighty Kong* (1998). They are also known for having written the song "You're Sixteen" (1960), which was recorded both by Johnny Burnette (1934–1964) and by Ringo Starr (1940–). The Burnette recording peaked at number eight on the charts, while the version by the ex-Beatle reached number one. An earlier song by the duo, "The Things I Might Have Been" (1953), was recorded by Wade Ray (1913–1998), Kitty Wells (1919–2012), Willie Nelson (1933–), Johnny Mathis, Kris Kristofferson (1936–) and Rita Coolidge (1945–), Wanda Jackson (1937–), and Tom Morrell (1938–).

AWARDS, HONORS, AND PERSONAL LIVES

Richard and Robert Sherman won two Academy Awards, one for the score to *Mary Poppins*, and another for Best Song ("Chim Chim Cher-ee" from the same film). The duo has received several Best Song nominations: "Chitty Chitty Bang Bang," "The Age of Not Believing" (from *Bedknobs and Broomsticks*), "The Slipper and the Rose Waltz," and "When You're Loved" (from *The Magic of Lassie*). They have also been nominated in the Best Score category for *Bedknobs and Broomsticks*, *Tom Sawyer*, and *The Slipper and the Rose: The Story of Cinderella*.

The Sherman brothers have been nominated for several Golden Globe Awards: for *Mary Poppins*, *Chitty Chitty Bang Bang* (both Best Score and Best Song), *Tom Sawyer*, and *The Slipper and the Rose: The Story of Cinderella*. The soundtrack to *Mary Poppins* yielded the brothers a Grammy Award for Best Original Score. In 2014 the original cast soundtrack of *Mary Poppins* was inducted into the Grammy Hall of Fame. "Chim Chim Cher-ee" was awarded a Golden Laurel, while "That Darn Cat" from the film of the same name won third place in the Laurel Awards in 1966. The brothers were awarded second place in the category Music Men in the 1965 Laurel Awards, the same year that "Chim Chim Cher-ee" was honored.

The Slipper and the Rose was also nominated for a British Academy of Film and Television Arts Award. The brothers were nominated for an Annie Award in 2000 for the song "Round My Family Tree" from *The Tigger Movie*. Three years later, they were honored with the Winsor McCay Award, for lifetime achievement in the field of animated films. On May 21, 2011, their alma mater, Bard College, awarded the brothers honorary doctorates. A star on Hollywood's Walk of Fame was added for the duo on November 17, 1976, and they were inducted into the Songwriters Hall of Fame in 2005. On November 17, 2008, they garnered a National Medal of Arts awarded by President George W. Bush (1946–).

The Walt Disney Studios awarded the brothers a Mousecar in 1985 and named them as Disney Legends in 1990. Two decades later a window honoring them was unveiled at Disneyland's Main Street U.S.A. Richard Sherman once confided in Disney Historian Jim Korkis that one of the costs of being a Disney Legend is that every fan sends the songwriter items to autograph without sending return postage or packaging material.[76] Thus, Richard makes nearly weekly trips to the post office sending items to fans, paying for postage and packaging out of his own pocket.[77]

Working together for so many years caused the relationship between the brothers to be strained. Jeffrey Sherman, Robert's son, spoke of this in an interview in 2009: "I heard a lot of things. My dad would often come home, very upset, and maybe he wouldn't talk to me but you'd sure hear it. I knew there were issues and I'd hear him complaining."[78] At one point, Jeffrey asked his father why he continued to work with his brother when it made him so unhappy. Robert responded, "Because we're really good at it. We're successful, and I don't think I could do this with anybody else."[79]

Dee Dee Wood, a choreographer who worked with the Sherman brothers on *Mary Poppins* contrasted the their personas: "Richard was the forceful one and seemed to lead everything. Robert was sweet and laid back, and when he had something to add he would say it without having to jump into the conversation like Richard."[80] Wood added, "They both were very nice."[81]

Jeff Kurtti assessed, "Robert was hard to get to know . . . there was a structure to his life in terms of who he let in."[82] Kurtti went on to say that "he was reserved about how he parceled out his words, and he was a listener . . . he budgeted his words so carefully."[83] The author also wondered about whether the songwriter was happy with the way in which his career worked out:

> He was a complicated guy though. On a lot of occasions I thought, you know he had this extraordinary success professionally, and financially, and culturally, and I wondered a lot of the times though if it wasn't exactly the success he wanted . . . He yearned to write, and he yearned to write of serious things. He yearned to write a novel, or to write a great book . . . He was so multi-talented he was an artist, sculptor. It's almost like there weren't enough hours in the day for him to express all of the things that he held inside and held in such reserve.[84]

Kurtti felt that Robert's introspection served as a perfect complement to his brother's playfulness, resulting in one of the most successful songwriting duos of all time.[85]

Robert married his second wife, Joyce Sasner, on September 15, 1953. The couple had four children: Laurie Shane, Jeffrey Craig, Andrea Tracy, and Robert Jason. Jeffrey Sherman went on to write and produce movies and television. Robert J. Sherman helped his father adapt *Chitty Chitty Bang Bang* and *Mary Poppins* to stage musicals.[86] He became a composer, writing the musical *Bumblescratch*. Robert J. Sherman also took over management of World Music Corporation when his father died, in London on March 5, 2012.

Richard Sherman married Ursula Gluck on July 6, 1957. The couple has two children, Gregg and Victoria. Richard also has another daughter, Linda, from a previous marriage to Corinne Newman. Jeff Kurtti described the composer's personality: "Dick is ebullience, and he's talkative, and he's an entertainer, and he's got an upbeat personality, and it's very embracing."[87]

THE SWORD IN THE STONE

Leonard Maltin criticizes *The Sword in the Stone* for having its mind too much in the sixties.[88] This is perhaps most notable in the stylistically inconsistent opening title music. The most prominent melody during this sequence is "That's What Makes the World Go Round." The first orchestration of this melody features very light swing-style snare drumming, while the end of the bridge is punctuated by a trumpet line typical of musical theater (Figure 9.1). A later arrangement of the same tune in the opening drifts from a jazz piano incarnation to being accompanied by a bossa nova vamp.

Such popular influence is understandable in the first animated film from the Studios since *One Hundred and One Dalmatians*, another score written by Bruns and orchestrated by Marks. It is also easily explained by the fact that Merlin has traveled to the future, mentioning indoor plumbing and electricity. In fact, Merlin returns from the future at one point clad in a Hawaiian shirt, having come from Bermuda. Despite such justifications for stylistic inconsistency, the film does suffer a bit from disparity.

Figure 9.1. Trumpet line from "That's What Makes the World Go Round"—THAT'S WHAT MAKES THE WORLD GO ROUND—From THE SWORD IN THE STONE—Words and Music by Richard M. Sherman and Robert B. Sherman—© 1963 Wonderland Music Company, Inc.

Perhaps the best example of this dissimilarity can be heard in the difference between the vaguely jazzy title music and the music that accompanies the following storybook sequence. The utilization of the opening-book device harks back to films such as *Snow White and the Seven Dwarfs, Pinocchio, Cinderella*, and *Sleeping Beauty*. In *The Sword in the Stone*, this opening book is accompanied by a muted brass fanfare. It is followed by a ballad accompanied by solo guitar. While the orchestration for this ballad is unique, the singing style of the vocalist, Fred Darian (1927–), most closely recalls that of "Love Is a Song" from *Bambi*. A choir enters on the word "miracle" from the lyric "and that miracle appeared in London town."[89] This orchestrational change coincides with a heavenly beam of light shining down upon Excalibur. This recalls the entrance of the choir that accompanies the Prince's kiss at the end of *Snow White and the Seven Dwarfs*. Thus, in less than three minutes' time, the soundtrack stylistically alludes to over two decades' worth of Disney films.

The song in *The Sword in the Stone* that most clearly resembles a number from another Disney animated feature is "Higitus Figitus." This song is similar in style and function to "Bibbidi-Bobbidi-Boo" from *Cinderella*. Not only are both magic songs in compound duple meters, both use nonsense words, and help establish the characters as absentminded. This bumbling nature softens the image of both the magician and the Fairy Godmother.

Like other songs in Disney animated films, "Higitus Figitus" is introduced with rhyming dialog. While the song is not used as a leitmotif, a jazzy version of "Higitus Figitus" appears later in the film when Merlin casts a spell to get the dishes to wash themselves. Another vague reference to the tune occurs shortly before the song appears in the film. When Merlin offers Wart a cup of tea, the self-animated sugar bowl that sweetens the boy's beverage is accompanied by music with a similar compound duple rhythmic feel as "Higitus Figitus."

The Sherman brothers were very fond of using made-up words in their songs. While "Higitus Figitus" is saturated with such imaginative vocabulary, it is not the only song in the film to contain invented words. "A Most Befuddling Thing" contains words such as "discombooberation," "hodge-podgical," and "confusiling."[90] Likewise, "Mad Madam Mim" features the magical phrase "Zim zabberim zim."[91]

In terms of the moral of the film, "That's What Makes the World Go Round" is the movie's central song. In it, Merlin tells Wart, "You see, my boy, it's nature's way / Upon the weak the strong ones prey."[92] He goes on to say, "The strong will try to conquer you … unless you use your intellect."[93] The message of the song is also to aspire to better things, to "set your sights upon the heights, don't be a mediocrity."[94] This line is followed by a criticism of predestination, "Don't just wait and trust to fate, and say 'That's how it's meant to be.'"[95]

The Sherman brothers returned to this idea in their movie musical *Tom Sawyer*. In it the character Muff Potter communicates the opposite view to this sentiment to Tom and Huck in the song "A Man's Gotta Be (What He Was Born to Be)." Potter states it is useless to strive for a better future, since, "It's a matter of destiny, who'll you'll be ... There ain't no fightin' fate."[96] Potter's portrayal in the film is of a ne'er-do-well drunk, allowing Tom to realize the error of the inebriate's point of view by the end of the film, thus imparting a similar moral lesson as "That's What Makes the World Go Round."

There were two songs that the Sherman brothers wrote for *The Sword in the Stone* that were not used in the film. "Blue Oak Tree" was to be sung by the Knights of the Round Table. The song expresses senseless devotion to an empty symbol, as well as the brute power pledged to this symbol without reason. In contrast, "The Magic Key," which features a very Gilbert and Sullivan–esque flavor, was a song that Merlin would sing to Wart to express the importance of education. While not included in the movie, both songs were released on the Disneyland Records album *All the Songs from "The Sword in the Stone"* (1963).

RECEPTION

The Sword in the Stone was the first animated film that the Sherman brothers worked on. They were enthusiastic about the project, as Robert related:

> We enjoyed it immensely, because with animated films the songs seem so much more important to the entire story line of the film. For example, the song "Higitus Figitus" was written to both establish Merlin's rather bumbling character and to advance the story line of the film. That's something you don't get to do when just writing popular songs.[97]

While the Sherman brothers enjoyed working on *The Sword in the Stone*, they were not satisfied with the movie, stating, "*The Sword in the Stone* has many delightful moments, but we've never been happy with it as a whole."[98] Among other things, the songwriters were disappointed that the melodies of their songs were not worked into the score as leitmotifs.[99]

Ultimately, the Sherman brothers wrote music for four Disney animated features, *The Sword in the Stone, The Jungle Book, The Aristocats,* and *The Tigger Movie.* A fifth animated Disney feature, *The Many Adventures of Winnie the Pooh,* was assembled out of several shorts for which they wrote songs. The two also wrote music for three non-Disney animated features: *Snoopy, Come Home, Charlotte's Web,* and *Little Nemo: Adventures in Slumberland.* They even wrote songs for the DePatie-Freleng Enterprises animated television short *Goldilocks* (1971).

The Sherman brothers' songs were seen as a strong selling point for *The Sword in the Stone.* In fact, the original promotional poster for the film enthuses,

"It's HIGITUS-FIGITUS for magical mirth and music!"[100] Premiering in New York City on Christmas Day, 1963, the movie performed well at the box office, grossing 4.5 million dollars. The film received a single Academy Award nomination, for Best Score.

There was an inadvertent timeliness to the release of the film, slightly more than a month after the assassination of President John Fitzgerald Kennedy (1917–1963). An interview with Jacqueline Kennedy (1929–1994) appeared in *Life* magazine on December 3.[101] In the article the president's widow connected her late husband to the legend of Camelot.[102] She mentioned that JFK had been a classmate of Alan Jay Lerner while at Harvard, and that the president had been a fan of the musical *Camelot*.[103] She then directly associated her husband's legacy to King Arthur, stating, "There will be great presidents again, but there will never be another Camelot."[104] From that moment on, Americans would always connect the name Camelot with the beloved first family. A little more than three weeks later, Disney's animated feature premiered.

The Sword in the Stone has never entered the pantheon of classic Disney animated features. Perhaps the reason is that the film lacks an emotional center. The closest the movie comes to such a moment is when Wart begins to cry after Sir Ector drives Merlin away. However, this moment is not reinforced with song.

The Sword in the Stone is a unique film in the catalog of Disney animated features. The movie's emphasis on the importance of education makes it one of the Studios' best films in terms of positive messages. Likewise, the subplot of Sir Kay's bullying of Wart lends the story a David-and-Goliath-like appeal.

THE JUNGLE BOOK

Bill Peet, who had been a storywriter for *The Sword in the Stone*, approached Walt with the idea of using *The Jungle Book* by Rudyard Kipling (1865–1936) for the Studios' next animated film. Peet worked on the project with little supervision from Walt and stayed relatively close to the original Kipling, resulting in a fairly dark story. Due to the demands of creating Disneyland, and starting two television series, Walt had spent little of his time supervising the Studios' animated features. However, he decided to become more involved with *The Jungle Book*.[105] He felt Peet's script was too dark, and an argument over the project ensued between the writer and the studio head. Peet resigned and was replaced by Larry Clemmons (1906–1988).

A similar process happened with music. Originally, Terry Gilkyson (1916–1999) was hired to write the songs for the project, which was tentatively titled *Jungle Boy*. The songwriter, who had composed the theme song for *The Scarecrow of Romney Marsh* (1963), wrote relatively dark songs for the film. Again, Walt was not pleased with the tone of the songs, so he was replaced with the

Sherman brothers. However, one song by Gilkyson, "The Bare Necessities," was used in the film, as the animators loved it, and they implored Walt to let it appear in the movie.[106] Out of respect for the duo that had quickly became his favorite songwriters, the filmmaker asked permission from the Sherman brothers to include the song in the movie.[107] They consented. "The Bare Necessities" was rearranged by Van Dyke Parks (1943–), and the other songs for the film were written by the Sherman brothers. The score to the movie was composed by George Bruns, with orchestrations by Walter Sheets (1911–2001). Bruns helped prepare for the score by watching at least one film that featured an Indian music soundtrack.[108]

The title sequence of *The Jungle Book* utilizes the opening-book device that starts numerous Disney animated films. Accompanying this beginning is a theme (Figure 9.2) presented in the bass flute that is associated with Mowgli's journey. In the Disney Music Group's cue sheets (appendix), this melody is referred to as "Jungle Beauty." Bruns would also feature the bass flute prominently in the overture to the Pirates of the Caribbean attraction, which was in production around the same time.

"Jungle Beauty" appeared under the title "Serengeti Serenade" when it was first presented to the public as part of the area music for the International Gardens for the Ford pavilion at the 1964 World's Fair.[109] Regardless of the name of the tune, it represents Mowgli's journey. The theme also occurs when Bagheera takes the man-cub from the wolf pack to bring Mowgli to the village, and it recurs when the boy leaves Bagheera after an argument, shortly before Mowgli meets Baloo. The melody occurs a fourth time when the man-cub is on his own, shortly before Kaa sings "Trust in Me."

Like the song "Blue Oak Tree," an unused song from *The Sword in the Stone*, "Colonel Hathi's March" frames aspects of military drilling as being senseless. In their book *Walt's Time*, the Sherman brothers noted that "Colonel Hathi's March" was their "'tribute' to the pointlessness of constant drilling."[110] These musical expressions of the inanity of drilling may come from the fact that both brothers served in the U.S. Army. "Colonel Hathi's March" also reflects the Victorian era of British colonialism consistent with Kipling's worldview.

Shortly before Mowgli meets Baloo, the man-cub is on his own, and alone. He notices the quiet of the jungle, represented by silence in the soundtrack, and

Figure 9.2. Theme representing Mowgli's journey—JUNGLE BOOK SCORE from THE JUNGLE BOOK—Music by George Bruns—© 1967 Wonderland Music Company

is disquieted by the stillness. This tension is increased by the sound of rustling in the bushes, which is reinforced by accompanying tense music. However, this unease is quickly dispelled by Baloo, who emerges while scatting, "Well it's a doobidy doo, yes it's a doobidy doo."[111] This scatting is similar in concept to material written for an earlier draft of "The Bare Necessities."[112] The manner in which Baloo puts Mowgli at ease through his scatting puts music at the center of the dramatic arc of the scene.

"The Bare Necessities" establishes the character of Baloo, depicting the bear as being carefree and lazy. This portrayal is made most clear through lyrics like "If you act like that bee acts, uh-uh you're working too hard."[113] Other lines confirm Baloo's lack of aspirations: "And don't spend your time lookin' around / For something you want that can't be found / When you find out you can live without it / And go along not thinkin' about it."[114]

This characterization functions to create a mismatched duo of substitute parents in Bagheera and Baloo. The two are thrown together by a shared concern for Mowgli. Thus, the duo, which under any other circumstance would want nothing to do with each other, is forced to work together. In fact, the scene that follows "I Wan'na Be Like You," features ersatz pillow talk between the bear and the panther as Mowgli sleeps. Here Baloo is cast in the role of father, remarking, "That's my boy,"[115] while Bagheera, with his concern for Mowgli, represents an overly protective mother.

Given the jazzy nature of "The Bare Necessities" and Baloo's use of jazz vernacular, the pairing of Bagheera and Baloo presents a contrast between high-class and low-class individuals.[116] Furthermore, the improvisatory nature of the jazz is expressed through Baloo as impulsiveness, and further still as a lack of responsibility, contrasting greatly with Bagheera's character. Meanwhile, Sebastian Cabot's (1918–1977) proper British accent reads as intelligent, wise, and dignified, providing strong contrast with the lovable yet irresponsible bear.

While Bagheera embodies reason, Baloo is driven by impulse. On two occasions the bear enters a trancelike state. Both occur during jazzy numbers: during the scratching sequence of "The Bare Necessities" and during "I Wan'na Be Like You." While the musical settings are quite different, the former sequence descends from a montage of ursine scratching from the True-Life Adventure *Bear Country.*

The sentiments expressed in "The Bare Necessities," namely, that one should be satisfied with what one has, rather than striving for better things, can also be seen in "Under the Sea" from *The Little Mermaid* (1989) and "Hakuna Matata" from *The Lion King.* In all three instances, the songs are well-intentioned pieces of advice that each film ultimately makes clear are bad long-term advice for the protagonist. Thus, they all import the moral lesson that good things are worth working for by expressing the opposite viewpoint, and later showing it to be ineffective, insufficient, or counterproductive. This point of view is reinforced in *The Jungle Book* by having Baloo nearly inadvertently drop a rock on Mowgli's head during "The Bare Necessities." It is further supported by the fact that as the movie progresses it becomes clearer that Bagheera's point of view, that Mowgli should return to the man village, is more in line with the man-cub's best interests than Baloo's opinion that Mowgli should remain in the jungle.

In order to produce a light film like Walt had requested, the Sherman brothers decided to take the darkest part of the story, Mowgli's kidnapping by the king of the apes, and transform it into a fun scene. The resulting song, "I Wan'na Be Like You," is one of the highlights of the movie. The Sherman brothers traveled to Las Vegas in order to play the song for Louis Prima (1910–1978), who would ultimately be performing King Louie, a character who in an early continuity draft was referred to as Lunatic Louie.

While the moniker King Louie works as a double reference to both Prima and to Louis XIV (1638–1715), the powerful French monarch, the character was actually named for Louis Armstrong.[117] The Sherman brothers had initially envisioned Armstrong in the role, until someone mentioned that casting an African American as a monkey could be perceived as racially insensitive.[118]

Jimmy Johnson of Walt Disney Records suggested casting Louis Prima in the part of King Louie:

> I recommended him to Walt, who was a bit dubious. But Louis really wanted the part, so he brought his entire band down to Burbank at his own expense to audition for Walt and the animators. They set up on one of the sound stages and went into their regular Vegas act. As part of the act, Louis' drummer puts on a rubber ape mask and drums away with a whole fistful of sticks, flipping them into the air, catching them, then drumming all over the room on chairs, on the floor, on other instruments. It's a hilarious bit and the animators broke up.[119]

Animator Floyd Norman (1935–) said of Prima, "He was really into being King Louie."[120]

While "I Wan'na Be Like You" is a fun, light romp, the meaning of the song is rather dark. As the lyrics relate, King Louie feels he has reached his limits as an ape and wants to become a man. However, the character believes that the route to manhood is through the ability to make fire. This assertion has doubly sinister overtones. First, it shows King Louie as a character who desires power and dominion. Secondly, it indicates a view of man from the vantage of the animal kingdom, namely, that what separates man from animal is his destructive power.

During the brainstorming session that resulted in "I Wan'na Be Like You," the brothers struggled with finding a way to make the song light. One breakthrough was the idea of incorporating an ape's grunting into the song by using the line,

"I wanna be like you-oo-oo,"[121] to evoke grunting. Richard related another way that using apes as a concept led to the song: "What does an ape do? He swings in a tree. Well, if an ape swings in a tree, we call him the king of the apes, let's call him the king of the swingers. Wow! We were off and running."[122] Thus, the song is used not simply as entertainment, but to help establish the character of King Louie.

Some of the content of "I Wan'na Be Like You" was provided by the performers. Originally, the Sherman brothers intended Baloo to repeat each scat line sung by King Louie.[123] However, when Phil Harris (1904–1995) was brought in to record the part, the musician objected, stating that it would be natural to improvise something different.[124] The brothers agreed with the idea.[125] Among other lines, Harris came up with line, "Get mad, baby!" after King Louie's growl.[126]

Furthermore, when Louis Prima auditioned with his band for the role of King Louie, the Studios filmed the audition. Director Woolie Reitherman (1909–1985) had the animators use this footage as a source for some of the antics of the monkeys in the number.[127] In particular, the sequence contains a serpentine parade of marching ape musicians. Prima was known for having his band follow him single file, as he marched through the audience.

By Floyd Norman's estimation, the George Bruns arrangement of "I Wan'na Be Like You" was much more conservative than Prima's:

> The original tracks recorded by Louis and his band are indeed over the top.
> I don't exaggerate when I say Prima and his band went ape. The final tracks
> you hear on the movie's soundtrack have been toned down. And I mean way,
> way down. Louis Prima at full tilt was more than Disney moviegoers of the
> sixties would have been able to handle.[128]

This assessment of the arrangement of "I Wan'na Be Like You" fits the mold of a tendency in Disney films to lean strongly toward the conservative side of popular music.

Despite Norman's appraisal of the Bruns version as conservative, the sequence contains a humorous endorsement of hotter brands of jazz. During the first solo section of "I Wan'na Be Like You," a small white-tufted ape improvises a legato, lyrical melody. King Louie reacts to this with visual disgust, not only due to the fact that he does not like sharing the spotlight with the ape, but also because he feels the style is too square. This latter point is evidenced by King Louie covering his ears with his hands in combination with the rhythmic, gutteral scat performed by Louie after quieting the smaller ape.

The character Kaa is associated aurally with melodic material (Figure 9.3) in Phrygian mode, played by the bass flute. According to Paul J. Smith's niece, the bass flute part was played by Smith's brother Arthur.[129] "Trust in Me" is the only song in the film that is sung by Kaa, who was voiced by Sterling Holloway.

Figure 9.3. Phrygian music representing Kaa—JUNGLE BOOK SCORE from THE JUNGLE BOOK—Music by George Bruns—© 1967 Wonderland Music Company

Figure 9.4. "Trust in Me"—TRUST IN ME from THE JUNGLE BOOK—Words and Music by Richard M. Sherman and Robert B. Sherman—© 1967 Wonderland Music Company, Inc.

While the song is not written in Phrygian mode, the melody's chromaticism (Figure 9.4) lends it a similar exoticism.

In *The Jungle Book*, "Trust in Me" functions as a lullaby, as Kaa uses the song to lull Mowgli into slumber. Robert Sherman's lyrics for the song focus on alliterate sibilants such as those from the bridge: "Slip into silent slumber / Sail on a silver mist / Slowly and surely your senses / Will cease to resist."[130] These lyrics not only help portray Kaa as a snake but also work well with Holloway's distinctive vocal qualities.

The idea for the sequence was successfully pitched by Floyd Norman and Vance Gerry (1929–2005) to Walt during the summer of 1966.[131] Walt decided that the scene needed a song, and tasked the Sherman brothers with creating one.[132] The duo was able to deliver "Trust in Me" less than week later, as lyrics were added to the preexisting melody for "Land of Sand" which was an unused song from *Mary Poppins*.

Danny Alguire, who assisted Woolie Reitherman, mentioned the vultures in relationship to the crows from *Dumbo* in a storyboard meeting from June 29, 1965. He felt that the vultures at the meeting were ugly in comparison to the crows, but that both sets of characters served similar functions, namely, being sympathetic to the protagonists while having a little bit of fun at their expense.[133] Alguire even mentioned Cliff Edwards as a possible voice actor for one of the vultures.[134] He also brought up Jimmy Durante but added that such a choice would be "reaching too much."[135]

Walt commented that "a Beatle-type group would do if they can handle lines."[136] The concept evolved to use the Beatles themselves in the sequence. Under this plan, the vultures were to be a finger-snapping gang called the Buzzniks.[137] In fact, in an early draft of the scene, "That's What Friends Are For" is generically referred to as "Buzzniks Song," which would have utilized a Watusi dance sequence.[138]

Legend has it that the group's manager, Brian Epstein (1934–1967), met with Walt in 1965 and arranged for the group's appearance in the film. Apparently, John Lennon, who had been upset by the ABC animated series *The Beatles* (1965–1969), vetoed the idea and suggested that Elvis Presley (1935–1977) should do the project. Another version of the story has Walt getting cold feet on including the Beatles in the film, as he felt it would date the film too much.[139]

The vultures that were to sing "That's What Friends Are For" had already been modeled after the Fab Four, and it was decided to keep the character design as well as the Liverpudlian accents. The style of the song was changed from rock and roll to a barbershop quartet, which seems particularly anachronistic in a film that mainly features jazz and exotic music. In his version of the story, Floyd Norman stated that it was Walt's idea to use a barbershop quartet arrangement.[140] However, a bit of rock and roll remains, as the first appearance of the vultures is accompanied by electric bass, bluesy electric guitar, and punctuating snare.

While the vultures are portrayed in the film as being honestly friendly to Mowgli, the Sherman brothers wrote the lyrics in such a way that it could be interpreted as being either earnest or ironic, perhaps indicating an earlier plan to cast the quartet as being villainous. In fact, in their book *Walt's Time*, the brothers describe the vultures as "heavies."[141] The concept of "friends to the bitter end"[142] suggests mortality, and lyrics like, "who comes around to pluck you up"[143] reflect the vultures' nature as scavengers. Likewise, "When you're lost in dire need / Who's at your side in lightning speed?"[144] can be interpreted as the desire for a fresh meal. This is followed by a potential culinary assessment: "We never met an animal we didn't like."[145]

The last song of the film, "My Own Home," embodies the central concern of *The Jungle Book*. Richard Sherman even called the tune "the main theme of the show."[146] The Richard M. and Robert B. Sherman Papers at the University of Wyoming contain a lyric manuscript of the song dated November 11, 1965.[147]

Sung by Darlene Carr (1950–), "My Own Home" is a work song, a siren song, and a sweetly sad lullaby. The first verse presents the girl's frustration with the repetitive toil of her existence. The second verse relates that her best hope is to someday ascend the hierarchy slightly to obtain her mother's position. The bleak nature of the girl's dreams is outdone only by the fact that, like "I Wan'na Be Like You," the song is about power. In this case the desire is to not be on the bottom of society's hierarchy. Robert J. Sherman posits that "My Own Home" even hints at the restrictive caste system of Indian society.[148]

The song is also about the inevitability of life cycles. In this manner, the song is a fitting end of the movie, reflecting the natural order that Mowgli join his own people in order to continue the circle of life. This cyclical theme is portrayed in the repetition inherent in lyrics such as, "'Til I'm grown."[149] This

Figure 9.5. "My Own Home" (lyrics from second verse)—MY OWN HOME from THE JUNGLE BOOK—Words and Music by Richard M. Sherman and Robert B. Sherman—© 1967 Wonderland Music Company, Inc.

recurrent theme is also reflected in the arpeggiation of the melody, as well as the oscillation between the accompanying tonic and dominant harmonies (Figure 9.5). The life cycle theme is reinforced by the melody's appearance early in the film when Bagheera leaves Mowgli with the wolves.

The melody also represents the inevitability of Mowgli's return to the man village. This connection is made when the tune occurs after the man-cub's encounter with Colonel Hathi, when Bagheera tells the boy that the panther is going to take him the man village. It is also reinforced when the melody accompanies Baloo as he tries to convince Mowgli to return to the man village. The downward minor-chord arpeggiation that begins "My Own Home" complements the upward minor-chord arpeggiation that is featured in Mowgli's Journey Theme (Figure 9.2). This musical relationship suggests a connection between the man-cub and the girl, and by extension, Mowgli and the man village.

"My Own Home" is also a siren song. The girl who sings the song acts in a coy manner after she spots Mowgli in the tree. Since the Sherman brothers were instructed not to follow the book, they had to devise an ending for the film. The duo decided that the protagonist should be enticed into the man village by a girl.[150] After coming up with the idea, the brothers told animator Ken Anderson (1909–1993) about their idea for the ending of the movie.[151] Anderson brought the duo to his office to show them that he had come up with the same concept and had already begun creating a storyboard for it.[152]

In some ways the narrative of the film seems like a reflection of *Alice in Wonderland*. In *Alice* the protagonist's journey becomes one of trying to find her way home out of the foreign world of Wonderland. In *The Jungle Book*, Mowgli's narrative is to find a way to stay in the jungle, the only home he has known. Yet it becomes increasingly evident that the man cub is unsuited to the dangerous life of the jungle, particularly when he is outside the protection of Bagheera or Baloo. However, when Mowgli encounters the girl, the previously foreign world of the man village is recast as home.

Numerous songs had been written for *The Jungle Book* but not used. While many of these were written by Terry Gilkyson, one song, "Baloo," was written by George Bruns with Bill Peet acting as a lyricist.[153] This song, which was first put to paper on September 19, 1963, would have introduced the bear in the film.[154]

Around the same time that "Baloo" was written, Disney brought Gilkyson in to be a songwriter for the project.[155] The composer wrote half a dozen songs for the project, only one of which made its way to the completed film. The version of "The Bare Necessities" that became part of *The Jungle Book* was actually the third draft of the song.[156] As previously stated, an earlier version of the song included lyrics similar to scatting that Baloo performs as he first meets Mowgli.[157]

One unused song by Gilkyson is "Brothers All." This tune features dark lyrics such as "Give us our freedom or soon we die."[158] "Kalaweeta Kallana" was written to be a lullaby sung by the mother wolf to an infant Mowgli.[159] Written on September 13, 1963, "The Song of the Seeonee" would have been sung by the wolves.[160] "Monkey See—Monkey Do" had a band of simians bragging about themselves to Mowgli.[161] Gilkyson also wrote a waltz where Mowgli tells Bagheera a dream about finding his home and human mother.[162]

RECEPTION AND SUMMARY

The Jungle Book was released on October 18, 1967, a little over ten months after the death of Walt Disney. The film earned 13 million dollars at the box office in its initial domestic release.[163] The movie was generally well received, due in part to nostalgia over the death of the Studios' head.

"The Bare Necessities" was nominated for an Academy Award for Best Song. *The Jungle Book* won best feature film for children in the 1968 Gijón International Film Festival and was awarded fifth place in the category of comedy in the 1968 Laurel Awards. After adjusting for inflation, the feature has made over 585 million dollars for the Studios, making it the twenty-ninth-most-successful film of all time.[164]

"The Bare Necessities" has been recorded by Louis Armstrong, Astrud Gilberto (1940–), and Harry Connick, Jr. (1967–). "I Wan'na Be Like You" was covered by the bands Phish, Los Lobos, Big Bad Voodoo Daddy, and the Morning Benders. "Trust in Me" was recorded by Siouxsie Sioux (1957–). The Record Industry Association of America awarded a Gold Record to the Storyteller record for the film.[165] According to Jimmy Johnson, the Swedish-language version of the Storyteller record was the bestselling record in the history of Sweden, selling more than 300,000 copies.[166]

The Sword in the Stone and *The Jungle Book* were the eighteenth and nineteenth animated feature films produced by The Walt Disney Studios. In addition, the latter film was the last animated film that Walt worked on, before his death on December 15, 1966. Given that Walt was integrally involved in so much of the Studios' output, it is not surprising that changes followed his passing. Jimmy Johnson summarized how Walt's death affected individuals:

Some seemed to bloom creatively, more free to express themselves without his sometimes authoritarian rule. Many others, however, were diminished in their abilities. They had relied heavily on Walt to make that final decision and were incapable of doing so themselves.[167]

The Sherman brothers described being confronted by a scenario similar to the latter situation in conjunction with their work on *Bedknobs and Broomsticks*: "Walt had been replaced by 'The Committee.' We called them 'The Board of Indecision.'"[168]

Perhaps the most noticeable change musically speaking to the Studios' output once Walt passed came from the Sherman brothers leaving the Studios. Robert Sherman described the situation in his posthumously published memoirs, *Moose*:

> The once nurturing environment that had been The Walt Disney Studios suddenly seemed limiting and oppressive. Dick and I were no longer receiving the Studios' "A list" project assignments. Adding salt to the wound, we were suddenly expected to share songwriting duties on films with other teams. This meant that we no longer possessed the sort of creative autonomy which we had enjoyed while Walt was alive. This treatment was not reserved for us alone. Much of Walt's favorite talent was punished in this way, after Walt died.[169]

While the duo would occasionally return to work as independent contractors on specific projects such as *Bedknobs and Broomsticks*, *The Aristocats*, and music for various EPCOT attractions, the brothers were the last in-house songwriters employed full-time by the Studios.

Since the release of *Winnie the Pooh* (2011), 3-D CGI animation has been the predominant approach to animation at Disney. The company's CEO, Bob Iger (1951–), recently announced, "To my knowledge we're not developing a 2D or hand-drawn feature animated film right now."[170] The predominance of 3-D CGI films in the Studios' output has caused many animation fans to be critical of the trend.

Numerous reviewers criticized the animation of *Frozen* (2013). In an online review of *Frozen*, Michael Barrier lamented that he "saw not a hint of progress toward making CGI human characters look more like real beings and less like plasticine dolls," adding, "I don't think I'll see *Frozen* again."[171] Keith Uhlich of *Time Out New York* echoed Barrier's sentiment, characterizing the visuals as "plasticine CG animation."[172] Tasha Robinson of *The Dissolve* notes that "much of *Frozen* feels mighty familiar, right down to the character models . . . Disney's CGI heroines pretty much have the same face."[173]

Conversely, as of late March, 2014, the *Frozen* soundtrack sold 1.4 million copies and was the first album to sell over a million copies in 2014.[174] The soundtrack knocked Beyoncé's (1981–) eponymous album out of the number one position on the *Billboard* charts.[175] The soundtrack is Disney's first number one since *Pocahontas* (1995).[176] The *Frozen* soundtrack has become the Studios' longest-running number one soundtrack from an animated feature, breaking the record previously held by *The Lion King*.[177]

Frozen's "Let It Go" was awarded an Academy Award for Best Original Song. The award allowed Robert Lopez (1975–), who cowrote the song with his wife, Kristen Anderson-Lopez, to become one of only one and half dozen individuals in entertainment history to have EGOT, that is, to win an Emmy, a Grammy, an Oscar, and a Tony. Furthermore, if you discount Barbra Streisand (1942–), who was awarded a noncompetitive Special Tony Award, Lopez is the individual who has earned an EGOT in the least amount of time, taking only ten years from his first award to achieve his fourth. In addition to being an award-winning song, "Let It Go" has been tremendously successful. Idina Menzel's (1971–) recording of the song has sold 1.8 million copies, while Demi Lovato's (1992–) cover has sold 738,000 downloads.[178]

Frozen is a deservedly acclaimed film. The story weaves several narratives. At the center of these stories are two sisters with dramatically contrasting personalities. The elder sister, Elsa, suffers from crippling anxiety that stems from fear. Elsa feels pressure to perform a public role that is different from her true self. This character fears that if people knew her true self, she would be rejected, an all too common fear not limited to teenagers.

"Let It Go" is a power anthem in which Elsa finds the courage to assert that she would rather be alone as her true self than hide in public. Elsa's potentially dark plot line touches on anxiety, depression, and fear surrounding acceptance, conforming, and passing. However, this narrative is told in a family-friendly manner that ultimately preaches self-confidence, self-acceptance, and self-love. Kristen Anderson-Lopez stated, "I was really excited to write an anthem that said 'Screw fear and shame, be yourself, be powerful.'"[179] Furthermore, the sisters' story is one where the two gradually learn the importance of unconditional love, forgiveness, and sacrifice. This narrative is arguably the most compassionate message in a Disney Princess film.

"Let It Go" also had the power to change the plot of *Frozen*. Originally, Elsa was the villain of the film.[180] However, after writing "Let It Go," the couple realized they had found the root of the character's motivations and had humanized her in a manner that was inconsistent with the nature of an antagonist. Thus, the songwriters set aside all the songs they had written thus far for the project, and forged ahead with codirectors Jennifer Lee (1971–) and Chris Buck (1960–) to retool the plot with both Anna and Elsa as protagonists.[181] Lee claims, "The minute we heard the song for the first time, I knew that I had to rewrite the whole movie."[182] This integration of songwriting and screenwriting descends from the earliest animated features to come from The Walt Disney Studios.

Frozen, like the overwhelming majority of the movies covered in this volume, is told through music. The songs in the film are more than mere entertainment. They convey the narrative, establish character, and reinforce the emotional arc of the story. While many recent Disney animated movies use music in this same manner, the songs in *Frozen* are so tightly integrated with the film's narrative that the story would simply not be the same without them.

The Academy Award for Best Animated Feature was first awarded in 2001. If you omit films created by Pixar, Disney has won the award only twice to date, for *Frozen* and *Big Hero 6*. No Disney picture has ever won an Academy Award for Best Picture, and only two, *Mary Poppins* and *Beauty and the Beast* (1991), have been nominated. However, eight movies from the Studio have been awarded Best Score Oscars, and another ten songs from Disney films have earned Academy Awards for Best Original Song.

The movies covered in this volume, and Disney's record of Academy Award nominations and wins, suggest where the heart and soul of the Studios' films are centered. The essence of a Disney animated feature is not drawn by a pencil, pen, paint, or pixels. Rather, it is written in notes, orchestrated to provide action and emotional subtext, and vocalized in lyrics that establish character and tell a story.

Appendix

COMPOSER CREDITS IN
ANIMATED FEATURES

The information in this appendix largely comes from cue sheets created by the Disney Music Group.

SNOW WHITE AND THE SEVEN DWARFS

Production: 2001   Film Duration: 82:54   Music Duration: 82:09

SEQ	CUE	TITLE	TIMING	COMPOSERS
1	1-A 1–28	"One Song"	1:28	Morey/Churchill
2	1-A 28-	"Some Day My Prince Will Come"	:49	Morey/Churchill
3	1-B 20-	"Mirror, Mirror"	1:23	Harline
4	2-A 2–69	"I'm Wishing"	1:52	Morey/Churchill
5	2-A 69–77	"Interlude"	:11	Harline
6	2-A 77-	"One Song"	:24	Morey/Churchill
7	2-A 1-	"Queen Theme"	:45	Churchill
8	3-A 1–11	"One Song"	:24	Morey/Churchill
9	3-A 11–51	"Hello There"	:58	Churchill
10	3-A 51–154	"Dramatic Music"	1:04	Smith
11	3-A 154-	"Montage"	:26	Churchill/Smith
12	3-B 103–186	"Animal Friends"	1:50	Churchill/Harline
13	3-B 186-	"With a Smile and a Song"	2:30	Morey/Churchill
14	3-C 249–283A	"Discovery"	:51	Churchill
15	3-C 283A-301	"Exploration"	:36	Smith
16	3-C 301A-	"In the Cottage"	1:37	Churchill
17	3-D	"Whistle While You Work"	3:24	Morey/Churchill
18	4-A	"Heigh-Ho"	2:04	Morey/Churchill

19	4-C 1–12	"Wondering"	:13	Churchill
20	4-C 12–22	Turtle Theme	:11	Smith
21	4-C 22–42	"Wondering"	:33	Churchill
22	4-C 42–60A	"Lullaby"	:24	Churchill/Smith
23	4-C 60-	"Heigh-Ho"	:46	Morey/Churchill
24	4-D 1–14	"Heigh-Ho"	:16	Morey/Churchill
25	4-D 14–24	Interlude	:13	Churchill/Harline
26	4-D 41–87	"Sneak"	1:28	Harline
27	4-D 87–241	Incidental #1	2:39	Harline
28	4-D 241–260	Dopey's Theme	:27	Churchill
29	4-D 260-	Incidental #2	1:18	Harline
30	5-A 2–11	Incidental #3	:22	Harline
31	5-A 11–22	"Perplexity"	:13	Churchill
32	5-A 22–67	Incidental #4	1:05	Harline/Churchill
33	5-A 67–69	"Hurry"	:04	Harline
34	5-A 69–96	Incidental #5	:43	Churchill
35	5-A 96–104	"Interrogation"	:33	Harline
36	5-A 104–118	"Happy Man"	:19	Churchill
37	5-A 118-	Incidental #6	1:50	Churchill/Harline
38	5-B 337–17	"In the Kitchen"	:23	Churchill
39	5-B 17–27B	"Food"	:21	Churchill
40	5-B 27B-90D	"Bad News"	1:42	Churchill
41	5-B 90D-	"March"	:27	Churchill
42	5-B 92-	"Defiance"	:29	Churchill
43	6-A 143–173	"Sissy Stuff"	:43	Churchill
44	6-A 173–244C	"Bluddle-Uddle-Um-Dum"	2:02	Morey/Churchill
45	6-A 244C-245	"Conspiracy"	:12	Churchill
46	6-A 245D-254	"Bluddle-Uddle-Um-Dum"	:21	Morey/Churchill
47	6-A 254–273A	"Fight"	:17	Churchill
48	6-A 273A-296	Dopey's Theme	:43	Churchill
49	6-A 354-	"Bluddle-Uddle-Um-Dum"	:19	Morey/Churchill
50	7-A 1A-36	"Magic Mirror"	1:36	Harline
51	7-A 36–69	"Steps Going Down"	:36	Harline
52	7-A 69-	"Transfiguration Music"	2:36	Harline
53	8-A A-262	"The Silly Song"	4:16	Morey/Churchill
54	8-B 16-	"Some Day My Prince Will Come"	1:49	Morey/Churchill
55	8-C 46–53	"Off to Bed"	:09	Smith
56	8-C 53–85	"Pleasant Dreams"	:52	Churchill
57	8-C 85-	Dopey's Theme	:25	Churchill
58	8-C 112-	"Prayer at Evening"	2:09	Smith
59	9-A 1–91	"Theme Sinister"	5:58	Harline

60	9-A 91-	"Foggy Morning"	:43	Harline
61	10-A 1–49	"Morning in the Country"	1:04	Churchill/Harline
62	10-A 49–71	Dopey's Theme	:29	Churchill
63	10-A 71–92	"Heigh-Ho"	:24	Churchill/Morey
64	10-A 92–113	Grumpy's Theme	:25	Churchill/Harline
65	10–1 130-	"Heigh-Ho"	:21	Morey/Churchill
66	10-B 1-	"Theme Sinister"	:32	Harline
67	13-A 18–63	"Some Day My Prince Will Come"	:52	Morey/Churchill
68	13-A 63–89	"Theme Sinister"	1:01	Harline
69	13-A 89–102	"Hurry #1"	:12	Harline
70	13-A 102–166	"Theme Sinister"	:42	Harline
71	13-A 166-	"Woodland Hurry"	:07	Harline
72	14-B 100–102	"Woodland Hurry"	:03	Harline
73	14-B 102–1	"Heigh-Ho"	:28	Morey/Churchill
74	14-B 1-	"Woodland Hurry"	:25	Harline
75	14-C 1-	"Theme Sinister"	:31	Harline
76	14-D 1–51	"Woodland Hurry"	:22	Harline
77	14-E 51-	"Dwarfs to the Rescue"	:28	Harline
78	14-F 1-	"Theme Sinister"	:31	Harline
79	14-G 1-	"Dwarfs to the Rescue"	:13	Harline
80	14-H 1–5 / 14 J	"Theme Sinister"	:52	Harline
81	14-J 6B-146	"Dramatic Chase"	1:27	Harline
82	15-A 1-	"Chorale"	1:04	Churchill
83	15-B 99-	"Transitional Music"	:29	Churchill/Harline
84	16-A 1A-16A	"One Song"	1:07	Morey/Churchill
85	16-A 1–5	"Transitional Music"	:22	Harline
86	16-A 5–35	"Some Day My Prince Will Come"	:29	Morey/Churchill
87	16-A 35–64	"Transitional Music"	:21	Churchill
88	16-A 64-	"Some Day My Prince Will Come"	1:04	Morey/Churchill
89	16-A 16-END	"Some Day My Prince Will Come"	:23	Morey/Churchill

PINOCCHIO

Production: 2003   Film Duration: 87:28   Music Duration: 87:15

SEQ	CUE	TITLE	TIMING	COMPOSERS
1	M. 1–15	"Little Wooden Head"	:26	Washington/Harline
2	M. 15–38A	"When You Wish Upon a Star"	1:04	Washington/Harline

3	Takes 1–4, M. A-25	"When You Wish Upon a Star"	1:42	Washington/ Harline
4	Take 5, M. 26–41	"Hop Along"	:22	Harline/Smith
5	Takes 6–11, M. 41–111	Cricket Theme	1:25	Harline
6	Takes 1–3, M. 1–38	"Little Wooden Head"	1:11	Washington/ Harline
7	Takes 4–5, M. 38–59	"Old Geppetto"	:42	Harline
8	Takes 6–9, M. 97A-155	"Little Wooden Head"	2:05	Washington/ Harline
9	Take 10, M. 156–171	Kitten Theme	:28	Harline
10	M. A-Y	"Clock Theme"	:56	Harline/Rees
11	Take 11, M. 171–179	"Old Geppetto"	:13	Harline
12	Takes 11–12, M. 179–203	Kitten Theme	:38	Harline
13	Take 13, M. 203–246	"Little Wooden Head"	1:12	Washington/ Harline
14	Take 14, M. 246–269	Kitten Theme	:37	Harline
15	Take 15, M. 269–276	"When You Wish Upon a Star"	:24	Washington/ Harline
16	M. 276–295	"Little Wooden Head"	:40	Washington/ Harline
17		"Clock Sequence"	1:08	Harline/Rees
18	Take 1, M. 1–11	Fairy Theme	:30	Harline/Smith
19	Takes 2–3, M. 11–46A	"When You Wish Upon a Star"	1:30	Washington/ Harline
20	Take 4, M. 72A-84	Cricket Theme	1:06	Harline
21	Take 5, M. 85–92	"When You Wish Upon a Star"	:22	Washington/ Harline
22	Take 1, M. 1–33	Cricket Theme	1:00	Harline
23	Takes 2–3, M. 33–82	"Give a Little Whistle"	1:52	Washington/ Harline
24	Take A, M. 1–13	"Geppetto's Nightmare"	:27	Harline/Smith
25	Take B, M. 1–15	"Geppetto's Sneak"	:48	Harline
26	Take C1, M. 1–9	"Old Geppetto"	:15	Harline
27	Take C1, M. 10–25	"Canon in the Octave"	:13	Harline
28	Take C2, M. 26–45	"Perplexity"	:31	Harline/Smith
29	Take D, M. 1–45	"Old Geppetto"	:38	Harline
30	Takes 1–5, M. 157–347B	"Turn On the Old Music Box"	1:07	Washington/ Harline
31	Take 6, M. 1–15	"Fire, Fire"	:08	Harline
32	Takes 6–7, M. 15–42	Cricket Theme	:32	Harline
33	Take 8, M. 42–61	"Little Wooden Head"	:43	Washington/ Harline
34	Take 1, M. 1–37	"Village Awakening"	:52	Harline

35	Take 2, M. 37–92	"Turn On the Old Music Box"	1:00	Washington/Harline
36	Takes 1–3, M. 1–40	"Four Flushers"	:42	Harline
37	Takes 4–7, M. 40–112	"Turn On the Old Music Box"	1:15	Washington/Harline
38	Take 8, M. 112–137	"So Sorry"	:25	Harline
39	Take 8, M. 137–143	"Turn On the Old Music Box"	:11	Washington/Harline
40	Take 10, M. 144–153	"On to the Theatre"	:10	Harline
41	Takes 11–12, M. 153–176	"So Sorry"	:27	Harline
42	Take 13, M. 383–422C	"Hi-Diddle-Dee-Dee"	:36	Washington/Harline
43	Take 14, M. 1–18	Cricket Theme	:12	Harline
44	Take 15, M. 210–250	"Hi-Diddle-Dee-Dee"	:36	Washington/Harline
45	Take 16, M. 1–30, Take 17, M. 1–18	"The Jitters"	:30	Harline/Smith
46	Take 18, M. 1–8	"So Sorry"	:13	Harline
47	Takes 19–21, M. 1 of 19–4 of 21	"The Jitters"	:28	Harline/Smith
48	Takes 22–23, M. 1 of 22–14 of 23	"So Sorry"	:31	Harline
49	Take 24, M. 367–384	"Hi-Diddle-Dee-Dee"	:22	Washington/Harline
50	Takes 1–11, M. 80–256H	"I've Got No Strings"	4:20	Washington/Harline
51	Takes 1–2, M. 1–13	Kitten Theme	:52	Harline
52	A-M	"I've Got No Strings"	:11	Washington/Harline
53	Takes 1–3, M. 1–52	"Sinister Stromboli"	3:15	Harline
54	Take 1, M. 1–21	Cricket Theme	:37	Harline
55	Take 2, M. 1–18	"Sad Reunion"	1:24	Harline
56	Take 1, M. 1–13	"Little Wooden Head"	:38	Washington/Harline
57	Take 1, M. 1–16	"Sad Reunion"	:45	Harline
58	Take 2, M. 16–24	Fairy Theme	:18	Harline
59	Take 2, M. 24–30	"When You Wish Upon a Star"	:22	Washington/Harline
60	Take 3, 4, M. 1–28	"Lesson in Lies"	1:20	Harline
61	Take 4, M. 28–36	"When You Wish Upon a Star"	:22	Washington/Harline
62	Take 5, M. 1–7	"Old Geppetto"	:06	Harline
63	Take 5, M. 7–20	"I've Got No Strings"	:08	Washington/Harline

64	Take 5, M. 21–33	"Old Geppetto"	:11	Harline
65	Take 1, M. 1–3	"Fog Music"	:05	Harline/Smith
66	Take 2, M. 1–16	"Hi-Diddle-Dee-Dee"	:17	Washington/ Harline
67	Takes 3–4, M. 1–40	"Fakers"	1:03	Harline/Smith
68	Takes 5–6, M. 41–79	"Deviltry"	1:10	Harline/Smith
69	Takes 1–2, M. 1–63	"Turn On the Old Music Box"	:53	Washington/ Harline
70	Take 3, M. 1–39	"The Jitters"	:38	Harline/Smith
71	Take 4, M. 1–8	"Swinging Shutters"	:12	Harline/Smith
72	Takes 5, 5A, 6, M. 1–11	"The Cure"	:39	Harline/Smith
73	Take 7, M. 1–93	"Hi-Diddle-Dee-Dee"	1:58	Washington/ Harline
74	Take 1, M. 1–9	"Who's Da Beetle"	:17	Harline
75	Take 2, M. 1–24	"Honest John"	:15	Harline
76	Take 3, M. 1–12	"Who's Da Beetle"	:25	Harline
77	Take 4, 4A, M. 1–24	"Hi-Diddle-Dee-Dee"	:23	Washington/ Harline
78	Takes 1–4, M. 1–33	"No Fun"	2:05	Washington/Harline/Rees/Smith/ Wolcott (arranger)
79	Takes 5–9, M. 34–105	"Angry Cricket"	1:46	Harline
80	Take 1, M. 1–12	"Angry Cricket (Continued)"	:24	Harline
81	Take 2, M. 13–50	"Tragic Happenings"	1:04	Harline
82	Take 1, M. 1–31	"Transformation"	:59	Harline
83	Takes A–D, M. 1–20	"Jackass Frenzy"	:38	Harline/Smith
84	Take E, M. 1–22	"To the Rescue"	:49	Harline/Smith
85	Take 2, M. 1–40	"Out of the Sea"	1:15	Harline/Smith
86	Take 2A, M. 1–6	Fairy Theme	:26	Harline/Smith
87	Take 3, M. 1–22	"To the Rescue"	:13	Harline/Smith
88	Take 3, M. 1–22	"Monstro the Whale"	:18	Harline
89	Take 4, M. 1–16	"Away Together"	:25	Harline/Smith
90	Takes 1–7, M. 1–40	"Deep Ripples"	3:18	Harline/Smith
91	Take 8, M. 1–30	"Sea Horses"	:32	Harline/Smith
92	Take 9, M. 1–6	"Deep Ripples"	:12	Harline/Smith
93	Take 1, M. 1–5	"The Terror"	:22	Harline
94	Takes 2–3, M. 1–16	Desolation Theme	1:19	Harline
95	Take 4, M. 1–8	"Monstro Awakens"	:18	Harline
96	Takes 5–11, M. 506–547	"Tuna"	2:10	Harline
97	Take 12, M. 1–24	"Little Wooden Head"	:53	Washington/ Harline

98	Take 13, M. 1–15	"Understanding"	:32	Harline/Smith
99	Take 14, M. 15–29	Cricket Theme	:14	Harline
100	Take 15, M. 1–25	"Hopeless"	:53	Harline/Smith
101	Take 16, M. 26–32	"Smoke"	:15	Harline/Smith
102	Take A-7A, M. A-F, 1–44	"Whale Chase"	3:45	Harline/Plumb
103	Take X, M. 1–10	Desolation Theme	:36	Harline
104	Take 1, M. 1–13	"When You Wish Upon a Star"	:45	Washington/ Harline
105	Take 2, M. 1–53	"Turn On the Old Music Box"	1:14	Washington/ Harline
106	Take 3, M. 1–26	"When You Wish Upon a Star"	1:06	Washington/ Harline

DUMBO

Production: 2006   Film Duration: 64:00   Music Duration: 49:43

SEQ	CUE	TITLE	TIMING	COMPOSERS
1	1–92	"Dumbo" Main Title	1:14	Wallace
2	1–62	"Look Out for Mr. Stork"	2:10	Washington/ Churchill
3	1–12	"Loading"	:09	Wallace
4	13–17	"Casey Junior"	:03	Washington/ Churchill
5	17–39	"Loading"	:17	Wallace
6	39–43	"Casey Junior"	:03	Washington/ Churchill
7	43.87	"Loading"	:33	Wallace
8	1–53	"Casey Junior"	:44	Washington/ Churchill
9	1–15	"Stork on Cloud"	:18	Wallace
10	15–29	"Rock-a-Bye Baby"	:21	Effie Canning/Wallace (arranger)
11	1–28	"Stork on Cloud"	:24	Wallace
12	1–36	"Casey Junior"	:30	Washington/ Churchill
13	1–20	"Gossips"	:21	Wallace
14	23–28	"Stork Clears Throat"	:09	Wallace
15	1–4	"Eyes of Blue"	:04	Wallace
16	5–8	"Straight from Heaven"	:04	Wallace
17	1–10	"Happy Birthday to You"	:34	Mildred & Patty Hill
18	1–5	"Casey Junior"	:04	Washington/ Churchill

19	1–9	"This Is a Proud Day"	:10	Wallace
20	10–27A	"Dumbo Looks 'Em Over"	:14	Wallace
21	1–13	"Dumbo Serenade"	:18	Wallace
22	1–5	"Shocked Gossips"	:05	Wallace
23	2–17	"Dumbo Serenade"	:25	Wallace
24	1–8	"Casey Junior"	:13	Washington/ Churchill
25	22	"Casey Junior"	:24	Washington/ Churchill
26	1–34	"Unloading"	:33	Wallace
27	35–142	"Song of the Roustabouts"	2:29	Washington/ Churchill
28	1–10	"Dawn"	:08	Wallace
29	104	"It's Circus Day Again"	1:28	Churchill
30	1–63	"Dumbo Serenade"	1:29	Wallace
31	44–73	"It's Circus Day Again"	:43	Churchill
32	81–131	"Berserk"	:52	Wallace
33	1–11	"Dumbo Serenade" (Paraphrase)	:29	Wallace
34	1–11	"Dumbo Serenade"	:55	Wallace
35	1–8	"Timothy Steps on 'Em"	:09	Wallace
36	1–16	"Timothy Steps on 'Em"	:19	Wallace
37	1–41	"Enticing"	:49	Wallace
38	7	"Casey Junior"	:05	Washington/ Churchill
39	1–26	"Enticing"	:33	Wallace
40	1–3	"Fanfare #1"	:04	Wallace
41	1–2	"Depressed Fanfare"	:05	Wallace
42	1–4	"Enticing"	:07	Wallace
43	1–24	"Scherzo"	:31	Wallace
44	1–14	"Shadow Music"	:17	Wallace
45	1–3	"Fanfare #2"	:03	Wallace
46	1–140	"Building the Pyramid"	1:40	Wallace
47	1–3	"Fanfare #2"	:03	Wallace
48	1–3	"Fanfare #2"	:03	Wallace
49	1–3	"Fanfare #2"	:03	Wallace
50	1–3	"Fanfare #2"	:03	Wallace
51	1–68	"Catastrophe"	1:36	Wallace
52	12	"Casey Junior"	:17	Washington/ Churchill
53	36–39	"Elephant Blues"	:14	Wallace
54	112	"Fireman Save My Child"	1:29	Wallace
55	1–27	"Dumbo Serenade"	1:15	Wallace

56	1–32	"Baby Mine"	2:02	Washington/ Churchill
57	C–F	"Dumbo Serenade"	:11	Wallace
58	C–F	"Baby Mine"	:11	Washington/ Churchill
59	3–16	"Clown Song"	:57	Wallace
60	1–5	"Dumbo Serenade" (Sad & Happy Paraphrase)	:19	Wallace
61	1–47	"Dumbo Serenade" (Hiccups Paraphrase)	1:07	Wallace
62		Vocal Improvisation	:00	Brophy
63	1–66	"Pink Bubbles"	1:54	Wallace
64	103	"Pink Elephants on Parade"	6:25	Washington/ Wallace
65	1–15	"Timothy's Awakening"	:19	Wallace
66	93–97	"Morning Afternoon"	:06	Wallace
67	102–103	"Surprise"	:05	Wallace
68	1–4	"The Walkaway"	:06	Wallace
69	112D-118	"Pink Elephants on Parade"	:14	Washington/ Wallace
70	1–6	"Pink Elephants on Parade"	:16	Washington/ Wallace
71	1–8	"The Happy Thought"	:10	Wallace
72	40	"When I See an Elephant Fly"	1:33	Washington/ Churchill
73	1–20	"Lament"	1:08	Wallace
74	1–23	"An Elephant Flies"	:36	Wallace
75	6	"When I See an Elephant Fly"	:20	Washington/ Churchill
76	72	"Fireman Save My Child"	:49	Wallace
77	A1–26	"Triumph"	:21	Wallace
78	26–80	"Spread Your Wings"	:39	Churchill
79	1–33	"Victorious"	:22	Wallace
80	2–75	"When I See an Elephant Fly"	:51	Washington/ Churchill

BAMBI

Production: 2002   Film Duration: 69:33   Music Duration: 62:07

SEQ	CUE	TITLE	TIMING	COMPOSERS
1		Main Title—Part I	:11	Plumb
2		Main Title—Part II	:05	Morey/Churchill
3	1A-V/1B-V	"Love Is a Song"	2:39	Morey/Churchill
4	1C	"Awakening"	:45	Churchill

5	1D	"Magpies"	:13	Churchill
6	1D	"Sleepy Morning"	:27	Churchill
7	1E	"Hurry to the Thicket"	:53	Churchill
8	1F	Bambi Theme	:05	Churchill/Plumb
9	1G	"Bambi Gets Up"	:05	Churchill
10	1H	Walking Theme	:33	Churchill
11	1H	Bambi Theme	:17	Churchill/Plumb
12	1J-V	"Love Is a Song"	:58	Morey/Churchill
13	1K	Walking Theme	:39	Churchill
14	1K	Thumper Theme	:08	Churchill
15	1K	Walking Theme	:03	Churchill
16	1K	Thumper Theme	:09	Churchill
17	1K	Walking Theme	:04	Churchill
18	1K	Mole Theme	:15	Churchill
19	1K	Walking Theme	:13	Churchill
20	2A	"Bambi Gets Up"	:05	Churchill
21	2B	Walking Theme	:19	Churchill
22	2C	"Through the Woods"	:05	Churchill
23	2D	Thumper Theme	:03	Churchill
24	2E	"Through the Woods"	:44	Churchill
25	2F	"Bambi Gets Up"	:04	Churchill
26	2G	"Through the Woods"	:03	Churchill
27	2H	"Bambi Gets Up"	:20	Churchill
28	2H	Thumper Theme	:21	Churchill
29	2J	"Say Bird"	:51	Churchill
30	2J	"Happy Birds"	:17	Churchill
31	2K	Thumper Theme	:35	Churchill
32	2K	Flower's Theme	:05	Churchill
33	2K	Thumper Theme	:09	Churchill
34	2K	Flower's Theme	:11	Churchill
35	2K	"Walking Theme"	:08	Churchill
36	2L,M,N,O-V	"Little April Shower"	3:52	Morey/Churchill
37	3A	"Walking Theme"	:46	Churchill/Plumb
38	3B	"The Meadow"	:10	Plumb
39	3C	"Danger"	:04	Plumb
40	3D/3E	"Mysterious Meadow"	:19	Plumb
41	3F	"Bambi Scared"	:07	Plumb
42	3G	"Mysterious Meadow"	:13	Plumb
43	3H	"All's Clear"	:10	Plumb
44	3H	Bambi Theme	:14	Churchill/Plumb
45	3H	"Looking for Romance"	:55	Morey/Churchill

46	3J-3K	"Bambi Curious"	:13	Plumb
47	3L,3M,3N,3O	"Reflection"	:24	Churchill
48	3P	"Bambi Sees Faline"	:05	Plumb
49	3Q,3R,3S	Faline's Theme	:30	Churchill
50	3T	"Bambi Is Bashful"	:13	Churchill
51	3U-3V	Faline's Theme	:14	Churchill
52	3W	"Pantomime"	:04	Plumb
53	3X-3Y	"Bambi Says Hello"	:14	Churchill
54	3Z	Faline's Theme	:09	Churchill
55	3AA	"Bambi Is Annoyed"	:29	Churchill/Plumb
56	3BB	"Bambi Is Annoyed"	:24	Churchill/Plumb
57	3CC-1	"Fanfare"	:03	Churchill
58	3CC-1	"Fanfare Echo"	:03	Churchill
59	3CC	"Gallop of the Stags"	1:05	Churchill
60	3DD-3EE	"The Stag"	:37	Churchill
61	4A	"The Stag"	:25	Churchill
62	4B-V	"Love Is a Song"	:35	Morey/Churchill
63	4C-4D	Man's Theme	1:28	Churchill/Plumb
64	4E	Man's Theme	:34	Churchill/Plumb
65	4F-V	"Transition into Autumn"	:09	Plumb
66	4G-V	"Autumn"	:13	Plumb
67	4H	Bambi's Theme	:21	Plumb
68	4J-V	"End of Autumn"	:39	Plumb
69	4K	"Bambi's First Snow"	:48	Churchill
70	4K-1	"The Snowplow"	:39	Churchill
71	4L	"Fun on Ice"	:29	Churchill
72	4L-4M	"Skater's Trouble"	:18	Churchill
73	4M	"Fun on Ice"	:07	Churchill
74	4N	"Skater's Trouble"	:10	Churchill
75	4O-4P	"Fun on Ice"	:33	Churchill
76	4O-4P	"Skater's Trouble"	:27	Churchill
77	4R	"Fun on Ice"	:25	Churchill
78	5A	"Caught in the Snowdrift"	:11	Churchill
79	5A	Flower's Theme	:49	Churchill
80	5B-V	"Winter"	1:01	Plumb
81	5C	"Love Is a Song"	:30	Morey/Churchill/ Plumb (arranger)
82	5D	"Food Theme"	:17	Churchill/Plumb
83	5E	Man's Theme	:37	Churchill/Plumb
84	5F	"Bambi Escapes"	:16	Plumb
85	5G-V	"Winter"	:41	Plumb

86	5H	"Love Is a Song"	:21	Morey/Churchill/ Plumb (arranger)
87	5J-V	"Let's Sing a Gay Little Spring Song"	1:35	Morey/Churchill
88	5K-V	"Let's Sing a Gay Little Spring Song"	:14	Morey/Churchill
89	5L	"Let's Sing a Gay Little Spring Song"	:20	Morey/Churchill
90	5L	"Sleepy Owl"	:10	Churchill
91	5M	"Earthquake"	:17	Churchill
92	5N	"Let's Sing a Gay Little Spring Song"	:15	Morey/Churchill
93	6A	"Twitterpated"	:26	Churchill
94	6B	"Your Head's in a Whirl"	:07	Churchill
95	6B	"You're Walking on Air"	:15	Churchill
96	6B	"You're Knocked for a Loop"	:08	Churchill
97	6C	"Let's Sing a Gay Little Spring Song"	:32	Morey/Churchill
98	6D	"Let's Sing a Gay Little Spring Song"	:21	Morey/Churchill
99	6D	Flower's Theme	:20	Churchill
100	6D	"Flower Is Attracted"	:09	Churchill
101	6D	"Let's Sing a Gay Little Spring Song"	:05	Morey/Churchill
102	6D	"Flower's Theme"	:20	Churchill
103	6E	"Let's Sing a Gay Little Spring Song"	:14	Morey/Churchill
104	6F	"Flower's Theme"	:20	Churchill
105	6F	"Let's Sing a Gay Little Spring Song"	:13	Morey/Churchill
106	6F	"Thumper Is Attracted"	:05	Churchill
107	6G-V	"Let's Sing a Gay Little Spring Song"	:13	Morey/Churchill
108	6H	"Thumper Is Twitterpated"	:15	Churchill
109	6J-V	"Let's Sing a Gay Little Spring Song"	:13	Morey/Churchill
110	6K	"Thumper Is Twitterpated"	:09	Churchill
111	6K	"Thumper Thumps"	:05	Churchill
112	6K	"Thumper Is Twitterpated"	:06	Churchill
113	6L	"Bambi on His Way"	:05	Churchill
114	6M-V	"Let's Sing a Gay Little Spring Song"	:08	Morey/Churchill
115	7A	"Bambi at the Pool"	:11	Churchill
116	7A-7B	Faline's Theme	:29	Churchill
117	7C	"Bambi Twitterpated"	:19	Churchill
118	7D	"Let's Sing a Gay Little Spring Song"	:13	Morey/Churchill
119	7E	"Rondo Menaces"	:23	Plumb
120	7F	"Bambi Grows Up"	:11	Plumb
121	7F	"Bambi Charges"	:11	Plumb
122	7G	"Bambi Is Dazed"	:09	Plumb
123	7H	"Bambi Returns to Battle"	:16	Plumb
124'	7J	Bambi's Theme	:04	Churchill/Plumb
125	7J	"Bambi Victorious"	:16	Plumb
126	7K	Bambi's Theme	:17	Churchill/Plumb

127	7L-V	"Night Wind"	:15	Churchill
128	7L-V/7M-V	"Looking for Romance"	1:24	Morey/Churchill
129	7N	"Falling Petals"	:10	Churchill
130	7O-V	"Looking for Romance"	:20	Morey/Churchill
131	7T	"Bambi Senses Man"	:50	Plumb
132	7U	"Man's Camp"	:19	Plumb
133	7V	"Follow Me"	:04	Plumb
134	7W	"Away to Faline"	:09	Plumb
135	7X	Man's Theme	1:24	Churchill/Plumb
136	7Y	"Terror"	:10	Plumb
137	7Y	"Man's Hunting Call"	:27	Churchill/Plumb
138	8A-8B	"The Dogs"	:36	Churchill/Plumb
139	8C	"To the Rescue"	:10	Plumb
140	8D	"Fight with the Dogs"	:21	Churchill/Plumb
141	8D	"Faline Gets Away"	:09	Plumb
142	8E	"Bambi Gets Away"	:18	Plumb
143	8F	"Bambi Wounded"	:13	Plumb
144	8G	"Spreading Fire"	:19	Plumb
145	8G-1	"The Deeper Forest"	:19	Plumb
146	8H	"The Fire Rages"	:11	Plumb
147	8J	"The Power of the Stag"	:32	Plumb
148	8K	"The Fire Enters"	:09	Plumb
149	8L	"Bambi and the Stag Gain Speed"	:07	Plumb
150	8M	"Distant Fire"	:08	Plumb
151	8N	"Flames Everywhere"	:12	Plumb
152	8O-8P	"Through the Molten River"	:12	Plumb
153	8Q,8R-8S	"Crashing Trees"	:18	Plumb
154	8T-V	"Aftermath"	:29	Plumb
155	8U-V	"Love Is a Song"	1:10	Morey/Churchill/Plumb (arranger)
156	8V	"Hurry to the Thicket"	:58	Churchill
157	8W-V	"Love Is a Song"	1:23	Morey/Churchill

CINDERELLA

Production: 2063   Film Duration: 74:08   Music Duration: 68:22

SEQ	CUE	TITLE	TIMING	COMPOSERS
1	10.12	Main Title Part 1-Introduction	:12	Smith
2	10.30	Main Title Part 2-"Cinderella"	1:09	Livingston/David/Hoffman
3	11.34	Prologue Part 1	:17	Smith/Wallace

4	11.34	Prologue Part 2—(Paraphrase on "Cinderella")	:41	Livingston/David/Hoffman
5	11.34	"Prologue Part 3"	:56	Wallace
6	13.08	"Wake Up! Cinderella"	:27	Wallace
7	13.49	"Lovely Morning"	:15	Wallace
8	13.49	Introduction to "A Dream Is a Wish Your Heart Makes"	:21	Livingston/David/Hoffman
9	14.03	"A Dream Is a Wish Your Heart Makes"	1:09	Livingston/David/Hoffman
10	15:42	"A Dream Is a Wish Your Heart Makes"	:10	Livingston/David/Hoffman
11	15.59	"A Dream Is a Wish Your Heart Makes"	1:27	Livingston/David/Hoffman
12	17.31	"In the Trap"	:03	Wallace
13	20/12	Paraphrase on "Work Song"	:13	Livingston/David/Hoffman
14	20.12	"Gus in Trap"	:19	Wallace
15	20.12	Paraphrase on "Work Song"	:22	Livingston/David/Hoffman
16	20.12	"Gus Dressed Up"	:24	Wallace
17	21.29	"Preliminary Training"	:23	Wallace
18	21.29	Paraphrase on "Work Song"	:13	Livingston/David/Hoffman
19	21.29	"Lucifer Asleep"	:15	Wallace
20	22.13	Lucifer's Theme	:03	Wallace
21	22.23	"Lucifer the Villain"	:17	Wallace
22	22.49	"Lucifer the Villain" (Continued)	:16	Wallace
23	23.73	"Gus the Challenger"	:13	Wallace
24	22.73	"Work Song" Motive	:05	Livingston/David/Hoffman
25	22.73	"Bruno Dreaming"	:19	Wallace
26	22.73	Paraphrase on "Dream Is a Wish"	:28	Livingston/David/Hoffman
27	22.73	"Friendly Enemies"	:21	Wallace
28	24.03	"Arch Villain Lucifer"	:08	Wallace
29	24.26	"Bad Boy Bruno"	:24	Wallace
30	24.63	"Breakfast Time, Everybody Up!"	:31	Wallace
31	25.10	"Jaques' Plan"	1:01	Wallace
32	26.20	"Jaques' Sneak Approach"	:09	Wallace
33	26.16	"Opening Attack"	:33	Wallace
34	26.65	"Jaques's Success"	:25	Wallace
35	27.04	"A Dream Is a Wish Your Heart Makes" (Humming)	:12	Livingston/David/Hoffman
36	27.26	"Breakfast Is Served"	:30	Wallace

37	27.26	"Work Song" Motive	:04	Livingston/David/Hoffman
38	27.26	"Extra Morsels for Gus"	:12	Wallace
39	27.95	"Jaques' Signals"	:07	Wallace
40	28.06	Mice Running "Work Song" Motive	:11	Livingston/David/Hoffman
41	28.06	"Slow Poke Gus"	:23	Wallace
42	28.57	"Watch Out for Lucifer!"	:27	Wallace
43	29.03	"Gus Escapes"	:11	Wallace
44	30.16	"Lucifer's Shell Game"	:39	Wallace
45	30.16	Paraphrase on "Work Song"	:20	Livingston/David/Hoffman
46	30.16	"Lucifer's Shell Game"	:19	Wallace
47	31.32	Paraphrase on "Work Song"	:44	Livingston/David/Hoffman
48	31.98	"Cinderella's Morning Chores"	:50	Wallace
49	32.73	"Lucifer Catches Gus"	:09	Wallace
50	32.73	Paraphrase on "Work Song"	:16	Livingston/David/Hoffman
51	33.11	"Lucifer Releases Gus"	:57	Wallace
52	34.61	"Hard Work for Cinderella"	:23	Wallace
53	34.96	"The Royal Palace"	:16	Smith
54	35.20	"The King's Plans"	:55	Smith
55	36.02	"A Silly Idea"	:08	Smith
56	36.14	"The King's Plan" (Continued)	:38	Smith
57	36.14	"So This Is Love"	:13	Livingston/David/Hoffman
58	36.14	"It Cannot Fail!"	:09	Smith
59	37.04	"Strict Orders"	:15	Smith
60	37.35	"Oh, Sing Sweet Nightingale"	1:36	Livingston/David/Hoffman
61	38.70	"Bad Boy Lucifer"	:08	Smith
62	38.82	"A Mean Old Thing"	:07	Smith
63	38.93	"A Message from His Majesty"	:15	Smith
64	39.23	"Oh, Sing Sweet Nightingale"	:19	Livingston/David/Hoffman
65	40.13	"Royal Invitation"	1:20	Smith
66	41.45	Paraphrase on "Dream Is a Wish"	:33	Livingston/David/Hoffman
67	41.96	"Too Much Work"	:19	Wallace
68	42.24	Introduction to "Work Song"	:09	Wallace
69	42.24	"The Work Song"	:22	Livingston/David/Hoffman

70	42.24	"The Work Song" (Continued)	:24	Livingston/David/Hoffman
71	43.05	"The Work Song" (Continued)	:42	Livingston/David/Hoffman
72	43.68	Paraphrase on "Work Song"	:16	Livingston/David/Hoffman
73	43.93	"Secret Passage"	:05	Wallace
74	44.00	"Arguments"	:34	Wallace
75	44.52	Paraphrase on "Work Song"	:32	Livingston/David/Hoffman
76	44.52	"A Mad Scramble"	:14	Wallace
77	45.26	"Lucifer Hides Beads"	:37	Wallace
78	45.82	Strategy (Based on "Dream Is a Wish")	:40	Livingston/David/Hoffman
79	46.45	"Entanglements"	:44	Wallace
80	46.45	Paraphrase on "Work Song"	:14	Livingston/David/Hoffman
81	47.33	"Introduction to Dress Building"	:06	Wallace
82	47.42	"A Dream Is a Wish" (Dress Building Part 1)	1:16	Livingston/David/Hoffman
83	48.56	"A Dream Is a Wish" (Dress Building Part 2)	:19	Livingston/David/Hoffman
84	48.84	"Palace at Evening"	:31	Smith/Wallace
85	50.12	Paraphrase on "Work Song"	1:19	Livingston/David/Hoffman
86	50.12	"Dress for the Ball"	1:14	Smith
87	52.60	"A Dream Is a Wish" (Dramatic)	:23	Livingston/David/Hoffman
88	52.94	"A Dream Is a Wish," Voice A Capella	1:07	Livingston/David/Hoffman
89	53.92	"A Dream Is a Wish" (Strings)	:20	Livingston/David/Hoffman
90	54.24	"The Missing Wand"	:28	Smith
91	54.24	"Bibbidi-Bobbidi-Boo" (Introduction)	:11	Livingston/David/Hoffman
92	54.83	"Bibbidi-Bobbidi-Boo" (The Magic Song)	:45	Livingston/David/Hoffman
93	55.50	Paraphrase on "Bibbidi-Bobbidi-Boo"	:48	Livingston/David/Hoffman
94	56.21	Paraphrase on "Bibbidi-Bobbidi-Boo"	:48	Livingston/David/Hoffman
95	56.93	"Coach Is Ready"	:17	Smith
96	56.93	Paraphrase on "Bibbidi-Bobbidi-Boo"	:20	Livingston/David/Hoffman
97	56.93	"A New Dress"	:13	Smith

98	56.93	Paraphrase on "Dream Is a Wish" (Humming)	:34	Livingston/David/Hoffman
99	58.21	"Bibbidi-Bobbidi-Boo" (Finale Part 1)	:12	Livingston/David/Hoffman
100	58.40	"Bibbidi-Bobbidi-Boo" (Finale Part 2)	:15	Livingston/David/Hoffman
101	60.12	"Royal Fanfare"	:12	Smith
102	60.30	"Reception at Palace"	1:30	Smith
103	61.66	"No Hope"	:24	Smith
104	61.66	Enter Cinderella ("A Dream Is a Wish" Motive)	:19	Livingston/David/Hoffman
105	62.31	"New Hopes"	:13	Smith
106	62.74	"So This Is Love" (Orchestra)	1:36	Livingston/David/Hoffman
107	63.57	"So This Is Love"—King Humming	:07	Livingston/David/Hoffman
108	63.57	"Wedding March"	:05	Mendelssohn/Smith (arranger)
109	64.18	"So This Is Love" (Duet)	1:45	Livingston/David/Hoffman
110	65.85	"Midnight Chase"	1:21	Wallace
111	67.06	"So This Is Love" (Humming)	:42	Livingston/David/Hoffman
112	70.59	"The Royal Bed Chamber"	:11	Smith
113	70.76	"Twinkle, Twinkle Little Star"	:06	Smith (arranger)
114	70.86	"The Duke's Message"	:33	Smith
115	70.86	"Wedding March"	:08	Mendelssohn/Smith (arranger)
116	70.86	"The Duke's Message" (Continued)	:10	Smith
117	71.71	"The King's Slipper"	:30	Smith
118	72.41	"The Glass Slipper"	:36	Smith
119	72.96	"A Proclamation"	:10	Smith
120	73.13	"Stepmother's Dilemma"	:54	Smith
121	73.97	"Stepmother's Plans"	1:05	Smith
122	74.95	"A Different Story"	:14	Smith
123	75.25	"Luck for Cinderella"	:10	Smith
124	75.41	"So This Is Love"—(Cinderella Humming)	:20	Livingston/David/Hoffman
125	75.70	Paraphrase on "Work Song"	:17	Livingston/David/Hoffman
126	75.70	"So This Is Love"—(Cinderella Humming)	:17	Livingston/David/Hoffman
127	76.23	"Locked in Attic"	:32	Smith
128	80.28	"Trumpet Call"	:11	Wallace

129	80.28	Paraphrase on "Work Song"	:26	Livingston/David/Hoffman
130	80.28	"A Visit from the Duke"	:22	Smith
131	81.14	"Whose Slipper Is It?"	:31	Smith
132	82.59	"Anastasia Tries Slipper"	:38	Smith
133	83.17	"Work Song" Motive	:11	Livingston/David/Hoffman
134	83.17	"Hot Stuff"	:14	Smith
135	83.17	Paraphrase on "Work Song"	:37	Livingston/David/Hoffman
136	84.21	Paraphrase on "Work Song"	:18	Livingston/David/Hoffman
137	84.48	Paraphrase on "Work Song"	:18	Livingston/David/Hoffman
138	84.48	"Dream Is a Wish" Motive	:04	Livingston/David/Hoffman
139	84.81	"Lucifer versus Gus"	:12	Smith
140	84.81	Paraphrase on "Work Song"	:29	Livingston/David/Hoffman
141	85.45	Paraphrase on "Work Song"	:38	Livingston/David/Hoffman
142	86.01	"Misfit"	:31	Smith
143	86.49	Paraphrase on "Work Song"	:13	Livingston/David/Hoffman
144	86.49	"Bruno to the Rescue"	:26	Smith
145	87.21	"Cinderella Appears on Stairs"	:19	Smith
146	87.21	"Dream Is a Wish" Motive	:05	Livingston/David/Hoffman
147	87.21	"The Slipper Breaks"	:27	Smith
148	87.96	"Perfect Fit"	:16	Smith
149	88.34	Finale Part 1 (Wedding Bells)	:17	Wallace
150	88.34	Finale Part 2 ('A Dream Is a Wish Your Heart Makes")	:37	Livingston/David/Hoffman

ALICE IN WONDERLAND

Production: 2069   Film Duration: 75:02   Music Duration: 68:13

SEQ	CUE	TITLE	TIMING	COMPOSERS
1	M10.12	Main Title Part 1—Introduction	:15	Wallace
2	M10.35	Main Title Part 2—"Alice in Wonderland"	1:26	Hilliard/Fain
3	M11.35	"Alice in Wonderland"—Song	:51	Hilliard/Fain
4	M12.41	"Alice" background	:25	Wallace
5	M12.78	Introduction to "In a World of My Own"	:32	Wallace

6	M13.25	"In a World of My Own"	1:18	Hilliard/Fain
7	M14.43	Paraphrase on "I'm Late"	:43	Hilliard/Fain
8	M15.07	"Alice" Background	:21	Wallace
9	M16.44	Paraphrase on "I'm Late"	:15	Hilliard/Fain/Wallace (arranger)
10	M16.66	"I'm Late"	:05	Hilliard/Fain
11	M16.66	"Alice" Theme	:05	Hilliard/Fain
12	M16.81	"Alice" Background	:48	Wallace
13	M17.63	Paraphrase on "Alice"	:43	Hilliard/Fain
14	M17.63	"Alice" Background	:09	Wallace
15	M18.43	"Alice" Background	:06	Wallace
16	M18.56–69	"Alice" Background	:11	Wallace
17	M18.77	"Alice" Background	:11	Wallace
18	M18.94	"Alice" Background	:35	Wallace
19	M18.94	"Alice" Background	:15	Wallace
20	M20.32,79	"Sailor's Hornpipe"	:35	Traditional/Wallace (arranger)
21	M20.87	"Alice" Background (Including 21.01)	:09	Wallace
22	M21.02	"Row, Row, Row Your Boat"	:07	Traditional/Wallace (arranger)
23	M21.02	"Alice" Background	:08	Wallace
24	M21.23	"The Caucus Race"	1:16	Hilliard/Fain
25	M22.37,50,73	"Alice" Background (Tweedle Dum & Dee Section)	:37	Wallace
26	M23.04	"Alice" Background (Dee & Dum Dance)	:07	Wallace
27	M23.28	"How D'Ya Do and Shake Hands"	:09	Coben/Wallace
28	M23.50	"Alice" Background (Dee & Dum) (Including: 23.55, 65, 69, 77)	:31	Wallace
29	M23.94	"Alice" Background (Dee & Dum) (Including: M24.13)	:24	Wallace
30	M24.41	"The Walrus and the Carpenter"	1:07	Carroll/Hilliard/Fain
31	M25.40,48	"Alice" Background	:08	Wallace
32	M25.53	"The Walrus and the Carpenter" (Theme)	:23	Carroll/Hilliard/Fain
33	M25.53	"The Walrus and the Carpenter"	:18	Carroll/Hilliard/Fain
34	M26.16,46	"The Walrus and the Carpenter"	:42	Carroll/Hilliard/Fain
35	M26.77	"The Walrus and the Carpenter" (Theme) (M27.18)	:38	Carroll/Hilliard/Fain
36	M27.39	"Alice" Background (Walrus)	:32	Wallace
37	M27.86	"The Walrus and the Carpenter"	:23	Carroll/Hilliard/Fain

38	M28.18	"The Walrus and the Carpenter"	:25	Carroll/Hilliard/Fain
39	M28.70	"The Walrus and the Carpenter" (Theme)	:09	Carroll/Hilliard/Fain
40	M28.85	"The Walrus and the Carpenter" (Tag)	:05	Carroll/Hilliard/Fain
41	M29.14	"Old Father William"	:23	Carroll/Wallace
42	M30.15	"Alice" Theme	:15	Hilliard/Fain
43	M30.34	"I'm Late"—Theme	:06	Hilliard/Fain
44	M30.34	"Alice" Background	:13	Wallace
45	M30.67	"I'm Late"—Theme	:18	Hilliard/Fain
46	M31.11	"Alice" Background	:16	Wallace
47	M31.48	"We'll Smoke the Blighter Out" (Theme) (Including M31.61)	:08	Hibler/Sears/Wallace
48	M31.67	"Alice" Background	:18	Wallace
49	M31.98	"We'll Smoke the Blighter Out" (Theme)	:11	Hibler/Sears/Wallace
50	M32.11	"We'll Smoke the Blighter Out" (Theme)	:20	Hibler/Sears/Wallace
51	M31.98	"Alice" Background	:12	Wallace
52	M32.11	"We'll Smoke the Blighter Out" (Theme)	:21	Hibler/Sears/Wallace
53	M32.93	"Alice" Background (Including M33.00, 17, 43)	:41	Wallace
54	M33.53	"We'll Smoke the Blighter Out"	:39	Hibler/Sears/Wallace
55	M34.10,21	"Alice" Background	:29	Wallace
56	M34.53	"I'm Late" (Theme)	:17	Hilliard/Fain
57	M34.78	"We'll Smoke the Blighter Out" (Theme)	:09	Wallace
58	M34.91	"I'm Late" (Theme)	:03	Hilliard/Fain
59	M34.94	"Alice" Background	:17	Wallace
60	M35.21	Paraphrase on "Alice in Wonderland"	:45	Hilliard/Fain
61	M36.01	Vocalizing	:10	Wallace
62	M36.16	"All in the Golden Afternoon"	1:19	Hilliard/Fain
63	M37.35	"All in the Golden Afternoon"	1:05	Hilliard/Fain
64	M38.41	Paraphrase on "Alice in Wonderland"	:43	Hilliard/Fain
65	M39.09	"Alice" Background (Including M39.20, 28)	:32	Wallace
66	M40.15	"Alice" Background	:18	Wallace
67	M40.39	"A-E-I-O-U (Caterpillar Song)" (Including 41.22)	1:00	Wallace
68	M41.29	"Alice" Background (Caterpillar)	:49	Wallace
69	M42.10	"Alice" Background (Including M42.24–M44.54)	3:03	Wallace
70	M44.85	"Alice" (Theme)	:20	Hilliard/Fain

71	M45.28,36	"Alice" Background (Bird in Trees Material)	1:01	Wallace
72	M46.24	"Alice" Material	:11	Wallace
73	M46.24	"Alice" (Theme)	:19	Hilliard/Fain
74	M46.69	"'Twas Brillig"	:17	Carroll/De Paul/ Raye
75	M47.25	"'Twas Brillig"	:09	Carroll/De Paul/ Raye
76	M47.43	"'Twas Brillig"	:11	Carroll/De Paul/ Raye
77	M47.43	"Alice" Background ('Twas Brillig Material)	:21	Wallace
78	M47.43	"'Twas Brillig"	:10	Carroll/DePaul/ Raye
79	M48.04	"Alice" Background ('Twas Brillig Material)	1:00	Wallace
80	M49.07	"'Twas Brillig"	:07	Carroll/DePaul/ Raye
81	M50.12	"The Unbirthday Song"	:54	David/Hoffman/ Livingston
82	M50.94,96	"Alice" Background (Tea Party)	:07	Wallace
83	M51.20–42	"Alice" Background (Tea Party)	:52	Wallace
84	M51.98	"Unbirthday" Theme	:09	David/Hoffman/ Livingston
85	M52.11–55	"The Unbirthday Song"	:51	David/Hoffman/ Livingston
86	M53.12=46	"Alice" Background (Tea Party)	:39	Wallace
87	M53.93–55.68	"Alice" Background (Tea Party)	1:57	Wallace
88	M55.70	"I'm Late" (Theme)	:09	Hilliard/Fain
89	M55.91	"Alice" Background (Tea Party)	:21	Wallace
90	M57.17	"Unbirthday" Theme	:09	David/Hoffman/ Livingston
91	M57.31	"The Unbirthday Song"	:05	David/Hoffman/ Livingston
92	M57.39	"Alice" Background (Tea Party)	:03	Wallace
93	M57.40	"Tea Party Finale"	:16	David/Hoffman/ Livingston
94	M60.12–63.90	"Alice" Background (Tulgey Wood)	3:16	Wallace
95	M63.07	"Alice" Theme	:18	Hilliard/Fain
96	M63.34–63.53	"Alice" Background (Tulgey Woods)	:21	Wallace
97	M63.72	"Very Good Advice"	2:09	Hilliard/Fain
98	M65.66	"'Twas Brillig"	:08	Carroll/De Paul/ Raye
99	M65.79	"'Twas Brillig"	:40	Carroll/De Paul/ Raye
100	M66.43–66.59	"Alice" Background (Tulgey Woods)	:16	Wallace
101	M70.13	"Painting the Roses Red"	:55	Hilliard/Fain

102	M70.94	"Alice" Background (Painting Roses)	:07	Wallace
103	M70.94	"Painting the Roses Red"	:35	Hilliard/Fain
104	M71.58	"Trumpet Fanfare"	:03	Wallace
105	M71.62	"Alice" Background (Painting Roses)	:09	Wallace
106	M71.76	"March of the Cards"	1:01	Fain
107	M72.74	"Rabbits Call (Bugle)"	:07	Wallace
108	M72.84	"I'm Late" (Theme)	:17	Hilliard/Fain
109	M73.07	"Painting the Roses Red" (Queen's Chorus)	:31	Hilliard/Fain
110	M73.56–73.76	"Alice" Background (Painting Roses)	:17	Wallace
111	M73.81	"Painting the Roses Red"	:09	Hilliard/Fain
112	M74.15–74.30	"Alice" Background (Painting the Roses)	:56	Wallace
113	M74.99	"Trumpet Call"	:03	Wallace
114	M75.04	"March of the Cards"	:47	Fain
115	M75.76–75.93	"Alice" Background (Croquet)	:13	Wallace
116	M75.95	Paraphrase on "March of the Cards"	:16	Fain
117	M76.20	Paraphrase on "March of the Cards"	:23	Fain
118	M76.54	"Alice" Background (Croquet Game)	:13	Wallace
119	M76.73	"Painting the Roses Red" (Theme)	:15	Fain
120	M76.96–77.67	"Alice" Background (Croquet Game)	:56	Wallace
121	M77.81	"'Twas Brillig" (Theme)	:17	Carroll/De Paul/ Raye
122	M78.09–78.22	"Alice" Background (Croquet Game)	:16	Wallace
123	M78.29	"'Twas Brillig" (Theme)	:11	Carroll/De Paul/ Raye
124	M80.14–36	"Alice" Background (Croquet)	:33	Wallace
125	M80.62–80.23	"Alice" Background (Trial)	1:47	Wallace
126	M82.30	"Dialogue & Celeste"	:06	Wallace
127	M82.42–82.53	"Alice" Background (Trial)	:21	Wallace
128	M82.89	"Introduction to Song"	:04	Wallace
129	M82.95	Reprise of "Unbirthday Song"	:21	David/Hoffman/ Livingston
130	M83.45–84.57	"Alice" Background (Trial)	1:26	Wallace
131	M84.74	"Alice" Background (Chase)	:11	Wallace
132	M84.74	"March of the Cards" (Theme)	:09	Fain
133	M84.74	"Alice" Background (Chase)	:13	Wallace
134	M84.74	"The Caucus Race" (Theme)	:11	Hilliard/Fain
135	M84.74	"The Unbirthday Song" (Theme)	:11	David/Hoffman/ Livingston
136	M84.74	"Alice" Background (Chase)	:09	Wallace
137	M85.69–85.98	"Alice" Background (Chase Concluded)	:45	Wallace
138	M86.47	"Dialogue & Celeste"	:15	Wallace
139	M86.59–86.78	"Alice in Wonderland"—Song (Finale)	:30	Hilliard/Fain

| 140 | M86.78 | "Alice in Wonderland"—End Title | :11 | Wallace |
| 141 | M87.21 | "Alice in Wonderland"—Credit End Title | :40 | Hilliard/Fain |

PETER PAN

Production: 2074   Film Duration: 76:30   Music Duration: 70:58

SEQ	CUE	TITLE	TIMING	COMPOSERS
1	Opening Theme	Main Title—Part I "Peter Pan" Introduction	:33	Wallace
2	Opening Theme	Main Title—Part II "The Second Star to the Right"	1:15	Cahn/Fain
3	1.A	"The Second Star to the Right"	:31	Cahn/Fain
4	1.1	"Your Mother and Mine"	:20	Cahn/Fain
5	1.2–10	"Peter Pan" Background	1:53	Wallace
6	1.11	"Peter Pan" Background	:12	Wallace
7	1.12–14	"Peter Pan" Background	:29	Wallace
8	1.15–16	"Peter Pan" Background	:19	Wallace
9	1.17	"Your Mother and Mine"—Theme	:11	Cahn/Fain
10	1.18–24	"Peter Pan" Background	1:17	Wallace
11	1.25–27	"Peter Pan" Background	:29	Wallace
12	1.28	"Peter Pan" Background	1:29	Wallace
13	1.28–30	"Peter Pan" Background	:44	Wallace
14	1.31	Peter Pan Theme	:26	Wallace
15	1.32	Peter Pan Theme (Developed)	:11	Wallace
16	2.1	Peter Pan Theme	:21	Wallace
17	2.1	"Peter Pan" Background	:30	Wallace
18	2.1	Peter Pan Theme	:05	Wallace
19	2.1	"Peter Pan" Background	:07	Wallace
20	2.2	Peter Pan Theme	:09	Wallace
21	2.2	"Peter Pan" Background	:09	Wallace
22	2.2	Peter Pan Theme (Developed)	:12	Wallace
23	2.3–4	Peter Pan Theme	:33	Wallace
24	2.5–6A	"Peter Pan" Background	:27	Wallace
25	2.6B	Peter Pan Motif	:05	Wallace
26	2.7–9	"Peter Pan" Background	:51	Wallace
27	2.10	"Your Mother and Mine"	:18	Cahn/Fain/Wallace (arranger)
29	2.1.1	Peter Pan Theme	:22	Wallace
30	2.1.2–3	"Peter Pan" Background	:35	Wallace
31	2.1.4–5	"Peter Pan" Background	:25	Wallace
32	2.1.6–7	"You Can Fly! You Can Fly! You Can Fly!"	:43	Cahn/Fain/Wallace (arranger)

33	2.1.8	"Peter Pan" Background	:06	Wallace
34	2.1.9	"You Can Fly! You Can Fly! You Can Fly!"	:18	Cahn/Fain/Wallace (arranger)
35	2.1.10	"Peter Pan" Background	:07	Wallace
36	2.1.11	"You Can Fly! You Can Fly! You Can Fly!	:15	Cahn/Fain/Wallace (arranger)
37	3.1–2	Introduction to "You Can Fly"	:13	Wallace
38	3.3	"You Can Fly! You Can Fly! You Can Fly!"	1:17	Wallace
39	3.4	Bridge to "You Can Fly"	:18	Wallace
40	3.3A-4	"You Can Fly! You Can Fly! You Can Fly!"	:30	Cahn/Fain
41	3.3A-4	Peter Pan Theme	:11	Wallace
42	4.A	"A Pirate's Life"	:29	Penner/Wallace
43	4.B	"Peter Pan" Background (Including "Irish Washer Woman"–Public Domain)	:37	Wallace
44	4.C	"Peter Pan" Background	:09	Wallace
45	4.1	"Peter Pan" Background	:58	Wallace
46	4.2	"A Pirate's Life"	:24	Penner/Wallace
47	4.3–5	"Peter Pan" Background	:46	Wallace
48	4.6	"Never Smile at a Crocodile"—Crocodile Theme	1:11	Churchill
49	4.7	"A Pirate's Life"	:33	Penner/Wallace
50	4.8–10	"Peter Pan" Background	1:19	Wallace
51	4.11A	Peter Pan Theme and Background	:41	Wallace
52	4.12	"Peter Pan" Background and Theme	:35	Wallace
53	5.1–9	Peter Pan Theme Background (Including "Follow the Leader")	2:19	Hibler/Sears/ Wallace
54	5.10	"Peter Pan" Background	:01	Wallace
55	5.11	"Your Mother and Mine"	:17	Cahn/Fain/Wallace (arranger)
56	5.12–14	"Peter Pan" Background	:49	Wallace
57	5.15	"Peter Pan" Background	:09	Wallace
58	6.1	"Following the Leader (Tee-Dum, Tee-Dum)"	1:25	Hibler/Sears/ Wallace
59	6.2–8	"Peter Pan" Background	1:08	Wallace
60	6.9–10	"Following the Leader (Tee-Dum, Tee-Dum)"	:35	Hibler/Sears/ Wallace
61	7.1	"Peter Pan" Background (Mermaid Theme)	:24	Wallace
62	7.1A	Peter Pan Theme	:14	Wallace
63	7.2	"Peter Pan" Background (Mermaid Theme)	:27	Wallace
64	7.4–5B	"Peter Pan" Background	:30	Wallace
65	7.6	"Peter Pan" Background (Mermaid Theme)"	:05	Wallace
66	7.7	"Peter Pan"	:13	Wallace

67	7.7	"The Elegant Captain Hook"	:07	Cahn/Fain/Wallace (arranger)
68	7.7	"Never Smile at a Crocodile"	:15	Churchill/Wallace (arranger)
69	7.8	Peter Pan Theme (Developed)	:11	Wallace
70	8.1–2	Peter Pan Theme (Developed)	:41	Wallace
71	8.3A	"Peter Pan" Background	:08	Wallace
72	8.4–8	"Peter Pan" Background	1:21	Wallace
73	8.10	"Peter Pan" Background	:25	Wallace
74	8.11–14	Peter Pan Theme (Developed) / "Peter Pan" Background	:51	Wallace
75	8.15–18	"Peter Pan" Background	:47	Wallace
76	8.19	"Never Smile at a Crocodile"	:17	Churchill
77	8.19	"Peter Pan" Background	1:15	Wallace
78	8.24	Peter Pan Theme (Developed)	:19	Wallace
79	9.1A	"Never Smile at a Crocodile"	:39	Churchill/Wallace (arranger)
80	9.2	"A Pirate's Life"	:03	Penner/Wallace
81	9.3–6	"Peter Pan" Background	:16	Wallace
82	9.7	"Never Smile at a Crocodile"	:16	Churchill/Wallace (arranger)
83	9.8–15	"Peter Pan" Background	1:33	Wallace
84	10.1–5	"What Made the Red Man Red?"	1:53	Cahn/Fain
85	10.6	"What Made the Red Man Red?" (Developed)	:41	Cahn/Fain
86	11.A	Piano Improvisation on "A Pirate's Life"	1:09	Wallace
87	11.A	Piano Improvisation on "Flower Song"	:18	Lange/Wallace (arranger)
88	11.1–2	Piano Improvisation on "Flower Song"	:20	Lange/Wallace (arranger)
89	11.3–11	"Peter Pan" Background	1:40	Wallace
90	12.1	"What Made the Red Man Red?" (Developed)	:27	Cahn/Fain/Wallace (arranger)
91	12.2–6A	"Peter Pan" Background	:50	Wallace
92	12.7	"What Made the Red Man Red?" (Developed)	:11	Cahn/Fain/Wallace (arranger)
93	12.7	"Peter Pan" Background	:23	Wallace
94	12.8	"Peter Pan" Background	:13	Wallace
95	12.9	Introduction to "Mother Song"	:07	Wallace
96	12.10	"Your Mother and Mine"	1:51	Cahn/Fain
97	12.11	"Your Mother and Mine" (Developed)	:22	Cahn/Fain/Wallace (arranger)
98	12.12–13	"Peter Pan" Background	:17	Wallace
99	12.14A	Peter Pan Theme	:18	Wallace

100	12.15	"Peter Pan" Background	:35	Wallace
101	13.1–2	"The Elegant Captain Hook"	1:18	Cahn/Fain
102	13.3–4	"Peter Pan" Background	:43	Wallace
103	13.5–8	"Peter Pan" Background	2:32	Wallace
104	14.A	"Peter Pan" Background	:13	Wallace
105	14.1–10A	"Peter Pan" Background	2:31	Wallace
106	14.11	"Peter Pan" Background	:19	Wallace
107	14.11	Peter Pan Theme	:07	Wallace
108	14.12–16A	"Peter Pan" Background	1:31	Wallace
109	14.17	"Hook Is a Cod Fish" ("A Tisket, A Tasket")	:09	Traditional/Wallace (arranger)
110	14.17–19	"Peter Pan" Background	:17	Wallace
111	14.20	"Peter Pan" Background	:09	Wallace
112	14.20	"Never Smile at a Crocodile"	:27	Churchill/Wallace (arranger)
113	15.1	Peter Pan Theme (Developed)	:16	Wallace
114	15.2–5	"Peter Pan" Background	:35	Wallace
115	15.6	"You Can Fly! You Can Fly! You Can Fly!"	:25	Cahn/Fain/Wallace (arranger)
116	15.7–9	"Peter Pan" Background	:17	Wallace
117	15.10	Peter Pan Theme (Developed)	:35	Wallace
118	15.10	"You Can Fly! You Can Fly! You Can Fly!"– Motif	:10	Cahn/Fain/Wallace (arranger)
119	15.10	"Hook Is a Cod Fish" ("A Tisket, A Tasket")	:09	Traditional/Wallace (arranger)
120	15.11	"You Can Fly! You Can Fly! You Can Fly!"– Motif	:10	Cahn/Fain/Wallace (arranger)
121	15.11	Peter Pan Theme (Developed)	:11	Wallace
122	15.11AB	"Peter Pan" Background	:10	Wallace
123	15.12A	Introduction to Finale	:11	Wallace
124	15.12B	Finale: "You Can Fly!" And Peter Pan Theme	:34	Cahn/Fain/Wallace

LADY AND THE TRAMP

Production: 2079   Film Duration: 75:38Music Duration: 67:43

SEQ	CUE	TITLE	TIMING	COMPOSERS
1	A/B	Main Title—Parts 1 & 2	:14	Wallace
2	C	Main Title—Part 3: "Bella Notte"	1:23	Burke/Lee
3	1.0	"Dedication"	:22	Wallace
4		"Peace on Earth"	1:00	Burke/Lee

5	1 1-B	"Lady & Tramp" Background	:33	Wallace
6	1 A	Lady (Theme)	1:08	Fine/Penner/ Wallace
7	1 BC-G	"Lady and the Tramp" Background	1:58	Wallace
8	1 H	Lady (Theme)	:22	Fine/Penner/ Wallace
9	1 JKL	"Lady and the Tramp" Background	1:07	Wallace
10	1 M	Lady (Theme)	1:16	Fine/Penner/ Wallace
11	1 N	"Lady and the Tramp" Background	:16	Wallace
12	1 O	Lady (Theme)	:21	Fine/Penner/ Wallace
13	1 P-Q	"Loch Lomond"	:24	Traditional/Wallace (arranger)
14	1 R	"Lady and the Tramp" Background	:03	Wallace
15	1 S	Lady (Theme)	:28	Fine/Penner/ Wallace
16	1 T-Z	"Lady and the Tramp" Background	1:50	Wallace
17	1 BB-CC	Lady (Theme)	:49	Fine/Penner/ Wallace
18	1.1 1	Lady (Theme)	:37	Wallace
19	1.1 2	"Bella Notte"	:15	Burke/Lee
20	1.1 3	"Lady and the Tramp" Background	:17	Wallace
21	1.1 4	"Zu Lauterbach" ("Where, Oh Where Has My Little Dog Gone?")	:27	Traditional/Wallace (arranger)
22	1.1 5	"Lady and the Tramp" Background	:46	Wallace
23	1.1 6	Tramp (Theme)	:23	Wallace
24	2 1–3	"Lady and the Tramp" Background	:35	Wallace
25	2 4	"La La Lu"	:15	Burke/Lee
26	2 4A/B	"Lady and the Tramp" Background	:18	Wallace
27	2 5	Lady (Theme)	:34	Fine/Penner/ Wallace
28	2 5A-7A	"Lady and the Tramp" Background	:37	Wallace
29	2 8	"La La Lu"	:29	Burke/Lee
30	2 9–10	"Lady and the Tramp" Background	1:27	Wallace
31	2/3	"Lady and the Tramp" Background Sequence 2.11-15, Sequence 3 1-8	3:12	Wallace
32	3.2 A-1	"Lady and the Tramp" Background	:23	Wallace
33	3.2 2	"What Is a Baby"	1:11	Burke/Lee
34	3.2 2	"La La Lu"	1:20	Burke/Lee
35	4.1 1	"Lady and the Tramp" Background	:53	Wallace
36	4.1 2	Lady (Theme)	:06	Fine/Penner/ Wallace
37	4.1 3	"Lady and the Tramp" Background	:17	Wallace

38	4.1 4	Lady (Theme)	:21	Fine/Penner/ Wallace
39	4.1 5	"Rock-a-Bye Baby"	:17	Canning/Wallace (arranger)
40	4.1 6	"Siamese Cat Song"	1:55	Burke/Lee
41	4.1 7	"Lady and the Tramp" Background	:59	Wallace
42	5 1–13	"Lady and the Tramp" Background	:55	Wallace
43	5 3–6	"Lady and the Tramp" Background	3:09	Wallace
44	6 7–8	Beaver Theme	:49	Wallace
45	6 8A–10A	"Effects"	:43	Wallace
46	6 12	Beaver Theme	:14	Wallace
47	6 13–19	"Lady and the Tramp" Background	:52	Wallace
48	7 1	"Lady and the Tramp" Background	:24	Wallace
49	7 2	Tramp (Theme)	:39	Wallace
50		"Bella Notte" (Italian Lyrics)	:16	Burke/Lee
51	7 3–7	"Lady and the Tramp" Background	1:39	Wallace
52	7 8	"Bella Notte" (Duet)	1:15	Burke/Lee
53	7.1 2	"Bella Notte" (Mixed Chorus)	1:16	Burke/Lee
54	8 1	"Lady and the Tramp" Background	:23	Wallace
55	8 2	"Had I Known"	1:15	George/Wallace
56	8 3	"La La Lu"	:15	Burke/Lee
57	9 1	"Zu Lauterbach" (Where, Oh Where Has My Little Dog Gone?")	:07	Traditional/Wallace (arranger)
58		"Bella Notte"	:08	Burke/Lee
59	9 2–6	"Lady and the Tramp" Background	1:34	Wallace
60		"Lady and the Tramp" Background	:11	Wallace
61	10 1	"Home Sweet Home"	1:30	Bishop
62	10 2–9	"Lady and the Tramp" Background	1:55	Wallace
63	10 10	"He's a Tramp"	:47	Burke/Lee
64	10 11	"He's a Tramp"	1:34	Burke/Lee
65	10 12	"Lady and the Tramp" Background	:40	Wallace
66	11 / 12	"Lady and the Tramp" Background Sequence 11 1-11, Sequence 12 1-6A	7:16	Wallace
67	12 7	"Lady and the Tramp" Background	1:11	Wallace
68	12 9–10	"Lady and the Tramp" Background (Chase)	2:44	Wallace
69	12.1 1–2	Tramp (Theme)	:48	Wallace
70	12.1 3	"Lady and the Tramp" Background	:42	Wallace
71		Lady (Theme)	:37	Fine/Penner/ Wallace
72	12.1 4	"Peace on Earth" (Including End Title)	:27	Burke/Lee

SLEEPING BEAUTY

Production: 2082   Film Duration: 74:56   Music Duration: 74:16

SEQ	CUE	TITLE	TIMING	COMPOSERS
1		Main Title Part 1	:05	Bruns
2		Main Title Part 2	:07	Bruns
3		"Once Upon a Dream"—Main Title Part 3	:39	Fain/Lawrence
4		"Sing a Smiling Song"—Main Title Part 4	:09	Adair/Bruns
5		Main Title Part 5	:37	Bruns/ Tchaikovsky
6	1A	"My Beloved"	:33	Gil George/Bruns
7	1B	"Sweet Aurora"	:05	Bruns
8	1C	"Sunshine"	:24	Bruns
9	1D	"On That Joyful Day"	:11	Bruns
10	1E	"Hail to the Princess Aurora"	1:05	Adair/Bruns
11	1F	"Hail to the Princess Aurora"	:13	Adair/Bruns
12	1G	"Fanfares"	:07	Bruns
13	1H	"The Royal Highness"	:33	Bruns/Tchaikovsky
14	1J	"Fanfares"	:06	Bruns
15	1K	"Fairies Enter"	:26	Bruns/Tchaikovsky
16	1K	"Sing a Smiling Song"	:35	Adair/Bruns
17	1L	"Sleeping Beauty Song"	:29	Adair/Bruns
18	1M	"Sleeping Beauty Song"	:19	Adair/Bruns
19	1N	"Sleeping Beauty Song"	:31	Adair/Bruns
20	1O	"Maleficent Appears"	1:25	Bruns
21	1P	"Maleficent Bestows Her Gift"	1:11	Bruns
22	1Q	"Sleeping Beauty Song"	:36	Adair/Bruns
23	1R/2A	"Burn the Wheels"	:31	Bruns/Tchaikovsky
24	1R/2A	"Burn the Wheels"	:09	Bruns/Tchaikovsky
25	2B	"Tea Time"	1:09	Bruns/Tchaikovsky
26	2C	"Fairy Conference"	1:26	Bruns/Tchaikovsky
27	2D	"Raise the Child"	1:21	Bruns/Tchaikovsky
28	3A	"Goons"	1:28	Bruns/Tchaikovsky
29	3B	"Cradles"	1:13	Bruns/Tchaikovsky
30	3C	"In the Woods"	:21	Bruns/Tchaikovsky
31	3D	"Briar Rose"	:15	Bruns
32	3E	"A Surprise Party"	1:55	Bruns/Tchaikovsky
33	3F	"Dance of the Leaves"	:23	Jackman/Bruns
34	3F/3F-1/3F-2	"Dance of the Leaves"	:47	Jackman/Bruns
35	3G	"Fitting the Dress"	1:08	Bruns
36	3H	"Bluebird"	1:27	Bruns

37	3J	"In the Woods"	:13	Bruns
38	3K	"Briar and the Prince"	:17	Bruns
39	3L/3?-1/3L2	"Let's Find Out"	:49	Bruns
40	4A	"I Wonder"	1:27	Hibler/Sears/Bruns
41	4B	"Treat Me Like a Child"	:51	Bruns
42	4C	"I Wonder"	:37	Hibler/Sears/Bruns
43	4D/4D-1/4D-2	"Woodland Symphony"	:33	Bruns
44	4E	"You Know, Sampson"	:20	Bruns
45	4F	"Building Scare Crow"	:27	Bruns/Tchaikovsky
46	5A	"Scare Crow Walks"	:21	Bruns/Tchaikovsky
47	5B/5C	"Once Upon a Dream"	1:07	Fain/Lawrence
48	5D	"I'm Sorry"	:20	Bruns/Tchaikovsky
49	5E	"Once Upon a Dream"	:56	Fain/Lawrence
50	5F	"Who Are You?"	:31	Bruns
51	5G	"Bake a Cake"	1:33	Bruns/Tchaikovsky
52	5H1/23456	"Sing a Smiling Song"	2:40	Adair/Bruns
53	5J/5J-1	"Once Upon a Dream"	:20	Fain/Lawrence
54	5K	"Aunt Flora"	:49	Bruns/Tchaikovsky
55	5L/6A	"Once Upon a Dream"	1:05	Fain/Lawrence
56	5L/6A	"Aurora Crying"	:13	Bruns
57	6B	"The Kings"	:57	Bruns
58	6C	"Skumps"	:18	Adair/Penner/ Bruns
59	6D	"Skumps"	:25	Adair/Penner/ Bruns
60	6E	"Skumps"	:24	Adair/Penner/ Bruns
61	6F	"Skumps"	:57	Adair/Penner/ Bruns
62	6F	"The Plans"	1:07	Bruns
63	6G	"Lute Snoring Sequence"—(Musical Effects)	:20	Ad lib.
64	6H	"His Royal Highness"	:36	Bruns
65	6J	"Once Upon a Dream"	:40	Fain/Lawrence
66	6J/6J-1	"I've Met Her"	1:08	Bruns
67	7A	"Off to the Castle"	1:09	Bruns
68	7A	"Sleeping Beauty Song"	:19	Adair/Bruns
69	7A	"Unhappy Aurora"	:19	Bruns/Tchaikovsky
70	7B	"Maleficent Evil Spell"	:48	Bruns/Tchaikovsky
71	7C	"Maleficent Evil Spell"	1:38	Bruns/Tchaikovsky
72	7D	"Maleficent Evil Spell"	:14	Bruns
73	7E	"Simple Fools"	:37	Bruns
74	7F	"On the Throne"	:21	Bruns

75	7G	"Fanfares"	:11	Bruns
76	7H	"Hail to the Princess Aurora"	:15	Adair/Bruns
77	7J	"Fairies Cry"	1:01	Bruns
78	7K	"Sleeping Beauty Song"	1:40	Adair/Bruns
79	7L	"Minstrel Goes Down"	:40	Bruns/Tchaikovsky
80	7M	"Let's Go—(Dance Vertigo)"	:27	Tchaikovsky/Bruns (arranger)
81	8A	"Once Upon a Dream"	:18	Fain/Lawrence
82	8B	"Once Upon a Dream"	:19	Fain/Lawrence
83	8B	"Prince Gets Off"	:53	Bruns/Tchaikovsky
84	9C	"Dance Vertigo"	:25	Bruns/Tchaikovsky
85	8D	"Fairies in the Cottage"	:20	Bruns/Tchaikovsky
86	8E-1/8E-1A-C	"Bacchanal"	2:54	Bruns/Tchaikovsky
87	8E2	"Suspense"	:33	Bruns
88	8E3	Maleficent's Theme	:14	Bruns/Tchaikovsky
89	8E4	"My Beloved"	1:29	Gil George/Bruns
90	9A	"In the Dungeon"	1:19	Bruns
91	9B-1	"Escape"	:48	Bruns/Tchaikovsky
92	9B-2	"Escape"	:03	Bruns/Tchaikovsky
93	9B-3	"Phillip Escapes"	:49	Bruns/Tchaikovsky
94	9C	"Stone"	:11	Bruns
95	9D-1/9D-1A	"Battle with the Forces of Evil"	1:57	Tchaikovsky/Bruns (arranger)
96	9D-2/9D-3	"Battle with the Forces of Evil"	1:05	Tchaikovsky/Bruns (arranger)
97	9D-4	"Battle with the Forces of Evil—Ending"	:16	Bruns
98	9E	"My Beloved"	1:03	Gil George/Bruns
99	9E	"Hail to the Princess Aurora"	:43	Adair/Bruns
100	9F	"Trumpets Call"	:59	Bruns/Tchaikovsky
101	9G	"Once Upon a Dream"—End Title	1:39	Fain/Lawrence

ONE HUNDRED AND ONE DALMATIANS

Production: 2110 Film Duration: 79:04   Music Duration: 61:37

SEQ	CUE	TITLE	TIMING	COMPOSERS
1		Main Title Part 1 (Buena Vista)	:05	Bruns
2		Main Title Part 2 (Walt Disney Presents)	:08	Bruns
3		Main Title Part 3 (Spots)	:10	Bruns
4		Main Title Part 4 (Dalmatians)	:09	Bruns
5		Main Title Part 5 (Dogs)	:07	Bruns
6		Main Title Part 6 (Jazz)	:46	Bruns
7		Main Title Part 7 (Bloop Bleep)	:24	Bruns

8		Main Title Part 8—"Playful Melody"	:26	Dunham/Bruns
9		Main Title Part 9 (Peter)	:13	Bruns
10		Main Title Part 10 (Our Song)	:37	Bruns
11	1A	"Remember When"	3:25	Jackman/Marks
12	1B	"Playful Melody"	:46	Dunham/Bruns
13	1C	"My Love"	:17	Bruns
14	1D	"Pongo Struts"	:13	Bruns
15	1E	"Sitting on a River Bank"	:24	Bruns
16	1F	"Girl Looks"	:15	Bruns
17	1G	"Girl Not Amused"	:22	Bruns
18	1H/2A	"I'm Not Giving Up"	1:17	Bruns
19	2B	"I Love You Dear"	:18	Bruns
20	2C	"Cruella De Vil"	1:16	Leven
21	2D	"Cruella De Vil"	:26	Leven
22	2E	"Cruella De Vil"	1:56	Leven
23	2G	"Cruella De Vil"	:36	Leven
24	2H	"Happy Home"	:43	Bruns
25	2J	"Playful Melody"	:18	Dunham/Bruns
26	2K	"Eleven Puppies"	:47	Bruns
27	2L	"Playful Melody"	:33	Dunham/Bruns
28	2M	"My Song"	:19	Bruns
29	3A	"Get Lost"	1:24	Bruns
30	3A	"Playful Melody"	:13	Dunham/Bruns
31	3B	"Get Them"	:33	Bruns
32	3C	"What Ya Gonna Do Dad?"	:35	Bruns
33	3D	"I'm Shot"	:53	Bruns
34	3E	"Thunder Always Wins"	:45	Bruns
35	3F	"Kanine Krunchies Kommercial"	:17	Leven
36	3G	"To Bed"	:35	Bruns
37	3H	"Kanine Krunchies Kommercial"	:09	Leven
38	3J	"Playful Melody"	:27	Dunham/Bruns
39	3K	"I've Got the Knob for It"	:41	Bruns
40	3L	"Excuse Me"	:49	Bruns
41	3M	"Let Me Out"	:55	Bruns
42	4A	"Puppies Stolen"	1:05	Bruns
43	4B	"Slams Phone"	1:18	Bruns
44	4C	"Sad, Sad, Sad"	:37	Bruns
45	4D	"All Dog Alert"	:06	Bruns
46	4E	"Sound Alert"	:07	Bruns
47	4H	"It's an Alert"	:26	Bruns
48	4I	"Bugle Call" (Traditional British)	:16	Bruns (arranger)

49	5A	"Oh, I Do Hope So"	1:14	Bruns
50	5B	"Whispering Flowers"	1:44	Von Blon/Stalling (arranger)
51	5C	"Horace"	:18	Bruns
52	5D	"Can You Leave Tonight?"	:46	Bruns
53	5E	"Out of Tunnel"	1:11	Bruns
54	5F	"Snow"	:45	Bruns
55	5G	"Ker-Boom"	:33	Bruns
56	6A	"Let's Get on with It"	1:15	Bruns
57	6B	"Playful Melody"	:24	Dunham/Bruns
58	6C	"Playful Melody"	:35	Dunham/Bruns
59	6D	"To the Rescue"	:55	Bruns
60	6E	"Follow Me"	1:07	Bruns
61	6F	"Dog Fights Man"	:51	Bruns
62	6G	"Playful Melody"	1:09	Dunham/Bruns
63	6H	"Colonel Speaks"	1:03	Bruns
64	6K	"Hit Me Again"	:38	Bruns
65	6L	"Dogs on Ice"	:35	Bruns
66	6L	"Playful Melody"	:12	Dunham/Bruns
67	7A	"Snow Scene"	:47	Bruns
68	7B	"Survival"	1:54	Bruns
69	7C	"I'm Hungry"	:33	Bruns
70	7C	"Playful Melody"	:10	Dunham/Bruns
71	7D	"Tired"	:56	Bruns
72	7E	"On the Road"	1:00	Bruns
73	7F	"Well!"	:33	Bruns
74	7G	"Dogs Arrive"	:48	Bruns
75	7G	"Playful Melody"	:25	Dunham/Bruns
76	7H	"Sooty Pups"	:41	Bruns
77	7J	"Fun, Fun"	:23	Bruns
78	7K	"Wheels"	:37	Bruns
79	8A	"The Escape"	1:31	Bruns
80	8B	"Hurry, Perdi"	1:00	Bruns
81	8C	"Snowfall"	1:04	Bruns
82	8D	"Car Chase"	1:26	Bruns
83	8E-V	"Cruella De Vil"	:11	Leven
84	8F	"X-Mas Cheer"	:25	Bruns
85	8G	"They're Here"	1:11	Bruns
86	8G	"Playful Melody"	:26	Dunham/Bruns
87	8H-V	"Dalmatian Plantation"	:49	Leven
88	8H-V	End Title	:05	Bruns

THE SWORD IN THE STONE

Production: 2138   Film Duration: 79:28   Music Duration: 56:23

SEQ	CUE	TITLE	TIMING	COMPOSERS
1		Buena Vista Distributor's Credit	:05	Bruns
2		Main Title—Part 1	:21	Bruns
3		Main Title—Part 2—"That's What Makes the World Go Round"	:30	Sherman/Sherman
4		Main Title—Part 3	:43	Bruns
5	1A	Introduction to Song	:11	Bruns
6	1AV/1AV-1	"The Legend of the Sword in the Stone"	1:09	Sherman/Sherman
7	1B	"Fifth Century"	1:20	Bruns
8	1D	"Bubble Pot"	:48	Bruns
9	1E	"On the Limb"	:07	Bruns
10	1E	"Faster"	:24	Bruns
11	1F	"Wolf and the Boy"	:45	Bruns
12	2A	"Drop in for Tea"	:01	Bruns
13	2B	"Wizard"	:23	Bruns
14	2C	"Sugar, Please"	:06	Bruns
15	2D	"Manners First"	:45	Bruns
16	2E	"Chart"	:04	Bruns
17	2F	"Sugar"	:01	Bruns
18	2GV	"Higitus Figitus"—(Merlin's Magic Song)	:10	Sherman/Sherman
19	2H	"Teapot"	:05	Bruns
20	2IV	"Higitus Figitus"—(Merlin's Magic Song)	:30	Sherman/Sherman
21	2JV	"Higitus Figitus"—(Merlin's Magic Song)	:29	Sherman/Sherman
22	2K	"Beard in Door"	:35	Bruns
23	2L	"Travelin' Light"	:26	Bruns
24	2M	"Up the Hill"	:49	Bruns
25	2N	"Tweet, Tweet"	:03	Bruns
26	3A	"Castle"	:16	Bruns
27	3B	"Demonstrate"	:40	Bruns
28	3C	"Be Seated"	:04	Bruns
29	3D	"Brush Off"	:29	Bruns
30		"Dancing Dishes"	:13	Bruns
31	3D	"Brush Off"	:24	Bruns
32		"Dancing Dishes"	:05	Bruns
33	3D	"Brush Off"	:08	Bruns
34	3E	"Rain on the Castle"	:11	Bruns
35	3F	"Up"	:01	Bruns
36	3G	"Water in the Bowl"	:03	Bruns

37	3H	"Water Falls"	:01	Bruns
38	3I	"Bridge Down"	:13	Bruns
39	3J	"Pellinor"	:11	Bruns
40	3K	"Pellinor Walks"	:10	Bruns
41	3K-1	"Down the Steps"	:03	Bruns
42	4B	"Here's to London"	:41	Bruns
43	4C	"My Back"	:47	Bruns
44	4D	Wart's Theme	1:19	Bruns
45	4E	"Flies from Branch"	:06	Bruns
46	4F	"Dancing Dishes"	:06	Bruns
47	4F	"Let's Go"	:23	Bruns
48	5A	"In the Swim"	1:21	Bruns
49	5BV	"That's What Makes the World Go 'Round"	:46	Sherman/Sherman
50	5C	"Bug"	:21	Bruns
51	5DV	"That's What Makes the World Go 'Round"	:27	Sherman/Sherman
52	5EV	"That's What Makes the World Go 'Round"	:41	Sherman/Sherman
53	5F	"Let's Go"	:32	Bruns
54	5GV	"That's What Makes the World Go 'Round"	:26	Sherman/Sherman
55	5H	"Snap"	1:08	Bruns
56	5J	"Fish Fry Chase"	1:21	Bruns
57	5K	"Dancing Dishes"	:12	Bruns
58	5K	"Out of Water"	:17	Bruns
59	6A	"Dancing Dishes"	:09	Bruns
60	6A	"I'm Wet"	1:12	Bruns
61	6BV	"That's What Makes the World Go 'Round"	:13	Sherman/Sherman
62	6C	"Dancing Dishes"	:48	Bruns
63	6D	"In the Woods"	:40	Bruns
64	6E	"Wild Life"	1:17	Bruns
65	6F	"Wild Life"	:39	Bruns
66	6G	"Wild Love"	:48	Bruns
67	6HV	"A Most Befuddling Thing"	:51	Sherman/Sherman
68	6I	"The Squirrel Hop"	:44	Bruns
69	6JV	"A Most Befuddling Thing"	:17	Sherman/Sherman
70	6K	"Old Love"	1:29	Bruns
71	7A	"Oh, My"	1:10	Bruns
72	7B	"The Magic"	:03	Bruns
73	7C	"Faded Love"	:52	Bruns
74	7D	"Dancing Dishes"	:20	Bruns
75	7E	"Dancing Dishes"	:16	Bruns
76	7F	"Dancing Dishes"	:47	Bruns
77	7G	"Gone"	1:03	Bruns

78	7H	"Banished"	1:01	Bruns
79	7I	"Spin Me"	:04	Bruns
80	8AA	"Smoke Ring"	:03	Bruns
81	8A	"First the 'A'"	:10	Bruns
82	8B	"Now the 'D'"	:10	Bruns
83	8C	"Wild Head Paws"	:05	Bruns
84	8D	"Let's Fly"	:13	Bruns
85	8E	"Man Will Fly"	:38	Bruns
86	8F	"Ouch"	:31	Bruns
87	8G	"Love to Fly"	:36	Bruns
88	8H	"Help, the Hawk"	:32	Bruns
89	9A	"Dance, Madam"	:05	Bruns
90	9B	"Menace Madam"	:11	Bruns
91	9CV	"Mad Madam Mim"	:47	Sherman/Sherman
92	9D	"You're on My Broom"	:35	Bruns
93	9EV	"Mad Madam Mim"	:30	Sherman/Sherman
94	9F	"Witch Dance"	:39	Bruns
95	9G	"Bird and Cat"	:23	Bruns
96	9H	"Drums—Prescored"	:31	Unknown
97	9I	"Drums—Prescored"	:08	Unknown
98	9K Thru 9Q	"Wizard's Duel"	3:36	Bruns
99	9R	"Sick"	1:31	Bruns
100	10AV	"Blue Oak Tree"	:19	Sherman/Sherman
101	10C	"Down the Steps"	:14	Bruns
102	10D	"I'm Nobody"	:41	Bruns
103	10E	"Charge"	:11	Bruns
104	10F	"Joist Me"	:18	Bruns
105	10G	"Swords"	:35	Bruns
106	10IV	"Pull It Out"	:18	Bruns
107	10J	"Hold Everything"	:03	Bruns
108	10KV	"Go Ahead Son"	:25	Bruns
109	10L	"Hail King Arthur"	:33	Bruns
110	10M	"Wish Merlin Was Here"	:28	Bruns
111	10NV	"Hail King Arthur"—End Title	:45	Bruns

THE JUNGLE BOOK

Production: 2179   Film Duration: 78:07   Music Duration: 59:21

SEQ	CUE	TITLE	TIMING	COMPOSERS
1		Buena Vista	:05	Bruns
2	1A	Main Title—"Jungle Beauty"	2:33	Bruns
3	1B	"Baby"	1:49	Bruns
4	1C	"My Own Home"	:24	Sherman/Sherman
5	1D	"The Meeting"	:24	Bruns
6	1E	"Jungle Beauty"	1:29	Bruns
7	1FV-1	"Rock-a-Bye Snake"	:12	Bruns
8	1FV	"Snake Pit"	1:06	Bruns
9	2A	"Asleep"	:14	Bruns
10	2B	"In the Tree"	:26	Bruns
11	2CV	"Colonel Hathi's March"	1:46	Sherman/Sherman
12	2D	"Colonel Hathi's March"	:40	Sherman/Sherman
13	2E	"Collide"	:10	Bruns
14	2F	"I've Had It"	:52	Bruns
15	2F	"My Own Home"	:14	Sherman/Sherman
16	3A	"Jungle Serenade"	:46	Bruns
17	3B	"Who's There"	:10	Bruns
18	3BBV	"Doo-Bee-Dee-Doo"	:12	Bruns
19	3C	"Slap"	:06	Bruns
20	3D	"Jungle Drums"	:16	Bruns
21	3E	"Growl"	:36	Bruns
22	3F	"Jungle Drums"	:20	Bruns
23	3G	"Spank"	:03	Bruns
24	3H	"Boy"	:11	Bruns
25	3J	"Jungle Drums"	:12	Bruns
26	3K	"Fall Bear"	:02	Bruns
27	3L	"My Cub"	:30	Bruns
28	3L	"The Bare Necessities"	:41	Gilkyson
29	3M/3N	"The Bare Necessities"	4:07	Gilkyson
30	3OV	"Jungle Blues"	:40	Bruns
31	4A	"Why You!"	1:11	Bruns
32	4B	"Baloo"	:05	Bruns
33	4CV	"Jungle Blues"	1:33	Bruns
34	4DV/4EV/4FV	"I Wan'na Be Like You"	2:49	Sherman/Sherman
35	4G	"Monkey Chase"	1:21	Bruns
36	5A	"Jungle Beauty"	1:08	Bruns
37	5B	"Sleep Baby"	:21	Bruns

38	5C	"Why Not"	:50	Bruns
39	5D	"Love the Kid"	1:33	Bruns
40	5EV	"The Bare Necessities"	:23	Gilkyson
41	5F	"Tell Him"	1:01	Bruns
42	5F	"My Own Home"	:16	Sherman/Sherman
43	5G	"The Boy Runs"	:56	Bruns
44	6A	"Tiger"	:45	Bruns
45	6BV	"Colonel Hathi's March"	:55	Sherman/Sherman
46	6C	"Halt"	:03	Bruns
47	6D	"Tiger"	:51	Bruns
48	6E	"Mother"	:10	Bruns
49	6F	"Lost"	:48	Bruns
50	6G	"Attention"	:12	Bruns
51	6H	"Tiger"	:09	Bruns
52	6J	"Colonel Hathi's March"	:23	Sherman/Sherman
53	7A	"Jungle Beat"	1:19	Bruns
54	7B	"Hello Snake"	:19	Bruns
55	7CV	"Trust in Me"	1:33	Sherman/Sherman
56	7D	"Snake Home"	:19	Bruns
57	7E	"Trust in Me"	:13	Sherman/Sherman
58	7F	"Trust in Me"	:33	Sherman/Sherman
59	8A	"What'cha Wanna Do"	1:17	Clemmons/Bruns
60	8B	"Little Boy"	:20	Bruns
61	8C	"Little Fella"	:20	Bruns
62	8D	"I Don't Care"	1:09	Bruns
63	8EV	"That's What Friends Are For"	2:03	Sherman/Sherman
64	8F	"One"	:24	Bruns
65	8G	"Tiger Fight"	2:15	Bruns
66	9A	"Poor Bear"	1:04	Bruns
67	9B	"The Bare Necessities"	:57	Gilkyson
68	9C	"He's Alive"	1:01	Bruns
69	9DV/9EV/9FV	"My Own Home"	3:28	Sherman/Sherman
70	9GV	"The Bare Necessities"	:47	Gilkyson

NOTES

FOREWORD

1. Leonard Maltin, liner notes, *Stay Awake: Various Interpretations of Music from Vintage Disney Films*, A&M, B000002GFM, 1988.
2. John Hench, interview with Katherine and Richard Greene, 1998.
3. Richard Sherman, interview with Jeff Kurtti, 2000.

INTRODUCTION

1. Michael Barrier, *Hollywood Cartoons: American Animation in Its Golden Age* (New York: Oxford University Press, 2003) 120.
2. David Tietyen, *The Musical World of Walt Disney* (Milwaukee: Hal Leonard, 1990) 10.
3. "The Disneyland Story," *Disneyland*, ABC, 27 October 1954.
4. Larry Timm, *The Soul of Cinema: An Appreciation of Film Music* (Upper Saddle River: Prentice Hall, 2003), 28.
5. Ibid., 28.
6. Barry Cooper, "The Compositional Act: Sketches and Autographs," *The Cambridge Companion to Beethoven*, ed. Glenn Stanley (Cambridge: Cambridge University Press, 2000) 38.
7. Jimmy Johnson, *Inside the Whimsy Works: My Life with Walt Disney Productions*, ed. Greg Ehrbar and Didier Ghez (Jackson: University Press of Mississippi, 2014) 106–7.
8. While MGM was readily associated with their movie musicals, these films were but a fraction of the studio's output, and they were known for their musicals for only three decades, while the tendency for songs and music to play a prominent role in Disney animated features continues.

CHAPTER 1: MICKEYS

1. "The Disneyland Story," *Disneyland*, ABC, 27 October 1954.
2. Bob Thomas, *Walt Disney: An American Original* (New York: Disney Editions, 1994) 90.
3. Michael Barrier, *Hollywood Cartoons: American Animation in Its Golden Age* (New York: Oxford University Press, 2003) 50.
4. Ibid., 55.
5. Ibid., 35.
6. Ibid., 57.
7. Ibid., 52.
8. Ross Care, "Cinesymphony: Music and Animation at the Disney Studio 1928–42," *Sight and Sound* 46 (July–October 2002): 41.

9. Thomas, *Walt Disney*, 90.

10. Ub is the Americanized version of the original spelling of the artist's name, Ubbe. I will use Ub throughout, save when quoting a written source using the original spelling.

11. Thomas, *Walt Disney*, 91.

12. Ibid.

13. Ibid.

14. Barrier, *Hollywood Cartoons*, 52.

15. Neal Gabler, *Walt Disney: The Triumph of the American Imagination* (New York: Alfred A. Knopf, 2006) 118.

16. Ibid.

17. Ibid.

18. Ibid., 119.

19. Ibid.

20. Ibid.

21. Ibid.

22. Corinne F. Grewe, *The Orchestration of Joy and Suffering: Understanding Chronic Addiction* (New York: Algora, 2001) 159.

23. Michael Barrier, *The Animated Man: A Life of Walt Disney* (Berkeley: University of California Press, 2007) 68.

24. Mike Barrier, "An Interview with Carl Stalling" *The Cartoon Music Book*, ed. Daniel Goldmark and Yuval Taylor (Chicago: A Capella Books, 2002) 57.

25. Ibid.

26. Ibid., 56.

27. Wilfred Jackson, *Steamboat Willie*, The Walt Disney Studios, bar sheet, 1928, Walt Disney Archives, 2.

28. Ibid., 4.

29. Thomas, *Walt Disney*, 91.

30. Barrier, "Interview with Carl Stalling," 38.

31. Barrier, *Animated Man*, 63.

32. Tracey Birdsall, email to the author, 6 August 2014.

33. Birdsall, email to the author, 25 November 2013.

34. United States, Census Bureau, Elbert Lewis, Belvidere, Los Angeles, California, United States, Enumeration District 10, sheet 35B, 1920.

35. Gabler, *Walt Disney*, 45.

36. Thomas, *Walt Disney*, 91.

37. Gabler, *Walt Disney*, 121.

38. Ibid., 122.

39. Ibid.

40. Ibid.

41. Ibid., 123.

42. Thomas, *Walt Disney*, 94.

43. Bob Thomas, "Ub Iwerks (1901–1971): Interviewed by Bob Thomas around 1956," *Walt's People*, vol. 10, ed. Didier Ghez (Bloomington: Xlibris, 2011), 44.

44. Barrier, *Hollywood Cartoons*, 54.

45. Ibid.

46. Ibid.

47. Ibid.

48. Ibid.

49. Jim Korkis, *How to Be a Disney Historian* (Orlando: Theme Park Press, 2016) 30.

50. "United States World War II Draft Registration Cards, 1942," Elbert Clifford Lewis, 1942.

51. Birdsall, email to the author, 25 November 2013.

52. United States, Census Bureau, Charles Lewis, Topeka Ward 1, Shawnee, Kansas, United States, Enumeration District 144, sheet 185A, 1900.

53. Angeles Township, Los Angeles, California, United States. Enumeration District 60–1247, sheet 1A.

54. United States, Census Bureau, Charles Lewis.

55. Birdsall, email to the author, 25 November 2013.

56. "Elbert Lewis," Kansas City, Missouri, City Directory (1914) 1248.

57. Birdsall, email to the author, 25 November 2013.

58. Barrier, *Hollywood Cartoons*, 65.

59. Jack Kinney, *Walt Disney and Other Assorted Characters* (New York: Harmony Books, 1988) 205.

60. United States, Census Bureau, Elbert Lewis.

61. Ibid.

62. Thomas, *Walt Disney*, 96.

63. Barrier, "Interview with Carl Stalling," 39.

64. Mordaunt Hall, "The Screen," *New York Times* 19 November 1928: 16.

65. Gabler, *Walt Disney*, 128.

66. Barrier, *Hollywood Cartoons*, 57.

67. Maltin, *Disney Films*, 2.

68. Barrier, *Hollywood Cartoons*, 59.

69. Gabler, *Walt Disney*, 228.

70. Thomas, *Walt Disney*, 100.

71. Ibid., 96.

72. Tighe Zimmers, *Tin Pan Alley Girl: A Biography of Ann Ronell* (Jefferson: McFarland, 2009) 23.

73. Ibid.

74. "Irving Berlin, Inc.: Statement of Royalties," Ann Ronell, 31 December 1933.

75. Mack Gordon and Harry Revel, "It's the Animal in Me," Brunswick, 7591A, 1935.

76. Cole Porter, "You're the Top," WB Music Corp., 1934.

77. Barrier, "Interview with Carl Stalling," 57–58.

78. Ibid.

79. Bert Lewis, *Mickey Cuts Up*, manuscript, 1931, arr. by Carl Stalling, Carl W. Stalling Papers, Collection Number 5725, American Heritage Center, University of Wyoming, 1.

80. Bert Lewis, *Mickey Steps Out*, manuscript, 1931, arr. by Carl Stalling, Carl W. Stalling Papers, Collection Number 5725, American Heritage Center, University of Wyoming, 1.

81. Bert Lewis, *Fishin' Around*, manuscript, 1931, arr. by Carl Stalling, Carl W. Stalling Papers, Collection Number 5725, American Heritage Center, University of Wyoming, 8.

82. Jeremy Barham, "Recurring Dreams and Moving Images: The Cinematic Appropriation of Schumann's Op. 15, No. 7," *19th-Century Music* 34.3 (Spring 2011): 272.

83. Ibid.

CHAPTER 2. THE SILLY SYMPHONIES

1. Leonard Maltin, *The Disney Films*, 3rd ed. (New York: Hyperion, 1995) 4.

2. Ross Care, "Symphonists for the Sillies: The Composers for Disney's Shorts," *Funnyworld* 18 (Summer 1978): 39.

3. Mike Barrier, "Interview with Carl Stalling," *The Cartoon Music Book*, ed. Daniel Goldmark and Yuval Taylor (Chicago: A Capella Books, 2002) 57.

4. Ibid., 41.

5. Ibid., 40.

6. Ibid., 41.

7. Bob Thomas, *Walt Disney: An American Original* (New York: Disney Editions, 1994) 99.

8. Care, "Symphonists for the Sillies," 39.

9. Michael Barrier, *The Animated Man: A Life of Walt Disney* (Berkeley: University of California Press, 2007) 69.

10. Thomas, *Walt Disney*, 99.

11. Michael Barrier, *Hollywood Cartoons: American Animation in Its Golden Age* (New York: Oxford University Press, 2003) 61.

12. Ibid.

13. Ibid., 59.

14. Ibid.

15. Neal Gabler, *Walt Disney: The Triumph of the American Imagination* (New York: Alfred A. Knopf, 2006) 132.

16. *The Fifty Greatest Cartoons as Selected by 1,000 Animation Professionals*, ed. Jerry Beck (Atlanta: Turner, 1994) 92.

17. Gabler, *Walt Disney*, 133.

18. Barrier, "Interview with Carl Stalling," 55.

19. Ibid.

20. Linda Britt, email to the author, 9 May 2014.

21. Barrier, "Interview with Carl Stalling," 55.

22. Ibid., 56.

23. Ibid.

24. Ibid.

25. Ibid.

26. Daniel Goldmark, *Tunes for 'Toons: Music and the Hollywood Cartoon* (Berkeley: University of California Press, 2005) 166.

27. Ibid., 165.

28. Linda Britt, email to the author, 21 May 2014.

29. Ibid.

30. "United States World War I Draft Registration Cards, 1917–1918," Carl William Stalling, 5 June 1917.

31. Goldmark, *Tunes for 'Toons*, 166.

32. "Missouri Marriage Records," Carl Stalling and Gladys Baldwin, 16 June 1917.

33. "Carl Stalling," Kansas City, Missouri, City Directory (1924) 1999.

34. Barrier, "Interview with Carl Stalling," 38.

35. Ibid.

36. Ibid., 39.

37. Ibid., 51.

38. Ibid., 45.

39. Ibid., 47.

40. Barrier, *Animated Man*, 64.

41. Ibid.

42. Barrier, "Interview with Carl Stalling," 42.

43. Ibid., 47.

44. Ibid., 44.

45. Ibid., 42.

46. Ibid., 57.

47. Gabler, *Walt Disney*, 73.

48. Ibid., 82–83.

49. Barrier, *Animated Man*, 77.

50. Barrier, "Interview with Carl Stalling," 47.

51. Gabler, *Walt Disney*, 352.

52. Barrier, "Interview with Carl Stalling," 41.

53. Ibid., 46.

54. Ibid., 42.

55. Ibid., 43.

56. Ibid., 44.

57. Ibid.

58. Ibid., 43, 58.

59. Ibid., 46.

60. Barrier, *Hollywood Cartoons*, 65.

61. Barrier, "Interview with Carl Stalling," 46.

62. Ibid.

63. Ibid.

64. Britt, email to the author, 21 May 2014.

65. Bar rier, "Interview with Carl Stalling," 48.

66. Ibid., 48–49.

67. Goldmark, *Tunes for 'Toons*, 11.

68. Britt, email to the author, 9 May 2014.

69. Britt, email to the author, 8 May 2014.

70. Ibid.

71. Ibid.

72. Ibid.

73. Goldmark, *Tunes for 'Toons*, 166.

74. Britt, email to the author, 21 May 2014.

75. Goldmark, *Tunes for 'Toons*, 166.

76. Britt, email to the author, 9 May 2014.

77. Britt, email to the author, 21 May 2014.

78. Barrier, *Hollywood Cartoons*, 101.

79. Ibid., 80.

80. Ibid.

81. Gabler, *Walt Disney*, 181.

82. Ibid., 181–182.

83. Barrier, *Hollywood Cartoons*, 100.

84. David Tietyen, *The Musical World of Walt Disney* (Milwaukee: Hal Leonard, 1990) 29.

85. Thomas, 118.

86. Ibid.

87. Barrier, "Interview with Carl Stalling," 47.

88. Ibid.

89. Thomas, 118–19.

90. Steven Watts, *The Magic Kingdom: Walt Disney and the American Way of Life* (Columbia: University of Missouri Press, 1997) 78.

91. Ibid.

92. Barrier, *Hollywood Cartoons*, 106.

93. Jon Newsom, "'A Sound Idea': Music for Animated Films," *Wonderful Inventions: Motion Pictures, Broadcasting, and Recorded Sound at the Library of Congress*, ed. Iris Newsom (Washington: Library of Congress, 1985) 65.

94. *Fifty Greatest Cartoons*, 73.

95. Gabler, *Walt Disney*, 184.

96. David Tietyen, "Charles Wolcott (1906–1987): Interviewed by David Tietyen on September 26, 1978," *Walt's People*, vol. 8, ed. Didier Ghez (Bloomington: Xlibris, 2009) 161.

97. Ibid.

98. "Piglets' Tune," *Time*, 25 September 1933: 30.

99. Tighe Zimmers, *Tin Pan Alley Girl: A Biography of Ann Ronell* (Jefferson: McFarland, 2009) 123.

100. Ibid., 122.

101. Ibid., 126.

102. Ibid.

103. Ibid., 127.

104. Ibid., 122.

105. Ibid., 132.

106. "Piglets' Tune," 30.

107. Ross B. Care, "Threads of Melody: The Evolution of a Major Film Score—Walt Disney's *Bambi*," *Wonderful Inventions: Motion Pictures, Broadcasting, and Recorded Sound at the Library of Congress*, ed. Iris Newsom (Washington: Library of Congress, 1985) 84.

108. "Irving Berlin, Inc.: Statement of Royalties," Ann Ronell, 31 December 1933. New York Public Library

109. J. B. Kaufman, *The Fairest One of All: The Making of Walt Disney's* Snow White and the Seven Dwarfs (San Francisco: The Walt Disney Family Foundation Press, 2012) 66.

110. "Piglets' Tune," 30.

111. Thomas, *Walt Disney*, 118.

112. John Gabriel Hunt, *The Inaugural Addresses of the Presidents* (New York: Gramercy Books, 1997) 377.

113. Zimmers, *Tin Pan Alley Girl*, 24.

114. Ibid., 25.

115. Ibid.

116. Clifford McCarty, *Film Composers in America: A Filmography, 1911–1970* (New York: Oxford University Press, 2000) 366.

117. Joseph Machlis, *Introduction to Contemporary Music*, 2nd ed. (New York: W. W. Norton, 1979) 86.

118. Richard Taruskin and Piero Weiss, *Music in the Western World: A History in Documents* (New York: Schirmer Books, 1984) 417.

119. Tim Hollis and Greg Ehrbar, *Mouse Tracks: The Story of Walt Disney Records* (Jackson: University Press of Mississippi, 2006) 6.

120. Ibid.

121. Ibid.

122. Rick Shale, "Ward Kimball (1914–2002): Interviewed by Rick Shale on January 29, 1976," *Walt's People*, vol. 5, ed. Didier Ghez (Bloomington: Xlibris, 2007), 43.

123. Barrier, *Hollywood Cartoons*, 100.

124. Ibid., 101.

125. Ibid.

126. Ibid., 102.

127. Ibid., 92.

128. Ibid.

129. Ibid., 117.

130. Ibid.

CHAPTER 3: SNOW WHITE AND THE SEVEN DWARFS

1. Richard Holliss and Brian Sibley, *Walt Disney's* Snow White and the Seven Dwarfs *& the Making of the Classic Film* (New York: Hyperion, 1994) 5.

2. David Tietyen, *The Musical World of Walt Disney* (Milwaukee: Hal Leonard, 1990) 36.

3. Neal Gabler, *Walt Disney: The Triumph of the American Imagination* (New York: Alfred A. Knopf, 2006) 215.

4. Thomas Inge, "Walt Disney's *Snow White*: Art, Adaptation, and Ideology," *Journal of Popular Film and Television* 32.3 (Fall 2004): 134.

5. J. B. Kaufman, Snow White and the Seven Dwarfs: *The Art and Creation of Walt Disney's Classic Animated Film* (San Francisco: The Walt Disney Family Foundation Press, 2012) 15.

6. Ibid.

7. Bob Thomas, *Walt Disney: An American Original* (New York: Disney Editions, 1994) 134.

8. Michael Barrier, *Hollywood Cartoons: American Animation in Its Golden Age* (New York: Oxford University Press, 2003) 124.

9. Ibid., 126.

10. Ibid.

11. Ibid.

12. J. B. Kaufman, *The Fairest One of All: The Making of Walt Disney's* Snow White and the Seven Dwarfs (San Francisco: The Walt Disney Family Foundation Press, 2012) 90.

13. Barrier, *Hollywood Cartoons*, 206.

14. Kaufman, *The Fairest One of All*, 93.

15. Barrier, *Hollywood Cartoons*, 127.

16. Ibid., 151.

17. Jan Boles, email to the author, 12 March 2015.

18. R. Vernon Steele, "Fairyland Goes Hollywood: An Interview with Leigh Harline," *Pacific Coast Musician*, 20 November 1937): 10.

19. Ibid.

20. Ibid.

21. Kaufman, *Fairest One of All*, 93.

22. United States, Census Bureau, Andrew Churchill, Los Angeles Assembly District 64, Los Angeles, California, United States, Enumeration District 219, sheet 3A, 1920.

23. United States, Census Bureau, 1930, Andrew Churchill, Los Angeles, Los Angeles, California, United States, Enumeration District 42, sheet 9B, 1930.

24. Ross B. Care, "Threads of Melody: The Evolution of a Major Film Score—Walt Disney's *Bambi*," *Wonderful Inventions: Motion Pictures, Broadcasting, and Recorded Sound at the Library of Congress*, ed. Iris Newsom (Washington: Library of Congress, 1985) 84.

25. Ross Care, "Symphonists for the Sillies: The Composers for Disney's Shorts," *Funnyworld* 18 (Summer 1978): 41.

26. Care, "Threads of Melody," 84.

27. Ross Care, "Disney Unlocks the Music Vault," *Scarlet Street* 27 (Spring 1998): 45.

28. Care, "Threads of Melody," 86.

29. Ibid.

30. Care, "Symphonists for the Sillies," 44.

31. Michael Barrier, Milton Gray, and Bob Clampett, "Wilfred Jackson: An interview by Michael Barrier, Milton Gray and Bob Clampett," *MichaelBarrier.com*, 31 July 2015, Web, 3 August 2015 <michaelbarrier.com/Interviews/Jackson1973/Jackson1973.html>.

32. Ross Care, "Make Walt's Music: Music for Disney Animation, 1928–1967," *The Cartoon Music Book*, ed. Daniel Goldmark and Yuval Taylor (Chicago: A Capella Books, 2002) 26.

33. Jack Kinney, *Walt Disney and Assorted Other Characters* (New York: Harmony Books, 1988) 84.

34. Ibid.

35. Jimmy Johnson, *Inside the Whimsy Works: My Life with Walt Disney Productions*, ed. Greg Ehrbar and Didier Ghez (Jackson: University Press of Mississippi, 2014) 115.

36. Ibid.

37. "California, County Marriages, 1850–1952," Frank E. Churchill and Leona J. Milligan, 6 July 1922, Orange, California.

38. United States, Census Bureau, Andrew Churchill.

39. Ibid.

40. "Frank Churchill," Los Angeles, California, City Directory (1939) 440.

41. Kaufman, *Fairest One of All*, 93.

42. Ibid.

43. Ibid.

44. Ibid.

45. "'Big Bad Wolf' Creator Suicide," *Los Angeles Times* 15 May 1942: A12.

46. Ibid.

47. Ibid.

48. John Boston, "The Mysterious Death of a Disney Oscar Winner in Castaic," *West Ranch Beacon*, 7 December 2011, Web, 17 August 2012 <westranchbeacon.com/2011/12/the-boston-re port-the-mysterious-death-of-a-disney-oscar-winner-in-castaic/>.

49. Gabler, *Walt Disney*, 397.

50. Ibid.

51. "California, County Marriages, 1850–1952," Donald Frederick Durnford and Carolyn Shafer Churchill, Los Angeles, 20 November 1943.

52. David Lesjak, post to The Disney History Institute Group, *Facebook*, 14 May 2016.

53. Rose Heylbut, "The Music of the Walt Disney Cartoons: A Conference with Paul J. Smith," *Etude Magazine* (July 1940): 438.

54. Leonard Maltin, *The Disney Films*, 3rd ed. (New York: Hyperion, 1995) 30.

55. Gabler, *Walt Disney*, 254.

56. Ibid.

57. *Snow White and the Seven Dwarfs*, dir. David Hand, Walt Disney Productions, 1937.

58. Ibid.

59. Ibid.

60. Kaufman, *Fairest One of All*, 120.

61. Ibid.

62. Ibid., 90.

63. Ibid.

64. Ibid., 90.

65. Ibid., 106.

66. *Snow White and the Seven Dwarfs*.

67. Ibid.

68. Later in the film, "Heigh-Ho" uses the same trick of having the characters sing in alternation with their echo.

69. *Snow White and the Seven Dwarfs*.

70. Ibid.

71. Barrier, *Hollywood Cartoons*, 195.

72. Kaufman, *Fairest One of All*, 45.

73. Ibid.

74. Marge Champion, conversation with the author, 14 August 2013.

75. Gabler, *Walt Disney*, 253.

76. Kaufman, *Fairest One of All*, 106.

77. Ibid., 48.

78. *Snow White and the Seven Dwarfs.*

79. Kaufman, *Fairest One of All*, 90.

80. Maltin, *Disney Films*, 30.

81. Kaufman, *Fairest One of All*, 92.

82. *Snow White and the Seven Dwarfs.*

83. Tietyen, *Musical World of Walt Disney*, 40.

84. Gabler, *Walt Disney*, 254.

85. Tietyen, *Musical World of Walt Disney*, 40.

86. Ibid.

87. Kaufman, *Fairest One of All*, 179.

88. Ibid.

89. Ibid.

90. Ibid., 184.

91. Holliss and Sibley, *Walt Disney's* Snow White and the Seven Dwarfs, 15.

92. Gabler, *Walt Disney*, 254.

93. Kaufman, *Fairest One of All*, 181.

94. Ibid., 181–82.

95. Ibid., 184.

96. Ibid., 178.

97. Ibid., 164.

98. Ibid.

99. Ibid.

100. Ibid.

101. Ibid.

102. Ibid.

103. Ibid.

104. Ibid., 174.

105. Ibid., 175.

106. Ibid.

107. Ibid., 174–75.

108. Ibid., 176.

109. Ibid.

110. Ibid.

111. Ibid., 175–76.

112. Ibid., 176.

113. Ibid.

114. Ibid.

115. Ibid.

116. Ibid.

117. Ibid.

118. Ibid.

119. Ibid.

120. Ibid., 177.

121. Ibid.

122. Ibid.

123. Ibid., 181.

124. Ibid.

125. Ibid., 177.

126. Martin Krause and Linda Witowski, *Walt Disney's* Snow White and the Seven Dwarfs: An Art in Its Making (New York: Hyperion, 1994) 53.

127. Barrier, *Hollywood Cartoons*, 229.

128. Krause and Witowski, 63.

129. Gabler, *Walt Disney*, 268.

130. Holliss and Sibley, *Walt Disney's* Snow White and the Seven Dwarfs, 35.

131. Ibid.

132. Ibid.

133. Gabler, *Walt Disney*, 272.

134. Ibid.

135. Ibid.

136. Krause and Witowski, *Walt Disney's* Snow White and the Seven Dwarfs, 60.

137. Gabler, *Walt Disney*, 276.

138. Barrier, *Hollywood Cartoons*, 229.

139. Ibid.

140. Gabler, *Walt Disney*, 276.

141. Barrier, *Hollywood Cartoons*, 229.

142. "News of the Screen," *New York Times*, 31 January 1938: 15.

143. Gabler, *Walt Disney*, 277.

144. Ibid.

145. Thomas, *Walt Disney*, 143.

146. Maltin, *Disney Films*, 32.

147. Box Office Mojo, "All Time Box Office Adjusted for Ticket Price Inflation," *Box Office Mojo*, 8 September 2011, Web, 8 September 2011 <boxofficemojo.com/alltime/adjusted.htm>.

148. Tim Hollis and Greg Ehrbar, *Mouse Tracks: The Story of Walt Disney Records* (Jackson: University Press of Mississippi, 2006) 7.

149. Kaufman, Snow White and the Seven Dwarfs, 120.

150. David Sheff, "Playboy Interview: John Lennon and Yoko Ono," *Playboy* 28.1 (January 1981): 112.

151. It is unknown whether the ballad "Snow White" had been intended for use in the film *Snow White and the Seven Dwarfs*. The song has been released on LP on *The Songs from Walt Disney's*: Snow White and the Seven Dwarfs (Pickwick International, HT-1039) & *15 Walt Disney Favorites* (Pickwick International, SPC 5119).

152. Gabler, *Walt Disney*, 285.

153. Thirty-fourth-best film on the 2007 list, it was listed as the forty-ninth on the 1998 list.

154. Kaufman, Snow White and the Seven Dwarfs, 8.

155. Ross Care, "The Film Music of Leigh Harline," *Filmmusic Notebook* 3.2 (1977): 36.

156. Ross Care, "Record Rack: *Snow White and the Seven Dwarfs* and *Pinocchio*; The First," *Scarlet Street* 12 (Fall 1993): 52.

157. Care, "Record Rack," 53.

158. Thomas, *Walt Disney*, 145.

159. Kaufman, Snow White and the Seven Dwarfs, 27.

CHAPTER 4: PINOCCHIO

1. Ross B. Care, "Threads of Melody: The Evolution of a Major Film Score—Walt Disney's *Bambi*," *Wonderful Inventions: Motion Pictures, Broadcasting, and Recorded Sound at the Library of Congress*, ed. Iris Newsom (Washington: Library of Congress, 1985) 88.

2. Maxine Hof, email to the author, 18 April 2013.

3. Ross Care, "The Film Music of Leigh Harline," *Filmmusic Notebook* 3.2 (1977): 38.

4. Ibid.

5. United States, Census Bureau, Carl Harline, Wilford, Salt Lake, Utah, United States, Enumeration District 79, sheet 5B, 1910.

6. David Lesjak, *Facebook* message to the author, 11 January 2014.

7. Carolyn Catherine Shafter, "Society News," *The Mickey Mouse Melodeon: House Organ of the Disney Studio* 1.3 (January 1933): 3.

8. Ross Care, "Symphonists for the Sillies: The Composers for Disney's Shorts," *Funnyworld* 18 (Summer 1978): 44.

9. Care, "Film Music of Leigh Harline," 34.

10. R. Vernon Steele, "'Fairyland Goes Hollywood': An Interview with Leigh Harline," *Pacific Coast Musician*, 20 November 1937: 10.

11. Ibid.

12. Care, "Film Music of Leigh Harline," 39.

13. "Leigh Harline: Obituary" *Los Angeles Times,* 11 December 1969: D4.

14. Ibid.

15. Rose Heylbut, "The Music of the Walt Disney Cartoons: A Conference with Paul J. Smith," *Etude Magazine* (July 1940) 438.

16. Neal Gabler, *Walt Disney: The Triumph of the American Imagination* (New York: Alfred A. Knopf, 2006) 304.

17. *Pinocchio*, dir. Hamilton Luske and Ben Sharpsteen, Walt Disney Productions, 1940.

18. Ibid.

19. Ibid.

20. Ibid.

21. Ibid.

22. Heylbut, "Music of the Walt Disney Cartoons," 494.

23. Ibid., 438.

24. Ross Care, "Make Walt's Music: Music for Disney Animation, 1928–1967," *The Cartoon Music Book*, ed. Daniel Goldmark and Yuval Taylor (Chicago: A Capella Books, 2002) 30.

25. Russell Schroeder, *Disney's Lost Chords: More Hidden Treasures from the Walt Disney Music Library Archives*, vol. 2 (Robbinsville: Voigt, 2008) 353.

26. Ibid.

27. Ibid.

28. Ibid.

29. Leigh Harline and Ned Washington, "Figaro and Cleo," manuscript, n.d., Leigh Harline Papers, 1938–1968, US-86-22, Archives and Rare Books Library, University of Cincinnati, Cincinnati, Ohio.

30. Leigh Harline, *After M.B*, manuscript sketch from *Pinocchio*, n.d., Leigh Harline Papers, 1938–1968, US-86-22, Archives and Rare Books Library, University of Cincinnati, Cincinnati, Ohio.

31. Leigh Harline, *After "It's Getting Late" Dialog*, manuscript sketch from *Pinocchio*, n.d., Leigh Harline papers, 1938–1968, US-86-22, Archives and Rare Books Library, University of Cincinnati, Cincinnati, Ohio.

32. Leigh Harline, *Untitled Sketch [Figaro in Bed Through Opening Window]*, manuscript, n.d., Leigh Harline Papers, 1938–1968, US-86-22, Archives and Rare Books Library, University of Cincinnati, Cincinnati, Ohio.

33. Heylbut, "Music of the Walt Disney Cartoons," 494.

34. Douglas W. Churchill, "Screen News Here and in Hollywood," *New York Times* 8 February 1940: 25.

35. Paul F. Anderson, "'The Funniest of Them All': Disney's *Snow White* vs. *Pinocchio*," *Dis-*

ney History Institute, 3 November 2009, Web, 11 September 2013 <www.disneyhistoryinstitute .com/2009/11/funniest-of-them-all-disneys-snow-white.html>.

36. Michael Barrier, *Hollywood Cartoons: American Animation in Its Golden Age* (New York: Oxford University Press, 2003) 269.

37. Ibid., 266.

38. Ibid., 272.

39. Box Office Mojo, "All Time Box Office Adjusted for Ticket Price Inflation," *Box Office Mojo*, 8 September 2011, Web, 8 September 2011 <boxofficemojo.com/alltime/adjusted.htm>.

40. David Tietyen, "Charles Wolcott (1906–1987): Interviewed by David Tietyen on September 26, 1978," *Walt's People*, vol. 8, ed. Didier Ghez (Bloomington: Xlibris, 2009), 163.

41. Ibid., 164.

42. "Jiminy Cricket" and "Three Cheers for Anything" were songs written for *Pinocchio* that were not used in the film.

43. Tim Hollis and Greg Ehrbar, *Mouse Tracks: The Story of Walt Disney Records* (Jackson: University Press of Mississippi, 2006) 112.

44. Neil Lerner, "Nostalgia, Masculinist Discourse, and Authoritarianism in John Williams' Scores for *Star Wars* and *Close Encounters of the Third Kind*," *Off the Planet: Music, Sound and Science Fiction Cinema*, ed. Philip Hayward (Eastleigh: John Libbey, 2004) 108.

45. Ibid., 105.

46. "I'm Wishing" from *Snow White and the Seven Dwarfs* expresses the specific dream of the protagonist, while "When You Wish Upon a Star" relates the merits of dreams without identifying character-specific wishes.

CHAPTER 5: DUMBO AND BAMBI

1. Bob Thomas, *Walt Disney: An American Original* (New York: Disney Editions, 1994) 159.

2. Ibid., 160.

3. Michael Barrier, *Hollywood Cartoons: American Animation in Its Golden Age* (New York: Oxford University Press, 2003) 271.

4. Ibid.

5. Ibid., 272.

6. Ross Care, "Melody Time: Musicians for Disney Animation 1941–1955," *Soundtrack* 8.31 (1989), 34.

7. *Dumbo*, dir. Ben Sharpsteen, Walt Disney Productions, 1941, film.

8. Ibid.

9. Ibid.

10. Ibid.

11. Ibid.

12. Ibid.

13. Ibid.

14. David Tietyen, *The Musical World of Walt Disney* (Milwaukee: Hal Leonard, 1990) 64.

15. Ibid.

16. Russell Schroeder, *Disney's Lost Chords*, vol. 2 (Robbinsville: Voigt, 2008) 329.

17. Ibid.

18. Ibid., 328.

19. Ibid., 346.

20. Ibid., 349.

21. Ibid.

22. Thomas, *Walt Disney*, 163.

23. Leonard Maltin, *The Disney Films*, 3rd ed. (New York: Hyperion, 1995) 49.

24. Barrier, *Hollywood Cartoons*, 309.

25. Ibid., 318.

26. Ibid.

27. Neal Gabler, *Walt Disney: The Triumph of the American Imagination* (New York: Alfred A. Knopf, 2006) 215.

28. Barrier, *Hollywood Cartoons*, 236.

29. Ibid.

30. Ibid.

31. Gabler, *Walt Disney*, 265.

32. Barrier, *Hollywood Cartoons*, 236.

33. Ibid., 244.

34. Gabler, *Walt Disney*, 327–28.

35. Ibid., 328.

36. Ross B. Care, "Threads of Melody: The Evolution of a Major Film Score—Walt Disney's *Bambi*," *Wonderful Inventions: Motion Pictures, Broadcasting, and Recorded Sound at the Library of Congress*, ed. Iris Newsom (Washington: Library of Congress, 1985) 82.

37. Gabler, *Walt Disney*, 302.

38. Care, "Threads of Melody," 88.

39. Ibid., 113.

40. Barrier, *Hollywood Cartoons*, 274.

41. Ibid.

42. Care, "Threads of Melody," 99.

43. "The Making of Bambi: A Prince Is Born," *Bambi*, Walt Disney Studios Home Entertainment, 2011. DVD, Disc 2.

44. David J. Fisher, "The Music of Disney: A Legacy in Song" liner notes, *The Music of Disney: A Legacy in Song* (Walt Disney Records, 1992) 17.

45. Paula Angle, *Biography in Black: A History of Streator, Illinois*, Web, 1 May 2014 <archive.org/stream/biographyinblackoofran/biographyinblackoofran_djvu.txt>.

46. Ibid.

47. Ibid.

48. Ibid.

49. Ibid.

50. Ibid.

51. Ibid.

52. "United States, Census Bureau, 1910," Levancia Plumb, Streator Ward 2, La Salle, Illinois, United States. Enumeration District 89, sheet 16A.

53. Care, "Threads of Melody," 84.

54. Ibid.

55. Ibid.

56. Ibid.

57. Ibid.

58. Ibid., 164–65.

59. Joe Campana, "Century Birthday: Edward Plumb," *Animation Who & Where*, 6 June 2007, Web, 12 May 2011 <animationwhoandwhere.blogspot.com/2007/06/century-birthday-edward-plumb.html>.

60. David Tietyen, "Charles Wolcott (1906–1987): Interviewed by David Tietyen on September 26, 1978," *Walt's People*, vol. 8, ed. Didier Ghez (Bloomington: Xlibris, 2009), 163.

61. Ibid.

62. Care, "Threads of Melody," 109.

63. "Story Conference on *Bambi*," Walt Disney Productions, 4 September 1937, Walt Disney Archives, 1.

64. Ibid., 7.

65. Tietyen, *Musical World of Walt Disney*, 66.

66. Care, "Threads of Melody," 82.

67. Ibid., 83.

68. Ibid.

69. Ibid.

70. Ibid.

71. Ibid., 85.

72. Ibid., 89.

73. Ibid., 91.

74. *Bambi*, dir. David Hand, Walt Disney Productions, 1942. Film.

75. *The Lion King*, dir. Roger Allers and Rob Minkoff, Walt Disney Pictures, 1994. Film.

76. Care, "Threads of Melody," 91.

77. Ibid., 87.

78. Ibid.

79. "Story Conference on *Bambi*," 1.

80. Care, "Threads of Melody," 97.

81. "Making of Bambi."

82. *Bambi*.

83. Ibid.

84. Care, "Threads of Melody," 109.

85. "Story Conference on *Bambi*," 2.

86. Ibid., 3.

87. Ibid., 2.

88. Ibid.

89. Russell Schroeder, *Disney's Lost Chords* (Robbinsville: Voigt, 2007) 11–15.

90. Ibid., 10.

91. Barrier, *Hollywood Cartoons*, 318.

92. Box Office Mojo, "All Time Box Office Adjusted for Ticket Price Inflation," *Box Office Mojo*, 8 September 2011, Web, 8 September, 2011 <boxofficemojo.com/alltime/adjusted.htm>.

93. William H. and Nancy K. Young, *World War II and the Postwar Years in America: A Historical and Cultural Encyclopedia*, vol. 1 (A–I) (Santa Barbara: ABC-Clio, 2010) 38.

94. Ibid., 37.

95. Jimmy Johnson, *Inside the Whimsy Works: My Life with Walt Disney Publications*, ed. Greg Ehrbar and Didier Ghez (Jackson: University Press of Mississippi, 2014) 62.

96. Ibid., 63.

97. J. B. Kaufman, *South of the Border with Disney: Walt Disney and the Good Neighbor Program, 1941–1948* (New York: Disney Editions, 2009), 129.

98. Ibid., 154, 156.

CHAPTER 6: *CINDERELLA*

1. Bob Thomas, *Walt Disney: An American Original* (New York: Disney Editions, 1994) 178.

2. "Package films" are features that comprise an anthology of loosely related segments, much like *Fantasia*.

3. Thomas, *Walt Disney*, 171.

4. Ibid., 201.

5. Michael Barrier, *The Animated Man: A Life of Walt Disney* (Berkeley: University of California Press, 2007) 206.

6. David Tietyen, "Charles Wolcott (1906–1987): Interviewed by David Tietyen on September 26, 1978," *Walt's People*, vol. 8, ed. Didier Ghez (Bloomington: Xlibris, 2009), 170.

7. Ibid., 170–71.

8. Thomas, *Walt Disney*, 209.

9. Jimmy Johnson, *Inside the Whimsy Works: My Life with Walt Disney Productions*, ed. Greg Ehrbar and Didier Ghez (Jackson: University Press of Mississippi, 2014) 40–41.

10. Ibid., 41.

11. Thomas, *Walt Disney*, 209.

12. Russell Schroeder, *Disney's Lost Chords*, vol. 1 (Robbinsville: Voigt, 2007) 114.

13. Arlynn Anderson, email to the author, 18 March 2015.

14. Ibid.

15. "Paul Smith: Bio," *d23.com*, Web, 8 August 2011 <d23.com/walt-disney-legend/paul-smith>.

16. Jan Boles, email to the author, 12 March 2015.

17. Ibid.

18. "Paul Smith: Bio."

19. Paul Joseph Smith, letter to Anne Ronell (estimated winter 1933–1934).

20. "The Musical Legacy of Paul Smith," dir. Les Perkins, *Walt Disney Presents: 20,000 Leagues Under the Sea*, 2003, DVD, Disc 2.

21. David Tietyen, *The Musical World of Walt Disney* (Milwaukee: Hal Leonard, 1990) 19.

22. Ross Care, "Melody Time: Musicians for Disney Animation 1941–1955," *Soundtrack* 8.31 (1989): 33.

23. Boles, email to the author, 12 March 2015.

24. Tietyen, *Musical World of Walt Disney*, 69.

25. Ibid., 116.

26. Theresa Smith Powers, conversation with the author, 18 July 2013.

27. Jerome Smith, conversation with the author, 29 July 2013.

28. Ibid.

29. "Musical Legacy of Paul Smith."

30. Ibid.

31. Ibid.

32. Ibid.

33. Jon Burlingame, "Buddy Baker (1918–2002) Interviewed by Jon Burlingame on May 10, 2001," *Walt's People*, vol. 5, ed. Didier Ghez (Bloomington: Xlibris, 2007) 159.

34. Ibid.

35. Ibid.

36. Howard Lucraft, "Buddy Baker: Hollywood Film Composer," Norman "Buddy" Baker Collection, box 39, Fales Library and Special Collections, Elmer Holmes Bobst Library, New York University, 2.

37. Tietyen, "Charles Wolcott (1906–1987)," 172.

38. David Tietyen, "George Bruns (1914–1983): Interviewed by David Tietyen in 1978," *Walt's People*, vol. 11, ed. Didier Ghez (Bloomington: Xlibris, 2011) 310.

39. Burlingame, "Buddy Baker (1918–2002)," 164.

40. Jan Boles, email to the author, 30 August 2012.

41. Arlynn Anderson, email to the author, 20 March 2015.

42. Anderson, email to the author, 18 March 2015.

43. Boles, email to the author, 30 August 2012.

44. Paul Joseph Smith, letter to Anne Ronell (estimated winter 1933–34), New York Public Library.

45. Ibid.

46. Paul Smith, "An Article on *Love Happy*: On Precision Timing," *Film Music Notes* 9.4 (March–April 1950): 10–12.

47. Boles, email to the author, 12 March 2015.

48. Powers, conversation with the author, 18 July 2013.

49. Ibid.

50. Ibid.

51. Ibid.

52. Smith, conversation with the author, 29 July 2013.

53. Powers, conversation with the author, 28 August 2012.

54. Ibid.

55. Ibid.

56. Jack Kinney, *Walt Disney and Assorted Other Characters* (New York: Harmony Books, 1988) 84.

57. Ibid.

58. Powers, conversation with the author, 28 August 2012.

59. Ibid.

60. David Tietyen, *Facebook* message to the author, 9 August 2011.

61. "MMC Crew: Paul Smith," *The Original Mickey Mouse Club Show*, Web, 8 August 2011 <www.originalmmc.com/paulsmith.html>.

62. Barrier, *Hollywood Cartoons*, 220.

63. Ibid.

64. Tietyen, *Musical World of Walt Disney*, 91.

65. Ibid.

66. Ibid.

67. Ibid.

68. *Cinderella*, dir. Clyde Geronimi, Wilfred Jackson, and Hamilton Luske, Walt Disney Productions, 1950. Film.

69. Ibid.

70. Ibid.

71. Ibid.

72. *Pinocchio*, dir. Hamilton Luske and Ben Sharpsteen, Walt Disney Productions, 1940. Film.

73. *Cinderella*.

74. Ibid.

75. Ibid.

76. Ibid.

77. Ibid.

78. Ibid.

79. Ibid.

80. Ibid.

81. Ibid.

82. Ibid.

83. Ibid.

84. Paula Sigman-Lowery, Liner notes, *Walt Disney Records Legacy Collection: Cinderella*, Walt Disney Records, D002066092, 2015.

85. *Cinderella*.

86. J. B. Kaufman, *The Fairest One of All: The Making of Walt Disney's* Snow White and the Seven Dwarfs (San Francisco: The Walt Disney Family Foundation Press, 2012) 106.

87. Schroeder, *Disney's Lost Chords*, vol. 1, 115.

88. Ibid., 116.
89. *Cinderella.*
90. Ibid.
91. Ibid.
92. Ibid.
93. Schroeder, *Disney's Lost Chords*, vol. 1, 117.
94. Ibid., 122.
95. Ibid., 122–23.
96. Ibid., 125.
97. Ibid., 115.
98. Ibid.
99. Ibid., 134.
100. Ibid., 138.
101. Ibid., 142.
102. Ibid., 146.
103. Barrier, *Hollywood Cartoons*, 221.
104. Ibid.
105. Tim Hollis and Greg Ehrbar, *Mouse Tracks: The Story of Walt Disney Records* (Jackson: University Press of Mississippi, 2006) 8.
106. Johnson, *Inside the Whimsy Works*, 43–44.
107. Ibid., 44.
108. Tietyen, *Musical World of Walt Disney*, 35.

CHAPTER 7: ALICE IN WONDERLAND AND PETER PAN

1. Russell Schroeder, *Disney's Lost Chords,* vol. 1 (Robbinsville: Voigt, 2007) 151.
2. Ibid.
3. Michael Barrier, *Hollywood Cartoons: American Animation in Its Golden Age* (New York: Oxford University Press, 2003) 372–73.
4. Ibid. 392.
5. Ibid.
6. Schroeder, *Disney's Lost Chords*, vol. 1, 151.
7. Jack Lavin, "Walt Disney Productions: Inter-Office Communication," message to Main File, 10 May 1949, Joseph Dubin, personnel file, Walt Disney Archives.
8. Jack Lavin, "Walt Disney Productions: Inter-Office Communication," message to Esther Haight, 25 May 1950, Joseph Dubin, personnel file, Walt Disney Archives.
9. Ross Care, "Melody Time: Musicians for Disney Animation 1941–1955," *Soundtrack* 8.31 (1989): 32.
10. Jimmy Johnson, *Inside the Whimsy Works: My Life with Walt Disney Productions*, ed. Greg Ehrbar and Didier Ghez (Jackson: University Press of Mississippi, 2014) 76.
11. "Disney Legends—Oliver Wallace," *D23.com*, Web, 18 March 2011 <d23.com/legend-oli ver-wallace>.
12. Care, "Melody Time," 33.
13. Ibid.
14. Jon Burlingame, "Buddy Baker (1918–2002) Interviewed by Jon Burlingame on May 10, 2001," *Walt's People*, vol. 5, ed. Didier Ghez (Bloomington: Xlibris, 2007) 160.
15. Ibid.
16. Ibid.
17. "Meeting Notes—Seq. 0.3.0 'Calendar,'" Walt Disney Productions, 24 March 1953, 7.
18. David Tietyen, "George Bruns (1914–1983): Interviewed by David Tietyen in 1978," *Walt's*

People, vol. 11, ed. Didier Ghez (Bloomington: Xlibris, 2011) 310.

19. Richard Hubler, "Bob Sherman (b. 1925): Interviewed by Richard Hubler on July 30, 1968," *Walt's People*, vol. 8, ed. Didier Ghez (Bloomington: Xlibris, 2009) 208.

20. Buddy Baker, "Priceless Moments with Walt," manuscript, Buddy Baker Collection, box 39, Fales Library and Special Collections, Elmer Holmes Bobst Library, New York University.

21. Ibid.

22. Ibid.

23. Ibid.

24. Ibid.

25. "United States Census, 1940," Oliver Wallace, Councilmanic District 1, Los Angeles, Los Angeles Township, Los Angeles, California, United States, Enumeration District 60–49, sheet 6A.

26. *Alice in Wonderland*, dir. Clyde Geronimi, Wilfred Jackson, and Hamilton Luske, Walt Disney Productions, 1951. Film.

27. David Tietyen, *The Musical World of Walt Disney* (Milwaukee: Hal Leonard, 1990) 96.

28. Schroeder, *Disney's Lost Chords*, vol. 1, 152.

29. Ibid., 154.

30. Ibid., 160.

31. Ibid.

32. Ibid., 159.

33. Ibid.

34. Ibid.

35. Ibid.

36. Ibid., 166.

37. Ibid., 162.

38. Ibid., 178.

39. Ibid., 173.

40. Ibid., 176.

41. Ibid., 169.

42. Steven Watts, *The Magic Kingdom: Walt Disney and the American Way of Life* (Columbia: University of Missouri Press, 1997) 367.

43. Thomas, *Walt Disney*, 221.

44. *The Walt Disney Story*, Walt Disney Productions, 1973. Film.

45. Leonard Maltin, *The Disney Films*, 3rd ed. (New York: Hyperion, 1995) 103.

46. Tim Hollis and Greg Ehrbar, *Mouse Tracks: The Story of Walt Disney Records* (Jackson: University Press of Mississippi, 2006) 23.

47. A second-cast, sometimes called a studio-cast, album is a recording where a group of vocalists different from those used in the film is hired to perform the music for release.

48. Russell Schroeder, *Disney's Lost Chords*, vol. 2 (Robbinsville: Voigt, 2008) 280.

49. Schroeder, *Disney's Lost Chords*, vol. 1, 182–83.

50. Jack Kinney, *Walt Disney and Assorted Other Characters* (New York: Harmony Books, 1988) 173.

51. Ibid.

52. Ibid., 174.

53. *Peter Pan*, dir. Clyde Geronimi, Wilfred Jackson, and Hamilton Luske, Walt Disney Productions, 1953. Film.

54. Ibid.

55. Sammy Cahn and Sammy Fain, "The Second Star from the Right," Walt Disney Music Company, 1951.

56. *Peter Pan*.

57. Ibid.

58. Ibid.

59. Cahn and Fain, "Second Star from the Right."

60. *Peter Pan*.

61. Ibid.

62. Ibid.

63. Ibid.

64. Schroeder, *Disney's Lost Chords*, vol. 2, 281.

65. Schroeder, *Disney's Lost Chords*, vol. 1, 184.

66. Schroeder, *Disney's Lost Chords*, vol. 2, 280.

67. Johnson, *Inside the Whimsy Works*, 44.

68. Box Office Mojo, "All Time Box Office Adjusted for Ticket Price Inflation," *Box Office Mojo* 3 February 2012 Web, 3 February 2012 <boxofficemojo.com/alltime/adjusted.htm>.

69. *Peter Pan*.

70. Ibid.

CHAPTER 8: DISNEY ANIMATED FEATURES 1955–1961

1. Russell Schroeder, *Disney's Lost Chords*, vol. 1 (Robbinsville: Voigt, 2007) 188.

2. "2079—'Lady & the Tramp': Seqs. 01.1–3.2—04.1–12.0–12.1: 3E-12–Meeting" Walt Disney Productions, 9 July 1954, Walt Disney Archives, 1.

3. "Meeting Notes—Seq. 0.3.0 'Calendar.'" Walt Disney Productions, 24 March 1953, 3.

4. Ibid., Walt Disney Archives, 2.

5. "2079—'Lady & the Tramp' Seq. 0.3.2—WHAT IS A BABY? Story Boards." Walt Disney Productions, 26 May 1953, Walt Disney Archives, 2.

6. Ibid.

7. "Mousetalgia—Episode 44," host Dave Breiland, *Mousetalgia*, 7 September 2009, MP3 file.

8. Ibid.

9. Ibid.

10. *Lady and the Tramp*, dir. Clyde Geronimi, Wilfred Jackson, Hamilton Luske, Walt Disney Productions, 1955, film.

11. Ibid.

12. See Daniel Goldmark and Utz McKnight, "Locating America: Revisiting Disney's *Lady and the Tramp*," *Social Identities* 14.1 (January 2008): 101–20.

13. Schroeder, *Disney's Lost Chords*, vol. 1, 190.

14. Ibid.

15. Ibid., 192–193.

16. Box Office Mojo, "All Time Box Office Adjusted for Ticket Price Inflation," *Box Office Mojo* 19 January 2012, Web, 19 January 2012 <boxofficemojo.com/alltime/adjusted.htm>.

17. "Singing ('Cause He Wants to Sing)" and "I'm Singing ('Cause I Want to Sing)" are different versions of the same song, with the perspective changed from third-person to first-person narrative.

18. Sonny Burke and Peggy Lee, "That Fellow's a Friend of Mine," Walt Disney Music Company, 1955.

19. Sonny Burke and Peggy Lee, "Singing ('Cause He Wants to Sing)," Walt Disney Music Company, 1955.

20. Schroeder, *Disney's Lost Chords*, vol. 1, 200.

21. Ibid.

22. Leonard Maltin, *The Disney Films*, 3rd ed. (New York: Hyperion, 1995) 154.

23. Ross Care, "George Bruns," *Cue Sheet* 18.3–4 (July–October 2002): 36.

24. Burt A. Folkart, "Writer of 'The Ballad of Davy Crockett' Dies," *Los Angeles Times* 26 May 1983: F8.

25. "MMC Crew: George Bruns" *The Original Mickey Mouse Club Show*, Web, 11 September 2011 <www.originalmmc.com/bruns.html>.

26. David Tietyen, "George Bruns (1914–1983): Interviewed by David Tietyen in 1978," *Walt's People*, vol. 11, ed. Didier Ghez (Bloomington: Xlibris, 2011) 309.

27. Care, "George Bruns," 34.

28. Ibid.

29. Tietyen, "George Bruns," 306.

30. Ibid., 306.

31. Jon Burlingame, "Buddy Baker (1918–2002) Interviewed by Jon Burlingame on May 10, 2001," *Walt's People*, vol. 5, ed. Didier Ghez (Bloomington: Xlibris, 2007) 160–61.

32. Tietyen, "George Bruns," 306.

33. Ibid., 307.

34. Ibid.

35. Ibid.

36. Richard Hubler, "George Bruns (1914–1983) Interviewed by Richard Hubler on July 23, 1968," *Walt's People*, vol. 5, ed. Didier Ghez (Bloomington: Xlibris, 2007) 153.

37. Tietyen, "George Bruns," 309.

38. Ibid.

39. Care, "George Bruns," 36.

40. Alex Rannie, "Hi-Ho, Come to the Fair! Disney's Music for the New York World's Fair of 1964–65," *Persistence of Vision* 6/7 (1997): 131–33, 137.

41. Jimmy Johnson, *Inside the Whimsy Works: My Life with Walt Disney Productions*, ed. Greg Ehrbar and Didier Ghez (Jackson: University Press of Mississippi, 2014) 76.

42. "George Bruns: Bio," *D23.com*, Web, 11 September 2011 <d23.com/walt-disney-legend/george-bruns>.

43. Tim Hollis and Greg Ehrbar, *Mouse Tracks: The Story of Walt Disney Records* (Jackson: University Press of Mississippi, 2006) 10.

44. Hubler, "George Bruns," 154.

45. Tietyen, "George Bruns," 308.

46. Hubler, "George Bruns," 154.

47. Burlingame, 159.

48. Ibid., 161.

49. Ibid.

50. Ibid.

51. Hubler, "George Bruns," 154.

52. Ibid., 155.

53. Ibid.

54. Ibid.

55. Tietyen, "George Bruns," 307.

56. Ibid.

57. Ibid.

58. Ibid.

59. Ibid.

60. Ibid.

61. Hubler, "George Bruns," 155.

62. Ibid.

63. Ibid.

64. Care, "George Bruns," 37.

65. Ibid.

66. Ibid.

67. Ibid.

68. Ibid.

69. Ibid.

70. "*Sleeping Beauty:* Meeting Notes," Walt Disney Productions, 11 February 1953, Walt Disney Archives, 1.

71. Ibid.

72. Ibid.

73. Ibid., 2.

74. Ibid.

75. Ibid.

76. Ibid., 3.

77. Ibid.

78. *Sleeping Beauty,* dir. Clyde Geronimi, Walt Disney Productions, 1959, film.

79. Ibid.

80. Ibid.

81. Ibid.

82. Russell Schroeder, *Disney's Lost Chords,* vol. 2 (Robbinsville: Voigt, 2008) 242.

83. Ibid., 246.

84. Ibid., 254.

85. Ibid., 257–65.

86. Ibid., 271.

87. Ibid., 241.

88. Ibid.

89. Ibid., 266.

90. "*Sleeping Beauty:* Meeting Notes," 6.

91. Ibid.

92. Ibid., 7.

93. Schroeder, *Disney's Lost Chords,* vol. 1, 206–8.

94. Schroeder, *Disney's Lost Chords,* vol. 2, 277.

95. Schroeder, *Disney's Lost Chords,* vol. 1, 202–5.

96. Tietyen, "George Bruns," 306.

97. Schroeder, *Disney's Lost Chords,* vol. 1, 201.

98. Maltin, *Disney Films,* 156–57.

99. Bosley Crowther, "Screen: *Sleeping Beauty,*" *New York Times,* 18 February 1959: 36.

100. Ibid.

101. Ibid.

102. Maltin, *Disney Films,* 155.

103. Ibid., 157.

104. Box Office Mojo, "All Time Box Office Adjusted for Ticket Price Inflation," *Box Office Mojo* 8 September 2011 Web, 8 September 2011 <boxofficemojo.com/alltime/adjusted.htm>.

105. Schroeder, *Disney's Lost Chords,* vol. 1, 222.

106. Ibid., 221.

107. Ibid., 224.

108. Box Office Mojo, "All Time Box Office Adjusted for Ticket Price Inflation."

CHAPTER 9: *THE SWORD IN THE STONE* AND *THE JUNGLE BOOK*

1. Robert J. Sherman, reply to author's post, *Facebook,* 30 May 2013.

2. David J. Fisher, "The Music of Disney: A Legacy in Song," liner notes, *The Music of Disney: A Legacy in Song* (Walt Disney Records, 1992) 28.

3. Robert B. Sherman and Richard M. Sherman, *Walt's Time: From Before to Beyond*, ed. Bruce Gordon, David Mumford, and Jeff Kurtti (Santa Clarita: Camphor Tree, 1998) 113.

4. Ibid.

5. Ibid.

6. Robert B. Sherman, *Moose: Chapters from My Life*, edited by Robert J. Sherman (Bloomington: AuthorHouse, 2013) 227.

7. Sherman and Sherman, *Walt's Time*, 114.

8. Ibid., 115.

9. Amy Booth Green, "Words & Music By . . .," *Disney Magazine* 35.2 (Summer 2000), 50.

10. Ibid.

11. Ibid.

12. "Mousetalgia Episode 177: Robert Sherman, John Carter," host Dave Breiland, *Mousetalgia*, 12 May 2013, MP3 file.

13. Sherman and Sherman, *Walt's Time*, 24.

14. Green, "Words & Music By . . .," 53.

15. Ibid.

16. Sherman and Sherman, *Walt's Time*, 62.

17. Ibid.

18. Michael Mallory, "The Fabulous Sherman Boys," *Disney News* 27.3 (Summer 1992): 48.

19. Green, "Words & Music By . . .," 50.

20. "Richard Sherman—Writing a Happy Song," *Pursuing Happiness* <vimeo.com/69947501>

21. "Mousetalgia Episode 126—Richard Sherman and Tony Walton on *Mary Poppins*," host Dave Breiland, *Mousetalgia*, 28 March 2011, MP3 file.

22. Sherman and Sherman, *Walt's Time*, 112.

23. Richard J. Sherman, *Facebook* message to the author, 30 March 2014.

24. Ibid.

25. Ibid.

26. Ibid.

27. Ibid.

28. "Episode 38—Richard M. Sherman," hosts Simon Barber and Brian O'Connor, *The Sodajerker on Songwriting*, Simon Barber and Brian O'Connor, 27 March 2013, MP3 file.

29. Ibid.

30. Ibid.

31. "#36 Tiara Talk's Interview with Gregg and Jeff Sherman," host Tammy Tuckey, *The Tiara Talk Show Podcast*, The Tiara Talk Show Podcast, 27 November 2012, MP3 file.

32. David Tietyen, *The Musical World of Walt Disney* (Milwaukee: Hal Leonard, 1990) 124.

33. Ibid.

34. Ibid.

35. Ibid.

36. Tim Hollis and Greg Ehrbar, *Mouse Tracks: The Story of Walt Disney Records* (Jackson: University Press of Mississippi, 2006) 52.

37. Tietyen, *Musical World of Walt Disney*, 124.

38. Jimmy Johnson, *Inside the Whimsy Works: My Life with Walt Disney Productions*, ed. Greg Ehrbar and Didier Ghez (Jackson: University Press of Mississippi, 2014) 117.

39. Ibid.

40. Ibid.

41. Ibid., 118.

42. Ibid.

43. Ibid.

44. Sherman and Sherman, *Walt's Time*, 39.

45. Ibid.

46. Ibid., 40.

47. Green, "Words and Music By . . . ," 52.

48. Johnson, *Inside the Whimsy Works*, 119.

49. Hollis and Ehrbar, *Mouse Tracks*, 79.

50. Richard Hubler, "Bob Sherman (b. 1925): Interviewed by Richard Hubler on July 30, 1968," *Walt's People*, vol. 8, ed. Didier Ghez (Bloomington: Xlibris, 2009) 202.

51. Ibid., 203.

52. Sherman and Sherman, *Walt's Time*, 14.

53. Ibid.

54. Ibid., 26.

55. Ibid.

56. Ibid.

57. Ibid.

58. Hollis and Ehrbar, *Mouse Tracks*, 55.

59. Sherman and Sherman, *Walt's Time*, 44.

60. Green, "Words & Music By . . . ," 52.

61. Sherman and Sherman, *Walt's Time*, 19.

62. Ibid.

63. Green, "Words & Music By . . . ," 52.

64. Ibid., 53.

65. Ibid.

66. Hubler, "Bob Sherman (b. 1925): Interviewed by Richard Hubler on July 30, 1968," 202.

67. Jérémie Noyer, "Buddy Baker (1918–2002): Interviewed by Jérémie Noyer on July 19, 2001 and January 26, 2002," *Walt's People*, vol. 5, ed. Didier Ghez (Bloomington: Xlibris, 2007) 171.

68. Hubler, "Bob Sherman (b. 1925)," 206.

69. Fisher, "Music of Disney," 34.

70. "Episode 38—Richard M. Sherman."

71. Ibid.

72. Sherman and Sherman, *Walt's Time*, 9.

73. Hollis and Ehrbar, *Mouse Tracks*, 127.

74. Ibid., 82.

75. Green, "Words & Music By . . . ," 50.

76. Jim Korkis, *How to Be a Disney Historian* (Orlando: Theme Park Press, 2016) 54.

77. Ibid.

78. Scott Wolf, "Interview: Jeffrey Sherman (Son of Disney Songwriter Robert B. Sherman)," *Mouse Clubhouse*, 12 October 2015, Web, 13 October 2016 <mouseclubhouse.com/interview-jeffrey-sherman/>.

79. Ibid.

80. Charles Tranberg, *Walt Disney & Recollections of the Disney Studios: 1955–1980* (Albany, GA: BearManor Media, 2012) 166.

81. Ibid.

82. "Mousetalgia Episode 177: Robert Sherman, John Carter."

83. Ibid.

84. Ibid.

85. Ibid.

86. "Redstring Productions, Inc." *Redstring Productions, Inc.*, Web, 3 February 2013 <www.redstring.com/frameset_3.htm>.

87. "Mousetalgia Episode 177: Robert Sherman, John Carter."

88. Leonard Maltin, *The Disney Films*, 3rd ed. (New York: Hyperion, 1995) 216.

89. *The Sword in the Stone*, dir. Wolfgang Reitherman, Walt Disney Productions, 1963. Film.

90. Ibid.

91. Ibid.

92. Ibid.

93. Ibid.

94. Ibid.

95. Ibid.

96. *Tom Sawyer*, dir. Don Taylor, Reader's Digest, 1973. Film.

97. David Tietyen, *The Musical World of Walt Disney* (Milwaukee: Hal Leonard, 1990) 128.

98. Sherman and Sherman, *Walt's Time*, 28.

99. "Music Magic: The Sherman Brothers," dir. Les Perkins, prod. Clare Baren, *The Sword in the Stone: 45th Anniversary Edition*, Buena Vista Home Entertainment, 2001. DVD. Disc 2.

100. *The Sword in the Stone*. Promotional poster, Walt Disney Productions, 1963.

101. James Piereson, "How Jackie Kennedy Invented the Camelot Legend after JFK's Death," *The Daily Beast* 12 November 2013, Web, 6 March 2016 <thedailybeast.com/articles/2013/11/12/how-jackie-kennedy-invented-the-camelot-legend-after-jfk-s-death.html>.

102. Ibid.

103. Ibid.

104. Ibid.

105. Bob Thomas, *Walt Disney: An American Original* (New York: Disney Editions, 1994), 343.

106. Floyd Norman, "The Making of *The Jungle Book* as Remembered by Floyd Norman in September 2006," *Walt's People*, vol. 5, ed. Didier Ghez (Bloomington: Xlibris, 2007), 309.

107. Russell Schroeder, *Disney's Lost Chords: Hidden Treasures from the Disney Music Library Archives*, vol. 1 (Robbinsville: Voigt, 2007) 273.

108. "*Jungle Book*: Walt Meeting—Storyboards on Opening—Seq. 001—Prod. #2179," 26 August 1966, Richard B. and Robert B. Sherman Papers, Collection Number 3222, American Heritage Center, University of Wyoming.

109. Alex Rannie, "Hi-Ho, Come to the Fair! Disney's Music for the New York World's Fair of 1964–65," *Persistence of Vision* 6/7 (1997): 132.

110. Sherman and Sherman, *Walt's Time*, 81.

111. *The Jungle Book*, dir. Wolfgang Reitherman, Walt Disney Productions, 1967. Film.

112. Russell Schroeder, *Disney's Lost Chords: More Hidden Treasures from the Walt Disney Music Library Archives*, vol. 2 (Robbinsville: Voigt, 2008) 220.

113. *Jungle Book*.

114. Ibid.

115. Ibid.

116. See Susan Miller and Greg Rode, "The Movie You See, The Movie You Don't," *From Mouse to Mermaid: The Politics of Film, Gender, and Culture*, ed. Elizabeth Bell, Lynda Haas, and Laura Sells (Bloomington: Indiana University Press, 1995) 86–103.

117. Koen Van Otterdijk, "Richard M. Sherman: Legendarische Componist," *Filmvalley* 45 (November 2007): 73.

118. Ibid.

119. Hollis and Ehrbar, *Mouse Tracks*, 70.

120. Norman, "Making of *The Jungle Book* as Remembered by Floyd Norman," 310.

121. *Jungle Book*.

122. "Episode 38—Richard M. Sherman."

123. George Bruns, Terry Gilkyson, Robert B. Sherman, Richard M. Sherman, *The Jungle Book*, Walt Disney Records, 60950–7, 1997.

124. Ibid.

125. Ibid.

126. Ibid.

127. Ibid.

128. Norman, "The Making of *The Jungle Book* as Remembered by Floyd Norman," 311.

129. Arlynn Anderson, email to the author, 20 March 2015.

130. *Jungle Book.*

131. Floyd Norman, email to the author, 16 August 2013.

132. Ibid.

133. "*Jungle Book*: Walt Meeting—Storyboards on 'Baloo Rejecting Mowgli,' 'The Vultures,' 'Rhino Sequence,'" 29 June 1965, Richard M. and Robert B. Sherman Papers, Collection Number 3222, American Heritage Center, University of Wyoming, 2.

134. Ibid.

135. Ibid.

136. Ibid.

137. "Vulture Sequence," *Jungle Boy*, Richard M. and Robert B. Sherman Papers, Collection Number 3222, American Heritage Center, University of Wyoming, 3.

138. Ibid., 3–4.

139. "'The Bare Necessities': The Making of *The Jungle Book*," *Walt Disney's* The Jungle Book: *40th Anniversary Edition*, Buena Vista Home Entertainment, 2007. DVD.

140. Norman, "The Making of *The Jungle Book* as Remembered by Floyd Norman," 315.

141. Sherman and Sherman, *Walt's Time*, 84.

142. *Jungle Book.*

143. Ibid.

144. Ibid.

145. Ibid.

146. "'Bare Necessities': The Making of *The Jungle Book.*"

147. Robert B. Sherman and Richard M. Sherman, "My Own Home," lyric manuscript, 11 November 1965, Richard M. and Robert B. Sherman Papers, Collection 3222, American Heritage Center, University of Wyoming.

148. Robert J. Sherman, *Facebook* message to the author, 25 January 2013.

149. *Jungle Book.*

150. Sherman and Sherman, *Walt's Time*, 85.

151. Ibid.

152. Ibid.

153. Schroeder, vol. 1, 274.

154. Ibid.

155. Ibid., 272.

156. Schroeder, vol. 2, 219.

157. Ibid., 228.

158. Ibid., 277.

159. Ibid., 220.

160. Ibid., 224.

161. Ibid., 233–35.

162. Ibid., 236–39.

163. Maltin, *Disney Films*, 256.

164. Box Office Mojo, "All Time Box Office Adjusted for Ticket Price Inflation," *Box Office Mojo*, 3 February 2012, Web, 3 February 2012 <boxofficemojo.com/alltime/adjusted.htm>.

165. Johnson, *Inside the Whimsy Works*, 131.

166. Ibid., 132.

167. Ibid., 166.

168. Sherman and Sherman, *Walt's Time*, 167.

169. Robert B. Sherman, *Moose: Chapters from My Life*, ed. Robert J. Sherman (Bloomington: AuthorHouse, 2013) 404.

170. Ben Child, "Disney Turns Away from Hand-Drawn Animation," *Guardian*, 7 March 2013, Web, 16 November 2014 <www.theguardian.com/film/2013/mar/07/disney-hand-drawn -animation>.

171. Michael Barrier, "'What's New' Archives: March 2014," *www.michaelbarrier.com*, 12 March 2014, Web, 16 November 2014 <www.michaelbarrier.com/Home%20Page/WhatsNew ArchivesMar14.html>.

172. Keith Uhlich, "*Frozen*: Movie Review," *TimeOut*, 26 November 2013, Web, 16 November 2014 <www.timeout.com/us/film/frozen-movie-review>.

173. Tasha Robinson, "*Frozen*," *The Dissolve*. 28 November 2013, Web, 16 November 2014 <thedissolve.com/reviews/407-frozen/>.

174. Keith Caulfield, "*Frozen* Won't Let Go of No. 1 as DVD Spurs Sales," *Billboard* 126.11 (29 March 2014): 45.

175. Marc Snetiker, "*Frozen* Is on Fire: Disney's Smash Now Has Oscar Cred and a Soundtrack Hotter than Beyoncé," *Entertainment Weekly* 1296/1297 (31 January 2014): 28.

176. Ibid.

177. Nolan Feeney, "Easter Gives *Frozen* Soundtrack Its Best Sales Week Yet," *Time.com*, 25 April 2014, Web, 23 November 2014 <time.com/74085/frozen-soundtrack-charts/>.

178. Suzy Evans, "Idina Menzel, Unfrozen," *Billboard* 126.11 (29 March 2014): 28–33.

179. Dorian Lynskey, "Why *Frozen*'s 'Let It Go' Is More than a Disney Hit—It's an Adolescent Aperitif" *guardian.com*, 10 April 2014, Web, 14 October 2015 <www.theguardian.com/music/ musicblog/2014/apr/10/frozen-let-it-go-disney-hit-adolescent-lgbt-anthem>.

180. Hillary Busis, "Disney's *Frozen*: Composers Talk Unexpected Influences (Gaga!) and Accidentally Aping *Arrested Development*" *ew.com*, 27 November 2013, Web, 14 October 2015 <www.ew.com/article/2013/11/27/frozen-composers-bobby-lopez-kristen-anderson-lopez>.

181. Ibid.

182. Melena Ryrik, "*Frozen* Evolved around 'Let It Go,'" *Houston News*, 25 February 2014, Web, 14 October 2015 <www.chron.com/entertainment/movies/article/Frozen-evolved -around-Let-It-Go-5266745.php>.

BIBLIOGRAPHY

BOOKS ABOUT DISNEY

Barrier, Michael. *The Animated Man: A Life of Walt Disney*. Berkeley: University of California Press, 2007.

Bell, Elizabeth, Lynda Haas, and Laura Sells, eds. *From Mouse to Mermaid: The Politics of Film, Gender, and Culture*. Bloomington: Indiana University Press, 1995.

Finch, Christopher. *The Art of Walt Disney from Mickey Mouse to the Magic Kingdoms*. Rev. and expanded ed. New York: Harry N. Abrams, 2004.

Gabler, Neal. *Walt Disney: The Triumph of the American Imagination*. New York: Alfred A. Knopf, 2006.

Ghez, Didier, ed. *Walt's People*. Vol. 5. Bloomington: Xlibris, 2007.

——, ed. *Walt's People*. Vol. 8. Bloomington: Xlibris, 2009.

——, ed. *Walt's People*. Vol. 9. Bloomington: Xlibris, 2010.

——, ed. *Walt's People*. Vol. 10. Bloomington: Xlibris, 2011.

——, ed. *Walt's People*. Vol. 11. Bloomington: Xlibris, 2011.

Hollis, Tim, and Greg Ehrbar. *Mouse Tracks: The Story of Walt Disney Records*. Jackson: University Press of Mississippi, 2006.

Holliss, Richard, and Brian Sibley. *Walt Disney's "Snow White and the Seven Dwarfs" & the Making of the Classic Film*. New York: Hyperion, 1994.

Jackson, Kathy Merlock. *Walt Disney: Conversations*. Jackson: University Press of Mississippi, 2006.

Johnson, Jimmy. *Inside the Whimsy Works: My Life with Walt Disney Productions*. Ed. Greg Ehrbar and Didier Ghez. Jackson: University Press of Mississippi, 2014.

Kaufman, J. B. *The Fairest One of All: The Making of Walt Disney's "Snow White and the Seven Dwarfs."* San Francisco: The Walt Disney Family Foundation Press, 2012.

——. *"Snow White and the Seven Dwarfs": The Art and Creation of Walt Disney's Classic Animated Film*. San Francisco: The Walt Disney Family Foundation Press, 2012.

——. *South of the Border with Disney: Walt Disney and the Good Neighbor Program, 1941–1948*. New York: Disney Editions, 2009.

Kinney, Jack. *Walt Disney and Assorted Other Characters*. New York: Harmony Books, 1988.

Korkis, Jim. *How to Be a Disney Historian*. Orlando: Theme Park Press, 2016.

Krause, Marin, and Witowski, Linda. *Walt Disney's "Snow White and the Seven Dwarfs": An Art in Its Making*. New York: Hyperion, 1994.

Maltin, Leonard. *The Disney Films*. 3rd ed. New York: Hyperion, 1995.

Schroeder, Russell. *Disney's Lost Chords: Hidden Treasures from the Walt Disney Music Library Archives*. Robbinsville: Voigt, 2007.

——. *Disney's Lost Chords: More Hidden Treasures from the Walt Disney Music Library Archives*. Vol. 2. Robbinsville: Voigt, 2008.

Smoodin, Eric, ed. *Disney Discourse: Producing the Magic Kingdom*. New York: Routledge, 1994.

Thomas, Bob. *Walt Disney: An American Original*. New York: Disney Editions, 1994.

Tietyen, David. *The Musical World of Walt Disney*. Milwaukee: Hal Leonard, 1990.

Tranberg, Charles. *Walt Disney & Recollections of the Disney Studios: 1955–1980*. Albany: Bear-Manor Media, 2012.

Watts, Steven. *The Magic Kingdom: Walt Disney and the American Way of Life*. Columbia: University of Missouri Press, 1997.

OTHER BOOKS

Barrier, Michael. *Hollywood Cartoons: American Animation in Its Golden Age*. New York: Oxford University Press, 2003.

The Fifty Greatest Cartoons as Selected by 1,000 Animation Professionals. Atlanta: Turner, 1994.

Goldmark, Daniel. *Tunes for 'Toons: Music and the Hollywood Cartoon*. Berkeley: University of California Press, 2005.

Goldmark, Daniel, and Yuval Taylor, eds. *The Cartoon Music Book*. Chicago: A Capella Books, 2002.

Grewe, Corinne F. *The Orchestration of Joy and Suffering: Understanding Chronic Addiction*. New York: Algora, 2001.

Heyward, Philip, ed. *Off the Planet: Music, Sound and Science Fiction Cinema*. Eastleigh: John Libbey, 2004.

Holman, Tomlinson. *5.1 Surround Sound Up and Running*. Boston: Focal Press, 2000.

Hunt, John Gabriel. *The Inaugural Addresses of the Presidents*. New York: Gramercy Books, 1997.

Machlis, Joseph. *Introduction to Contemporary Music*. 2nd ed. New York: W. W. Norton, 1979.

McCarty, Clifford. *Film Composers in America: A Filmography 1911–1970*. New York: Oxford University Press, 2000.

Newsom, Iris, ed. *Wonderful Inventions: Motion Pictures, Broadcasting, and Recorded Sound at the Library of Congress*. Washington: Library of Congress, 1985.

Sherman, Robert B. *Moose: Chapters from My Life*. Edited by Robert J. Sherman. Bloomington: AuthorHouse, 2013.

Sherman, Robert B., and Richard M. Sherman. *Walt's Time: From Before to Beyond*. Ed. Bruce Gordon, David Mumford, and Jeff Kurtti. Santa Clarita: Camphor Tree, 1998.

Stanley, Glenn. *The Cambridge Companion to Beethoven*. Cambridge: Cambridge University Press, 2000.

Taruskin, Richard, and Piero Weiss. *Music in the Western World: A History in Documents*. New York: Schirmer Books, 1984.

Telotte, J. P. *Animating Space: From Mickey to Wall-E*. Lexington: University Press of Kentucky, 2010.

Timm, Larry. *The Soul of Cinema: An Appreciation of Film Music*. Upper Saddle River: Prentice Hall, 2003.

Van Dyke, Dick. *My Lucky Life in and out of Show Business*. New York: Three Rivers Press, 2011.

Young, William H., and Nancy K. Young. *World War II and the Postwar Years in America: A Historical and Cultural Encyclopedia*. Vol. 1 (A–I). Santa Barbara: ABC-Clio, 2010.

Zimmers, Tighe E. *Tin Pan Alley Girl: A Biography of Ann Ronell*. Jefferson: McFarland, 2009.

MOVIE REVIEWS

"*Bambi*, a Musical Cartoon in Technicolor Produced by Walt Disney from the Story by Felix Salten, at the Music Hall." *New York Times* 14 August 1942: 13.

Churchill, Douglas W. "Screen News Here and in Hollywood." *New York Times* 8 February 1940: 25.

———. "Walt Disney Sighs for More Whirls." *New York Times* 9 January 1938: X5.

Crowther, Bosley. "A Disney Dilemma." *New York Times* 22 February 1959: X1.

———. "Disney's *Snow White*, Reissued, Proves Itself Forever New—Other Films." *New York Times* 9 April 1944: X3.

———. "Forward with Walt Disney." *New York Times* 26 October 1941: X5.

———. "A Muchness of 'Alice.'" *New York Times* 29 July 1951: 73.

———. "Screen: Dogs and Lovers." *New York Times* 24 June 1955: 17.

———. "The Screen: Disney's *Peter Pan* Bows." *New York Times* 12 February 1953: 23.

———. "Screen: Eight New Movies Arrive for the Holidays." *New York Times* 26 December 1963: 33.

———. "The Screen." *New York Times* 13 February 1943: 8.

———. "The Screen." *New York Times* 5 February 1945: 20.

———. "The Screen in Review." *New York Times* 14 November 1940: 28.

———. "The Screen in Review." *New York Times* 30 July 1951: 12.

———. "Screen: *Sleeping Beauty*." *New York Times* 18 February 1959: 36.

———. "Walt Disney's Cartoon, *Dumbo*, a Fanciful Delight, Opens at the Broadway—*You'll Never Get Rich*, with Fred Astaire and Rita Hayworth, Is Seen at the Music Hall—New Film at Palace." *New York Times* 24 October 1941: 27.

———. "Yes, but Is It Art?" *New York Times* 17 November 1940: 141.

Downes, Olin. "Disney's Experiment." *New York Times* 17 November 1940: 143.

———. "*Fantasia* Discussed from the Musical Standpoint—Sound Reproduction Called Unprecedented." *New York Times* 14 November 1940: 28.

Hall, Mordaunt. "The Screen." *New York Times* 19 November 1928: 16.

"Latest Screen Journey to Never-Never Land." *New York Times* 8 February 1953: X5.

"Mr. Disney and *Fantasia*." *New York Times* 15 November 1940: 20.

"News of the Screen." *New York Times* 31 January 1938: 15.

Nugent, Frank S. "Jiminy Cricket! It's Disney!" *New York Times* 11 February 1940: 131.

———. "One Touch of Disney." *New York Times* 23 January 1938: 157.

———. "The Screen in Review." *New York Times* 14 January 1938: 21.

———. "The Screen in Review." *New York Times* 8 February 1940: 24.

Strauss, Theodore. "Donald Duck's Disney." *New York Times* 7 February 1943: X3.

———. "A Sorcerer, Not an Apprentice." *New York Times* 17 November 1940: 140.

OBITUARIES

"'Big Bad Wolf' Author Suicide in California." *New York Times* 15 May 1942: 24.

"'Big Bad Wolf' Creator Suicide." *Los Angeles Times* 15 May 1942: A12.

"Carl Stalling: Obituary." *Los Angeles Times* 1 December 1972: C24.

"Charles F. Wolcott, 80, Disney Film Composer." *New York Times* 30 January 1987: B8.

"Composer of 'Hindustan' Dies at 76." *Los Angeles Times* 17 September 1963: A1.

"Edward H. Plumb: Obituary." *Los Angeles Times* 20 April 1958: C10.

"Elbert C. Lewis." *Los Angeles Times* 3 December 1948: 23.

Folkart, Burt A. "Charles Wolcott; Musician, Baha'i Leader." *Los Angeles Times* 29 January 1987: 30.

Folkart, Burt A. "Writer of 'The Ballad of Davy Crockett' Dies." *Los Angeles Times* 26 May 1983: F8.

"George Bruns." *New York Times* 27 May 1983: B7.

"Leigh Harline: Obituary." *Los Angeles Times* 11 December 1969: D4.

Oliver, Myrna. "Obituaries: Irwin Kostal; Film, TV Orchestrator." *Los Angeles Times* 1 December 1994.

"Oliver Wallace Dies at 76; Composer of 'Hindustan.'" *New York Times* 17 September 1963: 35.
"Oscar-Winning Composer Paul Joseph Smith, 78, Dies." *Los Angeles Times* 1 February 1985: C3.

FROM *THE MICKEY MOUSE MELODEON*

Shafer, Carolyn Catherine. "The Animator's Prayer." *The Mickey Mouse Melodeon: House Organ of the Disney Studio* 1.4 (February 1933): 5.

——. "Clara Cluck's Column." *The Mickey Mouse Melodeon: House Organ of the Disney Studio* 1.1 (November 1932): 4.

——. "Clara Cluck's Column." *The Mickey Mouse Melodeon: House Organ of the Disney Studio* 1.2 (December 1932): 4.

——. "Clara Cluck's Column." *The Mickey Mouse Melodeon: House Organ of the Disney Studio* 1.4 (February 1933): 5.

——. "Dear Santa Claus." *The Mickey Mouse Melodeon: House Organ of the Disney Studio* 1.3 (January 1933); 4.

——. "Music Notes." *The Mickey Mouse Melodeon: House Organ of the Disney Studio* 1.1 (November 1932): 2.

——. "Our Ten Most Beautiful." *The Mickey Mouse Melodeon: House Organ of the Disney Studio* 1.4 (February 1933): 1.

——. "Society News." *The Mickey Mouse Melodeon: House Organ of the Disney Studio* 1.3 (January 1933): 3.

——. "What's Wrong with Production." *The Mickey Mouse Melodeon: House Organ of the Disney Studio* 1.2 (December 1932): 3.

OTHER ARTICLES

Barham, Jeremy. "Recurring Dreams and Moving Images: The Cinematic Appropriation of Schumann's Op. 15, No. 7." *19th-Century Music* 34.3 (Spring 2011): 271–301.

Care, Ross. "Cinesymphony: Music and Animation at the Disney Studio 1928–1942." *Sight and Sound* 46 (Winter 1976–1977): 40–44.

——. "Disney Music during the Classic Era: An Overview." *Cue Sheet* 18 (July–October 2002): 4–8.

——. "Disney Unlocks the Music Vault." *Scarlet Street* 27 (Spring 1998): 42–46, 49–50, 74.

——. "The Film Music of Leigh Harline." *Filmmusic Notebook* 3.2 (1977): 32–48.

——. "George Bruns." *Cue Sheet* 18.3–4 (July–October 2002): 34–37.

——. "Melody Time: Musicians for Disney Animation 1941–1955." *Soundtrack* 8.31 (1989): 32–40.

——. "Record Rack; *Snow White and the Seven Dwarfs* and *Pinocchio*; The First CD Releases." *Scarlet Street* 12 (Fall 1993): 52–53.

——. "Symphonists for the Sillies: The Composers for Disney's Shorts." *Funnyworld* 18 (Summer 1978): 38–48.

——. "Threads of Melody: The Evolution of a Major Film Score—Walt Disney's *Bambi*." *Quarterly Journal of the Library of Congress* 20.2 (Spring 1983): 76–98.

Caulfield, Keith. "*Frozen* Won't Let Go of No. 1 as DVD Spurs Sales." *Billboard* 126.11 (29 March 2014) 45.

"Disney Cinesymphony." *Time* (18 November 1940).

Evans, Suzy, "Idina Menzel, Unfrozen." *Billboard* 126.11 (29 March 2014): 28–33.

Goldmark, Daniel, and Utz McKnight. "Locating America: Revisiting Disney's *Lady and the Tramp*." *Social Identities* 14.1 (January 2008): 101–20.

Green, Amy Boothe. "Words & Music By . . ." *Disney Magazine* 35.2 (Summer 2000): 50–53.

Heylbut, Rose. "The Music of the Walt Disney Cartoons: A Conference with Paul J. Smith." *Etude Magazine* (July 1940): 438, 494.

Inge, M. Thomas. "Walt Disney's *Snow White*: Art, Adaptation, and Ideology." *Journal of Popular Film and Television* 32.3 (Fall 2004): 132–42.

Mallory, Michael. "The Fabulous Sherman Boys." *Disney News* 27.3 (Summer 1992): 47–48.

"Piglets' Tune." *Time* (25 September 1933): 30.

Pryor, Thomas M. "*Snow White* Sidelights: Censors Toppled and Business Boomed as the Dwarfs Went round the World." *New York Times* 5 February 1939: X4.

Rannie, Alex. "Hi-Ho, Come to the Fair! Disney's Music for the New York World's Fair of 1964–65." *Persistence of Vision* 6/7 (1997): 131–41.

Sheff, David. "Playboy Interview: John Lennon and Yoko Ono." *Playboy* 28.1 (January 1981): 75–76, 79, 82–84, 86, 88–89, 93–94, 96, 98, 101, 105, 107, 110, 112, 114, 144.

Smith, Paul. "An Article on *Love Happy*: On Precision Timing." *Film Music Notes* 9.4 (March–April 1950): 10–12.

Snetiker, Marc, "*Frozen* Is on Fire: Disney's Smash Now Has Oscar Cred and a Soundtrack Hotter than Beyoncé." *Entertainment Weekly* 1296/1297 (31 January 2014): 28.

Steele, R. Vernon. "Fairyland Goes Hollywood: An Interview with Leigh Harline." *Pacific Coast Musician* (20 November 1937): 10.

Van Otterdijk, Koen. "Richard M. Sherman: Legendarische Componist." *Filmvalley* 45 (November 2007): 72–73.

SCORES

Churchill, Frank. *Egyptian Melodies*. Manuscript (3 staves), 1931. Disney Music Legacy Libraries.

———. *Egyptian Melodies*. Manuscript (8 staves), 1931. Arr. by Carl Stalling. Carl W. Stalling Papers, Collection Number 5725, American Heritage Center, University of Wyoming.

Churchill, Frank, Leigh Harline, Larry Morey, and Paul Smith. *Walt Disney's "Snow White and the Seven Dwarfs" Master Score*. Burbank: Disney Music Legacy Libraries, 2015.

Darby, Ken. "A Mad Tea Party: Walt Disney, Preliminary Notes for *Alice in Wonderland*." Manuscript, n.d. Ken Darby Papers 1929–1992; Fine Arts and Communications; L. Tom Perry Special Collections, Harold B. Lee Library, Brigham Young University.

Harline, Leigh. *After "It's Getting Late" Dialog*. Manuscript sketch from *Pinocchio*, n.d. Leigh Harline Papers, 1938–1968, US-86–22, Archives and Rare Books Library, University of Cincinnati, Cincinnati, Ohio.

———. *After M.B.* Manuscript sketch from *Pinocchio*, n.d. Leigh Harline Papers, 1938–1968, US-86–22, Archives and Rare Books Library, University of Cincinnati, Cincinnati, Ohio.

———. *Cat on Floor*. Manuscript sketch from *Pinocchio*, n.d. Leigh Harline Papers, 1938–1968, US-86–22, Archives and Rare Books Library, University of Cincinnati, Cincinnati, Ohio.

———. *Elmer Elephant: Piano-Conductor*. Manuscript, 1936. Leigh Harline Papers, 1938–1968, US-86–22, Archives and Rare Books Library, University of Cincinnati, Cincinnati, Ohio.

———. *Music Land: Piano-Conductor*. Manuscript, 1935. Leigh Harline Papers, 1938–1968, US-86–22, Archives and Rare Books Library, University of Cincinnati, Cincinnati, Ohio.

———. *The Old Mill: Piano-Conductor*. Manuscript, 1937. Leigh Harline Papers, 1938–1968, US-86–22, Archives and Rare Books Library, University of Cincinnati, Cincinnati, Ohio.

———. *Untitled Sketch [Figaro in Bed Through Opening Window]*. Manuscript, n.d. Leigh Harline Papers, 1938–1968, US-86–22, Archives and Rare Books Library, University of Cincinnati, Cincinnati, Ohio.

Lewis, Bert. *Flowers and Trees*. Manuscript (3 staves), 1932. Disney Music Legacy Libraries.

———. *Fishin' Around*. Manuscript (2 staves), 1931. Arr. by Carl Stalling. Disney Music Legacy Libraries.

———. *Fishin' Around*. Manuscript (3 staves), 1931. Disney Music Legacy Libraries.

———. *Fishin' Around*. Manuscript (8 staves), 1931. Arr. by Carl Stalling. Carl W. Stalling Papers, Collection Number 5725, American Heritage Center, University of Wyoming.

———. *Mickey Cuts Up*. Manuscript (2 staves), 1931. Arr. by Carl Stalling. Disney Music Legacy Libraries.

———. *Mickey Cuts Up*. Manuscript (3 staves), 1931, Disney Music Legacy Libraries.

———. *Mickey Cuts Up*. Manuscript (6 staves), 1931. Arr. by Carl Stalling. Carl W. Stalling Papers, Collection Number 5725, American Heritage Center, University of Wyoming.

———. *Mickey Steps Out*. Manuscript (2 staves), 1931. Arr. by Carl Stalling. Disney Music Legacy Libraries.

———. *Mickey Steps Out*. Manuscript (3 staves), 1931. Disney Music Legacy Libraries.

———. *Mickey Steps Out*. Manuscript (7 staves), 1931. Arr. by Carl Stalling. Carl W. Stalling Papers, Collection Number 5725, American Heritage Center, University of Wyoming.

Smith, Paul J., and Oliver Wallace. *Cinderella: Piano-Conductor*. Manuscript, 1950, Robert E. Smylie Archives, College of Idaho.

Stalling, Carl. "Minnie's Yoo Hoo." Manuscript, 1930, Carl W. Stalling Papers, Collection Number 5725, American Heritage Center, University of Wyoming.

SONGS

Bagar, Robert, James Cavanaugh, and Milt Coleman. "The Wedding Party of Mickey Mouse." Stasny Music, 1931.

Benedict, Edward, C. E. J. Bresland, and Edith Andrew Burchell. "Hot Cha House." McKinley Music, 1933.

Burke, Sonny, and Peggy Lee. "Singing ('Cause He Wants to Sing)." Walt Disney Music Company, 1955.

———. "That Fellow's a Friend of Mine." Walt Disney Music Company, 1955.

Caesar, Irving. "What! No Mickey Mouse? What Kind of a Party Is This?" Irving Caesar, 1932.

Cahn, Sammy, and Sammy Fain. "The Second Star from the Right." Walt Disney Music Company, 1951.

Carlton, Harry, and Bert Reisfeld. "Micky Maus." Universum Verlags A.-G., 1930.

Churchill, Frank, and Larry Morey. "(The Dwarfs' Marching Song) Heigh-Ho." Irving Berlin Music., 1937.

———. "One Song." Irving Berlin Music, 1937.

———. "Some Day My Prince Will Come (Some Day I'll Find My Love)." Irving Berlin Music, 1937.

David, Lee, and Jack Meskill. "I'd Rather Stay Home with Mickey Mouse than Go Out with a Rat Like You." De Sylva, Brown, and Henderson, 1932.

David, Mack, Al Hoffman, and Jerry Livingston. "The Unbirthday Song." Manuscript, 28 June 1948. Disney Music Legacy Libraries.

Egan, Raymond B., Gus Kahn, and Richard A. Whiting. "Ain't We Got Fun." Jerome H. Remick, 1921.

Harline, Leigh, and Ned Washington. "Figaro and Cleo." Manuscript, n.d. Leigh Harline Papers, 1938–1968, US-86-22, Archives and Rare Books Library, University of Cincinnati, Cincinnati, Ohio.

Meyer, Joseph, Bob Rothberg, and Charlie Tobias. "Mickey Mouse's Birthday Party." Irving Berlin, 1936.

Porter, Cole. "You're the Top." WB Music, 1934.

Ronell, Ann. "In a Silly Symphony." Irving Berlin, 1933.

———. "Mickey Mouse and Minnie's in Town." Irving Berlin, 1933.

Sherman, Robert B., and Richard M. Sherman. "Colonel Hathi's March." Manuscript, 1966. Richard M. and Robert B. Sherman Papers, Collection Number 3222, American Heritage Center, University of Wyoming.

———. "I Wan'na Be Like You." Manuscript. 1966. Richard M. and Robert B. Sherman Papers, Collection Number 3222, American Heritage Center, University of Wyoming.

———. "My Own Home." Manuscript. 1966. Richard M. and Robert B. Sherman Papers, Collection Number 3222, American Heritage Center, University of Wyoming.

———. "That's What Friends Are For." Manuscript. 1966. Richard M. and Robert B. Sherman Papers, Collection Number 3222, American Heritage Center, University of Wyoming.

———. "Trust in Me." Manuscript. 1966. Richard M. and Robert B. Sherman Papers, Collection Number 3222, American Heritage Center, University of Wyoming.

FILMS AND VIDEOS

Alice in Wonderland. Dir. Clyde Geronimi, Wilfred Jackson, and Hamilton Luske. Walt Disney Productions, 1951. Film.

Bambi. Dir. David Hand, Walt Disney Productions, 1942. Film.

Cinderella. Dir. Clyde Geronimi, Wilfred Jackson, and Hamilton Luske. Walt Disney Productions, 1950. Film.

Dumbo. Dir. Ben Sharpsteen, Walt Disney Productions, 1941. Film.

The Grasshopper and the Ants. Dir. Wilfred Jackson, Walt Disney Productions, 1934. Film.

The Jungle Book. Dir. Wolfgang Reitherman, Walt Disney Productions, 1967. Film.

Lady and the Tramp. Dir. Clyde Geronimi, Wilfred Jackson, Hamilton Luske, Walt Disney Productions, 1955. Film.

The Lion King. Dir. Roger Allers and Rob Minkoff. Walt Disney Pictures, 1994. Film.

"'The Bare Necessities:' The Making of *The Jungle Book*." *Walt Disney's* The Jungle Book: *40th Anniversary Edition*. Buena Vista Home Entertainment, 2007. DVD.

"The Making of *Bambi*: A Prince Is Born." *Bambi*. Walt Disney Studios Home Entertainment, 2011. DVD.

"Music Magic: The Sherman Brothers." Dir. Les Perkins. Prod. Clare Baren. *The Sword in the Stone: 45th Anniversary Edition*. Buena Vista Home Entertainment, 2001, DVD. Disc 2.

"The Musical Legacy of Paul Smith." Dir. Les Perkins. *Walt Disney Presents: 20,000 Leagues Under the Sea*, 2003. DVD. Disc 2.

Peter Pan. Dir. Clyde Geronimi, Wilfred Jackson, and Hamilton Luske. Walt Disney Productions, 1953. Film.

Pinocchio. Dir. Hamilton Luske and Ben Sharpsteen. Walt Disney Productions, 1940. Film.

Sleeping Beauty. Dir. Clyde Geronimi. Walt Disney Productions, 1959. Film.

Snow White and the Seven Dwarfs. Dir. David Hand. Walt Disney Productions, 1937. Film.

The Sword in the Stone. Dir. Wolfgang Reitherman. Walt Disney Productions, 1963. Film.

The Walt Disney Story. Walt Disney Productions, 1973. Film.

WEB SOURCES

Anderson, Paul F. "'The Funniest of Them All': Disney's *Snow White* vs. *Pinocchio*." *Disney History Institute* 3 November 2009, Web. 11 September 2013 www.disneyhistoryinstitute.com/2009/ 11/funniest-of-them-all-disneys-snow-white.html>.

Angle, Paula. *Biography in Black: A History of Streator, Illinois*. Web. 1 May 2014 <archive.org/stream/biographyinblackoofran/biographyinblackoofran_djvu.txt>.

Barrier, Michael. "'What's New' Archives: March 2014." *www.michaelbarrier.com.* 12 March 2014. Web. 16 November 2014 <www.michaelbarrier.com/Home%20Page/WhatsNewArchives Mar14.html>.

Barrier, Michael, Milton Gray, and Bob Clampett. "Wilfred Jackson: An Interview by Michael Barrier, Milton Gray, and Bob Clampett." *www.michaelbarrier.com.* 31 July 2015. Web 3 August 2015 <michaelbarrier.com/Interviews/Jackson1973/ Jackson1973.html>.

Boston, John. "The Mysterious Death of a Disney Oscar Winner in Castaic." *West Ranch Beacon* 7 December 2011. Web. 17 August 2012 <westranchbeacon.com/2011/12/the-boston-report -the-mysterious-death-of-a-disney-oscar-winner-in-castaic/>.

Box Office Mojo. "All Time Box Office Adjusted for Ticket Price Inflation." *Box Office Mojo* 8 September 2011. Web. 8 September 2011 <boxofficemojo.com/alltime/adjusted.htm>.

Busis, Hillary. "Disney's *Frozen*: Composers Talk Unexpected Influences (Gaga!) and Accidentally Aping *Arrested Development.*" *ew.com.* 27 November 2014. Web. 14 October 2015 <www.ew.com/article/2013/11/27/frozen-composers-bobby-lopez-kristen-anderson-lopez>.

Campana, Joe. "Century Birthday: Edward Plumb." *Animation—Who & Where.* 6 June 2007. Web 12 May 2011 <animationwhoandwhere.blogspot.com/2007/06/century-birthday -edward-plumb.html>.

Child, Ben. "Disney Turns Away from Hand-Drawn Animation." *Guardian.* 7 March 2013. Web 16 November 2014 <www.theguardian.com/film/2013/mar/07/disney-hand-drawn-anima tion>.

"Disney Legends—George Bruns." *D23.com.* Web 11 September 2011 <d23com/walt-disney -legend/george-bruns>.

"Disney Legends—Oliver Wallace." *D23.com.* Web 18 March 2011 <d23.com/walt-disney -legend/oliver-wallace>.

Feeney, Nolan. "Easter Gives *Frozen* Soundtrack Its Best Sales Week Yet." *Time.com* 25 April 2014. Web 23 November 2014 <time.com/74085/frozen-soundtrack-charts/>.

Lynskey, Dorian. "Why *Frozen's* 'Let It Go' Is More than a Disney Hit—It's an Adolescent Aperitif." *guardian.com* 10 April 2014. Web 14 October 2015 <www.theguardian.com/music/ musicblog/2014/apr/10/frozen-let-it-go-disney-hit-adolescent-lgbt-anthem>.

"MMC Crew: George Bruns." *The Original Mickey Mouse Club Show.* Web 11 September 2011 <www.originalmmc.com/bruns.html>.

"MMC Crew: Paul Smith." *The Original Mickey Mouse Club Show.* Web 8 August 2011 <www .originalmmc.com/paulsmith.html>.

"Paul Smith: Bio." *D23.com.* Web 8 August 2011 <d23.com/walt-disney-legend/paul-smith>.

Piereson, James. "How Jackie Kennedy Invented the Camelot Legend after JFK's Death." *Daily Beast* 12 November 2013. Web 6 March 2016 <www.thedailybeast.com/articles/2013/11/12/ how-jackie-kennedy-invented-the-camelot-legend-after-jfk-s-death.html>.

"Redstring Productions, Inc." *Redstring Productions Inc.* Web 3 February 2013 <www.redstring .com/frameset_3.htm>.

"Richard Sherman—Writing a Happy Song," *Pursuing Happiness* <vimeo.com/69947501>.

Robinson, Tasha. "*Frozen.*" *The Dissolve.* 28 November 2013. Web 16 November 2014 <thedis solve.com/reviews/407-frozen/>.

Ryrik, Melena. "*Frozen* Evolved around 'Let It Go.'" *Houston News* 25 February 2014. Web. 14 October 2015 <www.chron.com/entertainment/movies/article/Frozen-evolved-around-Let -It-Go-5266745.php>.

Uhlich, Keith. "*Frozen*: Movie Review." *TimeOut.* 26 November 2013. Web 16 November 2014 <www.timeout.com/us/film/frozen-movie-review>.

Wolf, Scott. "Interview: Jeffrey Sherman (Son of Disney Songwriter Robert B. Sherman)." *Mouse Clubhouse.* 12 October 2015. Web 13 October 2016 <mouseclubhouse.com/interview -jeffrey-sherman/>.

CENSUS

United States. Census Bureau. Charles Lewis, Topeka Ward 1, Shawnee, Kansas, United States. Enumeration District 144, sheet 185A, 1900.

United States. Census Bureau. Carl Harline, Wilford, Salt Lake, Utah. United States. Enumeration District 79, sheet 5B, 1910.

United States. Census Bureau. Joseph J. Smith, Calumet, Houghton, Michigan. United States. Enumeration District 103, sheet 4B, 1910.

United States. Census Bureau. Levancia Plumb, Streator Ward 2, La Salle, Illinois. United States. Enumeration District 78, sheet 16A, 1910.

United States. Census Bureau. Ernest Stalling, Kansas Ward 14, Jackson, Missouri. United States. Enumeration District 205, sheet 2B, 1910.

United States. Census Bureau. Andrew Churchill, Los Angeles Assembly District 64, Los Angeles, California, United States. Enumeration District 219, sheet 3A, 1920.

United States. Census Bureau. Carl Harline, Precinct 3, Salt Lake, Utah, United States. Enumeration District 38, sheet 2A, 1920.

United States. Census Bureau. Elbert Lewis, Belvidere, Los Angeles, California, United States. Enumeration District 10, sheet 35B, 1920.

United States. Census Bureau. Joseph J. Smith, Caldwell Ward 2, Canyon, Idaho. United States. Enumeration District 58, sheet 7B, 1920.

United States. Census Bureau. S. Walter Plumb, Streator Ward 2, La Salle, Illinois, United States. Enumeration District 89, sheet 9B, 1920.

United States. Census Bureau. Carl Stalling, Kansas City Ward 13, Jackson, Missouri. United States. Enumeration District 200, sheet 1A, 1920.

United States. Census Bureau. Andrew Churchill, Los Angeles, Los Angeles, California, United States. Enumeration District 42, sheet 9B, 1930.

United States. Census Bureau. Albert Sherman, Tract 382, Beverly Hills, Beverly Hills Judicial Township, Los Angeles, California, United States. Enumeration District 19–45, sheet 24A, 1940.

United States. Census Bureau. Carl W. Stalling, Councilmanic District 2, Los Angeles, Los Angeles Township, Los Angeles, California, United States. Enumeration District 60–122, sheet 4B, 1940.

United States. Census Bureau. Edward H. Plumb, Councilmanic District 13, Los Angeles, Los Angeles Township, Los Angeles, California, United States. Enumeration District 60–1052A, sheet 18B, 1940.

United States. Census Bureau. Elbert Lewis, Councilmanic District 15, Los Angeles, Los Angeles Township, Los Angeles, California, United States. Enumeration District 60–1247, sheet 1A, 1940.

United States. Census Bureau. Frank E. Churchill, Councilmanic District 1, Los Angeles, Los Angeles Township, Los Angeles, California, United States. Enumeration District 60–78A, sheet 6A, 1940.

United States. Census Bureau. Leigh A. Harline, Councilmanic District 1, Los Angeles, Los Angeles Township, Los Angeles, California, United States. Enumeration District 60–81, sheet 4A, 1940.

United States. Census Bureau. Oliver Wallace, Councilmanic District 1, Los Angeles, Los Angeles Township, Los Angeles, California, United States. Enumeration District 60–49, sheet 6A, 1940.

MARRIAGE LICENSES, PHONE BOOKS, AND DRAFT REGISTRATIONS

"California, County Marriages, 1850–1952." Donald Frederick Durnford and Carolyn Shafer Churchill. Los Angeles, 20 November 1943.

"California, County Marriages, 1850–1952." Frank E. Churchill and Leona J. Milligan. Orange, 6 July 1922.

"California, County Marriages, 1850–1952." Richard Morton Sherman and Ursula Gluck. Los Angeles, 28 June 1957.

"California, County Marriages, 1850–1952." Robert Bernard Sherman and Joyce Ruth. Los Angeles, 15 September 1953.

"Carl Stalling." Kansas City, Missouri, City Directory (1910) 1448.

"Carl Stalling." Kansas City, Missouri, City Directory (1916) 1688.

"Carl Stalling." Kansas City, Missouri, City Directory (1917) 1944.

"Carl Stalling." Kansas City, Missouri, City Directory (1918) 1796.

"Carl Stalling." Kansas City, Missouri, City Directory (1919) 1901.

"Carl Stalling." Kansas City, Missouri, City Directory (1924) 1999.

"Elbert Lewis." Kansas City, Missouri, City Directory (1914) 1248.

"Frank Churchill." Los Angeles, California, City Directory (1939) 440.

"Missouri Marriage Records." Carl Stalling and Gladys Baldwin. County of Jackson, 16 June 1917.

"Missouri Marriage Records." Elbert Lewis and Maude Shinkle. County of Jackson, 14 June 1905.

"United States World War I Draft Registration Cards, 1917–1918." Carl William Stalling, Kansas City no. 13, Missouri, 5 June, 1917.

"United States World War I Draft Registration Cards, 1917–1918." Elbert Clifford Lewis. Kansas City, no. 8, Missouri, 12 September, 1918.

"United States World War II Draft Registration Cards, 1942." Carl William Stalling, Los Angeles, 1942.

"United States World War II Draft Registration Cards, 1942." Elbert Clifford Lewis, Los Angeles, 1942.

CORRESPONDENCE

Adamic, Margaret. Email to the author. 27 June 2011.

Anderson, Arlynn. Email to the author. 12 March 2015.

Birdsall, Tracey. Email to the author. 25 November 2013.

———. Email to the author. 6 August 2014.

Boles, Jan. Email to the author. 30 August 2012.

———. Email to the author, 12 March 2015.

Britt, Linda. Email to the author. 8 May 2014.

———. Email to the author. 9 May 2014.

———. Email to the author. 21 May 2014.

Champion, Marge. Conversation with the author. 14 August 2013.

———. Conversation with the author. 25 September 2013.

Hof, Maxine. Email to the author. 18 April 2013.

Jackson, Winifred (Jaxon). "Walt Disney Productions: Inter-Office Communication." Message to Ed Penner. 24 March, 1953, Walt Disney Archives.

Lavin, Jack. "Walt Disney Productions: Inter-Office Communication." Message to Esther Haight. 25 May 1950. Joseph Dubin. Personnel file. Walt Disney Archives.

———. "Walt Disney Productions: Inter-Office Communication." Message to Main File. 10 May 1949. Joseph Dubin. Personnel file. Walt Disney Archives.

Lesjak, David. *Facebook* messages to the author. 11 January 2014.

Norman, Floyd. Email to the author. 15 August 2013.

——. Email to the author. 16 August 2013.

——. Email to the author. 17 September 2014.

Powers, Theresa Smith. Conversation with the author. 28 August 2012.

——. Conversation with the author. 18 July 2013.

Sherman, Robert J. *Facebook* message to the author. 25 January 2013.

——. *Facebook* message to the author. 30 March 2014.

——. Reply to author's post. *Facebook*. 30 May 2013.

Smith, Jerome. Conversation with the author. 28 August 2012.

——. Conversation with the author. 29 July 2013.

Smith, Paul Joseph, letter to Ann Ronell, n.d. (estimated winter 1933–34). New York Public Library.

Stalling, David. Email to the author. 15 May 2014.

Tietyen, David. *Facebook* message to the author. 9 August 2011.

STORY, STORY BOARD, AND SWEATBOX MEETING NOTES

"2079—'Lady & the Tramp' Overall Showing for Walt." Walt Disney Productions. 10 September 1953. Walt Disney Archives.

"2079—'Lady & the Tramp' Seq. 0.3.2—WHAT IS A BABY? Story Boards." Walt Disney Productions. 26 May 1953. Walt Disney Archives.

"2079—'Lady & the Tramp' Seqs. 01.1—3.2—04.1—12.0—12.1: 3E-12—Meeting." Walt Disney Productions. 9 July 1954. Walt Disney Archives.

Jackson, Wilfred. *Steamboat Willie*. The Walt Disney Studios, bar sheet, 1928. Walt Disney Archives.

"*Jungle Book*: Walt Meeting—Storyboards on 'Baloo Rejecting Mowgli,' 'The Vultures,' 'Rhino Sequence.'" 29 June 1965. Richard M. and Robert B. Sherman Papers, Collection Number 3222, American Heritage Center, University of Wyoming.

"*Jungle Book*: Walt Meeting—Storyboards on Opening—Seq. 001—Prod. #2179." 26 August 1966. Richard M. and Robert B. Sherman Papers, Collection Number 3222, American Heritage Center, University of Wyoming.

"*Jungle Boy* [Story Meeting Notes]." *Jungle Boy*. 5 April 1965. Richard M. and Robert B. Sherman Papers, Collection Number 3222, American Heritage Center, University of Wyoming.

"'Lady & the Tramp'—Meeting." Walt Disney Productions. 10 September 1953. Walt Disney Archives.

"'Lady & the Tramp'—Meeting." Walt Disney Productions. 31 December 1953. Walt Disney Archives.

"'Lady & the Tramp'—Meeting: Seqs. 02.0 & 03.0." Walt Disney Productions. 23 September 1953. Walt Disney Archives.

"Meeting Notes—Seq. 0.3.0 'Calendar.'" Walt Disney Productions. 24 March, 1953. Walt Disney Archives.

"Meeting with Walt Disney on Prod. 2079 Seq. 3.2—'What Is a Baby.'" Walt Disney Productions. 6 October 1953. Walt Disney Archives.

"'Sleeping Beauty': Meeting Notes." Walt Disney Productions. 11 February 1953. Walt Disney Archives.

"Story Conference on *Bambi*." Walt Disney Productions. 4 September 1937. Walt Disney Archives.

"Story Conference on *Bambi*." Walt Disney Productions. 5 October 1937. Walt Disney Archives.

OTHER SOURCES

"#36 Tiara Talk's Interview with Gregg and Jeff Sherman." Host Tammy Tuckey. *The Tiara Talk Show Podcast*. 27 November 2012. MP3 file.

Baker, Buddy. "Priceless Moments with Walt." Manuscript. Buddy Baker Collection, box 39, Fales Library and Special Collections, Elmer Holmes Bobst Library, New York University.

Bruns, George, Terry Gilkyson, Robert B. Sherman, and Richard M. Sherman. *The Jungle Book*. Walt Disney Records, 60950–7, 1997.

"Continuity Outline." *The Jungle Book*. 5 April 1965. Richard M. and Robert B. Sherman Papers, Collection Number 3222, American Heritage Center, University of Wyoming.

"Continuity Outline." *Jungle Boy*. 26 March 1965. Richard M. and Robert B. Sherman Papers, Collection Number 3222, American Heritage Center, University of Wyoming.

"Continuity Outline." *Jungle Boy*. 31 March 1965. Richard M. and Robert B. Sherman Papers, Collection Number 3222, American Heritage Center, University of Wyoming.

"The Disneyland Story." *Disneyland*. ABC. 27 October 1954. Television.

"Episode 38—Richard M. Sherman." Hosts Simon Barber and Brian O'Connor. *The Sodajerker on Songwriting*. Simon Barber and Brian O'Connor, 27 March 2013. MP3 file.

Fisher, David J. "The Music of Disney: A Legacy in Song." Liner notes. *The Music of Disney: A Legacy in Song*. Walt Disney Records, 60957–2, 1992.

"Famous Music Corporation: Foreign Statement of Royalties." Ann Ronell. 30 June 1933. New York Public Library.

Gordon, Mack, and Harry Revel. "It's the Animal in Me." Brunswick, 7591A, 1935.

Harline, Leigh, Edward Plumb, Hal Rees, Paul J. Smith, and Ned Washington. *Walt Disney's Pinocchio: Remastered Original Soundtrack Edition*. Walt Disney Records, 0946 3 51035 2 6, 2006.

Hench, John. Interview with Katherine and Richard Greene, 1998.

"Irving Berlin, Inc.: Statement of Royalties." Ann Ronell. 31 December 1933. New York Public Library.

Leon, Michael, and Randy Thornton. "Polishing a Disney Gem: The Restoration of the *Snow White and the Seven Dwarfs* Soundtrack." Liner notes. *Walt Disney's Snow White and the Seven Dwarfs: Original Motion Picture Soundtrack*. Walt Disney Records, 60850–7, 1993.

Lesjak. Post to The Disney History Institute Group. *Facebook*. 14 May 2016.

Lucraft, Howard. "Buddy Baker: Hollywood Film Composer." Buddy Baker Collection, box 39, Fales Library and Special Collections, Elmer Holmes Bobst Library, New York University.

Maltin, Leonard. Liner notes. *Stay Awake: Various Interpretations of Music from Various Disney Films*, A&M, B000002GFM, 1988.

"Mousetalgia—Episode 44" Host Dave Breiland. *Mousetalgia*. 7 September 2009. MP3 file.

"Mousetalgia Episode 126—Richard Sherman and Tony Walton on *Mary Poppins*." Host Dave Breiland. *Mousetalgia*. 28 March 2011. MP3 file.

"Mousetalgia Episode 177: Robert Sherman, John Carter." Host Dave Breiland. *Mousetalgia*. 18 March 2012. MP3 file.

"Royalty Account with Edward B. Marks Music Corporation." Ann Ronell. 11 July 1933. New York Public Library.

Sherman, Richard M. Interview with Jeff Kurtti, 2000.

Sherman, Robert B., and Richard M. Sherman. "I Wan'na Be Like You." Lyric manuscript. Richard M. and Robert B. Sherman Papers, Collection Number 3222, American Heritage Center, University of Wyoming.

———. "My Own Home." Lyric manuscript. 11 November 1965. Richard M. and Robert B. Sherman Papers, Collection Number 3222, American Heritage Center, University of Wyoming.

———. "That's What Friends Are For." Lyric manuscript. Richard M. and Robert B. Sherman

Papers, Collection Number 3222, American Heritage Center, University of Wyoming.

Sigman-Lowery, Paula. Liner notes. *Walt Disney Records Legacy Collection: Cinderella*. Walt Disney Records. D002066092. 2015.

The Sword in the Stone. Promotional poster. Walt Disney Productions, 1963.

"Vulture Sequence." *Jungle Boy*. Richard M. and Robert B. Sherman Papers, Collection Number 3222, American Heritage Center, University of Wyoming.

INDEX